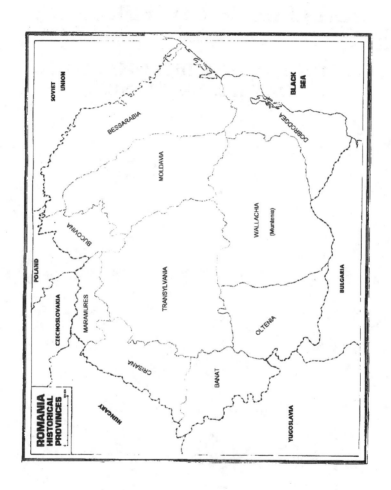

ROMANIA
HISTORICAL
PROVINCES

ROMANIA
AT THE
PARIS PEACE CONFERENCE:

A STUDY OF THE DIPLOMACY OF
IOAN I.C. BRĂTIANU

ROMANIA
AT THE
PARIS PEACE CONFERENCE:

A STUDY OF THE DIPLOMACY OF
IOAN I.C. BRĂTIANU

Sherman David Spector

THE CENTER FOR ROMANIAN STUDIES
THE ROMANIAN CULTURAL FOUNDATION
IAŞI, 1995

ROMANIAN CIVILIZATION STUDIES
VOL. VI
Series Editor: Kurt W. Treptow

ISBN 973-9155-72-3
Copyright © 1995 by Sherman David Spector
Printed in Romania

CONTENTS

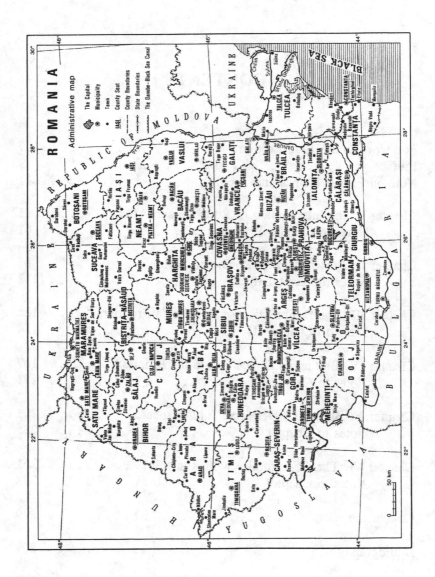

FOREWORD TO THE 1995 EDITION

In his just published one-volume *The First World War*, which the prolific British scholar Martin Gilbert subtitled "The Complete History," nowhere in his index is Romania cited! Is this the dust bin into which Rumania's pivotal role in that fateful conflict is to be consigned?

Forty years ago I undertook research into Romania's role in that war and its aftermath at the peace negotiations, intending to dramatize the critical part played by Ionel Brătianu (1864-1927), the National Liberal Party leader and dominating force in Romanian politics for the first quarter of this century. His family's influence on Romania began with his father Ion, who was instrumental in the anti-Turk 1848 revolution, unification of the two Danubian Principalities, establishment of the Hohenzollern-Sigmaringen monarchy after overthrowing the Alexandru Ioan Cuza regime, and the new nation's emergence as a small power in Eastern Europe. The eldest of his three sons, all destined to perpetuate the founding father's predominance in politics, doubled the size and population of the Romania the father originally created. In fact, the younger Ionel dominated Romania until the year of his death and my birth. Perhaps no non-dynastic family in Europe has ever exerted such influence over a nation's destiny as the Brătianu family did until Constantin (Dinu) was tried and condemned by the communist regime in 1947 — one century after his father ignited Romanian nationalism and after his brother had campaigned against the advance of Bolshevism into Central Europe in 1918-1919.

My 1962 study of Romania's moves during the First World War and at the subsequent Paris Peace Conference resulted from several years of research while I was a graduate student at Columbia University in the City of New York under the guidance of a fellow-tiller in the Romanian vineyard, Henry L. Roberts (1916-72), whose classic study *Rumania: Politics of an Agrarian State* (1951) inspired in me an urge to seek him out as a Ph.D. sponsor. My research efforts in the 1950s were frustrated by the silence experienced to the inquiries made to the community of historians and specialists in Bucharest. Not until my book was published in 1962 did I experience reactions from Romania. Those reactions were not laudatory because my appraisal of Brătianu did not coincide with the then official line. I hope the atmosphere has sufficiently changed so today's historians in Romania can accord to Brătianu the recognition I continue to maintain he earned. Trained as an engineer in École Polytechique in Paris, Brătianu engineered the creation of Greater Romania; without his policies and tactics such would not have materialized. I furthermore hope his contemporary colleagues in the other nations of the former socialist bloc who have been denied proper recognition by communist historians, e.g., Beneš in Czechoslovakia, Dmowski and Paderewski in Poland, Pašić and Trumbić in Yugoslavia, etc., will be accorded the honor and recognition they likewise earned during and after the First World War.

This book is about to appear in a Romanian translation and thus should be available to those in Romania denied access to it for more than thirty years. My profound thanks for the translation go to Professor Constantin Sorin Pârvu of the University in Iaşi, and to my dear friend for thirty years, Professor Ioan Aurel Preda of the University in Bucharest. I also thank Dr. Kurt W. Treptow of the University of Illinois and the Center for Romanian Studies of the Romanian Cultural Foundation in Iaşi for facilitating the publication of this English-language edition. Nothing in my 1962 book has been changed. Readers can thus acquire an awareness of what a young American concluded from his researches and analyses far from the time and place about which he was investigating. Whether his conclusions would have been different then or would be different now, if he were to conduct new researches and consequently reach new conclusions, is a daunting task an emeritus educator could not undertake. I ask readers to judge this 1962 book on its merit as the product of a non-Marxist bourgeois American graduate student fulfilling Ph.D. requirements at Columbia University in the City of New York, USA.

Sherman David Spector
Orange, Connecticut USA
March 1995

PREFACE

Twenty-eight years ago Harold Nicolson wrote that a history of the Paris Peace Conference "has yet to be written." He predicted it would be many years before complete materials could be made available or digested, and that "this documentary evidence (let us say in the year 1953) will be abundant and authentic."[1] Nicolson's optimism was not shared by Henry Wickham Steed who prophesied that "a full history of the Paris Peace Conference can never be written," and even when all documents and diaries have been published, and all contemporary records collated, "there will remain gaps that nobody can fill."[2]

I have found Steed, not Nicolson, correct in his prognostication. In this study concerned with negotiations between Romania and the Allied Powers, a paucity of documents and other materials from the Romanian side, scarcity of French and Italian sources, and a limited amount of American and British materials have restricted the scope and details of an analysis. The reader will become aware that in limiting the range of this study I have omitted certain important items. It has not been my purpose to provide an exhaustive analysis of the creation of "Greater Romania," but rather, after offering a survey of World War I developments, to select those events which either affected or were affected by Romania's policy.

I have tried to present the record for its own sake in an impartial manner without attempting to offer a particular thesis or point up a moral. Although the title of this study concerns events in 1919, it is important to go back to the origins of Romania's actions prior to her entry into the war in 1916. This procedure was adopted to provide a lucid account of Romania's wartime diplomacy; it is limited to those questions that became issues at the Peace Conference.

In preparing the materials for this study I have received assistance from many individuals and institutions. I wish to acknowledge the courtesy extended by the staff of The New York Public Library and the assistance given by that institution's Public Relations Office, which, by employing my wife, relieved me of the duties of breadwinner for two years so that I could devote full time to research. I thank the Institut Universitaire Roumain Charles Ier in Paris, whose directors assisted through correspondence in compensating for the disinclination of the Romanian government to answer my queries. The staff of the Edward M. House collection at Yale University was very cooperative. The Research Foundation of the State University of New York permitted me through its grant-in-aid to obtain materials from abroad.

I am indebted to many private persons who cheerfully answered queries. Among them are Mr. Vintilă Brătianu, Jr., Dr. Philip Marshall Brown, the late Charles Upson Clark, Dr. Alexander Crețianu, the late Leon Feraru, the Honorable Joseph C. Grew, Dr. John N. Hazard, Dr. David Mitrany, the Honorable Nicholas Roosevelt, Dr. Charles Seymour, Mr. Viorel V. Tilea, and Mr. Constantin Vișoianu.

To Frances and Robert Whitman for their advice and aid, to Dr. Jacob Hoptner for suggesting the topic, to Earl Aronson for editorial suggestions, and to Dr. Henry L. Roberts, Director of the Russian Institute of Columbia University, who, as my doctoral sponsor, shared the vicissitudes of this study's progress, I am especially grateful. Dr. Alexander Dallin read the entire manuscript and offered many helpful criticisms. A special word of appreciation is extended to Dr. Lewis A. Froman, President of Russell Sage College, whose financial assistance makes possible the publication of this study.

A pleasure a preface provides is the opportunity to acknowledge, however inadequately, my affectionate gratitude to Beryl, my wife, to whom this work is dedicated, for enduring the agonies of research and writing, for making many wise suggestions, and for her patient prodding without which this study would never have been completed.

Sherman David Spector
Troy, New York
March, 1962

NOTE ON PROPER NAMES
AND SPELLING

It is difficult to use a consistent method in spelling Romanian proper names without distortions. As a general rule, Romanian names are written in the Romanian spelling except where a word is more familiar in an English form. Although the true spelling of the country's name is "România," that rendition does not convey the precise English pronunciation; I therefore use "Romania," a widely accepted spelling approximating the precise sound. I have employed the English forms of the regional names, Moldavia (Moldova), Transylvania (Transilvania), Dobrodgea (Dobrogea), etc. Bucharest is the only city I have anglicized because the Romanian spelling of "Bucureşti" is unfamiliar to Americans and "Bucharest," the more familiar form, is rapidly being supplanted.

I have spelled Romanian words with their diacritical marks, following the system of Henry L. Roberts in his *Rumania: Political Problems of an Agrarian State* (New Haven: Yale University Press, 1951), p. xi. The English equivalents of accents and cedillas used in Romanian orthography are as follows:

â = has no exact equivalent in English. It is pronounced somewhat like the French *u*.

ă = like *e* in "father."

ş = like *sh* in "shall."

ţ = like *ts* in "tsar."

c = before *a, o,* and *u* as in English; before *e* and *i* as *ch* in "church." When *ci* or *ce* comes before *a, o,* or *u,* the *e* or *i* is not pronounced but the *c* has the sound of *ch* in "church." When *ch* comes before *e* or *i* the *h* is not pronounced but the *c* is as in English "can."

g = when followed by *e* or *i* it is pronounced *dj* as in "general"; otherwise as in "great."

u = is pronounced *oo* as in "too."

With regard to personal names, I have employed the original Romanian spellings instead of transliterating them into phonetic English.

Line of secret Allied-Rumanian Treaty (1916)

Neutral zone between Hungary and Rumania as proposed by the Allied Military Advisers to the Supreme Council

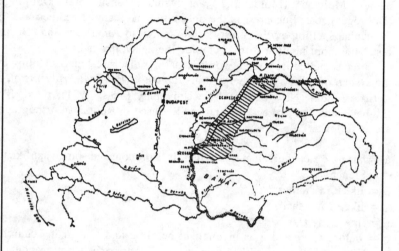

ROMANIA
AT THE
PARIS PEACE CONFERENCE:

A STUDY OF THE DIPLOMACY OF
ION I.C. BRĂTIANU

IOAN I.C. BRĂTIANU
(1866-1927)

Chapter I

THE INTERVENTION OF ROMANIA AND AFTER

"The Romanians aspire to create an independent state which is to include Bucovina, the Romanian portion of Transylvania and the Banat, with the Balkans as frontiers."

— Baron Prokesch-Osten at the Congress of Paris, 1856[1]

The Ties Which Bind

The step taken by the Kingdom of Romania in joining the Allied Powers in World War I resulted from a tediously negotiated agreement — the controversial Treaty of Alliance of Bucharest signed on August 17, 1916.[2] This pact remained the written declaration of Romania's aspirations, in spite of subsequent equivocations and wranglings. The secret political and military conventions comprising the Alliance were born in the Allies' desperate need for Romania's military assistance during decisive battles being waged on both fronts in the summer of 1916. Italy's decision to break her alliance with the Central Powers and join the Allies in 1915 prompted Romania to offer her intervention to the Allies at a cost they subsequently would regret.

The Alliance of 1916 was not born wholly out of Allied military disappointments; it was, rather, the product of two years of continuous discussions between Russian Foreign Minister Serge Sazonov, on behalf of the Allies, and Ioan I.C. Brătianu, President of the Romanian Council of Ministers. An almost complete account of these negotiations was published by the Soviet Government. The Romanian version remains secret. Recently published documents of the Italian Foreign Ministry fill in some gaps. An examination of the diplomatic correspondence of the Austro-Hungarian Foreign Ministry provides an account of the concurrent pourparlers with the Central Powers undertaken by Brătianu and Ottokar Czernin, Austro-Hungarian minister to Romania from 1913 to 1916. An abundance of memoirs and secondary accounts sheds further light on the archival materials.[3]

In 1914 Romania, like Italy, was a member of the Triple Alliance system. The relations of these so-called "Latin cousins" to their German partners (Germany and Austria-Hungary) were quite similar. Italy joined the alignment in 1882, Romania in 1883. The former had been attracted because of her envy and suspicion of French colonial gains in North Africa, and in the hope an alliance with Austria-Hungary would assuage or defer the burning question of "Italia Irredenta." Romania joined for similar motives. Hoping to secure protection from the menace of Russia and desiring to improve relations with Austria-Hungary, Romania believed an alignment with the German powers would alleviate the oppressive treatment of those Romanians living under Magyar rule and give her assurance against Russian encroachments.

Few in the Kingdom of Romania could ignore the fact that almost half of their co-nationals lived beyond the frontiers, under alien rule: approximately one million in Bessarabia under Russian rule; two hundred fifty thousand in Bucovina under Austria; about two million, five hundred thousand in Transylvania, Crişana, the Banat of Timişoara, and Maramureş under Hungary; and more than a half million scattered in Bulgaria, Macedonia, Serbia, and the Ukraine. Most lived near Romania's frontiers. Romania was too weak to liberate them by force. There was little possibility in Transylvania for irredentism to flare into open rebellion against Hungary. In the face of this situation, Romania pursued until 1914 her only possible course — to wait for a favorable opportunity to incorporate her co-nationals into the Kingdom.

A critical difference between Italy and Romania in the Triple Alliance system was that while the former was an open ally, the latter remained a secret partner. Only a handful of ministers in Bucharest knew of the 1883 alliance, which was considered a dynastic treaty between King Carol, the Hohenzollern-Sigmaringen monarch, and the rulers of the German states. Long before 1914, however, Italy had begun to swerve from the alignment, but Romania remained ostensibly faithful until the beginning of the war.

The assassination of Archduke Francis Ferdinand, in June 1914, produced the problem of fulfilling the terms of the Triple Alliance.

When Austria-Hungary decided that Serbia must be punished, Romania, like Italy, became alarmed and both reappraised the terms of the alliance. What was Romania's precise position in this treaty signed October 30, 1883, and renewed in 1888, 1892, 1896, 1902, and 1913? The treaty, never submitted to the Romanian Parliament for ratification as required by law, was essentially conservative and defensive. Romania had agreed not to enter into any engagements directed against any signatory power. If Romania, without provocation on her part, were attacked, Germany, Austria-Hungary, and Italy were to come to her assistance. If the latter powers were attacked under the same circumstances, Austria-Hungary reserving for herself the qualification "in a portion of her states bordering on Romania," the *casus foederis* would have arisen for Romania. Thus Romania was guaranteed against aggression by Russia, Bulgaria, Turkey, and Serbia. Austria-Hungary was assured of Romania's assistance if Russia attacked her eastern frontiers or if Serbia violated her southern borders. Romania was promised an equal voice in peace negotiations. The treaty did not accord Romania a special privilege that Italy had extracted from her allies. Germany and Austria-Hungary were required to take common counsel with Italy, not with Romania, immediately upon a *casus foederis*. Italy thus had a way out that Romania lacked.[4] Since Austria-Hungary and Germany were not attacked in 1914, the *casus foederis* did not arise. Austria-Hungary could only claim that her security was threatened by Serbian intrigues. Italy took advantage of this and "consultation in ample time" was begun. Romania did not receive such cordial treatment, but her subsequent refusal to intervene on the side of her allies was not the result of chagrin over being slighted. The decision to maintain a watchful neutrality was the result of the policy pursued by Ioan I.C. Brătianu.

Ioan I.C. Brătianu

Any study of Romania's policy during and after the World War hinges upon the personality and character of her premier, Brătianu. Most accounts of this policy are couched in such generalities as Romania's interest or lack of interest in her co-nationals beyond the Kingdom whom the mother-country did or did not wish to liberate, or in desire for economic gains by the unscrupulous National Liberal Party, or even in such flowery phrases as "irredenta, nationalism, sacred egoism, and national instinct." Brătianu did not indulge in such histrionics to achieve the union of all Romanians in East Central Europe.

Intractable, rigid, and ruthlessly calculating — such are words used to describe this leader. Foreign diplomats called him "The Sphinx"; others labelled him "La belle odalisque."[5] To one observer he had the round and charming face of a grand seigneur of Renaissance France with, as a fascinated woman put it, "eyes of a gazelle and the jaw of a tiger."[6] His magnificent brown eyes blazed and his leonine head, with classic forehead and curly, silvery hair, suggested indomitable energy. Others thought his physiognomy could not shield an oriental indolence and they likened him to a Tibetan-lama. Still others thought his olive complexion and long pointed beard hinted of a Byzantine Christ in morning coat and spats.[7] Yet one observer described him as a brilliant raconteur, supple, and full of gestures. His pensive and sometimes nonchalant appearance inspired respect."[8]

Queen Marie of Romania considered the Premier pleasantly ironical, watchful to the point of slyness, and never particular about his clothes. She enjoyed his company and found him witty. The Queen was not deceived, though. She realized this was only the façade of an unyielding personality. Yet she was constant in her public admiration for the Premier. She recalled that although her husband, the King, liked him, his admiration was mixed with a slight sense of apprehension as though Ferdinand were always suspicious of his first minister's actions. The wily Brătianu enchanted women in a somewhat oriental manner, but he was careful never to be the dupe. In her memoirs, Marie remembered a moonlit evening the two spent at a convent, at which time he told her he was always sentimental on such nights, even in a convent.[9]

Brătianu was born at Florica, his ancestral estate, in 1864, at a crucial moment in the life of his equally illustrious father. The anti-Cuza conspiracy was being plotted and the elder Brătianu was on the verge of a great triumph. Ioan C. Brătianu (1821-1891), founder of the family's prestige, is considered the architect of modern Romania. He was prominent in the movement that forced the abdication of Prince Bibescu in 1848, and promoted the election of Alexander Cuza as prince of the United Danubian Principalities in 1859. He was founder of the National Liberal Party. A radical in his early manhood, the elder Brătianu turned his extremism toward nationalist demands, playing a vital role in the dethronement of Cuza, the installation of the Hohenzollern-Sigmaringen dynasty in 1866, and the successful campaign for independence from Turkey in 1877. Brătianu worked for centralization of government power to develop Romania's primitive economy. Opposed to the entry of foreign capital, he developed the nucleus of a native middle class.

The elder's first-born son was called Ionel, diminutive of Ioan, the "el" corresponding to "junior." One of eight children, Ionel was the only son to inherit his father's physical and mental characteristics. The spade beard, the black brows, and the impressive stature were the same in both. The two other male progeny who became prominent, Vintilă and Constantin, were not of the same substances.[10] Ionel, who served as Premier five times from 1909 to 1927, pursued his father's policies less imaginatively, but with more power.

The younger Brătianu attended the preparatory school of the Colegiu Sfântul Sava in Bucharest before studying at the École Polytechnique in Paris for two years. He next enrolled in the École des Ponts et Chaussées for three years and received a degree in civil engineering. Returning home, he entered state service as an engineer and assisted in constructing the Cernavodă railway bridge over the Danube. This was a brief career for he soon entered politics and was elected to the Chamber of Deputies in 1895. Dimitrie Sturdza, who succeeded the elder Brătianu as chief of the National Liberals, appointed Ionel Minister of Public Works in 1896, a post he held until Sturdza resigned as premier, three years later. Brătianu's more active political life began in 1901 when Sturdza, upon recall to office, named him Foreign Minister, a post he held from January 1902 to December 1904.[11]

Brătianu married twice. His first wife, Marie Moruzi, bore his only son, Gheorghe, who was prominent in politics in the 1930s and earned considerable reputation as a historian. Ionel's second wife, Elise Ştirbei, had been married to his political rival, Alexandru Marghiloman, a leader of the Conservative Party. Her noble ancestry enhanced her second husband's prestige even though she was the grandniece of Prince Bibescu, whom Ionel's father had ousted. This marriage to a descendant of a boyar family would not have pleased the elder Brătianu whose policy had been to smash the strength of the great landowners. Ionel, nevertheless, became a great landed proprietor, the husband of a princess, and the brother-in-law of a noted prince, Barbu Ştirbei.[12]

Ionel returned to office in 1907 when Sturdza named him Minister of the Interior. His role in suppressing the famous peasant revolt that year remains controversial. His admirers credit him with appeasing the peasants and taking intelligent measures to produce a beneficial effect. Noted historian Robert W. Seton-Watson portrayed Brătianu's role as one of oppressive cruelty toward the peasants.[13] Whatever the nature of his role, it did not prevent Brătianu from succeeding the aged Sturdza as premier in 1909. He not only became leader of his father's political machine, but in January of that year assumed the combined offices of Premier and Foreign Minister which he retained until the end of 1912.

Brătianu thus began his independent political career. He was not given to any idealistic formulas for the fulfillment of his father's legacy. When one method proved unproductive, he turned conveniently to another. He switched alone; there was no reliance upon subordinates, all of whom he considered weak and inferior. Combining the characteristics of a fast-thinking businessman with the intuitive shrewdness of a peasant, Brătianu contrived to increase the immense wealth he had inherited from his father by controlling Romania's mineral resources and hence the entire economy. When one speaks of Romanian politics, the Brătianu family invariably appears as the real ruler of the country. The Liberal Party was synonymous with the family. The rabid chauvinism, the policy of exaggerated centralization, financial depreciation, and the bribery and corruption which pervaded the entire body politic — all stemmed from the hands of Ionel Brătianu who tolerated this situation.

Although rarely influenced by the opinions of others, Brătianu was at all times anxious to justify his decisions to those about him or to the world. Whereas the elder Brătianu leaned heavily upon King Carol and other close associates, Ionel's actions were his alone. Thus he alone must bear censure for failures and praise for triumphs.[14]

The Decision to Abstain

Bismarck once remarked that Romania's allegiance to the Triple Alliance would not outlive the span of King Carol's life.[15] This monarch, born in 1839 and ruling since 1866, tried to prevent this prophecy from materializing during the last months of his life, which was to end on October 10, 1914. Carol and those who still supported a German orientation for Romania were being swept up in a new diplomatic and political revolution. The Entente Powers were exerting strong influence over Romania in the spring and summer of 1914.[16] The 1883 treaty had been weakened by Austria's support of Bulgaria during the recent Balkan Wars. Russian diplomacy during those wars, and especially Russia's consent to the Romanian intervention, had reoriented thinking in Bucharest.

The Russian government, in an attempt to make the Romanians forget past abuses, sponsored a visit by Tsar Nicholas and his family to Constanţa in June 1914. At that time Russian Foreign Minister Sazonov held talks with Brătianu who had again assumed office on January 16, 1914, after an absence from politics during the Balkan Wars. This meeting marked the beginning of an unprecedented Russo-Romanian rapprochement.[17]

Germany and Austria-Hungary soon learned that Romania could not be relied upon in case of war. Carol advised the German envoy that he could no longer influence public opinion against the Entente in the face of successes achieved by Allied propaganda. He referred to Brătianu and the Liberals as Ententophiles who were making Romania's position in the Triple Alliance very precarious.[18]

When Czernin informed Carol, on July 24, that an ultimatum had been presented to Serbia, the King replied that Romania would maintain strict neutrality in case of war. Brătianu, after examining the famous ultimatum, warned Czernin that it proved Austria's desire for war. Romania, he declared, would never tolerate a dislocation of the Balkan balance of power which she had done so much to establish. He insisted Romania remain the leading power in the Balkans. Czernin concluded that Romania would not participate in any war against Serbia, but would remain neutral while awaiting the results of the struggles.[19] It should be noted that after the Balkan Wars Romania coveted the land of no other Balkan state and there was as yet no serious irredentist movement in Romania aimed at detaching the Romanian-inhabited regions of Austria-Hungary.

King Carol pleaded with Brătianu to remain friendly toward Vienna and Berlin, and the Premier promised to comply if the Magyars improved their treatment of Romanians residing in Hungary. Approaching the Central Powers with a request that they demonstrate their need for Romania's services by offering Bessarabia (to be detached, presumably, from a defeated Russia), and by forcing Hungary to accord her Romanian subjects certain political and cultural rights, Brătianu began two years of bazaar trading to acquire for Romania the highest rewards at the least possible sacrifice.[20]

When Vienna and Berlin could not coerce the inflexible Magyars into deferring to his wishes, Brătianu turned to Sazonov with whom he had struck up a friendship during their memorable automobile trip through Transylvania in June 1914.[21] Sazonov was convinced that Brătianu alone directed Romanian foreign policy. The Premier led Sazonov to believe he would go to war on the side that promised the most gains. Sazonov accepted the bait, and during the crisis over Vienna's ultimatum to Serbia, he worked to prevent Romania from joining the Central Powers. On July 29 Sazonov advised Brătianu that Romania would not be denied rewards if she joined the Allies. The next day he offered Transylvania without first consulting Britain or France. Without awaiting a reply from Brătianu, the impatient Sazonov, on July 31, instructed his envoy in Bucharest to sound out the Premier about non-intervention on either side. This was an irrevocable blunder which created a precedent for subsequent negotiations.[22] When Stanislas Poklevskii-Kozell, the Russian envoy, told Brătianu his position would be strengthened by Russia in exchange for a friendly attitude, the Premier asked if Russia would safeguard Romania's neutrality as an indication of friendship. Poklevskii interpreted Sazonov's instructions of July 31 to signify accession and he answered affirmatively. Poklevskii thus abandoned the chief bargaining point without receiving anything in exchange.[23]

The Romanian Premier had achieved a brilliant diplomatic victory by which he could maintain neutrality and, at the same time, be assured of territorial aggrandizement without the customary sacrifices. Germany had offered Bessarabia,[24] Austria-Hungary was noncommittal, but Russia was magnanimous. He could look to Transylvania promised to him without the prerequisite of intervention. France announced on August 1 support of Sazonov's territorial promise.[25] This led the elated Brătianu to advise Sazonov that Romania's position in the war would be determined by a joint discussion of the question by the leading statesmen of Romania.

The First Crown Council

Brătianu's decision to adopt a neutralist policy was reached before a crown council was convened on August 3 to discuss future action. Russia's offer of Transylvania in exchange for friendly neutrality could not be rejected in view of the paltry German offer of Bessarabia and the failure of Austria-Hungary to promise improved treatment of the Romanians in Hungary. When Fasciotti, Italian envoy to Romania, notified Brătianu of Rome's decision to abstain, this action strengthened the Premier's proposals to the Crown Council.[26]

Brătianu directed the session at Sinaia with Metternichean skill. He announced Italy's decision to remain neutral and his own determination to follow suit. The only opposition came from King Carol who muttered phrases about honor, and from aged Petre P. Carp, a former Conservative Premier, who insisted upon respect for the 1883 treaty.[27]

The Premier described Romania's role as one of armed preparation without commitments. The question of Transylvania had caused him to reconsider the commitments of the Triple Alliance and, after showing its text to the Crown Council, he said it did not oblige Romania to intervene. He intimated that the situation might have been different had Germany and Austria-Hungary consulted with their Romanian ally before deciding upon war:

> The Romanian State entered the alliance as a sovereign state, on a footing of equality. It cannot be treated in this manner [not being consulted before the ultimatum was handed to Serbia]. Those who thirty years ago tied our fate to the Triplice did not think of the future. Romania cannot take up arms in a war which has for its purpose the weakening of a small nation. The question of the Romanians of Transylvania dominates the entire situation. The entire government is involved in the ineluctable necessity of accounting for the rights of the irredentists and of the realization of our national ideal.... Right now one can make war if the national conscience approves of it. But it reproves it. Remain neutral then. Italy has taken the same attitude. The war will be long; wait for the march of events. We will have the chance to say our word.[28]

Brătianu concluded that Romania, surrounded by powerful neighbors, was not yet endowed with the ability to indulge in adventures. He refused to debate his decision, and the opposition leaders did not object.

The decision to abandon the Triple Alliance was a personal defeat for King Carol, inflicted by the son of the man who had made him ruler almost a half-century before. Carol expressed his embitterment in the following valedictory:

> Gentlemen, you cannot imagine how bitter it is to find oneself isolated in a country of which one is not a native.[29]

This abject confession produced no sympathy. Instead, pro-Entente Take Ionescu, leader of the Conservative Democrats, rebuked the King:

In peacetime it was possible for Your Majesty to follow a policy which was contrary to the sentiment of the country; but to make war in defiance of that sentiment is impossible.[30]

Perhaps Ionescu was exaggerating the Ententophilism prevalent in Romania. It was this attitude, however, which undoubtedly hastened the death of the King. In failing to fulfill what the monarch firmly believed was an alliance based on honor, Romania's statesmen, with the sole exception of Petre P. Carp, had repudiated their King. Carol died two months later, content he would not live to see intervention on the Allied side.[31]

The Accord With Italy

Having followed Italy's lead, Romania was now prepared to work in concert with Rome. An agreement was negotiated during August and September by which both states agreed to remain neutral, furnish prior notice if this condition changed, maintain contact in examining the situation and taking measures, and establish a common front when the time arrived to present demands for intervention. An unwritten understanding obliged both to thwart any Allied plan to create free Slav states such as Bohemia or Croatia, out of the anticipated ruins of the Habsburg Monarchy. Armed with a friendship treaty made on equal terms with a great power, Brătianu was now ready to extract from Russia a precise agreement to implement promises made by Sazonov.[32]

The Neutrality Treaty With Russia

Russian capture of Cernăuţi, capital of Austrian Bucovina, on September 15 stirred excitement in Bucharest toward joining the Russian march on Transylvania. Resisting interventionist clamorings, Brătianu asked Sazonov on September 21 for a written promise of Transylvania, Bucovina up to the Prut River, and Cernăuţi in exchange for Romanian neutrality.[33] Sazonov rejected these demands because of Russian victories over Austria-Hungary. Brătianu retreated by withdrawing his claim to most of Bucovina and by proposing a neutrality agreement lest Sazonov repudiate his earlier promise of Transylvania now that Russia was on the offensive. Sazonov agreed and, on October 1, he and Constantin Diamandy, the Romanian minister to Russia, signed a treaty in Petrograd.

This treaty, representing the first diplomatic recognition of Romania's claims by an Allied Power, provided that Russia would, in exchange for Romania's benevolent neutrality, recognize her right to annex Transylvania and sections of Bucovina inhabited by Romanian majorities. Sazonov yielded to Brătianu's claim to the ethnically Romanian part of Bucovina in order to assure continued Romanian friendship. Romania's neutrality was actually a misnomer because Brătianu agreed, in payment for the offer of Bucovinan territory, to permit passage of war matériel across Romania to Serbia and to prohibit shipment of arms from the Central Powers across Romania to Turkey.[34]

On October 8, Brătianu revealed to an applauding cabinet the texts of his agreements with Italy and Russia. He promised to march into Transylvania and to cooperate with the Russo-Romanian commission to delimit an ethnic frontier between the two states in Bucovina. This was to be undertaken at the most opportune time. He then showed the texts to Ionescu and Nicu Filipescu, leaders of the Conservative Democrat Party, who were impressed.[35] Brătianu was given *carte blanche* by Ferdinand, who had succeeded Carol on October 10, and the opposition leaders to pursue his announced policy. There was no longer the question of which side to join; the problem was when to intervene to reap still bigger harvests. In the meantime, Brătianu would let others do his fighting.

A Year of Wavering

Intervention depended upon the highest price the Allies were prepared to pay. Romania would step into the war only after two basic requirements were met: written guarantees by the Allies to (1) fight for Romania's maximum territorial demands, and to (2) provide for Romania's war matériel. Brătianu could plead with reason that his country was unprepared for war. Weapons, planes, and railway equipment were inadequate. Unless the Turkish Straits were forced open or contact with Britain and France were secured through still neutral Bulgaria, Romania would have to rely on Russia for supplies. Dependence upon Russia was a frightening prospect.

In order to obtain the greatest dividends at the least premium, Brătianu entertained the wooings of both sides during 1915. He haggled when the Allies pressed him for a definite promise, hinted at favoring promises of the Central Powers at another time, revived bogies about Bulgarian threats to his southern flank, and repeatedly cited the need to prepare public opinion at home before taking the irrevocable step into war.[36] The Premier bided his time, alternately eyeing Bulgaria and interventionist agitation in his own country which increased with every Allied victory, however inconsequential. Brătianu's decision would be determined exclusively by the balance of territorial advantages offered by each side. He could not afford to repeat the error made in 1877-78 when, in return for intervention against Turkey, Romania lost southern Bessarabia to Russia.[37] It was now essential for him to secure advantageous terms clearly specified and adequately guaranteed. Unless such terms outweighed those which he could obtain from the other side in return for mere inaction, Brătianu felt it was his duty to reject them.

Failure of the Anglo-French expedition to open the Turkish Straits in the spring of 1915 was ineffectively compensated for by the dispatch of Allied missions to Bucharest, to encourage intervention. The appearance of British and French generals, propagandists, and renowned Romanophiles left Brătianu unmoved.[38] Britain offered a loan as a lure and France promised forty aircraft. When this prodding became uncomfortable, the resourceful Premier increased his demands.

When the Allies began to woo Bulgaria and asked Brătianu to assist them by retroceding southern Dobrodgea, seized from Bulgaria by the Treaty of Bucharest of 1913, the Premier jacked up his demands. He raised the issue of the Straits, insisting that seaway be open to all ships, Constantinople placed under international protection, and Romania given representation on a commission to regulate free navigation through the Straits.[39] When Sazonov responded by promising to guarantee Romania's right to free passage in exchange for intervention, Brătianu raised his price again. This time he laid claim to the entire Banat of Timişoara, to which Serbia also aspired.

The Allies were constrained by conflicting Serbian and Romanian claims to the Banat. Brătianu aggravated the issue by claiming not only the Banat and the regions promised in his neutrality treaty with Russia, but also Bucovina as far north as the Prut River, including the capital of Cernăuţi, and the comitats (counties) of eastern Hungary comprising the region known as Crişana which were inhabited by Romanian majorities. Sazonov denounced these new demands and informed Britain and France of his refusal to wage war against Austria-Hungary for the exclusive purpose of Romania's aggrandizement.[40]

The haggling continued. Whenever Sazonov hesitated or when Russia's armies encountered reversals, Brătianu reminded him of his offer to intervene. Sazonov insisted that Brătianu consult with Serbia regarding a partition of the Banat. Brătianu countered with a demand for a military convention promising Romania a large quantity of Allied troops and munitions. Discouraged by the enemy recapture of Galicia and Bucovina in June 1915, Sazonov yielded to the pleas of the Russian General Staff and offered Bucovina as far north as the Prut, including Cernăuţi, Maramureş south of the upper Tisa River, and troops and supplies if Romania would retrocede southern Dobrodgea and intervene immediately. Sazonov had yielded even after learning Brătianu had refused to discuss the Banat with Serbia.[41]

Brătianu's audacity had been encouraged by Italy's success in April 1915 when the Allies negotiated the Treaty of London in return for Italian intervention.[42] Italy's ability to obtain promises of large territorial awards led Brătianu to increase his price for entry. Taking advantage of Russia's appeal for immediate intervention, Brătianu again asked for the entire Banat, this time with an Allied guarantee. Sazonov still held out for the Serbs, but Britain and France forced him to accept Brătianu's pledge that if the entire province were yielded, Romania would never fortify the river bank opposite Belgrade. Sazonov thereby consented to every territorial demand, but there still remained the question of military aid to Romania.[43]

Brătianu summoned a Crown Council session on August 9, 1915. A year had elapsed since the last meeting. He reported plans to intervene if the Allies withdrew a request for him to yield southern Dobrodgea. The Conservatives opposed war, but they were in support of the Premier's cautious neutralism. After the Council reviewed recent military developments — the Germans had captured Warsaw on August 7, Austro-Hungarian troops had recovered Galicia and Bucovina, and Anglo-French forces on Gallipoli could not advance — it was decided to postpone intervention indefinitely. Brătianu rejected the Conservative opinion that outright pacifism would suffice to permit Romania to obtain her territorial objectives. He was convinced that inaction would fail to seal the bargain he had made with Russia in October 1914, or guarantee acquisition of additional territories he had claimed in his subsequent negotiations with Sazonov. Realization of his maximum claims was predicated upon active intervention, not upon neutrality.[44]

The Romanian leader had truly earned the sobriquet "Sonnino of Eastern Europe," and he may have deserved Paul Cambon's description of him as "performing like a peddler in an oriental bazaar,"[45] or that of a British officer — "a master of *un marchandage balkanique*."[46] Despite his realization that the Allies were becoming irritated with his tactics, Brătianu would not be rushed into action.[47] He anticipated that the Allies, exhausted either by negotiations or military defeats, eventually would accede to all his demands, and perhaps a few more.

The Second Year of Caution

In September 1915 Bulgaria joined the Central Powers to secure territory in Macedonia from Serbia and southern Dobrodgea from Romania if the latter state intervened on the Allied side.[48] When the Bulgarians combined forces with the Central Powers to invade Serbia in October, Sazonov turned to Brătianu once more and appealed for intervention to save Serbia. The Premier, noting the embarrassing inability of the Allies to assist Serbia, increased his price again. This time he demanded, in addition to territories already promised, an adequate supply of munitions, resumption of the Anglo-French campaign at the Straits, and invasion of Bulgaria by British and French forces which had landed at Salonika on October 3. He also insisted the Russians resume their offensive on the entire Eastern Front, but he refused to permit them to cross Romania to reach the retreating Serbs. When the Allies were ready to yield, Brătianu, who had no intention of intervening while German and Austro-Hungarian troops were advancing through Serbia, increased the original number of troops which he demanded the Russians send to Bessarabia to protect his northern flank.[49]

The Premier knew the Russians could not satisfy his demands because they were powerless to rescue Serbia and unable to mount an offensive to distract German forces which, by the middle of December, had occupied Serbia. When he was accused at home of abandoning the Serbs, Brătianu replied that Romania's unpreparedness prevented him from intervening at a time when the fate experienced by Serbia would have been dealt to Romania.[50] The interventionists charged him with abandoning Romania's traditional role of preserving the status quo in the Balkans by failure to aid Serbia, to whom Romania was tied by the 1913 Treaty of Bucharest. Ionescu and Filipescu renounced their support of neutralism in a series of debates in the Chamber of Deputies. They accused Brătianu of "trafficking with one side and with the other, deceiving both, lying in wait watching for the best opportunity." Ionescu denounced him as a thief lacking in moral guidance, knowing nothing about duty or the demands of honor, and only waiting "the more conveniently to rifle pockets." The Conservative Democrats urged immediate entry as the only way to achieve Romania's national aspirations.[51]

Brătianu withstood these invectives, and continued his policy of cautious neutralism. This perhaps indicates most effectively the secondary role played by the interventionists in bringing Romania into the war. Brătianu defied their charges by negotiating trade treaties with Germany and Austria-Hungary early in 1916, making possible the sale of more than two million tons of grain to feed the Central Powers. So as not to anger the Allies, the Premier agreed to sell wheat and corn to Britain.[52]

The desperate Allied military situation early in 1916 encouraged a resumption of active negotiations. Serbia had been occupied, Bulgaria had entered the war, and Greece was still undecided. Russia needed supplies which could be shipped through the Straits, still held by Turkey. The Anglo-French army on Gallipoli was preparing to withdraw. If the Russian General Staff, planning a massive counter-attack against Austria-Hungary, expected to tip the scales of war, it would be necessary to secure Romania's entry or at least her assurance that she would not submit to strong German pressure to join the Central Powers. Although Alekseev, appointed Russian Chief of Staff in August 1915, was dubious about the value of Romania's intervention, he was prodded by the Allies to reopen talks regarding a military convention.[53] He sent a military mission to Bucharest, and Brătianu dispatched Nicu Filipescu to Petrograd as his representative.

Conservative Democrat Filipescu was received by the Tsar and Sazonov. He stressed the need for a Russian army to protect Romanian's southern flank by occupying Dobrodgea. This move would permit the Russians to engage the Bulgarians whose traditional friendship for Russia had always worried the Romanians. Sazonov and French ambassador Paleologue assured Filipescu that Russia no longer considered the Bulgarians as friends. Both urged him to press Brătianu into negotiating a military convention, but Filipescu reminded them that Brătianu "had not yet found the market good enough." Filipescu was told to warn the Premier that if he waited much longer the Germans would make Romania a vassal state since they were well acquainted with his negotiations with the Allies.[54]

Brătianu discussed military arrangements with Alekseev's representative in Bucharest. During these pourparlers, the Premier added more and more requirements to his already exorbitant claims to territory. He insisted Russia first occupy Dobrodgea, then reconquer Bucovina before Romania invaded Transylvania, and finally make contact in Dobrodgea with the Anglo-French forces, which were expected to march through Bulgaria. This strategy was designed to render Bulgaria incapable of menacing Romania, whose exclusive assignment would be the conquest of Transylvania.[55]

Alekseev rejected these conditions, and he warned Sazonov that Romania must acquire only those territories merited by her military efforts. Sazonov concurred despite French insistence that he yield.[56] He rebuffed Brătianu's demands and French intercession because he believed the Brusilov offensive, begun June 4, would entice Brătianu into intervening.

By June 18 the Russians had recaptured Cernăuţi. Their victory intensified interventionist clamorings. Ionescu appealed to the King for immediate entry, so that Romania could realize her "sacred union" with Transylvania, and he called for the formation of a coalition government to prosecute the war.[57]

Brătianu remained firm. If he yielded, he risked losing many of the promises made by the Allies, because Russia had never been generous while waging an offensive. Brusilov's armies, advancing toward Transylvania, trespassed on Romanian soil on June 11. This action was construed as a Russian attempt to force Romania to intervene, but Brătianu rejected the temptation and protested a violation of his territory. Sazonov replied peremptorily that Russia was entirely indifferent toward the possibility of Romania's assistance.[58] The Premier was momentarily shaken by this rejoinder for he feared Russia might grab Transylvania before Romania could. He told the French envoy:

> Russia does not neglect any occasion to aggravate our mis-
> trust, the principal cause of hesitation for which I am re-
> proached. You know that I can obtain guarantees which I
> judge indispensable and which the other Allies, with France at
> the head, should accord me.... How do you wish me to enter
> the war — to aid Russia to get Constantinople, that is to say,
> to encircle us? We are treated like an enemy, or at least
> suspected of being one.[59]

The French government shared this attitude and appealed to Sazonov again to submit and thereby bring Romania into the war to cover the southeastern flank of Brusilov's army. This plea came during the siege of Verdun and the anguished cry influenced Sazonov to act. On June 27 he formally invited Brătianu to intervene. His note pictured a wide-open road to Budapest and Timişoara for the Romanians. Brătianu now refused to move until the four Allied Powers agreed on military strategy. He was asking for what the Allies themselves had been unable to do since the beginning of the war.[60]

Fear of an imminent Russian invasion of Hungary led Vienna to offer Bucovina to Romania in return for intervention against Russia. Although Count Stephen Tisa, the powerful Magyar leader, opposed this offer, he was overruled by the Austro-Hungarian Foreign Ministry and General Staff. Brătianu, however, rejected the offer.[61]

Aristide Briand, the French premier, and General Joffre interceded directly with Brătianu to secure his entry. They promised an offensive from Salonika to check Bulgaria. This encouraged Brătianu to take a decisive step. On July 4, he informed Sazonov of his readiness to enter as soon as a formal political convention was signed, guaranteeing all territorial promises already made, and as soon as a long list of military conditions was satisfied. He demanded: (1) the arrival of the first munitions train at the Romanian frontier; (2) a promise to send a maximum of 300 tons of provisions daily, for the remainder of 1916; (3) stabilization of Russian positions in Galicia and Bucovina; (4) resumption of the offensive against Bulgaria; and (5) positive guarantees against an attack upon Romania by Bulgaria.[62]

Sazonov yielded on condition that Britain and France join him in an ultimatum to Brătianu, insisting he intervene immediately or risk losing all promises made since 1914.[63] When Brătianu learned of Sazonov's conditions, which also required him to retrocede southern Dobrodgea to assure Bulgaria's neutrality vis-à-vis Romania, he accused the Allies of reversing their responsibilities and charging him with their own sins.[64] He proposed to intervene in October or November, not in July or August, as Sazonov demanded.

Despite his most recent tergiversation, Brătianu was resolved to act while the Brusilov offensive was successful. On July 19 Russian troops crossed the Carpathians and were in view of the plains of Transylvania. But five days later (July 23) Sazonov was replaced by Boris Stürmer, whose attitude toward Romania was unknown to Brătianu.

Uncertain of the outcome of the ministerial change in Petrograd, Brătianu concluded a military agreement with the British and French general staffs at Chantilly promising that 150,000 Anglo-French troops would move against Bulgaria as soon as Romania intervened. Brătianu was determined to secure an irrevocable guarantee his troops would not be required to wage a two-front campaign.[65]

When entry appeared imminent, Brătianu threw another stumbling block into the path. He insisted Romania must not fight Bulgaria.[66] This caused Alekseev to hesitate again, but he was forced by Stürmer to comply after the Allied ambassadors advised that Germany would force Bulgaria to attack Romania anyhow. On August 5 Russia agreed that Romania's military efforts should be directed exclusively toward Transylvania. This was done to end Brătianu's hesitations and to fix the date of intervention for August 14.[67]

Brătianu still stalled, as hope for a quick Russian victory faded, and as the Germans were transferring fifteen divisions from the West to relieve Austria-Hungary. As the Brusilov offensive weakened, Brătianu began talks with Bulgaria regarding a neutrality treaty. When his approaches became known in Petrograd, the Allied ambassadors pleaded with Stürmer to yield even if it entailed postponing intervention.[68] Stürmer complied, on August 8, by communicating the draft of a political convention to the Allies and Romania. It provided for an entry date of August 21, at which time Romania must go to war or forfeit every territorial promise. The Allies accepted Stürmer's conditions, and on August 9 the four Allied envoys in Bucharest presented the convention to Brătianu. This was the first time that the four Allied Powers had acted in concert; heretofore Russia had negotiated on behalf of her allies.[69]

Brătianu agreed to all except Article 5 which provided that if any territory promised had not been conquered by the Allies or Romania then the regions were promised "only to the extent that this seems possible in connection with the general situation after the war." The enraged Premier saw in this article an opportunity for Hungary to save herself by signing a separate peace with the Allies who, in turn, would accord Romania mere bits of territory from that state. He categorically refused to sign.[70]

Stürmer rebuffed Brătianu's objections and asked the Allies to join him in presenting a stern démarche to Brătianu opposing any change in the terms.[71] Briand saved the day by proposing the conclusion of a secret Franco-Russian accord whereby "the annexations promised to Romania will be effective only as the general situation permits. The Great Powers reserve for themselves the big questions. The Banat question will be examined."[72] Briand predicted that the Allies would be so strong after the war that they could review their wartime promises, or they would be so weak that they could not enforce them. Stürmer was enchanted by this scheme and gave way by deleting Article 5 and even agreeing to extend the date of Romania's entry to August 27.[73]

The political convention was now in the form desired by Brătianu. The Allied envoys and military attaches met on August 17 with the Premier in a private house to avoid arousing the suspicion of German agents. After signing, Brătianu expressed hope that a new era of friendship and confidence between Russia and Romania had begun.[74]

The political convention provided that Romania would enter the war by August 28, or within eight days after the offensive from Salonika, scheduled to begin August 20, had opened against Bulgaria. Romania was obliged to fulfill the following conditions: (Art. 2) declare war on and attack Austria-Hungary according to terms of an accompanying military convention, and cease all diplomatic, economic, and commercial relations with Germany, Bulgaria, and Turkey; (Art. 4) leave a zone in the Banat opposite Belgrade free of fortifications and indemnify Serbs of the Banat who wished to emigrate to Serbia after the war; (Art. 5) refrain from concluding a separate or general peace with the enemy; and (Art. 7) preserve the secrecy of the convention until achievement of general peace.

The four Allied Powers guaranteed to: (Art. 1) safeguard the territorial integrity of the Kingdom of Romania "in all the extent of her present frontiers" (thus assuring Brătianu against any subsequent demand for retrocession of southern Dobrodgea to Bulgaria); (Art. 3) recognize Romania's right to annex territories of Austria-Hungary within the borders indicated in the convention (the regions assigned to Romania corresponded to Brătianu's maximum demands, including Bucovina as far north as the Prut River and Cernăuți); (Art. 5) refrain from concluding a separate or general peace unless jointly and simultaneously with Romania, and to see to it that at the treaty of peace the territories of Austria-Hungary promised to Romania "will be annexed to the Crown" of that state (this clause was inserted at Briand's suggestion); (Art. 6) promise Romania the same rights enjoyed by the four Allied Powers at the preliminaries and negotiations of the peace, as well as at discussions and questions to be submitted to the decision of the peace conference; and (Art. 7) maintain the secrecy of the convention until the achievement of general peace.[75]

The accompanying military convention assured Romania that Britain and France would begin their offensive against Bulgaria and Turkey no later than August 20. Russia undertook to advance toward Hungary from the northeast and protect the port of Constanța with her Black Sea fleet. Russia also promised to send troops to Dobrodgea to engage the Bulgarians. The Allies agreed to provide a minimum of 300 tons of supplies daily to be transported through Russia. Romania was obliged to act jointly with Russia against Bulgaria, but no condition was included requiring Romania to declare war on Bulgaria. The march on Budapest was reserved exclusively for the Romanians. Coordination between the Russian and Romanian general staffs was to be kept at a minimum, and a precise line of demarcation between the two armies barred Russian forces from operating as fighting units on Romanian soil. This agreement was obviously the sort concluded by two allies who did not trust each other. Article 16 proved ultimately to be of vital consequence for it provided that questions of armistices would be decided by general agreement between the Russian and Romanian general staffs.[76]

Brătianu's assumption that Article 6 conferred "great power" status on Romania was not absurd. Historical precedents show that Romania had cogent reasons to think herself no longer in the small power category. Adherence to the Triple Alliance in 1883 granted Romania the status of a co-equal with Germany, Austria-Hungary, and Italy, specifically in regard to their common undertaking that none would conclude a separate peace and all would participate equally in negotiating settlements arising out of a general war. No changes were made in the alliance whenever renewals were signed. Romania's obligations were no less than those of the other signatory powers, except that she was not privy to consultations whenever a *casus foederis* arose.[77]

Brătianu was unaware of the Franco-Russian understanding regarding postwar interpretation of the 1916 Alliance.[78] Article 6 guaranteed Romania equal rights with the four Allied Powers in the preliminary and final peace negotiations. This privilege actually contradicted the Briand-Stürmer formula, for it gave Brătianu a basis upon which to mount his claim to equality at the Paris Peace Conference. Article 5 prohibited Romania, as well as the Allied Powers, from concluding separate or general peace. These provisions ultimately caused serious trouble when the time arrived for the Allies to fulfill their promises to Romania.

Brătianu's decision to intervene did not cancel last-minute talks with the Austro-Hungarian and German envoys. Czernin, a more discerning judge of Brătianu's tactics than any of the Allied envoys, was instructed to prevent him from intervening. He repeatedly advised Vienna it was too late to change Brătianu's mind. Meeting with the Premier for the last time on August 26, Czernin learned that he wished to remain neutral, but future policy would be determined by a Crown Council the next day. This statement did not convince Czernin who described Brătianu as an incorrigible liar who had hypnotized Ferdinand into joining the Allies. German minister Bussche warned Brătianu that Germany would declare war if Romania attacked Austria-

Hungary. The Premier acknowledged this consequence, but he nevertheless appealed for a guarantee that German planes would not bomb Romanian cities.[79]

The Crown Council of 1916

Two years of temporizing had come to an end. Brătianu now wanted approval of the opposition leaders, but if this were not forthcoming he would still, in all probability, have intervened. The Conservatives and Conservative Democrats had not participated in the secret negotiations; the Premier had merely kept them politely informed. He was now ready to present to them written guarantees promising extensive territorial aggrandizement and elevation of Romania to the status of an equal Allied Power.

A Crown Council convened on August 27 at the Cotroceni Palace on the outskirts of Bucharest. The King and nineteen statesmen, including Brătianu and his cabinet, were joined by a few superannuated Liberals who had long since retired from politics. Rosetti, Carp, and Maiorescu, former Conservative premiers, represented the old guard of their party, while Marghiloman and Olănescu were there for the younger Conservatives. Ionescu, Filipescu, and Cantacuzino-Pașcanu represented the Conservative Democrats.

The King announced his intention to support Brătianu's decision and he asked the statesmen to cooperate in the war effort. He ruled out any debate. Brătianu explained his decision: he recalled how the Balkan crisis of 1912-13 had only prefaced an inevitable struggle with Austria-Hungary because Romania's interests had come into acute conflict with those of Vienna and Budapest; he cited Italy's decision to intervene as an example for Romania to follow, especially since the "Latin nations" were ranged against the Germans; he predicted defeat of the Central Powers with whom a continuation of the 1883 alliance was senseless; and he was convinced that his neutrality treaty with Russia must be implemented by active intervention if Romania were to secure positive guarantees instead of just assurances.

To obtain their support, Brătianu explained that his alliance with the Entente guaranteed Romania "equal rights with those of the other states at the peace congress." When asked about the territories promised, he promised to take territory "up to the Tisa, the Banat, Crișana, the Slav part of Maramureș, and Bucovina up to the Prut." His assertion that Romania would obtain the Tisa as her new frontier with Hungary was a distortion of the truth. The Alliance did not provide for it.

To a question about Germany's attitude, Brătianu replied he would declare war on Austria-Hungary only, not on other Central Powers. At this point, Petre P. Carp uttered his famous jeremiad to the interventionists: "I wish that you be conquered because your victory will be the ruin of the country!". Brătianu retorted, "Then take your sons and give them to the enemy army!" [80]

The session was then adjourned. Although failing to win support of the Conservatives, Brătianu wasted no time in fulfilling his obligations.[81] That afternoon martial law was proclaimed and in Vienna that evening the Romanian envoy handed a declaration of war to the Austro-Hungarian Foreign Ministry.[82] The next morning Brătianu visited his father's tomb at Florica. Upon returning, he told his wife, "I have just come from my father's grave — he would have done as I have done."[83]

Events which followed were not unexpected. Germany declared war on August 28, and Turkey did the same on August 31. To deter Bulgaria's declaration, Brătianu told Radoslavov, the Bulgarian premier, of his intention to support Bulgaria's claim to southern Dobrodgea and to use his good offices with the Allies to arrange a separate peace for the Bulgarians. He even promised to support Bulgaria's claim against Turkey for the Enos-Midia line. Radoslavov refused to haggle and declared war on September 1.[84]

Two years of negotiations made clear the deep-seated rift among the Allies with respect to Romania's destiny. Britain anticipated that an enlarged Romania would challenge Russian encroachments in the Balkans. To France, Romania could be a bulwark against German moves. For the Italians, Romania could be an ally against the Slavs who were destined to become a force after the defeat of Austria-Hungary. The Russians conceived of Romania as removed from the German economic orbit and able to provide easy access to the Slavic Balkans, and become, for the first time, a friendly neighbor.[85] Despite these differences the Allies were now obligated to fulfill one common aim — the dismemberment of Hungary for the purpose of enlarging Romania. But these dreams were somewhat dispelled when Romania's march into Transylvania turned into a rout in the fall of 1916. The reversals inflicted by the Central Powers appeared to some observers to be a just punishment for Brătianu's folly in intervening with a poorly equipped army.[86] To others it was a vindication of his efforts to create a "Greater Romania," with that added ingredient of martyrdom which no patriotic cause can neglect.

The Military Debacle

Romania's military operations, agreed to by the Allies, were based on too many contingencies. It was anticipated the Brusilov offensive would attract Austro-Hungarian forces to Bucovina while the Romanians crossed the Carpathians into southeastern Transylvania, the Russians in Dobrodgea and Anglo-French forces from Salonika would prevent Bulgaria from invading Romania, and the Italians would advance on the Isonzo River while the Germans would be fully occupied at Verdun and on the Somme. None of these prospects materialized.

The Allies' obligation to coordinate their strategy with respect to the Romanian campaign (Article 15 of the military convention) was not fulfilled. The Brusilov offensive stalled, permitting Austria-Hungary and Germany to advance unhindered against the Romanians. The Russians were able to send only 20,000 troops to Dobrodgea, the closest Russia ever came to Constantinople. The offensive from Salonika scarcely budged. By mid-September, after taking Braşov (German, Kronstadt) and Sibiu (German, Hermannstadt), the Romanians were caught in a gigantic pincer. Germany, taking advantage of the lack of Allied unity and purpose, coordinated Austro-Hungarian, Bulgarian, and Turkish forces with her own in a massive encircling movement against Romania, beginning September 27. Generals Falkenhayn and Mackensen led the counter-attack, the former crossing into western Wallachia from Transylvania on November 14, and the latter marching toward Bucharest from Bulgaria.

The Romanian army was forced to cease its advance into Transylvania and rush troops to the rear to meet Mackensen, who occupied Constanţa on October 23. A month later Mackensen crossed the Danube at a point forty miles from Bucharest. Exactly one hundred days after Romania's declaration of war the Central Powers were in control of one-half of the country. Bucharest surrendered on December 6, after the royal family, the government, and most of the army were evacuated from Wallachia to northern Moldavia.

This debacle could not be blamed on any single power. Romania's unpreparedness, her determination to grab Transylvania before the Russians could, and her subordination of military to political strategy combined to turn the scales against her. Russia's apathy, indecision, and exhaustion certainly contributed to the disaster.[87] The British and French must also be counted as partly responsible for they, even more than the Russians, had enticed Romania into war and were then unwilling and unable to fulfill their bargain to march from Salonika into Bulgaria.

By January 1917 the Romanians, with minimum Russian assistance, were able to stop the enemy advance. The battle line was stabilized along the Siret River, separating most of Moldavia from occupied Wallachia, where it remained for a year. Following a reorganization of her army by a French military mission led by General Henri Berthelot, Romania resumed hostilities in June 1917, and inflicted severe defeats upon the enemy at Mărești and Mărășești. These victories could not be followed up with an expulsion of enemy forces from Wallachia because the Russian army in Moldavia, upon which the Romanians relied, was *hors de combat*. Romania's position worsened as Bolsheviks agitated and revolutionaries clamoring for peace seized power in Petrograd in November 1917. The choice between complete subjugation through surrender to the Central Powers or continued resistance, without any Allied assistance, confronted Romania in the winter of 1917-18.

Indecision Again

The Romanian government functioned in unoccupied Moldavia while Brătianu labored to uphold the terms of the Alliance and to force the Allies to do likewise. He convened parliament in overpopulated Iași and reorganized his government on December 24, 1916. A coalition regime, he believed, would dispel growing defeatism and provide a solid front against the Central Powers, the pro-German Conservatives who remained in Bucharest to collaborate, and those in Iași ready to scrap the Alliance to save the country. Conservative Democrats Ionescu, Mihai Cantacuzino, Dimitrie Greceanu, and Constantin Istrati were appointed to the new cabinet. The Iași parliament voted the new cabinet emergency powers to continue the war, and Brătianu thereby enjoyed unquestioned power for the remainder of his term in office.[88]

Brătianu revealed to the parliament the contents of the 1916 Alliance, confident the Allies would never consider it a scrap of paper. He blamed the defeats squarely on the Russians, while expressing the complacent opinion that Anglo-French forces at Salonika would soon attack and speed to the rescue of Romania. The Premier praised the respect shown by the western Allies for the principles of small-power independence and freedom of all peoples:

> When the flag of the Entente was raised in a great war capable of changing the whole situation in Europe, all the sentiments and interests of the Romanians flocked to its colors. Romania could not stand by in this struggle watching her neighbors with indifference while they fought over issues affecting Romania's fate.[89]

The legislators responded by voting to continue resistance.

The March Revolution in Russia and the subsequent growth of the Bolshevik movement there led Brătianu to reform his domestic and foreign policies. In keeping with his decision to remain a belligerent and to assert his privilege of an equal ally, Brătianu had attended the Inter-Allied Conference in Petrograd in January-February 1917, even though he had not been invited. He appealed for aid, but received only words of consolation from the French delegation and words of desolation from the Russian General Staff.[90]

Brătianu, attempting again in May 1917 to secure military assistance, went to Petrograd to talk with the Provisional Government which had, like himself, decided to remain in the war. He was once more confronted with defeatism and even contempt for the Romanian war effort, especially from Foreign Minister Miliukov who made no secret of his preference for Bulgaria. Brătianu learned of the demands of the Petrograd Soviet for peace without annexations. Miliukov assured him the Soviet program did not bind the Provisional Government, but Brătianu was not convinced. Returning quite disillusioned to Iaşi, he told the French envoy that "...revolution is inevitable in Russia where it will be a witch's cauldron or a Pandora's box with all its evils and without Hope at the bottom.[91]

Since Russia appeared to be on her way out of the war, Brătianu could no longer look to her for the strength he lacked. The declaration of war by the United States in April 1917 had no practical importance for Romania; her fate was linked to that of Russia, not to that of the western Allies. If Russia withdrew, Romania inevitably would be forced to take steps to save herself, by surrender if necessary. Brătianu could not temporize in the fall of 1917 as he had done from 1914 to 1916. By seeking peace, the most drastic solution, he would be violating Article 5 of the Alliance and consequently forfeiting all treaty advantages. He now looked for a means to extract from the western

Allies a revision of the Alliance to enable him to conclude a temporary truce or peace without abandoning his status of an equal ally. At the same time he had to prevent Austria-Hungary from seeking a separate peace, lest the Habsburg Monarchy emerge intact from the war.

Before opening talks with the western Allies Brătianu decided to strengthen his position at home. The promise he had made in 1914 to enact agrarian and electoral reforms was fulfilled in June 1917 when, with the cooperation of the Conservative Democrats, Parliament introduced universal manhood suffrage and the expropriation and division of large landed estates. This was done to insure social stability threatened by radical propaganda in neighboring Russia.[92]

Brătianu approached the Provisional Government in October 1917, but the lateness of the hour, which did not permit Kerenskii to reply favorably to pleas for assistance, was illustrated by the declaration of the Petrograd Soviet on October 20. The Soviet called upon the Central Powers to evacuate Wallachia, but other points were not comforting. The Soviet's peace proposals called for plebiscites in all disputed areas of the Balkans, restoration of Romania to her pre-war frontiers on condition that she grant autonomy to the Bulgarians of Dobrodgea and permit a plebiscite in that region to determine its future status, fulfillment by Romania of the provisions of Article 44 of the Treaty of Berlin of 1878 obliging her to accord rights of citizenship and religious toleration to non-Orthodox peoples, and repudiation and denunciation of all secret treaties concluded during the war.[93]

It was clear that, if the Soviet overthrew the Provisional Government, the Bolsheviks would repudiate the 1916 Alliance and thus raise the question of its validity after one signatory had disavowed it. As events turned out, the Bolsheviks, after seizing power on November 7, decreed the abolition of all Tsarist commitments to the Allies. On November 8 the All-Union Congress of Soviets renounced the secret treaties and, on November 22, published the texts. Trotskii called for armistices on all fronts and the opening of peace talks based on national self-determination for all peoples. He then appealed to the people of all belligerent countries, including Romania, to force their governments to open peace negotiations.[94]

Brătianu turned to the Allies for guidance and was greeted with a request that he evacuate his government and army (as the Serbs had done two years before) into southern Russia, and then proceed through the Caucasus to join British forces in Mesopotamia. He explored this possibility in a visit to Odessa only to come away convinced that a struggle with Bolshevik sympathizers in the Ukraine would impede completion of the plan. His appraisal of the grave situation was confirmed by American and French officials and military officers who visited Romania and Russia in the fall of 1917. Pleading for tangible evidence of Allied solidarity, Brătianu was promised an American loan.[95] French minister Saint-Aulaire expressed his inability to obtain anything more than verbal assurances from the new premier of France, Georges Clemenceau, whose esteem for Romania had never been high. Barclay, the British minister, could not convince Brătianu of Lloyd George's sympathy after the Premier had learned that the British were responsible for abandoning the Salonika offensive. Italian envoy Fasciotti, whose country had all but been driven out of the war, could offer nothing more than consolation.[96]

Brătianu's approaches to the Americans were disappointing. President Wilson, in a note to Iaşi on November 28, promised that he would use his good offices to assure that Romania's integrity as a free and independent nation would be safeguarded after the war.[97] This message was the result of a mission sent to Washington by Brătianu to stimulate a movement for Romanian unity among natives of Transylvania and Romania living in the United States. When the three Transylvanian nationalists (Uniate priests Vasile Lucaciu and Ioan Moţa, and Captain Vasile Stoica, a Hungarian expatriate serving in the Romanian army) met with Secretary of State Robert Lansing on July 2 after their arduous trek across Siberia and the Pacific, Lansing refused to subscribe to any aim of dismembering Austria-Hungary when told that Romania's claims could be satisfied only if the Dual Monarchy lost territory.[98] The United States had not yet declared war on Austria-Hungary, but it did agree to lend Romania $5 million. Britain later agreed to lend 600,000 pounds, and France promised 2 million francs.[99] But these offers came too late; Brătianu had decided upon the armistice which the Allies were trying ineffectually to prevent.

The Armistice

Brătianu's decision to seek an armistice was the direct consequence of a speech made by Wilson to the Congress, on December 4, in which he requested a declaration of war on Austria-Hungary. The President stated that he did not wish to "impair or rearrange the Austro-Hungarian Empire," but only to release the peoples of the Balkans and Austria-Hungary from the "impudent and alien dominion of the Prussian military and commercial autocracy."[100] Thus Wilson refused to subscribe to the principal terms of the 1916 Alliance, fulfillment of which was predicated upon amputation of Hungary's territories.[101]

After having failed to obtain satisfactory responses from the western Allies, Brătianu turned to General Shcherbachev, commander of the Russian army in Moldavia, who wished to arrange an armistice because he could no longer control his Bolshevik-influenced troops. Shcherbachev proposed a truce to Mackensen on December 5, coincidental with the beginning of armistice negotiations at Brest-Litovsk between the Soviet Government and the Central Powers. Brătianu advised the Allies that if Russia concluded a truce or separate peace the Central Powers would be free to occupy Moldavia and install a pro-German puppet regime in Iaşi. He pleaded with the Allied envoys for approval to conclude a truce without violating the 1916 Alliance. The consequence of Allied refusal, he explained, would be the subjugation of Moldavia by German or Bolshevik forces.[102]

The Allies insisted again that Brătianu evacuate Moldavia, a course which the Premier steadfastly refused to consider, lest a pro-German or a Bolshevik regime replace him. He summoned a Crown Council to discuss the crisis. The Conservative Democrats favored an armistice if the terms coincided with those being considered at Brest-Litovsk. Ionescu desired a strictly military truce excluding any idea of a separate peace. Since Romania already was consulting with Shcher-bachev, who represented what remained of the Imperial Russian General Staff, the provisions of Article 16 of the military convention (joint discussion of questions of armistices) were not being violated. Shcherbachev, who attended the session, acknowledged this interpretation, as did General Berthelot. The council decided to open talks leading to an armistice.[103]

Brătianu assured the Allied ministers that the proposed armistice would permit him to assume a "wait and see" policy while Romania's military reserves would remain intact for future cooperation with the Allies. A truce would permit the royal family to remain in Iaşi despite demands for Ferdinand's abdication by pro-German Conservatives in Bucharest. Brătianu promised to resign if forced by the Allies to evacuate Moldavia. He complained of Allied indifference toward Romania's plight compounded by military defeats, a typhus epidemic, and deteriorating army and civilian morale.

The Romanian General Staff signed a cease-fire at Focşani on December 9. The armistice, effective for three months and terminable upon 72-hour notice, was not to be considered as a capitulation or separate peace by either side. Romania thus became the second of the

Allied and Associated Powers to take herself out of the war; Bolshevik Russia was the only other.[104] Allied reaction was instantaneously critical. Clemenceau instructed Saint-Aulaire to condemn the truce. Brătianu instructed Victor Antonescu, his envoy in Paris, to assure President Poincaré of Romania's intention to remain loyal. This approach was a tragic error, for Poincaré was Clemenceau's vigorous antagonist. Antonescu also called on William Sharp, American ambassador in Paris, who obtained from Lansing assurances that Washington intended to continue financial aid to Romania. To repair the damage Brătianu resorted to distortions to describe his armistice. He insisted falsely that the Focşani armistice did not really involve Romania, that it was purely a Russo-German agreement, and that he would conduct his own negotiations, avoiding any mention of peace. He did not reveal that General Lupescu of the Romanian General Staff had signed the armistice.[105]

Brătianu's skill in deception netted the desired results. The Allies accepted at face value his distortion of the facts. They decided at the Inter-Allied Conference in Paris on December 22-23, in response to Antonescu's appeal, to consider the Focşani armistice a temporary cease-fire and not a prelude to a separate peace. The Allies promised to send food and military supplies to Romania "to whom they felt bound by every obligation of honor."[106] Brătianu was thereby awarded a grace period as 1917 came to a close.

Brătianu's Resignation

No sooner had Brătianu received encouraging news from the West than he was demoralized by news of changes in Allied war aims in January 1918. He learned of British efforts to lure Austria-Hungary out of the war by a separate peace.[107] When Vienna balked, Lloyd George noted that Russia's defection had necessitated an Allied reexamination of territorial rearrangements in the secret treaties. Despite his avowals to honor British commitments to Romania, Lloyd George countermanded these assurances in his famous war aims speech of January 5 when he advised Austria-Hungary that Britain did not intend to dismember the Habsburg Monarchy, but only wished to see certain rights granted to Romanians and other nationalities within the empire.[108] Clemenceau endorsed this declaration. Briand, the premier who had secured Romania's intervention in exchange for a guarantee she would receive territories of the Dual Monarchy, complained that Clemenceau's action would deprive Romania of achieving her "legitimate aspirations."[109] But Briand was no longer in office. The only statesman in the Allied camp who had survived changes in governments was the Italian foreign minister, Baron Sidney Sonnino, and his statement to the Romanian envoy in Rome was hardly reassuring. He said that "in the worst of conditions Romania will never get consent from the Entente for a separate peace."[110]

A dramatic reversal of war aims occurred on January 8 when Wilson delivered his "Fourteen Points" address. Romania would stand to lose more than she would gain if she supported the Points. Point One, which denounced secret diplomacy, repudiated the bargaining and jeopardized the validity of the 1916 Alliance. Point Ten threatened the prospect of annexing Transylvania after Wilson called for the autonomous development of the peoples of Austria-Hungary, not for their incorporation into neighboring states. Point Eleven called for the evacuation and restoration of Romania, establishment of close relations among the Balkan states, and an international guarantee of the political, economic, and territorial independence and integrity of the Balkan nations. Thus Romania would be evacuated and restored; there was no mention of any territorial acquisitions.[111]

Wilson's address touched off a peace movement among Romanian army officers who were convinced that Wallachia would be recovered even if a separate peace were concluded.[112] This interpretation of Point Eleven was strengthened when Stephen Pichon, the French foreign minister, urged Brătianu to conclude a separate peace and promised it would not jeopardize Romania's status as an ally. When Pichon requested American concurrence, Lansing replied that he would uphold Wilson's message of November 28 and nothing more. Brătianu asked Lansing to explain the American position on the 1916 Alliance. The Secretary of State replied that the United States had no knowledge of the existence of any understanding between Romania and the Allies with regard to peace terms.[113] This avowal by Lansing of his ignorance of the Alliance came about one year after Wilson had been apprised of the contents of the secret treaties and two months after the Bolsheviks published them.[114] American indifference toward the 1916 Alliance complicated the settlement of future problems.

Brătianu was completely taken aback by the confusion in the Allied camp. He instructed the new Romanian envoy in Washington, Constantin Anghelescu (formerly Minister of Public Works in Brătianu's cabinet), to approach Wilson for a clarification of the muddle over war aims. The President told him on January 15 that the United States was "happy to have freed its arm for the like protection

of your country and your country's allies," and he expressed
confidence in the combined Allied effort. Wilson said nothing about the
1916 Alliance.[115]

Amid this confusion Brătianu found himself embroiled in a crisis
with Bolshevik Russia over the issue of Bessarabia. In December 1917
Romanian nationalists had proclaimed Bessarabia an autonomous
republic within Russia. The Sfatul Ţării (Council of the Land) of the
new republic appealed to Brătianu for protection against the Bolsheviks
and the Ukrainian nationalists. Saint-Aulaire and Berthelot urged him
to send troops to Chişinău to drive a Bolshevik force from that city. In
an action which Soviet historians term the first armed Allied intervention in Russia,[116] Romania occupied Bessarabia. The Petrograd
government, unable to recover the province, decided to avenge the
invasion by arresting Constantin Diamandy, the Romanian envoy to
Russia. This action provoked a diplomatic protest by the Allied
ambassadors who demanded that Lenin release the envoy. Diamandy
was released after two weeks in prison and forced to leave Russia, and
the Soviet government suspended diplomatic relations with Romania.[117]

While involved with the Bolsheviks, Brătianu faced a new crisis at
home. On January 20 Mackensen demanded an opening of peace talks.
His alternative was a German occupation of Moldavia. This ultimatum
aroused expectations in Iaşi that if Romania acceded, Germany would
evacuate Wallachia, detach only small sections of southern Dobrodgea
and a few passes in the Carpathians, and permit Romania to retain
Bessarabia. Thus a separate peace would not be as disastrous as Allied
propaganda was proclaiming it would be, and it would enable Romania
to take precautions, with German assistance, against Bolshevik threats.
Brătianu requested Allied permission to negotiate with Germany on the
basis of these assumptions, but the four envoys responded by asking
him to attack the Germans in order to reverse the situation. The
ministers believed the Premier would not sign a treaty unless Germany
invaded Moldavia. Brătianu rejoined that his country already had
followed similar advice by attacking the Bolsheviks in Bessarabia only
to arouse the wrath of Russia.[118]

The Allied envoys tried to dissuade Brătianu on February 5,
contending that the Germans could not mount an offensive against
Moldavia. The Premier did not think the Germans were accustomed to
making idle threats. General Ludendorff had that day ordered troops
transferred from the Western to the Eastern Front and instructed
Mackensen to extract a treaty from Romania.[119] The deadline for talks
to begin was set for February 10.[120]

Brătianu summoned his cabinet on February 7. The Conservative Democrats implored him to remain in the war at all costs and to reject Mackensen's ultimatum. Brătianu revealed his intention to open protracted talks while making some arrangement with the Bolsheviks before considering the risks of a separate peace. Rather than share the guilt of peace negotiations, the Conservative Democrats resigned from the coalition government on February 7.[121]

The ministerial crisis occasioned by the Conservative Democrat retreat culminated in Brătianu's resignation on February 8. He proposed that the King appoint General Alexandru Averescu to head a non-party government. Averescu was willing to carry out Brătianu's tactics of prolonged peace talks. Both agreed that negotiations would be undertaken as a consequence of the war aims speeches of Lloyd George and Wilson, whose words were interpreted to mean that even if the Allies won the war Romania would not obtain the territories promised in the 1916 Alliance.[122]

It remained to be seen whether the assurance Brătianu once gave to Barclay — that Romania's obligations would be binding upon his successor — would be fulfilled.[123] Averescu obtained a delay of the peace talks and soon became convinced of the inevitable triumph of the Central Powers. He accepted in good faith the promise of Emperor Charles that Austro-Hungarian troops would not advance into Moldavia if Romania accepted a treaty entailing no humiliation other than minor frontier rectifications.[124] When Averescu turned to the Allies for a lead he was met with the familiar demand for evacuation. He appealed to Vopicka, the American minister, for a common Allied approval of a separate peace. Vopicka complied by requesting Lansing to reject the evacuation proposal. Wilson instructed Lansing to inform Averescu on February 21 that the United States would consider null and void measures imposed on Romania by the Central Powers only insofar as they adversely affected that state's political and territorial integrity.[125]

Confronted with adamant Allied demands Averescu decided to meet with Kühlmann, the German foreign minister, and Czernin, now Austro-Hungarian foreign minister, to receive peace terms. He learned that all of Dobrodgea and undefined frontier passes in the Carpathians had to be ceded. Averescu had the King intercede with the foreign ministers on February 27, but Ferdinand failed to obtain a modification of the terms. Czernin hinted that a new government led by anti-interventionist Marghiloman, leader of the Conservatives, might secure better terms. Ferdinand agreed to explore this in exchange for a postponement of talks. He then summoned a Crown Council for March 1 to determine acceptance or rejection.[126]

The Decision to Make Peace

Three sessions of the Crown Council were required before Averescu won approval of his decision to make peace. He cited the inability of the army to renew hostilities, the failure of the Allies to outline a satisfactory solution, and Bolshevik infiltration. Brătianu offered two solutions: (1) resistance led by a coalition of Liberals, Conservative Democrats, and Averescu's cabinet; or (2) acceptance of the enemy terms under protest so as to preserve Romania's honor. If Averescu rejected both solutions, Brătianu advised, the King should summon Marghiloman, candidate of the Central Powers, to form a government which could "perhaps get better conditions." The Conservative Democrats appealed for acceptance of the Allied order to evacuate, but Ferdinand overruled it because the General Staff refused to fight the Bolsheviks in the Ukraine.

Ferdinand and Averescu, employing Brătianu's tactic of prolonging the talks, requested a revision of enemy terms. Czernin rejected a protraction of the discussions and demanded that Romania yield specific areas before formal negotiations began. He warned that the Central Powers would resume hostilities on March 5 if the Romanians refused to comply.[127] This ultimatum caused Ferdinand to yield to the terms, but Brătianu still urged him to appoint Marghiloman so that the Conservative leader could use his influence in Berlin and Vienna to mitigate the harsh terms. The Liberals and Conservative Democrats could protest publicly, even with "a knife at our throats," but they could not hope to elicit lenient conditions, Brătianu declared. Averescu revealed that the Central Powers would assist Romania in annexing Bessarabia in return for a treaty. This news tipped the scales in favor of peace; another determining factor was a report that the Soviet government had signed a peace treaty at Brest-Litovsk that day (March 3).[128] The Crown Council agreed, with the Conservative Democrats abstaining, to seek a provisional peace treaty.

When Czernin and Kühlmann returned from Brest-Litovsk with a very satisfactory treaty eliminating Russia from the war and permitting the transfer of troops from the Eastern to the Western Front, the two foreign ministers agreed to arrange a temporary treaty binding Romania against resuming hostilities and requiring her to permit the passage of German troops through Moldavia and Bessarabia to reach the grainfields of the Ukraine. The preliminary treaty was signed at Buftea on March 5. It contained mutual guarantees that the final peace would be concluded after the Central Powers had consolidated their positions in the Ukraine. Romania had to cede all of Dobrodgea to the condominium of the four Central Powers, she had to accept in principle certain frontier rectifications with Hungary, and her army was to be partially demobilized. Passage through Moldavia and Bessarabia of German and Austro-Hungarian troops was to be facilitated. All officers of the Allied military missions were to be expelled. Finally, Romania had to accept in principle all economic measures considered "adequate to the occasion" which would be imposed by the final peace.[129]

Averescu then turned to making peace with the Bolsheviks who desired to terminate the dispute over Bessarabia. In line with the action taken by the Soviet government at Brest-Litovsk, the Bolsheviks holding Odessa signed an agreement with Averescu on March 9, providing for evacuation of Bessarabia by troops of both sides within two months.[130] Averescu was pressed into yielding by the Germans so that pacification of Bessarabia would facilitate passage of troops into the Ukraine. Romania had no intention of honoring the provisions for within one month an opportunity arose to proceed with the formal annexation of Bessarabia. This was occasioned by the German occupation of the Ukraine and the resultant flight of the Bolsheviks.

Although the Buftea treaty by its very nature permitted Romania to protract negotiations for a final peace, Brătianu did not consider it lenient and he convinced Ferdinand to replace Averescu with Marghiloman. Marghiloman's appointment was based on two assumptions: (1) if the Allies won the war, his regime would be discredited for submission to the Central Powers, and it would be replaced by a Liberal government which could reassert Romania's claims and status as an allied state; and (2) if the Central Powers were victorious, Romania would at least retain Bessarabia and perhaps enjoy the benefits of a moderate peace. Brătianu gambled on the first assumption by retiring from politics in March so as to give the impression that he neither sponsored nor supported a government which proposed to arrange a final peace. The Liberal leader, nevertheless, was responsible for Marghiloman's appointment, and by the same token he must bear the onus of having made possible the Peace of Bucharest of May 7, 1918.[131]

The Peace of Bucharest

Marghiloman assumed office on March 18.[132] During his brief term, Romania formally annexed Bessarabia on April 9.[133] He concluded lengthy negotiations with the Central Powers on May 7, after certain harsh terms of the Buftea treaty were mitigated while others were intensified. The final peace was signed in the same room of the Cotroceni Palace in which the memorable Crown Council of August 2, 1916 had taken place. Total cession of territory amounted to more than 10,000 square miles with a population exceeding 800,000. One feature of the Peace of Bucharest should be noted — Article 9 of the Political-Legal section provided that Romania's membership in the Triple Alliance would be revived. But the most memorable aspect of the peace was Romania's complete submission to the economic control of Germany and Austria-Hungary.[134] The fate of Bessarabia was not mentioned except for permission to occupy the province.[135] Public protest from the Liberals and Conservative Democrats did not arise when the peace was published on May 8. It was not the lenient treaty Brătianu hoped Marghiloman would secure from his German friends. It nevertheless served a practical purpose for, by its extremely harsh economic character, Brătianu was able to convince the Allies that the imposed peace reflected German rapacity and Romania's helplessness. Marghiloman's anti-Liberal practice of recalling Romanian diplomats appointed by Brătianu, inciting press campaigns against the Liberals and Conservative Democrats, and supporting a plan to bring to trial the entire Liberal Party in the summer of 1918 served to enhance Brătianu and the policy he represented.[136]

The four Allied ministers exonerated Brătianu from responsibility for the separate peace. They described it as an example of the "insatiable greed and hypocrisy of German imperialism" which the Liberals would refuse to ratify in the vote Marghiloman promised to secure.[137] The envoys told Marghiloman, on May 14, that all treaty stipulations contrary to "principles the violation of which constrains the Entente to take up arms, and which are all contrary to the rights and interests of the Entente," should be considered null and void.[138] They requested their governments to affirm an Allied victory would erase the territorial provisions of the peace and, observing that no time limit was set for the exchange of ratifications, accurately predicted the Central Powers would delay ratifying in order to gain further advantages from a state of war which in theory still existed. The four ministers urged a close examination of the peace inasmuch:

as the German delegates informed the Romanian delegates, who were appalled at being required to accept such conditions, that they would appreciate their moderation when they learned those which could be imposed on the Western Powers after the victory of the Central Powers.[139]

Britain, France, and Italy yielded to their envoys' appeal and announced an intention to consider those stipulations of the peace which conflicted with the 1916 Alliance to be null and void. Clemenceau joined with Poincaré and Pichon to declare the separate peace did not cancel Romania's membership in the Entente.[140] Lloyd George pledged his support of a revocation, and Italian premier Orlando promised to undo the harsh terms.[141] Wilson did not respond to the appeal, but his statement of February 21 was interpreted to be still in effect.[142]

Brătianu and the Liberals, who were excluded from the elections to the new parliament, did not participate in the ratification process. The Chamber ratified the peace on June 28, the only opposition coming from Averescu's People's League. The vote indicated that 135 out of a possible 179 ayes were cast for ratification. The Senate ratified unanimously on July 4, after the King appealed for an end to bitter partisanship and a swift return of peace. Germany completed parliamentary ratifications on July 4.[143]

Several flaws affected the legality of the ratifications. Only two of the signatory powers, Romania and Germany, ratified the entire peace treaty, but the two ratifications were never exchanged even though Article 31 stated that exchanges should take place in Vienna "as soon as possible." The Romanian parliament had acted under threat of an occupation of Moldavia if ratification was not voted. Although no provision stipulated the required number of ratifications or the actual effective date of the terms, subsequent events indicated that none of the signatory powers put the treaty into effect. It is clear the binding force of the treaty was suspended until exchanges occurred, but neither Germany nor Romania fulfilled that treaty requirement. The moral effect of the peace was more influential than its terms. This evidence better substantiates the charge that the treaty was null and void than does Ferdinand's refusal to sign the ratification.[144]

Propaganda Abroad

The Peace of Bucharest ended temporarily Romania's military and diplomatic activities, but the treaty did not end propaganda efforts. The Liberals and Conservative Democrats were assisted by unwitting propaganda mills in Berlin and Vienna gloating over the conquest of Romania and boasting of plans to dominate East Central Europe forever. Public statements by Allied leaders assuring Romania of a treaty revision revived pro-Allied sentiments in Romania. Publicity surrounding the abortive treason trials of Brătianu and other Liberals in July 1918 aroused considerable indignation among Allied sympathizers.[145] But the most effective organs of propaganda designed to make the Allies forget the stigma of separate peace and have them uphold the 1916 Alliance were operated by Romanian intellectuals and émigrés who waged a paper war from Paris, London, and Rome.

Brătianu had early appreciated the value of a strong propaganda effort. After his first attempt at propagandizing abroad (the mission of Transylvanian nationalists to Washington in July 1917), he dispatched a group to the United States in November 1917. One member of the mission, Ludovic Mrazec, a petroleum expert, furnished the Department of State with an interpretation of the Peace of Bucharest.[146] In January 1918 Brătianu sent to Paris Alexandru Lăpedatu, a Transylvanian historian, and Nicolae Petrescu-Comnen, a member of the diplomatic service. The latter organized Romanian immigrants in Geneva and revived the works of Transylvanian nationalist Aurel Popovici for the cause.[147]

French statesmen and intellectuals were enlisted. Albert Thomas, former Minister of Armaments, and Pichon made no secret of their affection. Henri Franklin-Bouillon, a prominent leader of the Chamber of Deputies, lent support. The Sorbonne, from which many Liberals and Conservative Democrats had graduated, was represented by such proponents of "Latinity," as Georges Lacour-Gayet, Émile Picard, noted geographer Emmanuel De Martonne, and distinguished historians Charles Seignobos, Louis Léger, and Ernest Lavisse.

British sympathies, cultivated before the war, glowed in the writings of Robert W. Seton-Watson, the inveterate and influential publicist for the liberation of the nationalities of the Habsburg Monarchy. Henry Wickham Steed, prominent correspondent of the *Times*, provided contacts with the Foreign Office. An Anglo-Romanian Society was created to bring Romania's aspirations to the attention of indifferent British statesmen. By 1918, it included officials of the

Foreign Office and members of the House of Commons.[148] Seton-Watson and Steed were instrumental in convening the Rome Congress of Oppressed Nationalities in April 1918. Romania was represented by six émigrés.[149] The Congress gave the Romanians an opportunity to add their claims to those nationalities within the Habsburg Monarchy demanding dismemberment of that empire. Clemenceau endorsed the aspirations,[150] but Orlando was as yet unwilling to subscribe to them.[151]

Conferences held by European socialists during the war took up the question of Romanian aspirations. Christian G. Rakovskii, a founder of the Romanian Socialist Party, hoped to see Romania annex Transylvania. Another socialist, Nicolae Lupu, called for the satisfaction of Romanian claims on the basis of national self-determination.[152] British socialists, organized in the Union of Democratic Control, supported the Fourteen Points which went counter to Romanian aspirations.[153] American socialists were indifferent, but one self-styled socialist who spent the war years in Switzerland and who was considered Wilson's confidante, George D. Herron, was a strong advocate of dismemberment of the Habsburg Monarchy and was one of the first Americans to consider Romania a bulwark against Bolshevism. In a memorandum to the Department of State (May 25, 1918), Herron insisted the Peace of Bucharest was not the result of pro-German sentiment in Romania, but rather of the Allied failure to rescue the country. He tried to weaken pro-Bulgarian, and hence anti-Romanian sentiments in high circles, especially among State Department officials, but he was unsuccessful. Wilson and Lansing never called for war against Bulgaria, and diplomatic relations with that Central Power were never suspended.[154]

Pro-Romanian sympathies in the United States were insignificant contrasted with those for Serbs, Poles, Czechs, Croats, and others whose aspirations could be fulfilled only by a rearrangement of the map of Europe. This was partly due to the fact that relatively few Romanians had emigrated to the United States. About 145,000, principally from Transylvania, had come to America in the period 1899-1914. Most had settled in the Midwestern states where some ineffectual propaganda was produced. Several Romanian-language newspapers appeared, but they served more to present local news than propaganda. An English-language paper, *Romania,* published in Chicago, devoted some space to propaganda, but lack of business limited its existence to the year 1917.[155] Activities of the American Red Cross relief corps in Moldavia in 1917-18 were more widely known in the United States than aspirations of the Romanian government.[156]

The Romanian National Council

The Romanians found their most effective support in France where most of their intellectuals had been educated and where most of those unwilling to remain in Romania after the Peace of Bucharest had gravitated. The titular head of the large Romanian colony in Paris was Take Ionescu, who was permitted to leave Iaşi in June 1918 accompanied by pro-Allied statesmen, teachers, and bureaucrats. More than two hundred traveled on an "exile express" provided by the German General Staff. Their destination was to have been Switzerland, but Ionescu and his entourage soon found their way to Paris where they were greeted by earlier arrivals who had established the Romanian National Council and were publishing a weekly organ, *La Roumanie*. Ionescu was elected president of the council, became editor of the paper, and worked with leaders of national movements seeking freedom from Austria-Hungary.[157]

The council's executive committee included Brătianu, as an honorary president, Constantin Diamandy, Nicolae Petrescu-Comnen, Vasile Lucaciu, Mihai Cantacuzino, Octavian Goga, Ştefan Cicio-Pop, and others representing Romanians of the kingdom, Transylvania, Bessarabia, the Banat, and Bucovina. It appears quite apparent that Brătianu at first sponsored the work of the council even though Ionescu had preempted the role the Premier should have played had he decided to leave Iaşi. Such loyal followers of Brătianu as Diamandy, Victor Antonescu, Constantin Anghelescu, and other Liberals who had found refuge in Paris and who supported Ionescu publicly would not have joined the council if forbidden by the powerful Liberal leader.[158]

The aims of Ionescu and Brătianu were virtually identical; their tactics differed. Ionescu was as realistic, but he foresaw that the Allies might reject the 1916 Alliance because of Romania's defection. He knew most of Europe's leading statesmen and used his unofficial position as "roving ambassador" to regain their sympathy, even if this entailed a diminution of Brătianu's maximum demands.[159] After four months of discussions with Allied statesmen, Ionescu was convinced they did not intend to uphold the maximum promises of the Alliance. Greetings to the council and sympathetic words for Romania's plight from Lloyd George, Clemenceau, Balfour, Pichon, and Lansing did not amount to written reaffirmations of the Alliance.[160] Ionescu learned that they no longer considered the Alliance binding because Romania had technically violated it by concluding a separate peace. He then realized the need to reach an accord with leaders of the national movements within the Habsburg Monarchy and with Balkan statesmen so that they could present a united platform to the peace conference.[161]

Ionescu consulted with Premier Nikola Pašić of Serbia, Premier Eleutherios Venizelos of Greece, and Thomas Masaryk, spokesman of the Czech-Slovak movement. In October 1918 an agreement was reached on a stand to be taken before the peace conference. Although Ionescu was overreaching himself, since he held no official post, it is known that he and Pašić reached a settlement of the Serbo-Romanian dispute over the Banat, that they laid plans with Venizelos for a Balkan federation, and that all agreed to support each other's claims. Ionescu's efforts, however, were in vain because Brătianu was disinclined to cooperate with the small states of East Central Europe.[162]

Although Ionescu's efforts in 1918 proved stillborn, his council's activities succeeded in convincing the British of the military value of propaganda. In early 1918 Lloyd George had named Viscount Northcliffe, publisher of the *Times*, to be Director of Propaganda in Enemy Countries. Northcliffe was assisted by Wickham Steed, Seton-Watson, H. G. Wells, Sidney Low, and many expatriates from Austria-Hungary.[163] As a result of prodding by Romanian and other national groups, the Northcliffe Bureau gradually came to support dismemberment of the Habsburg Monarchy. Supervision of propaganda regarding dismemberment was under Seton-Watson, who found time to publish an influential weekly, *The New Europe,* containing frequent articles by Nicolae Iorga, the nationalistic Romanian historian, and Octavian Goga, the Transylvanian poet. In the opinion of a Transylvanian, Seton-Watson "became the focus of the nationalities and together with Steed can claim the honor of [placing] the British Government [in a position] to adopt as one of its peace aims the right of self-determination for the nationalities of Austria-Hungary."[164]

Romania's Second Intervention

Marghiloman steered a passive course under the surveillance of the Central Powers as long as the ratifications were not exchanged and Moldavia remained free of enemy troops. He was faithful in furnishing the food and petroleum demanded by the Central Powers. Germany and Austria-Hungary were reluctant to conclude the formalities of peace because such action would end requisitions and the unlimited issuance of occupation currency in Wallachia. The permission granted in the Buftea Treaty, by which enemy troops could cross Bessarabia to reach the Ukraine, would have been revoked if ratifications were exchanged.

Marghiloman realized that delivery of his ratification would void all chances for future mobilization of Romania's army, required to be fully demobilized after the exchanges. His hesitation gained the support of Brătianu who emerged from his cloistered life in September to make known his views about the first of several love affairs of Crown Prince Carol. Brătianu moderated the chagrin of King Ferdinand, who bristled at Carol's marriage to Zizi Lambrino, a commoner. Brătianu's claim that he, as leader of the Liberals, had to be consulted on questions of dynastic succession (Carol's qualifications were doubted for the first time) was recognized by Ferdinand and Marghiloman.[165] He soon regained influence over Romanian policy as an Allied victory appeared impending.

On October 7, Brătianu met with the Allied envoys for the first time since resigning eight months before. He informed them he would regain control of the government as soon as the King could exert his free will, and he predicted Romania would re-enter the war as soon as the Allied army advancing from Salonika signalled her to resume hostilities. Renewal of war, he believed, would revive Romanian prestige, render the Peace of Bucharest invalid, and restore Romania's status as an equal ally. The four envoys encouraged him.[166]

The military situation in East Central Europe was changing rapidly. Bulgaria surrendered on September 30 and was no more a threat. Austria-Hungary, in the process of disintegration, no longer presented any appreciable menace. Germany, however, was still a threat. Ludendorff had advised a resumption of hostilities against Romania if she refused to exchange ratifications in October; he was convinced an invasion of Moldavia would prevent Romania from joining the Allied army advancing toward Belgrade.[167] This threat could not be carried out; it was too late.

The German government offered Marghiloman certain privileges if he agreed to exchanges. Romania was promised restoration of Dobrodgea, retrocession of the Carpathian passes, formal recognition of the union of Bessarabia, full restitution for war damages, and revision of economic clauses of the Bucharest peace.[168] Brătianu manipulated this last-minute offer to his advantage by telling the Allies they must make a counter-offer, such as a written guarantee reaffirming the promises of the 1916 Alliance, so that he could regain his popularity and wrest control of Romania's destiny from Marghiloman. He hinted that public opinion, which favored a rapprochement with Germany, could be swayed by the Allies into supporting a second intervention against the Central Powers.[169]

Meanwhile Brătianu was trying to secure from the United States a promise to uphold the territorial guarantees of the 1916 Alliance. He had found little comfort in Wilson's address of September 27, in which the President referred to the "dishonorable and unjust" Peace of Bucharest, but said nothing about American recognition of his claims.[170] Not until Wilson replied on October 19 to the request of Emperor Charles for an armistice did Brătianu hear reassuring words. Wilson told the Habsburg monarch he had been compelled to amend Point Ten ("the freest opportunity for the autonomous development of the peoples of the Empire") to permit the nationalities to determine their own destinies, by separation if so desired.[171] Although Romania was not mentioned, Brătianu expected the new Wilsonian formula could be applied to Romanians within the Habsburg Monarchy.[172]

In response to his appeal for an Allied counter-offer, Clemenceau obliged by dispatching an encouraging message carried by Victor Antonescu to Salonika and thence to Iaşi. Speaking for the four Allied Powers, Clemenceau called upon Romania to re-enter the war and oust the Marghiloman regime before it concluded any arrangements with Germany, but he failed to include any *quid pro quo* to satisfy Brătianu.[173] The presence of twelve German divisions in Wallachia and five in the Ukraine could not be overlooked.[174] Ferdinand issued a secret order to his army on October 28 to prepare for an invasion of Transylvania, but he still hesitated to move.[175]

Brătianu held out for an official American declaration before urging the King to dismiss Marghiloman and to resume the war. This finally came on November 5, when Wilson sent a note to Iaşi endorsing the principle of Romanian national unity. Wilson's move coincided with speeches made in the Budapest parliament by Croat, Slovak, and Romanian deputies who demanded self-determination.[176] Although the President's note contained no reference to the 1916 Alliance, the following declaration was an important factor in encouraging Brătianu to act:

The Government of the United States is not unmindful of the aspirations of the Romanian people without as well as within the boundaries of the Kingdom. It has witnessed their struggles and sufferings and sacrifices in the cause of freedom from their enemies and their oppressors. With the spirit of national unity and the aspirations of the Romanians everywhere, the Government of the United States deeply sympathizes and will not neglect at the proper time to exert its influence that the just political and territorial rights of the Romanian people may be obtained and made secure from foreign aggression.[177]

The following day Brătianu, with the backing of the Allied envoys, induced the King to dismiss Marghiloman. An interim cabinet was appointed under General Constantin Coandă and proceeded to repeal all legislation enacted by the Marghiloman regime.[178] Three days later (November 9) General Berthelot led a force across the Danube into Romania. The King, Brătianu, Coandă, and the Allied envoys then met and it was decided to give Germany twenty-four hours to surrender her army in Wallachia. The reason given was that Germany had violated the Peace of Bucharest by increasing her forces in Wallachia beyond the agreed strength.[179] Mackensen's refusal to reply was followed by Romania's re-entry into war on November 10. The Romanians crossed into Wallachia and Transylvania without opposition from retreating German and Austro-Hungarian troops. Cernăuţi was occupied on November 11, in response to a reported request of the Romanians of Bucovina to have troops of the Ukrainian Republic ousted.[180]

Brătianu negotiated with the Allied envoys even though he was not yet officially a member of the government. He demanded on November 13 that Romania had moral and political rights to the realization of her claims on the basis of Wilson's speech of September 27, in which the President reportedly said:

> ...the solutions of war are born from the nature and circumstances of the war itself; all that statesmen or assemblies could do is to realize or betray them.[181]

Referring to the wish of Transylvanian nationalists for self-determination, Brătianu explained it had been encouraged by Allied pronouncements about principles of justice, independence, and liberty; by the circumstances of the war; and by the 1916 Alliance guaranteeing Romanian unity. He asserted that

> Romania fulfilled her part of the treaty, but the Allies shirked theirs. The Peace of Bucharest, which has never been sanctioned by the King nor ratified, should not cancel the engagements of the 1916 treaty because Romania did not submit until after the Peace of Brest-Litovsk and the subjugation of the Ukraine to the Central Powers, that is to say, before a state of right in which Russia, the representative of

the Allies in their negotiations with Romania, had promised
direct collaboration and then made an agreement with the
enemy. Romania resisted all proposals which, before the
Russian peace, could have made her situation easier.[182]

Brătianu reminded the envoys of their approval of Romania's action
against the Bolsheviks in Bessarabia and their promise it would be the
final military effort anyone could expect from his prostrate country. He
asked that all which followed the Brest-Litovsk peace (March 3, 1918)
be considered null and void because, as soon as the situation improved,
Romania resumed without delay her military collaboration with the
Allies, "dictated by the bonds which the King and the Romanians had
never considered as broken."[183]

The question of Romania's status could not be resolved by a simple
obliteration of the events which occurred since the signing of the 1916
Alliance. Just as Briand told Stürmer in August 1916, and just as
Wilson had declared on September 27, 1918, the war, which was about
to end, had altered the situation.

The Armistice With Hungary

When the Allies concluded an armistice with Austria-Hungary at
Padua on November 3, Romania was at peace by virtue of the Peace
of Bucharest. Consequently, that armistice did not mention Romania.
The Padua truce did not provide for the disposition of Bucovina.
Strictly military in character, it permitted the Allies to move freely
over Austro-Hungarian territory to occupy places deemed essential for
maintaining the truce. Austro-Hungarian troops were withdrawn from
Wallachia by November 7.[184]

The Supreme War Council of the Allied Powers, meeting in Paris
on November 4, took up the question of Romania's status in the
projected armistice with Germany. Brătianu's plan to declare war on
Germany was not yet known. Pichon asked that Romania be considered
an ally in the armistice terms in response to a request from Ionescu.[185]
Sonnino pointed out that since Romania was at peace the armistice
could not apply to her. A compromise was reached providing for the
Germans to evacuate Wallachia within three weeks after the armistice
and to desist from making any requisitions during that period. The
Council adopted a suggestion of Colonel Edward M. House, the
American representative, requiring Germany to renounce the "palpably
fraudulent" Peace of Bucharest.[186] The Allies agreed to permit all

nations which had "sacrificed heavily for the Allied cause" to participate in the peace conference, but the small powers, including Romania, would be limited to discussions relating to their own particular interests.[187]

When the assembled statesmen learned of Romania's reentry, the terms of the German armistice were not changed so as to permit Romania's participation in the negotiations. The armistice with Germany concerned Romania less than the one with Austria since it did not cover any territorial changes.[188]

The armistice with the new government of Hungary, concluded on November 13, was considered the most important truce by Brătianu. The old regime in Budapest had been overthrown on October 31 by Hungarian radicals led by Count Mihály Károlyi, who detached Hungary from Austria and proclaimed a republic.[189] Károlyi, wishing to secure Allied recognition of the new Hungary, sought a separate armistice from General Franchet d'Esperey, Supreme Commander of the Allied Army of the Orient, who had arrived in Belgrade. D'Esperey favored a separate truce permitting his troops to move across Hungary on their march to Vienna and Berlin. After six days of wrangling, an armistice was signed.[190] Károlyi's decision to capitulate hastened Romanian activities and, on the same day, Brătianu issued an ultimatum to Hungary demanding that her troops be withdrawn from Transylvania and that she recognize Romania's annexation of that territory.[191]

The terms Hungary had to accept in the Belgrade armistice provided for occupation of large sections of her southern and eastern territory. All Hungarian troops had to be evacuated north of a line following the valley of the upper Someş and Bistriţa rivers to their confluence with the Tisa. The line in Transylvania ran along the Mureş River.[192] D'Esperey's truce lines thus permitted Romania to occupy only the eastern half of Transylvania, but since he reserved the right to change the demarcation line, Romania could anticipate a signal to march into the entire region at a later time. To demilitarize Hungary, d'Esperey required demobilization of her army with the exception of six infantry and two cavalry divisions. Hungary was placed under Allied supervision and thus her dismemberment was assured. D'Esperey agreed to a plan of General Berthelot to organize the Romanian army for the occupation of Transylvania and other parts of Hungary.[193]

Romania, it will be recalled, had not been invited to participate in any armistice negotiations. None of the provisions called for her collaboration in enforcing the terms. On the other hand, none of the terms expressly forbade her military cooperation. Encouraged by d'Esperey and Berthelot, Brătianu capitalized on this loophole by occupying Bucovina and eastern Transylvania. Since Romania was not a signatory to the armistices, Brătianu could later claim that he was not obligated to abide by the conventions.

After having seized Bucovina and most of Transylvania, Brătianu was prepared to resume formal control of the government. He whipped up a press campaign calling for the appointment of the one man who could gain those territories for which Romania had sacrificed so much. Even though he had been negotiating with the Allies since October, he earnestly wished to stage a popular recall of the Liberals. The scene was set for the return to power of Brătianu and for the beginning of a second struggle to achieve his war aims.

NOTES

1. Émile Bourgeois, *Politique étrangère*, III, p. 425. Prokesch-Osten was Austrian ambassador to Constantinople.

2. Although the Julian Calendar was used in Romania until July 1918, I have taken the liberty of transposing dates to conform to the Gregorian Calendar.

3. The more significant primary sources are listed in the Bibliography.

4. The texts of the treaty and renewals are in A. F. Pribram (ed.), *The Secret Treaties of Austria-Hungary, 1879-1914*, I, pp. 79-83. For studies of the origins of the treaty see Sidney B. Fay, *The Origins of the World War,* I, pp. 83-84, and Robert William Seton-Watson, *A History of the Roumanians*, pp. 364-365. The Romanian viewpoint is given by Gheorghe I. Brătianu, "Bismarck și Ion C. Brătianu," *Revistă Istorică Română*, V-VI (1935-36), pp. 86-103; and Georges Sofronie, *La position internationale de la Roumanie*, pp. 46-47. A German view is in Ernst Ebel, "Rumänien und die Mittelmächte, 1877-1913," *Historische Studien*, Heft 351, 1939, pp. 24-42. See also Assen Smedovski, "La Roumanie et la triple alliance, 1883-1913," *Revue d'Histoire Diplomatique,* LII (1937), pp. 39-56.

5. Comte de Saint-Aulaire, "Un grand latin-Jean Brătianu,"*La Revue Hebdomadaire*, August 4, 1928, p. 11. Saint-Aulaire was French minister to Romania, 1916-19.

6. *Ibid.*, p. 10.

7. Eugene S. Bagger, *Eminent Europeans, p.* 18; Raymond Recouly, *Les heures tragiques d'avant-guerre*, pp. 231, 234.

8. Nicolas Pillat (Brătianu's nephew), *Silhouettes de ma famille*, p. 92. Lent to the author by Mr. Vintilă Brătianu, Jr. Brătianu was prone to ponder major problems while lolling on a sofa with a book of French fables in his hand for negligent perusal. See Princess Anne-Marie Callimachi, *Yesterday Was Mine,* p. 266.

9.Queen Marie of Roumania, *The Story of My Life*, pp. 422-423, 425.

10. Vintilă (1867-1930) was a graduate engineer of the École Centrale in Paris. He became Secretary-General of the Ministry of Finance in 1901, Director of the Bancă Națională (owned by the National Liberal Party) in 1910, Minister of

War 1917-18, and, following Ionel's death in 1927, Premier and chief of the Liberal Party. Constantin ("Dinu") was the youngest brother, likewise a trained engineer and a politician. Five daughters were born to the elder Brătianu; the most famous was Marie, mother of poet Ion Pillat. See Sabina Cantacuzino (Brătianu's sister), *Din viaţa familiei I. C. Brătianu: Războiul, 1914-1918.*

11. Miles, "M. Jean J. C. Bratiano: Silhouette de guerre," *Le Correspondant,* CCXXIX (1916), pp. 36-54.

12. Bagger, p. 161.

13. Gheorghe Adamescu, " Dictionar Istoric-Geografic," Part II of Aurel Candrea, *Dicţionarul Enciclopedic Ilustrat "Cartea Românească, "* p. 1541; Seton-Watson, A *History of the Roumanians*, p. 387.

    Brătianu's popularity was not universal. In 1909 a syndicalist tried to assassinate him. See Alexandru Marghiloman, *Note Politice,* 1897-1924, 1, p. 69.

14. Henry Wickham Steed, *The Antecedents of Post-War Europe,* p.75. A very hostile description is in D. D. Pătrăşcanu, *Vinovaţii,* 1916-1918, pp. 55-61.

15. Egon Gottschalk, "Rumänien und der Dreibund his zur Krise 1914," *Die Kriegsschuldfrage: Berliner Monatshefte füir Internationale Aufklärung,* V (1927), p. 632.

16. André Tardieu, foreign news editor of *Le Temps,* visited Bucharest in March 1914 to urge the Romanians to turn their attention toward Transylvania which he termed the "Alsace-Lorraine of Eastern Europe" (Marghiloman, *Note Politice,* I, pp. 213-214).

17. The Constanţa meeting is treated in the following: Constantin Diamandy, "La grande guerre vue du versant oriental: à Constanza," *Revue des Deux Mondes,* XLIII (1928), pp. 129-143; Paul Lindenberg, *König Karl von Rumänien*, II, pp. 240-248; Queen Marie, The *Story of My Life,* pp. 580-583; Serge Sazonov, *Fateful Years, 1909*-1916, pp. 107-115, 273.

    Anxiety in Vienna over the meeting is seen in Feldmarschall Conrad von Hötzendorf, *Aus meiner Dienstzeit,* III, pp. 481-482; and Count Ottokar Czernin, *In the World War*, p. 112.

18. Austria, Ministerium des Äussern, *Österreich-Ungans Aussenpolitik,* VIII, pp. 627-632, and *Österreichisch-Ungarisches Rotbuch,* pp. 2-3. See also Czernin, pp. 87-88, and Fay, I, pp. 491-492.

19. *Rotbuch,* pp. 2-3, and Czernin, p. 87.

20. *Aussenpolitik,* VIII, Nos. 9861, 9863, 9873, 9875, 9879. The talks with the German and Austro-Hungarian envoys are treated in Luigi Albertini, *The*

Origins of the War of 1914, I, pp. 529-530, and III, pp. 546-581. See also Fay, I, pp. 487-489, and Bernadotte E. Schmitt, *The Coming of the War, 1914,* 1, pp. 159-160.

The Magyar view is in Eugene Horváth, "La correspondence du comte Étienne Tisza," *Revue de Hongrie,* XXXVII (1927), No. 3, p. 194. Romania's attitude is in Victor G. Cădere, "Politica României in marele război," *Arhivă pentru Ştiintă şi Reformă Socială,* VIII (1929), pp. 270-272.

21. A. de Lapradelle and others, *Constantinople et les Détroits,* I, pp. 316-327, for Sazonov's report of the trip. For treatments of this tactless Russian sign of approval of Romanian irredentism, see Albertini, I, p. 531, citing Czernin's permission to Brătianu to make the journey; and G. P. Gooch, *Before the War: Studies in Diplomacy,* II, pp. 359-362.

22. Tsentrarkhiv, *Tsarskaia Rossiia v mirovoi voine,* pp. 143-153; Sazonov, pp. 265-267.

23. Alfred Rieber, "Russian Policy and Romania-August 1914 to August 1916," A. M. and Certificate Essay of the Russian Institute, Columbia University, pp. 10-11; and C. Jay Smith, *The Russian Struggle for Power, 1914-1917,* p. 24.

24. *Die Deutschen Dokumente zum Kriegsausbiuch,* IV, Nos. 506, 582, 743.

25. Friedrich Stieve (ed.), *Iswolski im Weltkriege,* pp. 28-30, for the French support.

26. Ministero degli affari esteri, *I documenti diplomatici italiani,* 5. Serie: 1914-1918, I, p. 20.

27. Carp asked, "Have the Romanians of Transylvania manifested a desire to be incorporated?" He predicted that "the first to fire on us will be the Romanian regiments of Transylvania." See Marghiloman, I, p. 231.

28. *Ibid.,* I, pp. 234-235.

29. *Ibid.,* I, p. 237.

30. *Ibid.,* I, pp. 237-238.

31. Seton-Watson, *A History,* p. 481. A French translation of the minutes of this Crown Council, taken from Marghiloman's notes, was prepared by Georges Fotino, "La neutralité roumaine: une séance historique au conseil de la couronne," *Revue des Deux Mondes,* LVIII (August 1930), pp. 529-541. Another French copy is in *Revue d'Histoire de la Guerre Mondiale,* VI (April 1928), pp. 157-161.

A personal account by Ionescu is in his *Some Personal Impressions,* pp. 40-48, 52, 212. Two descriptive accounts are in Nicolae Basilesco, *La Roumanie dans la guerre et dans la paix,* I, pp. 97-99, and Recouly, pp. 231-235. A picturesque view is given by Lindenberg, II, pp. 306-310. A recent treatment is by Georges I. Brătianu, *Origines et formation de l'unité roumaine,* pp. 270-272.

32. The negotiations with Italy are in *I documents diplomatici italiani,* 5. Serie: 1914-1918, I, pp. 20-21, 91-97, 133, 369, 390, 413-430, 450-451. The text of the September 17 accord is on pp. 419-420. Accounts of the talks are in Luigi Aldrovandi Marescotti, *Nuovi ricordi e frammenti di diario,* pp. 193-210; Diamandy, "La grande guerre vue du versant oriental: Ma mission en Russie," *Revue des Deux Mondes,* LX (1930), pp. 426-428; W. W. Gottlieb, *Studies in Secret Diplomacy,* p. 309; H. D. Napier, *The Experiences of a Military Attaché in the Balkans,* p. 4; Tommaso Tittoni, "La Bessarabia, la Romania, et l'Italia," *Nuova Antologia,* MCCCXXI (April 1927), pp. 265-266; and Mario Toscano, *Il patto di Londra,* pp. 55-56.

33. *Tsarskaia Rossiia,* p. 166.

34. The talks with Sazonov are recounted in Diamandy, "La grande guerre vue du versant oriental: Ma mission en Russie," *Revue des Deux Mondes,* XLIX (1929), pp. 813-817. The text of the treaty is in *Sbornik sekretnykh dokumentov iz arkhiva byvshago ministerstva inostrannykh del,* No. 72, p. 315; and in Heinrich von Triepel (ed.), *Nouveau recueil général de traités,* 3ème série, X, No. 111, pp. 340-341.

The treaty was approved by the French. See Raymond Poincaré, *Au service de la France,* V, p. 346.

Other accounts are in *Tsarskaia Rossiia,* p. 167, and Cădere, p. 273. In Bucovina, Romanians were in a majority south of the Siret River. The region north of that river, including Cernăuţi, was inhabited by a Ruthenian (Ukrainian) majority.

35. *I documents diplomatici italiani,* 5. Serie: 1914-1918, I, p, 549; Diamandy, "La grande guerre vue du versant oriental: Ma mission en Russie," *Revue des Deux Mondes,* LX (1930), p. 424; Georges I. Brătianu, *Origines et formation,* p. 278. See also Albert Pingaud, "L'Entente et les balkaniques aux premiers mois de la guerre," *Revue des Deux Mondes,* LIV (1929), pp. 65-73.

36. Brătianu had little to fear from the Romanian parliament in which his Liberals held 80 per cent of the seats in the Chamber and 70 per cent in the Senate. See I. Gheorghiu, "Relaţiile româno-ruse in perioada neutralităţii României," *Studii si Referate privind Istoria României,* II (1954), pp. 1452-1453, 1457. This article was written in accordance with the latest Marxian revisionism by a Romanian specialist whose sources are all available in the United States. It appears as if the archives of the Ministry of Foreign Affairs in Bucarest are either closed to native scholars or devoid of any materials relating to this period.

37. For an account of the elder Brătianu's hagglings in 1877 with Turkey and Russia, see B. H. Sumner, *Russia and the Balkans, 1870-1880* (New York: Oxford University Press, 1937), pp. 294-299.

38. For the mission of British general Paget, see David Lloyd George, *War Memoirs*, I, p. 433. For that of historians Seton-Watson and George M. Trevelyan, see Georges Moroïanu, *Les luttes des roumains transylvains*, pp. 95-98. The visit of French general Pau is recounted in Henri Mélot, *La mission du Général Pau aux Balkans et en Russie tzariste*, pp. 48-53.

39. Lapradelle, I, pp. 337-350. Romania's viewpoint is explained by Nicolae Daşcovici, "La question des Détroits et les nationalités du sud-est européen," *Les Annales des Nationalités*, IV (1915), No. 4, pp. 93-99.

40. *Tsarskaia Rossiia*, pp. 180-182. See also Rieber, p. 29, and Smith, pp. 291-292.

41. *Tsarskaia Rossiia*, pp. 182-188. See also Rieber, pp. 30-40, and Smith, pp. 301-302. A recent account of the Russo-Romanian negotiations based on familiar documents is by V.A. Emets, "Protivorechiia mezhdu Rossiei i soiuznikami po voprosu o vstuplenii Rumynii v voinu (1915-1916 gg.)," *Istoricheskie Zapiski*, No. 56 (1956), pp. 52-90.

42. For accounts leading to the Treaty of London of April 26, 1915, see René Albrecht-Carrié, *Italy at the Paris Peace Conference*, pp. 24-34; and Gottlieb, pp. 198-359.

43. *Tsariskaia Rossiia*, pp. 195-197. See also Smith, pp. 306-307.

44. This crown council is cited in Komissiia pri TsIK SSSR polzdaniiu Dokumentov Epokhi Imperializma, *Mezhdtinarodnye Otnosheniia v Epokhu Imperializma*, Series 3, VIII, 2, pp. 36-37. For other accounts see Emets, p. 57; Rieber, pp. 40-41; Smith, p. 308; and Harry N. Howard, *The Partition of Turkey*, 1913-1923, pp. 172-174.

45. Albert Pingaud, "Études diplomatiques: l'Entente et la Roumanie," *Revue des Deux Mondes*, LVII (1930), p. 152.

46. Lord Thomson of Cardington (British military attaché to Romania), *Smaranda*, p. 29.

47. Brătianu once told French minister Saint-Aulaire, "I know very well that in Allied camps they accuse me of blackmail when I ask for guarantees which are vital to us. More amiably, they compare me to a rug merchant." See Comte de Saint-Aulaire, *Confession d'un vieux diplomats*, p. 334.

48. The text of the secret treaty with Bulgaria, September 6, 1915, is in Ralph H. Lutz, *Fall of the German Empire, 1914-1918*, I, pp. 748-750.

49. *Mezhdunarodnye Otnosheniia*, VIII, 2, pp. 486-488, and IX, pp. 3-4, 18-19, 40, 86-87, 91-92, 112-113, 116, 131-132. Also *in Tsarskaia Rossiia*, pp. 202-203. Brătianu first asked Russia to send 200,000 troops and Britain and France to attack Bulgaria with 500,000. On November 10 he increased the number to 500,000 Russians. See Emets, p. 59; Poincaré, VII, pp. 192, 205; and Maurice Paléologue, *La Russie des tsars pendant la grande guerre*, II, pp. 96-97.

50. Brătianu was charged with a crime somewhat analogous to the action taken by his father in 1876. The elder Brătianu rejected Serbia's appeal for aid against the Turks and assured the Great Powers of Romanian neutrality. He likewise refused to permit the passage of Russian supplies across Romania to Serbia. In return for his anti-Serbian policy, he asked the Turks to recognize Romania's individuality as a state, conclude a trade treaty, and grant other privileges. See Richard V. Burks, "Romania and the Balkan Crisis of 1875-1878," *Journal of Central European Affairs*, II (1942), No. 2, p. 123.

51. Take Ionescu, *The Policy of National Instinct*, text of his speeches in the Chamber, December 16-17, 1915.

52. Brătianu's indifference is described in Georges I. Brătianu, *Origines*, p. 283. The trade treaties with the Central Powers are cited in Hans Peter Hanssen, *Diary of a Dying Empire*, pp. 147-148; and Howard, p. 174. The arrangement with Britain is mentioned in the *Times*, January 31, 1916; and U.S. Department of State, *Papers Relating to the Foreign Relations of the United States, The World* War, *1916, Supplement*, p. 13. This series will be cited hereinafter as *U.S. Foreign Relations*.

53. Emets, pp. 60-61. Gallipoli was evacuated in January 1916. Poincaré appealed to the Tsar to induce Romania to intervene (Paléologue, II, pp. 205-206).

54. Paléologue, II, pp. 203-205, 208-210.

55. *Ibid.*, II, pp. 245-246; *Tsarskaia Rossiia*, pp. 214-215.

56. Paléologue, II, pp. 275, 299, 301; *Tsarskaia Rossiia*, pp. 217-221. Brătianu's hesitations were not dispelled by French assurances of an offensive against Bulgaria beginning soon. He preferred to await the realization of this guarantee (Paléologue, II, p. 275).

57. This agitation is reported in British General Staff, War Office, *Daily Review of the Foreign Press*, July 6, 18, 21, 1916; and John C. Campbell, "Nicholas Iorga," *The Slavonic and East European Review*, XXVI (November 1947), p. 55.

Ionescu had apparently abandoned his attitude toward Russia whom he called in 1891 "Romania's eternal enemy." See his *La politique étrangère de la Roumanie*, p. 17.

58. *Tsarskaia Rossiia*, p. 217.

59. Saint-Aulaire, *Confession*, p. 324.

60. Paléologue, II, p. 299; *Sbornik*, No. 13, pp. 21-23, for the text of the French appeal; *Tsarskaia Rossiia*, p. 217, for Sazonov's note.

61. Count Stephen Burián von Rajecz, *Drei Jahre aus der Zeit meiner Amtsführung*, pp. 54-57.

62. *Tsarskaia Rossiia*, pp. 217-219.

63. *Ibid.*, p. 221. Briand agreed to the proposed ultimatum (Paléologue, II, p. 312).

64. *Tsarskaia Rossiia*, pp. 198-199. Brătianu told Saint-Aulaire that he could not rely upon the Allies because they had committed so many avoidable strategic errors. He cited their failure to stop the German cruisers Goeben and Breslau from sailing into the Bosporus in 1914, an act which encouraged Turkey to intervene, and their inability to defeat the Turks at Gallipoli because of British and French arguments over tactics (Saint-Aulaire, *Confession*, pp. 324, 327).

65. *Tsarskaia Rossiia*, pp. 221-223; Paléologue, II, pp. 323, 326; Lloyd George, II, p. 950.

66. Paléologue, II, pp. 329-331.

67. *Ibid.*, II, pp. 330-331. Stürmer could have heeded the moderating words of Marghiloman who told Eugene de Schelking, an official of the Russian Foreign Ministry who was visiting Bucarest in August that "Romania's stomach could not digest Transylvania and the Banat. In annexing Transylvania, which was culturally far more advanced than Romania, we should in time become Transylvanians and no longer Romanians.... Besides, we are not ready for military action, and our defeat.... would be a foregone conclusion." See Schelking, *Recollections of a Russian Diplomat, pp.* 204-205.

68. Paléologue, II, pp. 324, 326-331.

69. *Tsarskaia Rossiia*, pp. 223-225.

70. *Ibid.*, p. 225.

71. *Ibid.*, pp. 225-226. Also in F. Seymour Cocks, *The Secret Treaties and Understandings*, p. 53.

72. Albert Pingaud, *Histoire diplomatique de la France pendant la grande guerre*, II, pp. 194-195. Also cited in Emets, p. 77; and A.J.P. Taylor, *The Struggle for Mastery in Europe, 1848-1918*, pp. 550-551.

73. *Tsarskaia Rossiia*, p. 226.

74. *Ibid.*, pp. 230-231.

75. The text of the final political convention is in Stieve, *Iswolski im Weltkriege*, pp. 206-207; Triepel, X, pp. 342-343. A Romanian language text is in Nicolae Daşcovici, *Interesele şi Drepturile României în texte de internaţional public*, pp. 9-11. An abridged English version is in Harold W. V. Temperley (ed.), *A History of the Peace Conference of Paris*, IV, pp. 516-517.

76. *Tsarskaia Rossiia*, pp. 226-230.

77. As early as the 1880s Romania, the largest and strongest of Balkan states, was led to believe that the Great Powers looked favorably upon her. After entering the Triple Alliance, Romania became the training ground for future foreign ministers. Germany sent von Bülow and Kiderlen-Wächter as envoys, Austria-Hungary named Goluchowski, Aehrenthal, and Czernin, and Italy sent San Giuliano.

78. The Franco-Russian accord should not be emphasized. Evidence does not show that it was known to or considered binding upon Briand's successors. The Russian side of the agreement became invalid when the Bolsheviks made their separate peace. In any event, the Peace Conference did live up to the terms.

79. *Rotbuch*, p. 62; Marghiloman, II, pp. 164-166.

80. Carp was an unregenerate Germanophile. He once promised Prince von Bälow that whatever happened, he would be faithful to Germany. See Bernhard Fürst von Bälow, *Denkwärdigkeiten*, III, p. 142.

81. The minutes of the Crown Council are in Marghiloman, II, pp. 148-157. French translations appeared in Recouly, pp. 265-277; and *Revue d'Histoire de la Guerre Mondiale*, VI (April 1928), pp. 161-166. Queen Marie provided a brief description in her *Ordeal: The Story of My Life*, p. 51. For the version of Russian diplomat Schelking, who was in Bucharest at the time, see his *Recollections*, pp. 204-205. Cited also in Seton-Watson, *A History*, pp. 491-492, and Gheorghiu, p. 1515.

82. The text of the war declaration is in U.S. Department of State, *Declarations of War and Severances of Diplomatic Relations, 1914-1918*, pp. 55-58. A Romanian-language text is in Daşcovici, *Interesele şi Drepturile României*, pp. 16-19. The mobilization decree is in *Războiul dintre România şi Grupul Puterilor Centrale: Comunicatele Oficiale*, p. 5. The decision to go to war was known immediately. See *Tsarskaia Rossiia*, pp. 231-232; *U.S. Foreign Relations, The World War*, 1916, Supplement, American minister Vopicka to Lansing, August 27, p. 47.

83. Saint-Aulaire, "Un grand latin — Jean Brătiano," p. 12.

84. Marghiloman, II, p. 167. For further details see George Clenton Logio, *Bulgaria Past and Present*, p. 419.

85. Russian propagandists hailed the intervention, but they were careful to omit mention of the award of the entire Banat to Romania lest the news anger the Serbs. See G.I. Kapchev, *Sovremennaia Rumyniia i ee Zadachi*, pp. 14-60. Messages of congratulations were sent by Poincaré and Paul Deschanel, President of the Chamber of Deputies, quoted in G. Sterian, "La Roumanie: son passé, ses attachés françaises, les partis politiques," *La Revue Hebdomadaire*, September 9, 1916.

86. Hungarian denunciations of Brătianu are in *Revue de Hongrie*, XVIII (September 15, 1916), pp. 54-55. German descriptions of his perfidy are in Paul Herre, "Rumäniens Vertragsverhältnis zum Dreibund," *Historische Zeitschrift*, CXVIII (1917), 3, pp. 63-75.

87. Romania fulfilled Article 3 of the military convention by acting jointly with Russia against Bulgaria.

The last Romanian troops were pushed out of Transylvania in January 1917 (Temperley, IV, p. 44).

Alekseev's doubts about the value of Romania's intervention led him to renege on sending the promised number of troops to the southeastern front. See Général Broussilow (Brusilov), "L'Offensive de 1916," *Revue des Deux Mondes*, LI (May-June 1929), pp. 914-915.

88. The reorganization is discussed in Ion Rusu Abrudeanu, *Pacostea Rusească*, pp. 102-114; and Seton-Watson, *A History*, pp. 498-499.

Romania's government was supposedly based on the constitution of 1866 and its modifications of 1879 and 1884. See Ministère des affaires étrangères, *Constitution de 30 Juin/12 Juillet 1866, avec les modifications y introduites en 1879 et 1884*. For studies of the system in practice, see T. Crişan Axente, *Essai sur le régime représentatif en Roumanie*, pp. 235-436; Georges Tătăresco, *Le régime électoral et parlementaire en Roumanie*; and Alexandre-Radu F. Rădulesco, *Le contrôle de la constitutionnalité des lois en Roumanie*.

89. The text of his speech is in *Monitorul Oficial,* January 11, 1917, reprinted in Paul Nicorescu, *La Roumanie nouvelle.* The above excerpt was a paraphrase of his father's famous statement about Magyar oppression in Transylvania: "When there are quarrels in my father-in-law's house, that is not my affair; but when he raises the knife against his wife, that is not only my right to intervene, it is my duty." Quoted by David Mitrany in *The Balkans,* p. 315.

90. Paléologue, III, pp. 175-191; General Basil Gourko, *Memories and Impressions of War and Revolution in Russia,* pp. 243-244; and Aldrovandi Marescotti, *Guerra diplomatica,* pp. 92, 97.

91. Saint-Aulaire, *Confession,* p. 354. For Brătianu's talks in Petrograd see Paléologue, III, pp. 341-342; Cocks, pp. 57-58; Queen Marie, *Ordeal,* p. 162; and Robert D. Warth, *The Allies and the Russian Revolution,* pp. 19, 48.
  The peace declaration of the Soviet, issued April 10, is in G. Lowes Dickinson, *Documents and Statements Relating to Peace Proposals and War Aims,* p. 43.

92. The reforms are discussed in these works: Axente, pp. 420-424, 443-444; David Mitrany, *The Land and Peasant in Rumania: War and Agrarian Reform, 1917-1921*; Henry L. Roberts, *Rumania: Political Problems of an Agrarian State,* pp. 22-26; Seton-Watson, *A History,* pp. 463, 503-505. Press accounts of the legislative process are in *Daily Review of the Foreign Press, Allied Press Supplement,* May-October 1917, pp. 490-491.
  The impetus to introduce reforms is described by Wilbert E. Moore, *Economic Demography of Eastern and Southern Europe,* p. 239.

93. The text of the Soviet's declaration is in Dickinson, pp. 79-81.

94. The decree of November 8 is in Jane Degras (ed.), *Soviet Documents on Foreign Policy,* I: 1917-1924, pp. 1-3. The secret treaties began appearing in installments with the November 23 issue of *Izvestiia.* The complete texts were printed in *The Manchester Guardian* on December 13, and in *The New York Evening Post* on January 25, 1918. Trotskii's statements are in Degras, I, pp. 4-12, 18-21.
  The treaties were published in Iaşi in January 1918 in *Documente secrete din arhiva ministerului de externe din Petrograd,* a volume issued by Nicolae Iorga.

95. The plan to evacuate is in Saint-Aulaire, *Confession,* p. 421; and Victor S. Mamatey, *The United States and East Central Europe, 1914-1918,* pp. 127-128. For reports of the visits of American generals Judson and Scott to Romania, see *U.S. Foreign Relations, The World War,* 1917, Suppl. 2, I, p. 729; and U.S. *Foreign Relations, 1918, Russia,* I, p. 120.

96. Clemenceau's antipathy toward Romania was no secret. His newspaper, *L'Homme Enchainé*, had criticized Brătianu for bad faith and dishonesty before and after intervention.

97. *U.S. Foreign Relations*, 1917, Suppl. 2, I, p. 325.

98. *Ibid.*, Suppl. 2, I, pp. 723-726, 730-735. Stoica recounted his mission in *In America pentru cauza românească.* See Mamatey, pp. 123-124.

99. *U.S. Foreign Relations*, 1917, Suppl. 2, I, pp. 732-735; Mamatey, p. 167.

100. Dickinson, pp. 92-95. The declaration of war by Congress is in James Brown Scott (ed.), *Official Statements of War Aims and Peace Proposals*, p. 206.

101. Colonel House, Wilson's intimate adviser, learned in November that Lloyd George and Clemenceau opposed a separate peace for Romania. This lessened House's desire for America to assist the Romanians. See Charles Seymour (ed.), *The Intimate Papers of Colonel House*, III, p. 234; and Lloyd George, V, pp. 3002-3006.

102. *U.S. Foreign Relations*, 1917, Suppl. 2, I, pp. 456-457. In employing the convenient terms "Allied envoys" and "Allied ministers" to cite the diplomats of Britain, France, Italy, and the United States, it is not my intention to disregard the fact that the United States was not an "Allied Power"; she was, more precisely, an "Associated Power."

103. Constantin Kirițescu, *Istoria războiului pentru întregirea României*, III, pp. 19-23; D. Iancovici, *La paix de Bucarest, pp.* 40-41; and C. Xeni, *Take Ionescu*, p. 347.
    For continued Allied pressure, see *U.S. Foreign Relations, 1917*, Suppl. 2, I, pp. 459-460; Saint-Aulaire, *Confession*, p. 436; and Charles J. Vopicka (American envoy), *Secrets of the Balkans*, pp. 148-151.

104. The text of the Focșani armistice is in Scott, pp. 203-204. Brătianu's last-minute conversations with the Allied envoys is in *U.S. Foreign Relations*, 1917, Suppl. 2, I, pp. 469-470. An account of the negotiations with Mackensen is in Charles Upson Clark, *Greater Roumania*, pp. 216-219.

105. Saint-Aulaire, *Confession*, p. 440, for the French reaction. The American attitude is in *U.S. Foreign Relations*, 1917, Suppl. 2, I, pp. 474-475, 484.
    Brătianu informed the Allies on December 13 that he must have their unconditional support for his policy. The Allies could have noted his version of the armistice was inaccurate if they read *The New York Times* of December 11 containing the text of the truce. It is true the armistice also applied to the Russians since Shcherbachev signed it, too.

106. *U.S. Foreign Relations, 1918, Russia*, II, pp. 597-598. Clemenceau and Lord Milner agreed upon a division of spheres of influence in the East. The French acquired responsibility for organizing resistance in Romania; the British were to attend to the Caucasus. This convention was in part the outcome of a plan devised by General Berthelot to form an anti-Bolshevik crusade. See *U.S. Foreign Relations, 1918, Russia*, I, pp. 330-331. The text of the convention is in Louis Fischer, *The Soviets in World Affairs*, II, p. 836.

107. Lloyd George, V, pp. 2464, 2471, 2481-2488, for conversations between Jan Christiaan Smuts and Count Mensdorff in Switzerland in December. Also in Mamatey, pp. 151-152. Brătianu's anxiety is described in *U.S. Foreign Relations, 1918*, Suppl. 1, I, p. 752.

108. The text of Lloyd George's speech is in his *War Memoirs*, V, pp. 2515-2527. It was believed the speech called for autonomy or home rule for the Romanians of Transylvania, and it was considered to be incompatible with the secret treaties. For these interpretations, see Carlile A. Macartney, *National States and National Minorities*, p. 190; and Steed, *Through Thirty Years*, II, p. 268.

109. A. J. P. Taylor, "The War Aims of the Allies in the First World War," in Richard Pares and A. J. P. Taylor (eds.), *Essays Presented to Sir Lewis Namier*, pp. 492, 501.

110. Georges I. Brătianu, *Origines*, p. 290. Sonnino added that "Brătianu should know that the Church sometimes gives absolution after the sin, never before."

111. The text is in *U.S. Foreign Relations*, 1918, Suppl. 1, I, pp. 12-17. For an analysis of the effect upon Allied war aims caused by Russia's defection and America's intervention, see Arno J. Mayer, "The Politics of Allied War Aims," 2 vols., unpublished Yale University dissertation.

112. *U.S. Foreign Relations*, 1918, Suppl. 1, I, p. 752. The feeling in Iaşi is described by Nicolae Iorga in his *Memorii*, I, pp. 218-219.

113. *U.S. Foreign Relations*, 1918, Suppl. 1, I, pp. 751-752.

114. British Foreign Secretary Balfour revealed the terms to Wilson and House when he visited Washington in April 1917. House had already known about the Romanian treaty from Sir Edward Grey. Wilson's denial to the Senate Foreign Relations Committee on August 19, 1919 of his ever having seen the treaties has served to obscure the issue. See E. L. Woodward and Rohan Butler (eds.), *Documents on British Foreign Policy, 1919-1939*, First Series, V, pp. 1008, 1015-1017, for Balfour's confirmation. The following claim Wilson knew the terms: Lloyd George, III, pp. 1678-1686; Blanche E.D. Dugdale, *Arthur James Balfour*, II, pp. 200-201; Seymour, *House Papers*, III, pp. 40, 43, 47, 61; U.S. Department

of State, *The Lansing Papers*, 1914-1920, II, pp. 19-32; and Taylor, "The War Aims," p. 497.

115. *U.S. Foreign Relations*, 1917, Suppl. 2, 1, p. 737; and Ray Stannard Baker and William E. Dodd (eds.), *The Public Papers of Woodrow Wilson: War and Peace*, 1917-1924, I, pp. 163-164.

116. B. E. Shtein, *Russkii vopros no parizhskoi mirnoi konferentsii*, p. 305.

117. French urgings are related in *U.S. Foreign Relations, 1918, Russia*, II, pp. 707-708. The least controversial accounts of the Bessarabian dispute are in Seton-Watson, *A History*, pp. 509-512, 560-564; and "The Bessarabian Question and the Act of Union with Rumania," a study prepared by the Political Intelligence Department of the British Foreign Office, printed in David Hunter Miller, *My Diary at the Conference of Paris*, XX, pp. 299-312.

The episode over Diamandy's arrest is analyzed by George F. Kennan, *Soviet-American Relations, 1917-1920, I: Russia Leaves the War*, pp. 330-343. The rupture of Russo-Romanian relations, not to be resumed until 1934, was announced on January 26 (*Sobranie Uzakonenii i Rasporiazhenii Rabochevo i Krestian'skogo Pravitel'stva RSFSR*, 1917-1918, p. 237). The break made impossible Romania's recovery of her treasury and royal jewels sent to Moscow for safekeeping in 1916. See Gr. Romaşcanu, *Tezaurul Român dela Moscova*, and Paul Sterian, *La Roumanie et la réparation des dommages de guerre*, pp. 70-71.

118. *U.S. Foreign Relations, 1918, Russia*, II, pp. 707-710; *U.S. Foreign Relations*, 1918, Suppl. 1, I, p. 754; Vopicka, p. 170.

119. Ludendorff's plans are in his *The General Staff and its Problems*, II, pp. 438-439.

120. Vopicka, p. 170. Mackensen's deadline is in Kiriţescu, III, p.217. At a conference in Berlin on February 5, Ludendorff urged that Romania be presented with the alternative of making peace or of being crushed by force. See Gustav Gratz and Richard Schüller, *The Economic Policy of Austria-Hungary during the War*, p. 142.

121. Vopicka, p. 171. The envoys approached Ionescu suggesting he form a war government, but he pleaded lack of popular support for his party.

122. *U.S. Foreign Relations*, 1918, Suppl. 1, I, pp. 754-757; Abrudeanu, p. 343; Iancovici, p. 56; Kiriţescu, III, pp. 219-220; and Vopicka, pp. 172-173.

Averescu (1859-1938), native of Bessarabia, served in the war of 1877, studied strategy at Turin, was attaché in Berlin (1895-98) where he came to know Mackensen, became Minister of War in 1907, and was Chief of Staff in 1912-13. He was the hero of Mărăşti. See *Revue de Transylvanie*, IV (1937-38), Nos. 3-4, p. 468.

123. Uttered on September 18, 1915 *(Tsarskaia Rossiia,* pp. 200-201).

124. *U.S. Foreign Relations,* 1918, Suppl. 1, I, p. 761; Czernin, p. 319; and Alfred F. Pribram, *Austrian Foreign Policy,* 1908-18, p. 117.

Charles also promised to permit the Romanians to retain their dynasty (Czernin, p. 260; Karl Nowak, *The Collapse of Central Europe,* pp. 63-64). For efforts of the pro-German Conservatives to evict Ferdinand, see Seton-Watson, *A History,* pp. 505-506, 512.

125. *U.S. Foreign Relations,* 1918, Suppl. 1, I, pp. 758-761; Mamatey, pp. 207-208.

126. Abrudeanu, pp. 346-348; Czernin, pp. 263-265; Gratz and Schüller, pp. 152-153; and Marghiloman, III, pp. 367, 379.

127. The minutes of the Crown Council are in Abrudeanu, pp. 350-356, and Nicolae Iorga, "Acte privitoare la istoria marelui războiu: I. consiliile de coroană din Februar 1918," *Revistă Istorică,* XVIII (1932), pp. 193-215.

Additional terms were posted: (1) demobilization of eight army divisions with the remainder permitted to garrison Bessarabia; (2) permission for the Austro-Hungarian army to cross Moldavia to reach the Ukraine; and (3) ousting of all Allied military missions which would be given safe-conduct through enemy lines (Gratz and Schüller, p. 154).

128. The minutes of the last two Crown Councils are in Abrudeanu, pp. 357-364.

129. The text of the Buftea treaty is in Triepel, X, pp. 855-856. A Romanian-language copy is in Kirițescu, III, pp. 229-230. Marghiloman cited the terms as favorable *(Note Politice,* III, pp. 382-388). The negotiations are related in Gratz and Schüller, pp. 152-154.

130. The text of the treaty is in *U.S. Foreign Relations,* 1918; *Russia,* II, pp. 716-717, taken from *Izvestiia* of March 31, 1918. Also in *L'Ukraine Soviétiste,* pp. 51-55; and Andrei Popovici, *The Political Status of Bessarabia,* pp. 245-250.

Article 7 provided that the Romanian army would be given refuge and sustenance on Russian soil if forced to abandon Moldavia. This curious privilege showed that Averescu did not trust the Germans.

131. Marghiloman, III, pp. 413; Iorga, *Memorii,* I, pp. 326-328; and Seton-Watson, *A History,* p. 514.

Marghiloman had been talking with Mackensen in Bucharest since March 1 in an effort to modify terms. He met with Czernin for the same purpose. He claimed in his memoirs that the talks and his appointment were the result of a scheme devised by Ferdinand and Brătianu (II, pp. 117, 154-155, 224). Czernin substantiated this claim *(In the World War,* p. 266). According to Hans Peter Hanssen, Marghiloman was being blackmailed by the German Foreign Ministry which had involved him earlier in an illicit relationship with "a gay German woman" *(Diary of a Dying Empire,* p. 112). A recent Romanian account insisted Brătianu and Ferdinand summoned Marghiloman in the hope of "feudalizing" Romania. See Eugen C. Munteanu and Teodor Necşa, "Jefuirea petrolului românesc de către trusturile imperialiste in anii 1917-1923," *Studii şi Referate* (1954), II, pp. 1549-1586.

132. Abrudeanu, p. 373. The new government consisted chiefly of Conservatives from Bucharest.

133. For an American account of Marghiloman's participation in the Sfat vote, see *U.S. Foreign Relations, 1918, Russia,* II, p. 719. A British version is in "The Bessarabian Question and the Act of Union with Romania," Miller, *Diary,* XX, pp. 299-312. An objective treatment of the controversial vote is in Seton-Watson, *A History,* pp. 519-520. For a survey of the Bessarabian dispute, see my "The Question of Bessarabia in the Political Relations between Russia and Rumania, 1812-1935."

134. The most complete account of peace negotiations is in Gratz and Schüller, pp. 155-203. Both authors participated as economic advisers to the Austro-Hungarian delegation. The text of the peace is in Triepel, X, pp. 856-870; and U.S. Department of State, *Texts of the Roumanian Peace.*

Count Stephen Burián, who succeeded Czernin on April 15, signed the treaty and called it fair and due to the "wise and accommodating attitude of Marghiloman" *(Drei Jahre,* pp. 237-238). Emperor William conferred the Order of the Crown, First Class, on Kühlmann for his skill (J. Kreppel, *Der Friede im Osten,* pp. 276-277).

135. This omission was due in part to a dispute between Austria-Hungary and Romania, during the negotiations, with regard to delimitation of their common frontier in Bucovina. When Marghiloman protested the loss of Moldavian land, the Austrians retaliated by declaring the status of Bessarabia a question for future discussion.

That the Central Powers approved the union, a fact still disputed, may be seen in Czernin's speech to the Vienna Municipal Council on April 2. He claimed there were many indications the Romanian majority in Bessarabia desired union, and "if Romania will only adopt a frank, honorable, and friendly attitude toward us, we shall have no objection to meeting those tendencies in Bessarabia. Romania can gain in Bessarabia much more than she lost in the war" (Dickinson, pp. 177-178).

136. For Anghelescu's recall from Washington, see *U.S. Foreign Relations, 1918, Russia,* II, p. 719. Envoys to Britain and France were recalled in May *(Daily Review of the Foreign Press,* May 28, 1918, p. 219).

137. *U.S. Foreign Relations, 1918*, Suppl. 1, I, p. 771. A copy of the peace sent by Vopicka was received in Washington in two installments on May 19 and 22 *(Ibid.,* pp. 771-777, for text).

138. *Ibid.,* Suppl. 1, I, p. 778.

139. Great Britain, Foreign Office, Cmd. 9102, Misc. No. 15, 1918, *Observations by the Allied Ministers at Iassy with regard to Conditions of Peace Imposed* upon Roumania by *the Central Powers.* The quotation is a paraphrase of the memorable utterance of a high German officer: "A harsh peace? Just wait till you see what we are preparing for France and England!" (Marghiloman, III, p. 340).

140. Saint-Aulaire, *Confession,* p. 452.

141. *U.S. Foreign Relations, 1918*, Suppl. 1, I, p. 778; Vopicka, pp. 217-218.

142. *U.S. Foreign Relations, 1918*, Suppl. 1, I, p. 759.

143. Accounts of the ratification process are in Vopicka, pp. 218-222; Iorga, *Memorii,* I, p. 361, and II, p. 17; *La Roumanie* (Paris), No. 31, August 15, 1918. The text of Romania's ratification is in *Texts of the Roumanian Peace,* p. 7; that of Germany is in *Deutscher Reichsanzeiger,* June 5 and July 6, 1918. Austria-Hungary ratified the economic agreements only *(Die Zeit,* June 5, 1918).

144. According to Oppenheim, the mere signing of an instrument of ratification by the parties to a treaty is not enough to make it binding upon them. "It is necessary that the instruments of ratification should be exchanged between them or deposited in some agreed place, and they do not take effect until they have been exchanged or deposited." See L. Oppenheim, *International Law: A Treatise,* 6th edition edited by H. Lauterpracht, I, pp. 822-823.

145. Marghiloman told Ferdinand in March that his condition for accepting office required the exiling of Brătianu or a trial of the Liberal government before the Chamber (Marghiloman, *Note Politice,* III, p. 413). Charges were introduced in the Chamber on July 11, accusing the Liberals and Conservative Democrats of violating the constitution, of having failed to prepare for war, of sending the treasury to Moscow, of destroying the oilfields, etc. The accused refused to answer the charges and they were tried in absentia. Although convictions were voted, the King refused to sanction them and the matter was finally dropped *(Daily Review of the Foreign Press, Neutral Press Supplement,* VI, June-October 1918; Vopicka, pp. 226, 233-234).

146. For Mrazec's contributions, see Douglas W. Johnson, "The Geographic and Strategic Character of the Frontier Imposed on Roumania by the Treaty of Bucarest," *Texts of the Roumanian Peace,* pp. 181-184.

Vasile Stoica was also active in bringing Romania's aspirations to the attention of American officials. He appealed for an American statement favoring dismemberment of Hungary ("Comments of Vasile Stoica on the Transylvanian Question," Inquiry Document No. 554, The National Archives).

147. Popovici (1863-1917), a native of the Banat, was the author of *Die Vereinigten Staaten von Gross-Österreich,* an influential work calling for a reorganization of the Habsburg Monarchy into a federation of ethnic units to end the misdeeds of Dualism, Magyarism, and Pan-Slavism. He was a member of the Executive Committee of the Romanian National Party of Transylvania. His scheme found adherents in high circles, among whom were Archduke Francis Ferdinand, Czernin, and Nicu Filipescu. See Robert A. Kann, *The Multinational Empire,* II, pp. 197-207, and his "Count Ottokar Czernin and Archduke Francis Ferdinand," *Journal of Central European Affairs,* XVI (July 1956), p. 127.

148. Steed urged in 1916 that Romania be given the Romanian inhabited regions of Hungary and Bucovina "provided she helped effectively to liberate them" ("Programme for Peace," reprint from *The Edinburgh Review,* 1916, pp. 12-13).

Seton-Watson, as noted, was sent to Bucharest in February 1915 to induce intervention (*A History,* p. 477). He had apparently abandoned his admiration for Popovici's federalism. See "Tributes to R. W. Seton-Watson: A Symposium," *The Slavonic and East European Review,* XXX (June 1952), p. 356.

149. The Romanian delegates were Dimitrie Drăghicescu (former editor of the Liberal daily *L'Indépendance Roumaine*), Gheorghe Mironescu (Professor of Law at the University of Bucharest and a leading Conservative Democrat), Simion Mândrescu (Professor of German Literature at the University and President of the Association of Romanians of Transylvania and Bucovina), Ion Ursu (President of the League of Unity of the Romanians of Iaşi), Nicolae Lupu (physician, socialist, and Brătianu's emissary to the Petrograd Soviet in late 1917 where he tried in vain to secure sympathy), and Ioan Florescu (former Minister of Justice).

The Romanians were in distinguished company: Beneš, Stefanik, Dmowski, Mestrović, Trumbić, Franklin-Bouillon, and Mussolini attended. See *U.S. Foreign Relations, 1918,* Suppl. 1, I, pp. 795-796; Mamatey, pp. 238-245.

150. Eduard Beneš, *My War Memoirs,* p. 318.

151. The Romanians asked the Congress to support the 1916 Alliance. Orlando hesitated because Italy was not yet ready to propose a wholesale dismemberment of the Habsburg Monarchy. See Mironescu, *Aperçus sur la question roumaine,* cited in Moroïanu, pp. 204-205.

152. Emily Greene Balch, *Approaches to the Great Settlement,* pp. 32, 53-56; Kent Forster, *The Failures of Peace,* pp. 31, 86; Merle Fainsod, *International Socialism and the World War,* pp. 67-68, 71, 86, 116. Rakovskii was organizer of

Bolshevik opposition to Romania's seizure of Bessarabia. His life was quite melodramatic: native of Bulgarian Dobrodgea, graduate M.D. of Montpellier, influenced by Plekhanov, Liebknecht, and Dobrogeanu-Gherea (the high-priest of Marxism in Romania), in and out of Romania from 1894 to 1917, negotiator of the treaty on Bessarabia with Averescu in March 1918, alternately a pacifist and a militant Bolshevik, post-war chief of the Ukrainian Soviet government, Soviet ambassador to London and Paris in the 1920s, and tried, convicted, and sentenced at the purge trial of 1938. See G.D.H. Cole, *A History of Socialist Thought, III, Part 2: The Second International*, pp. 588-590; and Charles Upson Clark, *Bessarabia, Russia, and Roumania on the Black Sea*, pp. 180-188. Although the evidence is controversial, documents of the German Foreign Ministry for the period 1917-18 show that Rakovskii was in the pay of Germany to agitate against Romanian intervention. German envoy Bussche was permitted to give him 100,000 lei for this purpose (Z.A.B. Zeman, *Germany and the Revolution in Russia, 1915-1918*, pp. 85-86).

Lupu found it difficult, like many Romanian socialists, to bridge the gap between Marxism and efforts leading to capitalism, the latter phase a prerequisite for the advent of socialism. See his *Rumania and the War*, pp. 121-122, and "Rumania in the Mid-European Belt," *Asia*, XVIII (1918), pp. 1036-1043. A map showing his recommended frontiers is in the National Archives. His solicitation of aid from the Petrograd Soviet is treated in Joseph Noulens, *Mon ambassade en Russie soviétique, 1917-1919*, I, pp. 96-98.

153. The Union included Ramsay Macdonald, Philip Snowden, Arthur Ponsonby, Charles Roden Buxton, and G. Lowes Dickinson. See Balch, p. 269; Forster, p. 31; and Temperley, I, p. 217.

154. Mitchell Pirie Briggs, *George D. Herron and the European Settlement*, p. 126. Herron called himself a socialist in his *The Defeat in Victory*, p. xi. He proposed dismemberment as early as 1916 in an address to the third congress of the Union des Nationalités at Lausanne (*Annales des Nationalités*, V, Nos. 9-11, p. 268). Masaryk credited him with influencing Wilson's ultimate backing of dismemberment (*The Making of a State*, pp. 304-309).

Lansing was definitely pro-Bulgarian. See Baker and Dodd, *The Public Papers of Woodrow Wilson*, I, pp. 135-136; Mamatey, "The United States and Bulgaria in World War I," *The American Slavic and East European Review*, XII (April 1953), pp. 236-238. For the influence in Washington of American missionaries and teachers who had worked in Bulgaria, see Reuben H. Markham, *Bulgaria and the Y.M.C.A.*

155. Şerban Drutzu, *Românii în America*, p. 15; Christine Avghi Calitzi, *A Study of Assimilation among the Rumanians in the United States*, pp. 112-113. Theodore Roosevelt and Billy Sunday spoke up for Romanian aspirations (Kiriţescu, III, pp. 292-299).

156. Ernest P. Bicknell, *With the Red Cross in Europe, 1917-1922*, pp. 489-490; and Henry P. Davison, *The American Red Cross in the Great War*, pp. 231-249.

157. Averescu requested a safe-conduct pass for Ionescu from Mackensen who agreed to permit the departure of the Conservative Democrat leader and other "undesirables." Brătianu was asked to leave, but he insisted it was his duty to remain in Iaşi (Abrudeanu, p. 368; Vopicka, p. 188; and D. Iancovici, *Take Jonesco*, p. 146). Ionescu's reception in Paris is described in Iancovici, *Take Jonesco*, pp. 146-147; Abrudeanu, p. 371; and Albert Prahovan, "Take Ionesco anecdotique et intime," *La Revue*, CXXVII (Paris), 1918, Nos. 1920, p. 89.

158. Diamandy's hair-raising escape from Russia after his release from prison in January 1918 is related in Kennan, *Russia Leaves the War*, pp. 341-342.

159. As a result of his work, the Italian government permitted the formation of a legion of Romanian prisoners of war, who had served in the Hungarian army after being conscripted in Transylvania. This legion served on the final offensive on the Piave River. For details of the recruitment and operations of the Romanian Legion, see Sever Bocu, *Les légions roumains de Transylvanie*, and Valeriu Pop, "The Romanian Legion in Italy," *Revue de Transylvanie*, III (1936-37), No. 2, pp. 158-163. The text of the decree of the Italian government authorizing its formation is in *Actes et documents concernant la question roumaine*, pp. 58-61. Ionescu's letter thanking Sonnino is in *I documenti diplomatici italiani*, 6. Serie: 1918-1922, I, No. 54, p. 27.

160. These messages are in *La Roumanie*, No. 34, September 5; No. 35, September 12; No. 36, September 19; and No. 40, October 17. Trumbić of the Yugoslav Committee and Beneš of the Czech-Slovak National Committee added their good wishes *(Actes et documents concernant la question roumaine*, p. 55).

161. Ionescu was perhaps the most pro-Western of Romanian statesmen. He was born in Ploeşti in 1858, descendant of Macedo-Romanian (Vlach) stock, educated in law at the Sorbonne, and married to Bessie Richards, an English woman. From 1884 to 1908 he was a member of the Conservative Party, holding various ministries under Catargiu and Cantacuzino. Like Masaryk and Beneš in the first decade of the century, he called for federalizing the Habsburg Monarchy. In 1908 he broke with the Conservatives to form the Democrat wing of that party. He was a leading protagonist of Romania's anti-Bulgarian policy in 1913 and, as Maiorescu's Minister of Interior, cooperated with Serbia's leaders and Venizelos of Greece to force Bulgaria into signing the Treaty of Bucharest of that year. He was an advocate of Romanian hegemony in the Balkans. Unlike Brătianu, he did not possess a "Great Power fixation."

162. Romanian nationalists had close ties with the Czechs who, unlike the Serbs, had no claims opposed to those of Romania. Masaryk visited Iaşi in October

1917 and discussed with Brătianu and Ionescu the common plan to wrest territories from Austria-Hungary. See Masaryk, *The Making of a State,* pp. 186-188; and Iorga, *Memorii,* I, pp. 141-143.

For details of Ionescu's discussions, see the following: Seton-Watson, *A History,* pp. 537-538; Temperley, IV, pp. 221-222; Xeni, pp. 370-387. Masaryk's account is in *The Making of a State,* p. 364. Beneš speaks of it in his *My War Memoirs,* pp. 315-316. Of peripheral interest are Aurel Cosma, *La petite entente,* contending Ionescu negotiated a multilateral alliance, p. 17; Robert Machray, *The Little Entente,* pp. 85-86; Albert Mousset, *La petite entente,* p. 20; Felix Vondráček, *The Foreign Policy of Czechoslovakia,* pp. 162163; and Joseph S. Roucek, "The Little Entente," *Roumania,* VI (1930), No. 2, p. 18. Ionescu denied having concluded any arrangements ("La petite entente," *Revue des Balkans,* III, [1921], No. 26, pp. 189-190). According to Viorel V. Tilea, Ionescu and Pašić traced a partition of the Banat. See map in appendix of Tilea, *Acţiunea Diplomatică a României.*

163. For the work of the Northcliffe Bureau, see Sir Campbell Stuart, *Secrets of Crewe House,* especially pp. 33-35 for Balfour's instructions; Harold D. Lasswell, *Propaganda Technique in the World War,* pp. 174-175; Seymour, *Home Papers,* III, pp. 140-141, 338, 373-374. Steed's work is outlined in *The History of the "Times": The 150th Anniversary and Beyond,* Part 1, pp. 261, 284.

164. Viorel V. Tilea in "Tributes to R. W. Seton-Watson: A Symposium," p. 358.

According to Douglas W. Johnson, Professor of Geography at Columbia University attached to the group of scholars known as the "Inquiry" set up by Colonel House to prepare a peace program, Seton-Watson also worked for the Foreign Office. In an interview with Johnson in London on May 9, 1918, Seton-Watson said dismemberment of Transylvania from Hungary was absolutely necessary. He remarked, in reply to Johnson's observation that there was no enthusiasm in Transylvania for union with Romania, "That is all nonsense! You don't see the steam when you are sitting on a safety valve either." See "Memorandum of a conversation with R. W. Seton-Watson at the American Officers' Club, London," Inquiry Document No. 992, The National Archives.

165. Saint-Aulaire, *Confession,* pp. 450-451; Vopicka, p. 237. For side-lights of this affair, see Kim Beattie, *Brother, Here's A Man: The Saga of Klondike Boyle,* p. 296; A. L. Easterman, *King Carol, Hitler, and Lupescu,* pp. 33-35; and George Gay, *King Carol of Roumania,* pp. 26-27.

166. *U.S. Foreign Relations, 1918,* Suppl. 1, I, p. 783; Vopicka, p. 242.

167. Lutz, II, p. 487.

168. Marghiloman, IV, pp. 43-44, 51-53, 95-97, 120; Vopicka, p. 246; and Salamon Rosental, "Une page d'histoire roumaine: la Roumanie dans la grande guerre," *Revue d'Histoire Diplomatique,* LI (1936), pp. 439-442.

The Germans benefitted quite well from their occupation. According to Ludendorff, the highly serious food shortage in Germany was alleviated by the acquisition of Romanian grain *(The General Staff and its Problems,* II, pp. 491-498). Petroleum from the partially destroyed oilfields enabled German planes to remain in the air until the end of the war. See the testimony of General von Kuhl quoted by Lloyd George, VI, pp. 3216, 3355.

169. *U.S. Foreign Relations, 1918,* Suppl. 1, I, pp. 783-784; Vopicka, p. 246.

170. Dickinson, p. 227.

171. *Ibid.,* p. 252. For developments leading to Wilson's adoption of dismemberment as a war aim, see Kann, II, pp. 279-280; Mamatey, pp. 333-334; Nowak, pp. 348-349; and Seton-Watson, *A History,* p. 529.

House was won over to the aim of dismemberment through the efforts of Milenko Vesnić, Serbian envoy in Paris and later chief of a mission to Washington. Vesnić was a skilled diplomat, married to an American, could speak English fluently, and was held in high esteem by Mrs. Wilson. See Seymour, *House Papers,* III, pp. 333-336; and Henry Morgenthau, Sr., *All in a Life-Time,* p. 328.

172. Wilson had come a long way since February 8, 1917 when he told Lansing he did not like the Allied aim to dismember Austria-Hungary because a large measure of autonomy would suffice to guarantee peace and stability. He feared Austria-Hungary would fight harder if she thought she would be dismembered *(U.S. Foreign Relations, 1917,* Suppl. 1, I, p. 40).

173. *U.S. Foreign Relations, 1918,* Suppl. 1, I, p. 784; Saint-Aulaire, *Confession,* p. 468; Marghiloman, IV, p. 120.

174. Lutz, II, p. 473.

175. The text of the order is in Constantin Minesco, *L'Action diplomatique de la Roumanie pendant la guerre,* pp. 80-81.

176. For a treatment of the activities in Budapest, see Chapter II, p. 68.

177. *U.S. Foreign Relations, 1918,* Suppl. 1, I, p. 785.

178. Marghiloman, IV, pp. 117-118. The decree-law repealing the legislation and the text of a general amnesty signed by the King on November 6 are in *Monitorul Oficial,* No. 183, November 6, 1918.

Coandă had been an attaché to the Russian General Staff and had participated in negotiations culminating in the Peace of Bucharest. One of Brătianu's close friends, he acted as liaison officer between the King and Brătianu during the latter's absence from political life in 1918. The new cabinet consisted of generals (Iorga, *Memorii*, II, pp. 96-97).

179. *U.S. Foreign Relations, 1919, The Paris Peace Conference*, II, p. 385. This series will be cited hereinafter as *U.S. Foreign Relations, PPC*.

180. Seton-Watson, *A History*, p. 535. News of a Serbian advance toward the Banat may have accounted for Brătianu's impatience to get there first (Temperley, IV, p. 195).

181. This was a faulty translation and abbreviation of Wilson's actual words. This is what he did say: "At every turn of the war we gain a fresh consciousness of what we mean to accomplish by it. When our hope and expectations are most excited we think more definitely than before of the issues that hang upon it and of the purposes which we did not determine and which we cannot alter. No statesman or assembly created them; no statesman or assembly can alter them. They have arisen out of the very nature and circumstances of the war. The most that statesmen or assemblies can do is to carry them out or be false to them" (Dickinson, pp. 225-226).

182. *U.S. Foreign Relations, PPC*, II, pp. 387-388.

183. *Ibid.*, II, p. 388.

184. For the negotiations of the Padua armistice, see Gabriel Terrail (pseud. "Mermeix"), *Les négociations secrètes et les quatres armistices*, pp. 205-207; and Temperley, IV, pp. 126-127. The three Austro-Hungarian brigades quit Wallachia and withdrew into Transylvania (Edmund von Claise-Horstenau, *The Collapse of the Austro-Hungarian Empire*, p. 315).

185. A. de Lapradelle (ed.), *La paix de Versailles, XI: Questions militaires et navales*, p. 166; and Harry R. Rudin, *Armistice, 1918*, pp. 310-311.

186. Lapradelle, *La paix de Versailles*, XI, p. 167; *U.S. Foreign Relations, 1918*, Suppl. 1, I, pp. 409, 411; Miller, *Diary*, II, p. 74. According to David Hunter Miller, the American legal expert, the Allies were obliged to annul the Peace of Bucharest and require the Central Powers to repudiate it (*Diary*, II, pp. 323, 391-409, 419).

187. Seymour, *House Papers*, IV, p. 101.

188. The Supreme War Council consisted of Clemenceau, Lloyd George, Orlando, House, Venizelos, Pichon, Balfour, Sonnino, Vesnić, Beneš, and Marshal Foch. There was no Romanian representative. Serbia was permitted on October 31

to occupy all territory inhabited by the south Slavs (Lapradelle, *La paix de Versailles*, XI, p. 142).

189. Károlyi was unknowingly fulfilling a plan devised by Lansing on June 25, 1918. At that time Lansing proposed to Wilson adoption of a policy with regard to the nationalities of Austria-Hungary. He said that "it is wise to talk separate peace with Austria, even though it is contrary to the just claims of the nationalities within Austria-Hungary. However, since such a separate peace seemed no longer a possibility, [he] was in favor of declaring without reservation for an independent Hungary." Wilson approved the plan on September 27 (Baker, *Woodrow Wilson: Life and Letters*, VIII, p. 232).

190. An account of Károlyi's accession to power is provided by his close collaborator Oscar Jászi, *Revolution and Counter-Revolution in Hungary*. Károlyi's version is in his *Memoirs: Faith Without Illusion*, pp. 130-137. For additional accounts, see Francis Deák, *Hungary at the Paris Peace Conference*, pp. 8-11; Mamatey, pp. 351-352; and Temperley, I, pp. 352-353.

191. *U.S. Foreign Relations, PPC*, II, p. 393.

192. See map in endpaper of Deák, *Hungary at the Paris Peace Conference*.

193. The texts of the armistices are in Ministère des affaires étrangères, *Conventions d'armistice passées avec la Turquie, la Bulgarie, l'Autriche-Hongrie, et l'Allemagne*. Romanian-language texts of the German and Hungarian armistices are in Daşcovici, *Interesele şi Drepturile*, pp. 515-527.

Berthelot's scheme is in Général Paul Azan, *Franchet d'Esperey*, p. 232. It was supported by Poincaré *(Au service de la France*, X, pp. 408-409). It is treated in Sir Frederick Maurice, *The Armistices of 1918*, pp. 14-15. D'Esperey hoped to occupy Budapest with the help of the Romanians who were only too delighted to accommodate him. Not until December 22 was this plan quashed by the Supreme War Council *(U.S. Foreign Relations, PPC*, II, pp. 214-216).

Chapter II

PRESENTATION OF ROMANIAN CLAIMS

"M. Brătianu, you are here to listen, not to comment!"

— Clemenceau, 31 May 1919[1]

The Major Issues

The termination of hostilities and the anticipated convening of the Peace Conference presaged a restoration of stability in war-torn Europe. Notwithstanding Romania's emergence from the war as an allied state, the aspirations for which Brătianu had taken his people into the conflict had not yet been completely fulfilled. He was soon to realize that Romania's struggle had not ended with the armistices. Indeed, as will be shown presently, Romania was required to fight both on the battlefield and in the conference rooms to secure fulfillment of the 1916 Alliance. Having lost the war, Brătianu did not intend to lose the peace.

So far as this study is concerned, the chief questions confronting Romania at the beginning of the new year centered on the attitudes of the Allied Powers toward the 1916 Alliance and the Peace of Bucharest. An interpretation of the status of those two agreements affected discussions in Paris of issues emanating from the 1916 Alliance.

Brătianu's unfaltering reliance upon every word of the Alliance and his insistence that the Allies make good their promises dominated the issues he raised at the Peace Conference. In brief, the problems presented by his appearance at the Conference included, in order of presentation here: (1) fulfillment of the territorial promises contained in the 1916 Alliance and recognition of the annexation of Bessarabia; (2) tracing of Romania's new frontiers to provide her with maximum economic and strategic advantages; (3) recognition by the Allied

Powers of Romania as a co-equal entitled to act in East Central Europe as a Great Power; and (4) submission by the Allied Powers to Romania's demand that they reward her for services rendered in eliminating Magyar Bolshevism and holding back the advance of Russian Bolshevism.

Having been previously informed that he ought to find grounds other than the Alliance on which to base his claims, Brătianu, while refusing to release the Allies from their written guarantees, joined the ranks of those making appeals to Wilsonian idealism so as to conceal the territorial promises of secret treaties. He contrived to demonstrate that national self-determination, represented by the resolutions of the assemblies described below, was the principle underlying the 1916 Alliance.

Romanian nationalists in Transylvania, encouraged by the success of the Czech and Croat national assemblies, met in Oradea on October 12 to draft a resolution invoking the right of autonomous self-determination for Romanians inhabiting the Kingdom of Hungary. They called for the right to represent themselves at the peace conference. No call was made at the time for separation of the Romanian-inhabited regions from Hungary. The nationalists authorized Alexandru Vaida-Voevod, a deputy to the Budapest parliament, to present demands for autonomy to the Hungarian government. He did this in a memorable speech to the Hungarian chamber on October 18.[2]

After the Polish and Ruthenian provinces seceded from the Habsburg Monarchy, the Czech-Slovak republic was proclaimed in Prague, and the south Slavs declared their independence, the Romanian demand for autonomy was replaced by a call for separation from Hungary. The nationalists, who had not sponsored a secessionist movement before, now moved to declare for the independence of Transylvania, the Banat, and other regions of Hungary inhabited by Romanian majorities.[3] After establishing a Romanian national council, they informed Károlyi on November 10 of their assumption of political authority over thirty-three comitats.[4]

Károlyi negotiated with the nationalists, hoping to prevent the secession of Transylvania and other districts. The Romanians — Iuliu Maniu, Vaida-Voevod, Vasile Goldiş, and Ioan Erdélyi — had at first demanded broad autonomy with a loose connection to Hungary.[5] But after Károlyi yielded to d'Esperey's armistice on November 13, permitting the Allies to occupy most of Hungary, the nationalists rejected the liberal offers of Oscar Jaszi, Károlyi's minister of nationalities. The Romanians declared their right to the principle of national self-determination and proclaimed the separation from Hungary of Transylvania and other districts. They issued a manifesto calling for the freedom and independence of the regions of Hungary inhabited by Romanian majorities.[6]

The nationalists then arranged a mass demonstration calling for union with Romania of those districts inhabited by Romanians. More than 1,200 delegates and a reputed crowd of 100,000 observers gathered at Alba Iulia on December 1 to vote for the union of all Romanians in one state. The nationalists, however, were not prepared to join Romania without first securing from Bucharest definite guarantees of the rights for which they had struggled with their Magyar masters for so many years. They demanded the right to govern the Romanian districts of Hungary until a constituent assembly for "Greater Romania" could complete drafting a new constitution. Additional conditions for union were imposed: (1) full liberty for all peoples, Romanian and non-Romanian, and the right to be represented in the Romanian parliament; (2) full autonomy for all religious creeds; (3) use of native languages in administration, education, and justice; (4) universal manhood suffrage; (5) absolute freedom of press, assembly, association, and "free propagation of human thoughts"; (6) radical agrarian reform, the guiding principle of which would be "a social levelling and increased production"; (7) granting of the "same privileges to industrial workers as are secured to them by law in the most industrialized states"; and (8) "a purely democratic regime in all branches of public life."[7] The Alba Iulia national assembly called upon the peace conference to create a league of free nations to guarantee the rights and liberties of all peoples. The delegates reportedly recognized the right of the peace conference to settle "the definitive boundaries" of new Romania. This expression implied that the nationalists were prepared to accept rulings of the peace conference regarding the delimitation of the frontiers of "Greater Romania." The gathering requested the treatment of non-Romanians in enlarged Romania be regulated according to principles associated with Woodrow Wilson.[8]

The assembly empowered a Consiliu Dirigent (Directing Council) to act as interim government of the Romanian districts of Hungary. Maniu was named president, Vaida-Voevod minister of foreign affairs, Ştefan Cicio-Pop minister of war, Vasile Goldiş minister of education, and Aurel Vlad minister of finance. The Consiliu then sent a delegation to Bucharest to announce that union with Romania had been accomplished by the "spontaneous plebiscite" at Alba Iulia in accordance with the principle of self-determination. The Romanian government was asked to send troops to Transylvania to insure the liberation.[9] The Romanian nationalists in Bucovina held their assembly at Cernăuţi on November 28. The Ruthenian inhabitants were not represented. This assembly, unlike that at Alba Iulia, did not raise any conditions for union. The presence of Romanian troops in Cernăuţi since November 11 may have contributed to the decision for unconditional union.[10]

In line with the action at Cernăuţi, the Sfatul Ţării in Bessarabia decided to revoke the conditions imposed on the Romanian government in April 1918. Voting on December 10 to abrogate its list of demands for electoral and agrarian reforms, the Sfat proclaimed unconditional union. The last constitutional obstacle to union was thus removed.[11]

The final act of union was at Mediaş in Transylvania on January 8, when the Saxon Germans requested incorporation into Romania. This act, and those in Bucovina and Bessarabia, were carried out after Romanian troops had occupied the regions. Bessarabia had been occupied for a year, Bucovina was occupied on November 11, and Romanian troops had seized most of Transylvania by the end of December. These moves raise the question: were the acts of union spontaneous or were they arranged under the menacing or protecting guns of the Romanian army?[12] Evidence points to characteristics of both.

The Recall of Brătianu

King Ferdinand summoned Brătianu to take charge of the government on December 14. This move ended the life of the Coandă cabinet, which no one had considered a permanent fixture. It was felt generally that the man who had launched Romania into war should be entitled to the rewards of the 1916 Alliance. Brătianu returned to office amid great jubilation. The royal family, government officials, and the diplomatic corps left Iaşi on November 27, entering Bucharest in a triumphant procession on December 1. They were met by General Berthelot who had arrived with Allied troops. On a day described by Vopicka as "the greatest in Romania's history," Ferdinand promoted himself to field marshal and expressed joy that Romania would now be enlarged and that all peoples of the Romanian "race" would at last come together.[13]

Brătianu appointed to his government most of the Liberals who had served under him during the war. On December 18, he issued a decree-law accepting the union of Bucovina. This was followed on

December 26 by a similar law for the Romanian-inhabited regions of Hungary, which were permitted considerable self-government in deference to conditions laid down at Alba Iulia. Three members of the Consiliu Dirigent were appointed to his government. A week later, on January 1, the Bessarabian act of union was likewise accepted. Each act of union was duly ratified by the Romanian parliament on January 24.[14]

Demonstrations for union led Brătianu to demand that the Allies modify the armistice with Hungary to permit him to occupy the frontier promised in the 1916 Alliance. He insisted Magyar officials be removed from the regions east of the Tisa River and their authority transferred to the Consiliu Dirigent. Citing anti-Romanian atrocities committed by the Magyars, he demanded recognition of his right to occupy all of Transylvania. The Allied envoys advised their governments to yield to his demands so that the Romanian army could stem growing Bolshevik sympathies in Hungary.[15]

Occupation of most of the Banat by Serbian troops led Brătianu to incite a propaganda campaign against the new Kingdom of the Serbs-Croats-Slovenes. He accused Serbia of terrorizing Romanians of the Banat, preventing a return to that province of Romanians who had attended the Alba Iulia assembly, and financing a plot to murder Cicio-Pop, a native of the Banat and minister of war in the Consiliu Dirigent.[16] He summoned the Serbian chargé d'affaires to whom he handed a stern démarche. The chargé reminded the Premier that Serbia was not bound by the 1916 Alliance and that her troops were occupying the Banat at the request of the French General Staff.[17] The Allied envoys, caught up in this dispute, appealed to their governments to dispatch an inter-Allied force to the Banat to prevent an outbreak of hostilities.[18]

Similar difficulties arose over the question of southern Dobrodgea. When Bulgaria surrendered, that region was placed under Allied supervision. French and British troops occupied the region and prevented Romania from immediately recovering it. On November 29, however, Romanian troops crossed the Danube in an attempt to regain the province. This move defied the armistice, to which Romania was not a signatory. Compelled by the Supreme War Council, d'Esperey evicted the Romanians and restored Bulgarian authority. This proved temporary in deference to American insistence that the question of southern Dobrodgea be reserved for the peace table. Despite this reservation, General Berthelot permitted Romanian gendarmes to enter on December 8 to evict Bulgarian administrators. Bulgaria protested in vain and even staged a demonstration for the union of southern Dobrodgea with Bulgaria. By the end of December the Romanians had restored their sovereignty over all of Dobrodgea and silenced opposition there.[19]

By the middle of January 1919, Brătianu had enlarged Romania's holdings according to what he termed the "spontaneous expressions of popular feeling" generated by the ideals of Woodrow Wilson. The Premier now prepared to depart for Paris to take what he considered his rightful place among the Allied Powers to rearrange the map of Europe.[20]

The Romanian Delegation

Brătianu's delegation contained only those who supported his policy. To dignify the group, he invited nationalists of the new provinces to join. Vaida-Voevod represented the Romanians of former Hungarian comitats, Constantin Crişan spoke for the Romanians of the Banat, Neagoe Flondor for those of Bucovina, and Ioan Pelivan for Bessarabia. Brătianu's intimate collaborators, Coandă, Diamandy, Antonescu, and Danielopol, were given posts in the delegation. The Premier considered appointing Ionescu and made proper overtures, but Ionescu rejected the invitation unless Brătianu appointed Conservative Democrats to his government. Brătianu refused this condition and let it be known that Ionescu had forfeited his chances for appointment to the delegation because of his unauthorized negotiations with Pašić over a partition of the Banat. The Premier refused to compromise with the Serbs and rejected Ionescu's plan to establish a bloc of small powers at the peace conference. His disavowal of Ionescu's work did not lead to the latter's return to Romania. Ionescu remained in Paris to continue his efforts.[21] In his place Brătianu appointed Nicolae Mişu to be first deputy.[22]

The British suggested that Brătianu reconsider naming Ionescu, but the Premier accused him of being in league with Averescu, who was ostensibly plotting to seize power. Averescu was reportedly enjoying "clandestine relations" with the Germans. Brătianu threatened to resign if the Allies refused to recognize his rights as legal head of the Romanian government, and he warned that his resignation would be followed by a Bolshevik inundation of Romania.[23] This rejoinder was met by an Allied statement urging Brătianu to reach an understanding with Serbia before the conference opened. He agreed to stop in Belgrade on his way to Paris.[24]

Brătianu entrained for Paris on January 11.[25] He met with Prince-Regent Alexander in Belgrade and tried to convince him that Romania's claim to the entire Banat did not constitute an unfriendly act, but was merely intended to provide Romania with a defensible frontier along the Danube. He intimated a settlement was possible if the Serbs were willing to compromise. Alexander insisted Belgrade could not remain unprotected along the Serbo-Romanian frontier, and he claimed a bridgehead across the Danube in the Banat. Their meeting terminated without any reconciliation.[26]

Unknown to Brătianu was a development destined to cause an impasse in his attempts to acquire new territories. The French advised Lansing on January 4 that the decree-laws issued by Romania were illegal. Lansing was asked to subscribe to a joint démarche stating Allied opposition to annexations consecrated by Romania alone. The United States and Italy subscribed to the démarche.[27] This tripartite agreement appeared to be a revival of the Briand-Stürmer understanding by which the French and Russians proposed to dictate the peace. This demarche was the first indication of Allied disapproval of the actions taken by Romania to legalize her aggrandizement.

The Allied démarche was awaiting Brătianu when he arrived in Paris on January 13, the day Lansing agreed to the note. The Romanian delegation set up headquarters in the Romanian Legation at 77 Avenue des Champs-Élysées. The Peace Conference had opened the day before when Lloyd George, Clemenceau, Orlando, and Wilson, together with their foreign ministers, met at the Quai d'Orsay to discuss the question of small power representation. It was during this preliminary series of meetings that the question of Romania's status was raised.

Representation for Romania

Romania's status presented two related problems. The first concerned her position as an Allied and Associated Power. The three western Allies conceded that she had regained her allied status by re-entering the war on November 10. The American position was clarified in January after Brătianu succeeded in obtaining a loan for the purchase of foodstuffs. The Treasury Department hesitated before approving the loan because of the Peace of Bucharest which, it was contended, had made Romania a neutral state and, consequently, not entitled to a loan under terms of the Trading with the Enemy Act. Wilson interceded and

Lansing permitted the loan with the accompanying explanation of America's recognition of Romania as an ally:

> On November 9, 1918 the Romanian Government with the Allies' knowledge ordered the German army out in twenty-four hours. They did not leave. The Romanian army mobilized on the night of the 9th and hostilities were begun and continued until all German forces were taken prisoner of war or driven into Hungary. The Romanian Government, as stated above, mobilized on the 9th; hence the Romanian Government was once more in a state of war with Germany prior to the signing of the armistice on the 11th.... It is my understanding that the King of Romania never signed the Treaty of Bucharest and that the treaty was never promulgated. I am informed that according to Romanian law, no treaty is valid until promulgated following the royal signature. In view of the fact that the Allied Governments have never recognized the ·Treaty of Bucharest and that its validity is doubtful, that by the terms of the armistice the Germans were compelled to denounce the treaty and that from the point of view of the Associated Governments, the status of Romania is the same as if the treaty had never been made.... I consider that Romania is in a state of war with Germany and should be regarded as a belligerent within the meaning of the Act of Congress.[28]

This opinion was interpreted as official American recognition of Romania's right to participate in the conference. Furthermore, the United States thereby conceded that the Peace of Bucharest had not ended Romania's status as an allied state.[29] The Allied Powers concurred, and Romania was invited to participate.

The second problem concerned the number of plenipotentiaries for Romania. Prior to the opening of the conference the Allies considered various plans for representation. André Tardieu, Clemenceau's close associate, proposed that those nations that had been represented at the Inter-Allied Conference in December 1917, and that had participated in armistice negotiations, should be invited. Since this proposal eliminated Romania and other small powers that had not taken part in either circumstance, Tardieu's plan was rejected.[30]

In November 1918 the Supreme War Council adopted Lloyd George's suggestion to invite all states which had sacrificed heavily, but to limit participation of small powers to discussions relating to their particular interests.[31] This ruling enabled Romania to be represented, but subsequent decisions denied her an equal place with the Allies. None of the Allied leaders was willing to uphold Article 6 of the Alliance according Romania equality with the Great Powers. But the Quai d'Orsay intended to give Romania a greater voice than that proposed for other small powers. At the first meeting of the Supreme Council of the Peace Conference (January 12), Pichon urged that Romania be treated more favorably than other small powers because she had been forced out of the war and had later resumed her status as an ally. British Foreign Secretary Balfour did not oppose treating Romania as a reinstated ally for purposes of representation, but he did not wish thereby to renew every clause of the 1916 Alliance, which "Romania had broken by going out of the war."[32] Sonnino proposed a temporary postponement of discussions regarding the validity of the Alliance. He secured the Council's consent to the ruling that Romania be assigned the same number of seats as that given to other small powers.[33]

Pichon held out for a privileged position for Romania, proposing on January 15 that Romania be given three seats because she had fought against the enemy since 1914. Lloyd George corrected his chronological error and reminded Pichon that if the French insisted upon assigning seats only to those states which had entered the war in 1914, the United States would be eliminated. The Prime Minister was the most rigid advocate of placing control of the conference in the hands of the four Allied Powers, and he rejected a suggestion that Belgium be given three seats since the Allies, with a total population of over 100 million, were to have only five representatives each. He exclaimed that "after all, the delegates were here only to present their cases; and their cause could be presented just as well by two representatives as by three, and perhaps still by one only."[34] The Council adopted his ruling that small powers be given two seats each to lessen chances for jealousy.

An unanticipated uproar ensued when the allocations became known. Instead of maintaining their ruling, the Allied Powers took sides and thereby disrupted the entire plan for representation. Wilson forced through a revision in order to assign seats to Latin American states. Balfour secured two seats for the new Kingdom of the Hejaz. When the news leaked out, the small European powers objected to being treated like pariahs. Brătianu complained of being handled like "a poor wretch deserving pity and not like an ally who has a right to justice."[35] The Council permitted individual prejudices to intercede, and this produced an acrimonious atmosphere for the beginning of the conference. Clemenceau's argument won over the Allied leaders to his solution. He had them consider the loyalty of a state and its sufferings as criteria for assigning seats. He remarked that Belgium, "which could have done in 1914 as Romania did in 1918," should be given three seats, and the Serbs, whose losses had been terrible and whose manhood had been completely exhausted while she "fought on without counting her losses," should likewise get three seats.[36] Lloyd George yielded in return for termination of the debate. He expressed his vexation:

> If we were to occupy our time in making decisions and reversing them, and altering them, the Supreme Council would never come to an end. Tomorrow, when it will be learned that Belgium and Serbia have been given three representatives apiece, Greece, Romania, and even China with her population of 400 million, will undoubtedly protest. But if we are going to chop and change constantly, when would we come to the end of it?[37]

Romania would have two seats, while Belgium and Serbia, two allies who had fought without any written guarantees, enjoyed a superior status. Brătianu's only consolation came in the welcoming address of President Poincaré, who described how

> Romania resolved to fight only to realize her national unity, which was opposed by the powers of arbitrary force. Abandoned, betrayed, strangled, she had to submit to an abominable treaty, the revision of which you will exact....[38]

Brătianu soon learned the Allied Powers had reserved for themselves the chief questions which would then be submitted for final approval to plenary sessions. All that he could anticipate was the right to be heard at sessions of the Supreme Council when questions related to Romania were discussed. When the Council adopted Balfour's proposal (January 17) to establish various commissions to investigate issues, it was decided to give seats on those commissions to the small powers, whose delegates, Lloyd George pointed out, should be kept busy.[39]

The small powers were advised (January 25) about assignments to the commissions. Romania was not given a seat on the commission to discuss the establishment of the League of Nations. Brătianu expressed his disappointment in the first of his many challenges to the Supreme Council:

> I do not... wish to lose sight of the fact that at this moment the League is in question, and that it would be poor evidence of the interest felt by Romania in the formation of this League if I did not contribute to the explanations made by the representatives here. It is certain that in the representation of such a league the relative strength of each state has been kept in view, and it would be just to consider at the same time the interests which lead each state to favor the formation of this League, when it might perhaps be found that small states have more interest in it than great ones. In setting representatives in the League, both these points of view must be kept in mind. It is to express the interest which Romania feels in the principles of this League that she asks to be represented on this commission.[40]

Clemenceau reproached him for this expression of faithlessness in the intentions of the Supreme Council, reminding Brătianu that Romania would be permitted to present her case to every commission on which she had no representative. The larger a commission, he added, the less that could be accomplished. Brătianu was not appeased; he motioned to have the small powers meet in conclave to elect delegates to the League Commission and to discuss the question of more representatives.[41]

Having been denied a seat on the Supreme Council and the League Commission, Brătianu was determined to secure some satisfaction. He met with other small-power delegates (January 27) who were likewise disgruntled. They elected representatives to commissions, but Brătianu felt justifiably incensed when Romania failed to be elected to the Ports and Waterways Commission, which had as one of its tasks regulation of traffic on the Danube. It was undeniably incongruous to find Latin American states elected to that body, while a riparian state was not.[42] Brătianu and other frustrated delegates appealed for an increase in the size of commissions. Colonel House interceded for them, and the Council agreed to give the small powers more seats. The delegates were told the Allies would direct the work of each commission, and each state was to confine its attention to items for which its representation was authorized.[43]

Romania was assigned seats on seven commissions: Responsibility for the War, Aeronautical, Financial, Economic, Reparation of Damage, Ports and Waterways, and League of Nations. This increased privilege, enabling Romanian delegates to assist in drafting treaties, did not compensate for Brătianu's chagrin over being denied a seat on the Supreme Council. No less injurious to his pride was the Council's decision to deny representation to Romania, as well as to the other small powers, on commissions created to consider territorial questions and treaties for the protection of minorities. Interested states were invited to submit territorial claims in writing, but the Council later allowed the small powers to testify before the Allied leaders.[44]

The Council Asserts Its Authority

After experiencing a revolt of the small powers, the Supreme Council announced that the Allied Powers, who were undeniably responsible for victory, reserved the right to dictate the peace. This ruling originated in a request of the Quai d'Orsay to Britain, Italy, and the United States to join in a démarche to the small powers stopping them from grabbing territory before the conference determined the final awards of disputed regions.[45] Britain offered an amended version of the French request:

> In various districts.... armed unpleasantness for the possession of certain areas in dispute between certain nationalities has occurred.... We wish to declare that any attempt to anticipate peace conference decisions by seizing or occupying such areas with armed force will not only not assist the cause of those who have recourse to such methods, in the eyes of the Allies at the peace conference, but will certainly tend to prejudice it.[46]

This warning was directed especially against Romania's occupation of new territories and the union of these regions with the Romanian state. The United States concurred in the Anglo-French proposal after learning from Archibald Cary Coolidge, Professor of History at Harvard University and Chief of the American Commission of Study in Central Europe stationed in Vienna, that Romania was not observing the armistices with Hungary and Bulgaria and that she was committing provocations in the Banat and southern Dobrodgea.[47] This news led Wilson to present a resolution to the Council on January 25, which was adopted and transmitted throughout the world:

> The Council is deeply disturbed by the news which comes to it of the many instances in which armed force is being made use of, in many parts of Europe and the East, to gain possession of territory, the rightful claim to which the Peace Conference is to be asked to determine. They deem it their duty to utter a solemn warning that possession gained by force will seriously prejudice the claims of those who use such means. It will create the presumption that those who employ force doubt the justice and validity of their claim and propose to substitute possession for proof of right and set up sovereignty by coercion rather than by racial or national preference and natural historical association. They thus put a cloud upon every evidence of title they may afterwards allege and indicate their distrust for the Conference itself. Nothing but the most unfortunate results can ensue. If they expect justice, they must refrain from force and place their claims... in the hands of the Conference.[48]

This proclamation implied that the Principal Allied and Associated Powers, the title assumed by members of the Supreme Council, possessed the military capability to enforce peace settlements. As events turned out, the Council kept matters in its own hands, presenting completed treaties to lesser allies only when the time for signatures arrived. The plenary sessions, convoked for this purpose, were mere formalities. Small powers henceforth had to be satisfied with stating their cases before the tribunal of the Great Powers. The "Council of Ten," as it was informally called, consisted of the heads of government of Britain, France, Italy, Japan, and the United States, assisted by their foreign ministers. The Supreme Council, its formal title, was the real Peace Conference. Its size was reduced in March to the "Council of Four," the Japanese having decided to attend only those sessions of interest to them. While Clemenceau, Lloyd George, Orlando, and Wilson discussed major issues, their foreign ministers were assigned minor items.

Brătianu's Reaction

In attempting to rectify Council decisions, Brătianu approached Harold Nicolson, the British expert on the Balkans. Nicolson advised him it would be foolish to insist upon the validity of the 1916 Alliance "since it had been cancelled by Romania's making separate peace with Germany." Brătianu's irritation prompted the following observation by Nicolson:

> Brătianu is a bearded woman, a forceful humbug, a Bucharest intellectual, a most unpleasing man. Handsome and exuberant, he flings his fine head sideways, catching his whole profile in the glass. He makes elaborate verbal jokes, imagining them to be Parisian. He spends most of the luncheon inveighing against the Russians.... for not having rescued Romania in 1916.[49]

Brătianu then met with Colonel House (January 27). House listened to an interminable presentation of Romanian history, including a blistering attack upon Russian treachery. He finally interrupted to say he was entirely conversant with what Brătianu was relating. Brătianu, on the other hand, was quite pleased with the interview. When House expressed sympathy for his aspirations, the Premier replied that "it was the only encouraging word he had had since arriving in Paris."[50] House believed Brătianu to be a clever politician and diplomat of the "old and perhaps not too admirable school," whose career had incidents which

> ...a partial biographer would not bring into prominence. Perhaps for this very reason there can be no doubt but that he understands, as no one else, the intricacies of Romanian party life, and he has his finger on the pulse of popular feeling.[51]

House arranged for him to talk with Douglas Johnson, the American geographic expert, on January 28. Brătianu tried to convince Johnson that America was Romania's best friend and that France, from whom he had anticipated aid and friendship

> ...had missed a great opportunity when she failed to make herself the champion of the cause of the smaller nations. Colonel House's kind words gave me reason to hope that in

America we may find the friend we have not located elsewhere. I may characterize the interview with him as the
bright spot in the dark Romanian sky.[52]

The Premier assured Johnson he would refrain from expressing his
grievances because

I have the reputation of being a very bad character, who is
always making trouble by trying to secure too much. Therefore, I have been able to show the Allies that after all I am
not such a bad man and have preferred to ignore things
about which I might have complained.

But he nevertheless went on to criticize the assignment of only two
plenipotentiaries and to contrast Romania's importance with the
inferiority of Siam and the Hejaz, likewise given two seats each. He
predicted the Supreme Council would become a tribunal sitting in
judgement on the small powers.

Brătianu then proceeded to reconstruct history in insisting that
Romania had never willingly joined the Triple Alliance, but had been
forced into it by the British and French refusal to protect Romania
against Russia. He claimed he intended to remain neutral in 1914
despite tempting offers of the Central Powers. His negotiations with
Sazonov, "who was too Serbophile," produced his suspicions of
Russia's motives, and for that reason the Russians had accused him of
"talking too big." He concluded his harangue, delivered in perfect
French for one and one-half hours, with the lament:

It is a very bitter experience for us to have it even suggested
that the 1916 treaty stipulations are void.[53]

Brătianu Before the Council

After the Polish delegation won the privilege of presenting its
claims to the Supreme Council, the other small powers demanded the
same prerogative. When Brătianu requested permission to testify,
Wilson favored it but Lloyd George was distressed by the prospect of
listening to interminable declamations by the suppliant states:

Does it mean that the Supreme Council begins tomorrow
discussing territorial questions of Europe? He thought the

discussion on Czechoslovakia and Poland the other day was absolutely wrong. He would not use the term 'waste of time' because that was a very provocative one, and he could already see the glare in Woodrow Wilson's eye! Unless the Supreme Council began business with Romania and considered her claims, he did not think Romania's representatives ought to be present. If they came without intending to do business, it would be a waste of time.[54]

The Council, nevertheless, agreed to invite the Romanians and the Serbs to testify together on January 31.[55] To expedite the settlement of territorial questions Wilson proposed the creation of expert commissions to investigate claims. Balfour hailed this proposal:

> The Americans had done most of their work in the United States. The British had done their work in England and France. They had had books, but more than that they had seen the representatives of those countries. If they could come face to face with the actual living feelings of the peoples concerned, he felt it would be beneficial.[56]

The Council ruled that the territorial commission on Romanian frontiers should submit its findings to Brătianu for his opinions. In this way, it was anticipated, everything the experts and Brătianu agreed upon could be eliminated from Council discussions.

The forthcoming debate between Romanians and Serbs was not calculated to contribute toward making peace with the enemy (for which purpose the Peace Conference had originally been convened), but rather to preserve harmony between the two states.[57] It was Friday, January 31, at 3:15 P.M., when Brătianu and Mişu were admitted to La Salle d'Horloge in the Quay d'Orsay, the study of Pichon where the Council usually held its sessions. Seated at the table was Brătianu's formidable antagonist — Georges Clemenceau, a squat, round-shouldered man, with heavy white eyebrows and drooping mustache contrasting sharply with Brătianu's black beard and brows. The French premier was born in 1841, over twenty years before the name "Romania" became an actuality. Brătianu was certainly acquainted with Clemenceau's antipathies expressed vituperatively in his newspaper, *L'Homme Enchainé*. The two statesmen, nevertheless, were remarkably alike. Clemenceau's cynical realism in diplomacy, his distaste for idealism in politics, and his aversion to compromise found an equal in

Brătianu. Next to Clemenceau was Pichon, whom Brătianu could count as a friend. Also present was Philippe Berthelot, Director of the Diplomatic Cabinet and the powerful official at the Quai d'Orsay. No technical experts accompanied the French delegation.

The British delegation was headed by David Lloyd George, who once had accused Sir Edward Grey of ignorance of foreigners, but who would soon ask, "Where the hell is the Banat?".[58] Next to him was Arthur James Balfour, who once opposed Irish nationalism and now supported self-determination of small peoples. Two experts assisted the British leaders — Allen Leeper, an outspoken friend of the Romanians, and Harold Nicolson, who Brătianu knew was opposed to the 1916 Alliance.[59]

Vittorio Orlando, the reputedly warm-hearted Sicilian liberal, was there, attending sessions that were unintelligible to one who spoke no English, the *lingua franca* used by the others when they wished to ignore him. The roles in the Italian delegation were the reverse of those in the French. The latter was dominated by Clemenceau; the former was controlled by Foreign Minister Sonnino, the "evil genius of Italian obstruction," the apostle of *sacro egoismo*, who, distinguished by his bullet-shaped head, long mustache, and hawk-shaped nose, was probably the most disliked individual in the room, with the possible exception of Brătianu, with whom he shared similar objectives — fulfillment of a secret treaty and territorial aggrandizement. Like Clemenceau and Brătianu, Sonnino was a ruthless realist. He had come to Paris for one reason — to get everything promised by the Treaty of London, and perhaps more. Assisting the two Italian statesmen was Count Luigi Aldrovandi Marescotti, whom Brătianu had met at the Inter-Allied Conference in Petrograd in 1917. The Count interpreted for Orlando. Sonnino needed no translations; his English and French were perfect.

The Japanese delegates, Viscount Chinda and Baron Makino, were not accompanied by technical experts, nor were there any to assist the Italians. Both delegations knew precisely what they wanted. Advice, therefore, would have been superfluous.[60] In contrast was the American delegation headed by the most renowned man in the room, yet the most enigmatic — Woodrow Wilson. The Romanian Premier could not quite comprehend "Wilsonian Diplomacy." He once asserted, "I come from a race of peasants, and I never think the harvest is assured until I have the money for it in my pocket."[61] That statement expresses quite succinctly the essential difference between the two men. Assisting Wilson were Secretary of State Robert Lansing and these experts:

David Hunter Miller and Arthur Frazier (legal specialists), and Clive Day and Charles Seymour (experts on East Central Europe).

Brătianu sat in the gilded chair reserved for him directly in front of Clemenceau. Then, according to Nicolson's diary account, he opened his briefcase in dramatic fashion, as if to indicate to everyone present that he was by far the greatest statesman in the room.[62] He removed a lengthy document entitled "The Question of the Banat," which he proceeded to read. This is what he claimed: (1) Romania's right to the entire Banat as guaranteed in the 1916 Alliance by "our three great European allies"; (2) this claim was based on ethnic and historical rights, the Romanians having settled in the province in ancient times and now the largest nationality inhabiting it; (3) opposition to partition because it would destroy the geographical, economic, and political unity of the Banat; (4) the Swabian German inhabitants preferred Romanian to Serbian rule; (5) Serbia's fears would be overcome by Romanian promises not to erect fortifications along the Danube; (6) if the Serbs crossed the Danube (to acquire the one-third they claimed), there would "then be no end to the unappeasable appetites and disputes" involved in their desire for more territory; (7) Romania would guarantee the same rights to the Serbian minority if Serbia, in turn, did likewise for the Romanians living in the Timok valley of Serbia; and (8) having lost 335,000 soldiers and many more civilians in the war, Romania played a role "which cannot fail to confirm her right to the entire Banat." [63]

While Brătianu was reading, Balfour got up, "yawning slightly," to ask Nicolson for a map of British territorial recommendations. Leeper produced it, and Balfour then showed the map to Sonnino with "marked indifference."[64] Having completed his presentation by showing his own map of the Banat, which pointed to an absolute majority of Romanians in the central and eastern sections, Brătianu moved aside as the Serbian delegates entered the room.[65]

Nikola Pašić, Ante Trumbić (foreign minister of the new Kingdom of Serbs-Croats-Slovenes), and Milenko Vesnić (envoy to France) had not been present during Brătianu's reading.[66] Vesnić apologized for failing to bring a written statement, as Brătianu had done, because Serbia's invitation had been received too late for him to write out a speech. Nevertheless, he demonstrated a remarkable familiarity with what Brătianu had just related. He first assailed the 1916 Alliance as no longer valid, and added that Serbia, unlike Romania, had fought without asking for any written assurances because she firmly believed that peace would be concluded on the basis of self-determination.

Serbia, Vesnić continued, was not bound by the Alliance, and he complained of a refusal by the Quai d'Orsay to give him a copy. Clemenceau was surprised to learn that the Alliance had not been publicized. Brătianu explained that it was to be kept secret until the conclusion of peace, and Pichon confirmed this by reading Article 7. Vesnić deplored this provision and disputed the authority of the Allies to dispose of territory inhabited by Serbs without the consent of the Serbian government.[67] The Serbs then laid claim to the comitat of Torontál, western-most of the three comitats comprising the Banat, and the ethnically Serbian districts of the center comitat of Timiş. Vesnić commented that German and Magyar officials "had always shown greater favor to the Romanians because the latter had been allied to the Central Powers for nearly thirty years." This allusion to Romania's association with the Triple Alliance was not calculated to please Brătianu, nor was Vesnić's statement that, in parliamentary elections, the contests in the Banat were always between Serbs and Magyars, never between Romanians and Magyars.

Lloyd George asked if any Serbs of the Banat had been elected to the Budapest parliament. Vesnić replied that Serbs had been voted into office from districts inhabited by Serbian majorities.[68] Brătianu did not know the election results of the Banat, but he remarked that three million Romanians in Hungary were represented at Budapest by only five deputies, while the Serbs had three. He described the violence which invariably marked elections in Hungary, evidenced by the number of Romanian candidates thrown into prison to remove them from running.[69]

The Serbs then added historical rights to their claims, stating that the royal family had frequently found refuge in the Banat. Brătianu challenged this claim advanced on the basis of the Karageorgević dynasty gaining sanctuary there. He remarked

> ...otherwise the whole of Romania might as well be claimed by Serbia, since many of the members of the royal families of Obrenović and Karageorgević had taken refuge in Romania, and even M. Pašić himself, when the situation in Serbia was somewhat dangerous, had made his home in Romania.

As the debate grew heated, Trumbić interjected an additional demand for a plebiscite in the Banat, and he increased the Serbian claim by asking for the center comitat of Timiş in its entirety. He believed the Swabian German and Magyar minorities in Timiş would vote for incorporation into Serbia.[70] Brătianu was asked about a plebiscite. He prefaced his reply with an apology for speaking a third time, required because "the Romanians had only two representatives to pit against the three representatives of Serbia." He would not oppose a plebiscite, but he would never obey the results if the Banat were partitioned. The Premier closed with this pungent analogy:

> The work which the Conference was now called upon to carry out should be compared to that of an inter-Allied commission (had such a commission then been possible) appointed in the time of Charlemagne to adjudicate the question of the Rhine. Had the commission at that time decided that the Rhine should form the boundary between Germany and France, what untold benefits might have been conferred on the world, what influence such a decision might have had on the events leading up to the present war. The Conference was now in the same way settling the future of Eastern Europe.

Vesnić had the final word. He regretted that Brătianu had objected to Serbia's present occupation of the Banat, and reminded the Council that d'Esperey had ordered the Serbs to occupy the province where their troops had been welcomed as liberators. "At any rate," he concluded, "Serbia was not to blame if Romania had not entered the Banat either now or in 1916."

After the Romanian and Serbian delegates withdrew, Wilson, Lloyd George, and Clemenceau praised the Serbs for their judicious consideration of the Swabian German and Magyar interests in the Banat. But Orlando and Sonnino criticized this, not so much because "they had agreed with Romania to back her on condition she uphold the Treaty of London,"[71] but because of the favorable attitude shown the Serbs during the debate. It was clear that if the Serbs succeeded in getting support from the American, British, and French leaders for the establishment of a strong Slav state, a development contrary to the Italo-Romanian accord of 1914, the Treaty of London and its exorbitant promises of regions along the eastern Adriatic coast would probably be revised. A similar fate might be administered to the 1916 Alliance, which likewise encroached upon the territorial aspirations of the south Slavs.[72] The Serbian claim to more than one-third of the Banat was considered quite excessive and untenable from the point of view of ethnography.[73] The Serbs hoped the British, French, and Americans, who had made no secret of their admiration for Serbia's heroic role in the war, would yield to the increased claim posted by Trumbić. Their aspirations received considerable encouragement on February 5 when the United States granted recognition to the Kingdom of Serbs-Croats-Slovenes.

Brătianu, disconsolate at having come in second in the debate, revealed his chagrin at a dinner he gave for American experts Day, Johnson, and Seymour that evening (January 31). Mişu was sent to dine with the British experts.[74] The Americans heard Brătianu denounce the Council as a judge who had placed Romania on trial, but he was careful to name Britain, France, and Italy as his enemies, while citing the cordial treatment given by the Americans. Relapsing into his customary reconstruction of history, the Premier explained that the Focşani truce would never have been concluded had the Allies not urged him to do so. The three western Allies were therefore bound, he contended, by the 1916 Alliance which they had broken. He remarked:

> The fact that he was speaking did not prevent some of his auditors in the Supreme Council from sleeping, and the fact that they were sleeping would not prevent them from pronouncing judgment.[75]

When asked if he would accept a partitioned Banat, Brătianu warned of an inevitable conflict if the Serbs took the protective zone northeast of Belgrade. Serbia, he said, should not get any of the Banat because she would receive "enough new territory in the Balkans." When asked if he claimed the predominantly Magyar city of Debreczen, Brătianu replied he had never requested it.[76] He demanded the Council permit Dimitrie Drăghicescu, his territorial expert, to testify before the commission established to draw his frontiers.[77]

In appraising this encounter, Johnson and Seymour feared a delay in determining the Serbo-Romanian frontier would provoke a war. Seymour advised the tracing of a temporary boundary. Neither expert was impressed by Brătianu's expressions of affection for America. Both recommended he be told of the Allied determination to trust statistics of their own experts rather than accept those offered by Romania.[78]

Brătianu refused to accept any ideas that went counter to his maximum claims. He now prepared to make his second onslaught upon the Council to which he had been invited for another hearing on February 1.

Brătianu's Second Audition

There was little change in the scene at the Quai d'Orsay on February 1; the same participants (except the American experts, Leeper, and Viscount Chinda) were present. Just before Brătianu entered, the Council rejected Lansing's significant motion requiring members of the League of Nations to sign conventions to refrain from invading sovereign territory of other member states.[79] Brătianu was accompanied by Mişu, Alexandru Lăpedatu, and his nephew Constantin Brătianu. He prefaced reading his report with this bit of effrontery:

> This is the second time that he had to face a 'viva' examination in Paris. [The first time was for his engineering degree.] 'On that occasion my examiners knew more than I did.'[80]

With this tactless reference to the ignorance of his audience, the Premier launched into a lengthy statement of his steps leading to the signing of the 1916 Alliance: how Romania had been called into the Balkan War by Serbian and Greek appeals for aid against Bulgaria, how the Triple Alliance had been converted into an instrument of aggression thus absolving Romania of all responsibility to join the Central Powers, and how intervention against the Allies would have been contrary to Romanian national interests. He admitted having exported materials to the Central Powers, but stressed that the goods were not convertible to war matériel and that the Germans had paid him with arms and equipment "which were not available from the Allies." Romania, he claimed, aroused German hostility when the Russians sent supplies through his country to Serbia and when he prevented the passage of arms destined for the Turks on Gallipoli.[81]

Continuing his revised historical account, Brătianu related how the Russians, capitalizing on Romania's fear of the Central Powers, forced him into a neutrality treaty, how the Allies finally recognized the "justice of Romania's demands" after months of negotiations delayed by "causes... which did not emanate from the Romanian Government," whose attitude never varied, and how Romania "loyally fulfilled her duty" even though Russia failed to uphold her end of the bargain. Romania, he mourned, was discouraged by the "worst disappointments which did not always come from the side of the enemy." His nation was entitled to rewards commensurate with the sufferings she had endured. Brătianu then denounced Allied strategy:

Neither the Bulgarian attack, nor the possibility accorded to Germany by quiet on the other fronts of concentrating her efforts against Romania, nor the inactivity of her neighboring allies, who did not meet in Transylvania as arranged, nor the delay in Russian assistance which might have covered Bucharest and Wallachia, nor that, which from the material and moral points of view, represented the loss of two-thirds of the country, including the capital, shook the loyalty and devotion of the Romanians to the cause which they had made their own.

Brătianu tempered this charge with praise for the French military mission which rehabilitated his army, permitting it to resume hostilities in the summer of 1917 and, by defeating Mackensen at Mărăşeşti, preventing a German invasion of Russia from the southeast. He accused Russia of consorting with the Central Powers before the Bolsheviks seized power and, capitalizing on an assumption that the Allies were hostile toward Russia for making separate peace, the Premier described the horrors of Bolshevism and added that no Romanian platoon had succumbed to its propaganda. Romania, he boasted, had the distinction of being the first allied state to fight the Bolsheviks. He had obeyed the Allied summons to occupy Bessarabia, but could not continue against the Bolsheviks because the Germans had occupied the Ukraine, come down the Dniester River, threatened Romania's flank, and cut off the retreat of his army through southern Russia.[82] The Allies, he remarked, gave him permission to seek "a lull in a conflict which was to be resumed." The Peace of Bucharest, he affirmed, was this so-called lull, although neither legally, practically, nor morally were the Romanians ever really at peace with the enemy. The Premier had prudently omitted reference to the Focşani armistice and concealed the fact that he had participated in the preliminaries leading to the Buftea treaty. He chose instead to reveal that the Peace of Bucharest had been ratified by a parliament elected under German auspices when refugees and soldiers were denied the vote. Furthermore, "the Treaty was never sanctioned or ratified by the King." If the Allies had not made known their intention to disregard the Peace of Bucharest, Romania, he declared, would not have re-entered the war when requested by the Allies. Romanian troops, grateful to the Allied guarantee of the 1916 Alliance, remained in their trenches even after the peace was signed and thus forced the Germans to retain eight divisions in Wallachia instead of transferring them to the Western Front. Romania's claims, he insisted, were not imperialistic, but merely a reflection of the wishes of her brethren living outside of the Kingdom "who desired incorporation."

Turning next to his claims, Brătianu requested precisely what was promised in the 1916 Alliance.[83] He produced wearisome statistics, maps, and counter-charges to support his demands. The national assemblies at Alba Iulia, Chişinău, Cernăuţi, and Mediaş, he declared, provided evidence of the desire of the Romanians to be included in one nation. He did not reveal the presence of Romanian troops in Bucovina, Bessarabia, and eastern Transylvania when the referenda were held. In regard to Bessarabia, which was not promised him in the Alliance, the Premier claimed the province by rights of conquest and plebiscite. Romania's annexation would hinder future attempts by Russia to encroach upon the Balkans, Brătianu reassured the Council, and although Russia's dream of seizing the Balkans and Constantinople

> was perhaps cherished... at the beginning of the 19th century and the occupation of Bessarabia in 1812 was doubtless a step toward the occupation of Moldavia, Bulgaria, and Constantinople, it was a false political move. Bessarabia was, moreover, of no importance to Russia for there was scarcely a Russian in the country.

At this point Lloyd George questioned the nature of the national assemblies. Brătianu revealed that the Magyars had refused to vote for union, the Ruthenians had abstained, and the Romanians of Bessarabia had requested a special agrarian reform. The Prime Minister then inquired if Romania wished recognition of the annexations "purely and simply," or an Allied declaration that "in those regions regularly constituted assemblies should have the power to declare for union."[84] Brătianu requested recognition of the acts of union which had already been confirmed by the decree-laws of the Romanian parliament. Lloyd George was not convinced; he pressed the Premier to admit that minorities had not been permitted to participate in elections to the assemblies. This mistrust of the "spontaneous plebiscites" aroused Brătianu's wrath and he blurted out that

> Romania had fought in order to impose her national will on the Hungarian minority in Transylvania. It was certain, therefore, that if the Hungarians were asked to vote in favor of union with Romania, they would hardly be expected to do so. He did not think a special election should be held now.

As regards the situation created in Transylvania by the armistice, he considered that the question of principle had been decided by the war, and that these territories must be restored to Romania. The minorities would be given the greatest possible freedom in their future political life. But the vanquished could not now be expected willingly to unite themselves to a country which for a thousand years they sought to dominate.

The Premier thus disclosed that his iron ruthlessness was no longer shielded under a mask of modest affability giving lip-service to high-sounding principles. He had cast aside all dissimulation and laid his cards on the table.

Lloyd George warned Brătianu not to adopt notorious methods of repression so long associated with the Magyars in order to force minorities into line.[85] The Premier intimated that such a course might be necessary because the Magyars were organizing agitation "along Bolshevik lines" and proclaiming "Wilson's policy... to be nothing but a capitalist policy," which radicals in Hungary were using as propaganda for their program of a "division of wealth and the abolition of ranks." He requested permission to occupy territory beyond what he claimed so that Romania could wipe out Bolshevism, "a serious and contagious disease." The purpose of an immediate occupation of territory beyond the armistice line and the Tisa River would be to make the various nationalities "friendly and even fraternal." He pledged to make Romania a bulwark against Bolshevism if the Allies recognized his claims. Finally, he again asked the Allies to evict Serbian troops from the Banat, and he requested the Council to abandon any idea of forcing Romania to yield southern Dobrodgea to Bulgaria because he would reject efforts "to wrest a portion of territory from an allied state without such state having consented to an alteration of the frontier line."[86]

After Brătianu withdrew, Lloyd George proposed that his claims be examined by the territorial commission. Wilson agreed on condition that the commission refrain from discussing purely political questions since only the Allied leaders had the attributes of "tact and compromise" required to settle disputes between states. Orlando declared he was bound to Romania by the 1916 Alliance, although he did not wish to defend secret treaties which "indeed were now out of fashion." But the Alliance, he said, was not a secret pact; it was now a public treaty.[87]

Clemenceau declared that the Alliance, "by the common consent of the representatives of the Great Powers there in that room, had been cancelled." Romania's representation at the peace conference, he affirmed, did not validate every clause of the Alliance which "she had broken by going out of the war." Orlando could not recall any decision to cancel all or part of the Alliance, and he insisted Romania had been forced to sign the Peace of Bucharest, "a pistol agreement," that could not be binding. Lloyd George defended Clemenceau's argument and denounced Brătianu's exorbitant claims to territory not promised in the Alliance.[88]

To placate Orlando's sensitivities about secret treaties in general, Clemenceau agreed to postpone a discussion of the Alliance's validity. Orlando was relieved and agreed to support the work of the territorial commission on condition that his territorial demands would not be examined by any body of experts. He feared that if experts consulted the Romanians, they would become an examining tribunal constituting "the court of first instance, and the delegates of the Great Powers the final court of appeal."[89] Wilson interjected a bombshell at this point; he announced that "the United States were not bound by any of the treaties in question," but he was prepared to approve settlements based on the statistics of the Allied experts. In his opinion Romania's claims "frequently exceeded what was justified in the secret treaty." The Council decided to authorize a "Romanian Territorial Commission" to begin deliberations on Brătianu's claims and to report its findings to the Allied leaders.[90]

The Romanian Territorial Commission became the standard for other examining bodies. No special instructions were drawn up to guide its work, nor were the experts furnished any ruling on the validity of the 1916 Alliance. They were entrusted with pronouncing on the fairness of particular claims, not with recommending a general territorial settlement. The Council's eagerness to expedite proceedings resulted in failure to define precisely the commission's assignment. Its duties required an examination of historical, ethnographical, geographical, economic, strategic, but not political facts. Colonel House predicted a difficult course the commission had to follow: "To create new boundaries is always to create new troubles."[91]

Brătianu's Disillusionment

As Brătianu had predicted to his American guests on January 31, Romania had become a litigant before the Council, which had clearly established itself as arbiter of international disputes and as the real Peace Conference. Not only had the Council reserved for itself all questions requiring preliminary treatment, but its rights were also safeguarded by a rule providing for representation of Allied experts on all commissions. Although the small powers were given seats, they could engage in discussions only when questions affecting their interests arose. It was undeniably a bitter revelation for Brătianu to learn that the Allied leaders considered him to be precisely what he had often described himself to be, namely, "a bad character." They had demoted Romania from her exalted position as an equal ally to that of a second-rate state, in the same category as Siam and the Hejaz. The Alliance had become a scrap of paper.

Any confidence that Brătianu may have placed in the Italians to uphold his Alliance was shattered when Italy agreed to the establishment of the territorial commission. Since the commission was to have two experts from each Allied Power, the Italians would be outnumbered. As long as no commission would be appointed to examine Italy's claims, the Italians were safe. But Brătianu could not depend upon any Allied leader to support his Alliance. After all, it was Sonnino who had suggested an indefinite postponement of a discussion of its validity. The other statesmen viewed the Alliance with much skepticism. Clemenceau had opposed its creation in 1916.[92] Lloyd George had preferred the establishment of a bloc of Balkan powers, including Bulgaria, to intervene against the enemy in 1915.[93] And Wilson's aversion to secret treaties was universally known.

Brătianu's political opponents at home assailed his stubborn refusal to compromise. Ionescu insisted he seek an amicable solution to the Banat dispute by meeting the Serbs halfway.[94] Marghiloman wrote on February 2: "Ha! Romania gets less seats than Serbia. Brătianu thought he had the rights of a Great Power. The Alliance is worthless. I knew it."[95] Press reaction in Paris was as unfavorable. *Le Temps,* the semi-official organ of major influence, urged the Allies to find natural limits of the Banat and partition it. The left-wing *Populaire* advised Romania to conciliate Serbia in view of the acquisition of Bessarabia. Clemenceau's newspaper, *L'Homme Libre,* recommended partition according to strategic criteria.[96] Seton-Watson, for many years a champion of Romanian aspirations, criticized Brătianu's claim to the entire Banat in *The New Europe* (February 15).[97]

Brătianu failed to find any support for his determination to stand on the Alliance. He could not obtain any backing from the Allied leaders who rejected his demands for private interviews. His anxiety may have increased upon learning that Clemenceau had entertained Prince-Regent Alexander of Serbia who arrived in Paris in February. The French Premier assured Alexander that he would support Serbian claims to part of the Banat, and he praised the appointment of Vesnić as a delegate.[98]

The fate of Romanian claims was now in the hands of the Territorial Commission.

NOTES

1. E. J. Dillon, *The Inside Story of the Peace Conference,* p. 236.

2. The nationalists substituted Romanian names for cities in Transylvania. The session on October 12 was called in Oradea Mare (Nagy-Várad in Hungarian). Many years would pass before the more familiar German name of that city, Grosswardein, would be forgotten.
    Vaida-Voevod's speech is in *Daily Review of the Foreign Press, Enemy Press Supplement,* V, No. 1, November 7, 1918, p. 56; and Mircea Djuvara, *La guerre roumaine, 1916-1918,* pp. 313-322. He presented demands to Archduke Joseph of Habsburg, the first time since 1886 that a Romanian had been received by a Habsburg. Vaida-Voevod (1872-1950), a native of northern Transylvania, was a graduate physician of Vienna. He practiced in Karlsbad. He was elected to the Budapest chamber in 1906 from the Transylvanian district of Ighiu and later from that of Făgăraş. He was a friend of Archduke Francis Ferdinand to whom he had appealed for Romanian autonomy in Transylvania. He spent the war years in Vienna and Switzerland, returning to Budapest in the fall of 1918.

3. A treatment of the movement for autonomy among the Romanians lies beyond the scope of this study. For studies of this movement, see Kann, I, pp. 305-317, and II, pp. 197-207; Jászi, *The Dissolution of the Habsburg Monarchy,* pp. 397-402; Moroïanu, pp. 242-259; and Vaida-Voevod, "Slawen, Deutsche, Magyaren, und Rumänen," *Österreichische Rundschau,* XXIV (1913), pp. 8-12.

4. Seton-Watson, *A History,* p. 532; Temperley, IV, p. 102.

5. Maniu (1873-1951) was leader of the nationalists. He was born at Şimleul in Transylvania, studied law at Cluj, Budapest, and Vienna. A Uniate, he became legal adviser to the Uniate Metropolitan of Blaj and was elected to the Budapest chamber in 1906, where he worked with Slovak and Croat nationalists. He was silenced by the Hungarian government in 1918 by being drafted into military service, despite his parliamentary immunity. He later organized an insurrection of Romanian regiments stationed in Prague in November 1918.

6. For the negotiations with Jászi, see his *Revolution and Counter-Revolution,* pp. xvii, 59; Károlyi, p. 98; and Carlile A. Macartney, *Hungary and her Successors,* p. 275.
    The Council's declarations are in *Daily Review of the Foreign Press, Enemy Press Supplement,* V, No. 1, December 5, 1918, pp. 271-272. Jászi's counter-offer of self-government in a federated Hungary is in Royal Hungarian Ministry of Foreign Affairs, *The Hungarian Peace Negotiations,* I, pp. 209-216.

7. The text of this resolution is in *La Roumanie devant le congrès de la paix: Actes d'union des provinces de Bessarabie, la Bucovine, Transylvanie, Banat, et des régions roumaines de Hongrie avec le Royaume de Roumanie*, pp. 7-10. This brochure was an official memorandum of the Romanian delegation to the Peace Conference.

The nationalists had come a long way since 1914 when they petitioned Count Tisza for the right to use Romanian in the schools of Romanian districts, the appointment of judges who understood Romanian, freedom of association and state support for economic associations, and an end to press censorship. See David Mitrany, *The Effect of the War in Southeastern Europe*, p. 230.

8. Seton-Watson, A *History,* p. 533. The assembly's readiness to respect decisions of the peace conference was not included in the official brochure cited in Note 7 above.

9. *U.S. Foreign Relations, PPC,* II, pp. 396, 399; Vopicka, pp. 289-290; *La Roumanie,* No. 49, December 19, 1918; *Daily Review of the Foreign Press, Enemy Press Supplement,* V, No. 1, January 2, 1919, pp. 474-475.

Macartney, certainly no friend of the Romanians, maintains that the creation of the Consiliul Dirigent was a "clear enough expression of the will of the Romanians of Hungary" (*Hungary and her Successors,* p. 277). The request for Romania's protection is in *Daily Review of the Foreign Press, Enemy Press Supplement,* V, No. 1, December 19, 1918, p. 406.

10. The text of the Cernăuți resolution is in *La Roumanie devant le congrès de la paix: Actes d'union*, pp. 14-16.

11. This resolution is in La *Roumanie devant le congrès de la paix: Actes d'union*, p. 6. Bolshevik publicists charge that only 46 out of 162 deputies were present, and only 38 out of the 46 voted for union. See William Maxwell, "Bessarabia had Soviets," *Soviet Russia Today*, August 1940, p. 14.

12. The Mediaș resolution is in *La Roumanie devant le congrès de la paix: Actes d'union*, pp. 19-21. Romanian publicists denied the alleged interference of troops (Sofronie, p. 50). Magyar writers did not accuse Romania of forcing the resolutions. Their criticism was directed at the refusal of the nationalists to permit Magyars to participate. See Zsombor de Szász, *The Minorities in Roumanian Transylvania*, p. 22.

13. *U.S. Foreign Relations, PPC,* II, pp. 393-394.

14. Marghiloman, IV, pp. 173-174. Brătianu also took the post of Foreign Affairs. His cabinet included Mihai Pherekyde (Vice-Premier), Alexandru Constantinescu (Minister of Finance), Ioan Duca (Minister of Justice), Gheorghe Mârzescu (Minister of Interior), and a new appointee, General Artur Văitoianu, former commissioner general of Bessarabia (Minister of War).

The ratifications are described in *U.S. Foreign Relations, PPC,* II, pp. 396-397. The texts of the decree-laws are in *Monitorul Oficial,* No. 212 (December 26) for Transylvania; No. 217 (January 1) for Bucovina; No. 219 (January 1) for Bessarabia; and No. 206 (January 24), the ratifications. The King ratified the Transylvanian act of union, but never signed the others. It has never been finally determined what was the nature of the Transylvanian and other acts of union, nor how far the resolutions were legally binding.

15. *U.S. Foreign Relations, PPC,* II, pp. 396-397.

16. *Ibid.,* II, pp. 398. The American State Department verified this charge.

17. *Ibid.,* II, pp. 387, 396.

18. *Ibid.,* II, pp. 398-399, 401-403.

19. The text of the Bulgarian armistice is in *U.S. Foreign Relations, PPC,* II, pp. 241-242. Bulgarian protests are on pp. 251-253. American chargé Charles S. Wilson in Sofia hoped the peace conference would award southern Dobrodgea to Bulgaria in view of Romania's large acquisitions elsewhere (p. 256).

20. Sofronie, p. 49.

21. *Daily Review of the Foreign Press, Allied Press Supplement,* March 13, 1919, p. 561; Seton-Watson, *A History,* pp. 536, 538; Xeni, p. 387.

22. Mişu came from an old boyar family tracing its ancestry to the Macedo-Romanians (Vlachs). Educated in Germany, he was an expert in classical Greek literature. It was said he read a chapter of Thucydides every night before retiring. He was a linguist of remarkable ability, speaking modern Greek, French, English, German, and Bulgarian without trace of foreign accent. He could also use Magyar and Turkish as well as most Slavic tongues. He had served as envoy to Bulgaria, Turkey, Austria, and, since 1912, England. He had participated in negotiations with Bulgaria prior to Romania's entry into the Balkan War of 1913. Appointed foreign minister by Averescu in February 1918, he could not arrive home in time to take his post in the short-lived cabinet (Memorandum from House to Auchincloss, January 28, 1919, House Papers, Yale University Library).

23. *U.S. Foreign Relations, PPC,* II, p. 406; Georges I. Brătianu, *Origines,* p. 301.

24. *U.S. Foreign Relations, PPC,* I, pp. 265-266, and II, pp. 404-405.

25. Marghiloman (IV, p. 206) said Maniu accompanied Brătianu to Paris. There is no other evidence to substantiate this claim.

26. George I. Brătianu, *Origines*, p. 301; Ivo J. Lederer, "Yugoslavia and the Paris Peace Settlement," pp. 207-208.

27. *U.S. Foreign Relations, PPC*, II, pp. 404, 407; *I documenti diplomatici italiani, 6. Serie: 1918-1922*, I, pp. 430-431. As a result of the démarche, the French General Staff interposed a line of demarcation in the Banat between Serbian and Romanian troops.

28. *U.S. Foreign Relations, PPC*, II, pp. 721-722. Victor Antonescu had appealed for the loan (Miller, *Diary*, III, p. 113). Wilson's approval is in *U.S. Foreign Relations, PPC*, II, p. 724. He approved it with misgivings "regarding the legal authority of the present Romanian Government to negotiate foreign loans."

29. Wilson believed that if the East European states were provided with food, the Allies would not find it necessary to send troops to restore peaceful conditions in that region. He hoped to see Romania satisfied by a loan permitting her to buy food (*U.S. Foreign Relations, PPC*, II, p. 712).

30. *U.S. Foreign Relations, PPC*, I, p. 366. Tardieu's formula, "Sur le congrès de la paix," is discussed in Robert C. Binkley, "New Light on the Paris Peace Conference," *Political Science Quarterly*, XLVI (1931), pp. 340-343; Geoffrey Bruun, *Clemenceau*, pp. 184-185; and Frederick J. Cox, "The French Peace Plans, 1918-1919," in Cox and others, *Studies in Modern European History in Honor of Franklin Charles Palm*, pp. 71-104.

31. See p. 65 above, and Seymour, *House Papers*, IV, pp. 247-249.

32. *U.S. Foreign Relations, PPC*, III, p. 486.

33. *Ibid.*, III, pp. 486-487. Sonnino said he would view with caution any attempt to abrogate the 1916 Alliance (*I documenti diplomatici italiani, 6. Serie: 1918-1922*, I, p. 394). This statement was sent to Brătianu.

34. *U.S. Foreign Relations, PPC*, III, pp. 546-548; Tardieu, *The Truth about the Treaty*, pp. 88-91; and Temperley, I, p. 247. Wilson's legal advisers recommended two seats for Romania (Miller, *Diary*, I, p. 76, and III, p. 274).

35. *U.S. Foreign Relations, PPC*, I, p. 265, and III, pp. 590-600; Vopicka, p. 290.

36. *U.S. Foreign Relations, PPC*, III, pp. 601-604. Clemenceau's antipathy was well known. Sonnino had been apprised of it by the Italian envoy at Paris (*I documenti diplomatici italiani, 6. Serie: 1918-1922*, I, p. 380). Tardieu told Saint-Aulaire that his sympathy for Romania would encounter considerable opposition from Clemenceau "who does not pardon Brătianu for the separate peace" (Saint-Aulaire, *Confession*, p. 484).

37. *U.S. Foreign Relations, PPC,* III, p. 604.

38. *Ibid.*, III, p. 160. The rules of the conference provided for a new category — "small powers with special interests." Romania and the others were to be heard when topics related to their interests were discussed by the Supreme Council. See F. S. Marston, *The Peace Conference of 1919: Organization and Procedure,* pp. 264-267.

39. *U.S. Foreign Relations, PPC,* III, p. 604. Colonel House conceived of the value of commissions in December 1918 (Steed, *Through Thirty Years,* II, p. 264). When the Peace Conference terminated in January 1920, 58 commissions had been created (Tardieu, p. 97).

Romania was permitted to have only two plenipotentiaries at plenary sessions, but she could have more technical experts on the commissions.

40. *U.S. Foreign Relations, PPC,* III, pp. 194-195; and Miller, *Diary,* IV, pp. 230-231.

41. *U.S. Foreign Relations, PPC,* III, P. 201.

42. *Ibid.*, III, pp. 448-454; and Miller, *Diary,* XX, pp. 196-208. The election of Belgium, Brazil, China, Portugal, and Serbia to the League Commission distressed Brătianu. He disputed the right of Brazil, China, and Portugal to have seats since those states had contributed far less than Romania to the war effort.

Jules Cambon presided over the stormy session of small-power delegates. Steed praised his judicious handling of the disputatious delegates. He feared that "too many cooks might not only spoil the broth, but dangerously protract the cooking" *(Through Thirty Years,* II, p. 272).

43. *U.S. Foreign Relations, PPC,* III, p. 735; Seymour, *House Papers,* IV, p. 261. The process of appointing the commissions is neatly described in Almond and Lutz, *The Treaty of St. Germain,* pp. 3-5.

44. *U.S. Foreign Relations, PPC,* III, pp. 698-700; Temperley, I, p.252. Ray Stannard Baker contended that Clemenceau, alone of the Allied leaders, did not wish to consult with the small powers (*Woodrow Wilson and World Settlement,* I, p. 179). See also Binkley, p. 515.

45. See p. 74 above.

46. *U.S. Foreign Relations, PPC,* I, p. 415. The Foreign Office noted that Romanian troops were battling with Ruthenians in Maramureş.

47. *Ibid.*, XII, p. 372. Coolidge visited Budapest on January 16.

48. *Ibid.*, III, p. 715; Miller, *Diary,* XIV, pp. 16-17. This resolution was drafted by Allen W. Dulles, formerly Second Secretary of the legation in Berne. It contained these additional words: "The American Mission desires... to make clear that the employment of force to create a *fait accompli* may tend to raise rather than dispel doubts as to the justice of the territorial claims involved" (*U.S. Foreign Relations, PPC,* I, pp. 324-325; Miller, *Diary,* IV, p. 161). This proclamation appeared in the *Times,* London, January 25.

49. Nicolson, p. 248. Nicolson met earlier with Ionescu who said Brătianu's regime was not popular, that the Transylvanians were opposed to him although bound by his promise to obtain the entire Banat for them, and that he (Ionescu) had made an arrangement with the Serbs for a partition of the Banat, a deed which had infuriated Brătianu. Ionescu predicted Transylvania would never remain part of Romania unless Brătianu maintained a free and unfettered union (*Ibid.,* pp. 223-224).

50. Edward M. House, *Diary,* MSS, XV, January 1-May 1, 1919, pp. 24-25.

51. Memorandum, House to Auchincloss, January 28, House Papers.

52. According to Walter Lippmann, House was known all over Europe as the "Human Intercessor, the Comforter, the Virgin Mary. He's believed to be a little nearer this world than Woodrow Wilson, and a good deal nearer Heaven than Sonnino or Lloyd George" (Memorandum, Lippmann to Mezes, September 5, 1918, Mezes Papers, Columbia University Library).

53. Memorandum, Johnson to House, January 30, House Papers.

54. Miller, *Diary,* XIV, pp. 121-122.

55. *U.S. Foreign Relations, PPC,* III, pp. 814-815; Miller, *Diary,* XIV, pp. 125-126.

56. *U.S. Foreign Relations, PPC,* III, pp. 814-815; Miller, *Diary,* XIV, p. 126; Marston, p. 114.
Wilson had already instructed three American experts on Romania (Clive Day, Charles Seymour, and Douglas Johnson) to consult with specialists of the Allied Powers in order to submit joint recommendations to the Council. The President promised Seymour the Council would approve what the experts decided. See Seymour, *House Papers,* IV, pp. 274-275; James T. Shotwell, *At the Paris Peace Conference,* pp. 153-154; Nicolson, pp. 107, 126, 223, 226, 229-230, 247, for discussions between the Americans and the British.

57. According to Temperley (I, p. 257), the decision to hear the claimants was "a course of action which dissipated its [the Conference's] energies and aggravated the slowness of proceedings."

58. Lloyd George told Wilson that if Grey had been in good health the secret treaties would never have been negotiated. He explained how Asquith had concluded them and brought them to the Cabinet as *faits accomplis,* much to the despair of the ministers (Thomas W. Lamont, *Across World Frontiers,* p. 115).

59. Leeper, native of Australia, was an Assyriologist and Egyptologist, fluent in many languages, and honorary secretary of the Anglo-Romanian Society. An official of the Foreign Office, he wrote a pamphlet in 1917 in defense of Romanian aspirations — *The Justice of Romania's Cause.*

60. Brătianu established a legation in Tokyo in August 1917. His only significant contact with the Japanese before that was when he decorated General Nogi, hero of the battle of Mukden, with the Order of the Romanian Crown in 1911. See Velicu Dudu, "Misiunea secretă a unui nobil polon la curtea regelui Carol I," *Revistă Istorică Română*, VIII (1938), p. 188; and Marya Kasterska, "Le comte Bohdan Hutten-Czapski et la Roumanie, dans ses mémoires," *Revue historique du sud-est européen,* XVI (1939), Nos. 1-3, p. 7.

61. William Martin, *Statesmen of the War in Retrospect,* p. 160.

62. Nicolson, pp. 253-254.

63. *U.S. Foreign Relations, PPC,* III, pp. 830-834; Miller, *Diary,* XIV, pp. 132-144. Brătianu read portions of *La Roumanie devant le congrès de la paix: la question du Banat de Temeshvar.*

64. Nicolson, p. 254.

65. *Ibid.*

66. Pašić had resigned as Premier in December 1918. The new government was headed by his close associate Stojan Protić, who named him chief of the delegation. Trumbić, the Croat nationalist who had concluded the Pact of Corfu with Pašić in 1917, took the post of foreign minister. Vesnić, the leading spokesman of the Serb-Croat-Slovene delegation, was born in Novi-Bazar in 1863, earned his degree at Munich, began his diplomatic career in Turkey, and later became a law professor at Belgrade. He had been minister of justice and public instruction. In 1903 he became minister to Italy and later to France.

67. The text of the 1916 Alliance was published in *Le Temps* and the *Times* on February 4, 1919.

68. These districts were Versecz, Timişoara, Pancsova, Weisskirchen, and Nagy-Kikinda.

69. Brătianu could have mentioned that Octavian Goga had been a deputy from Kisjenö, Maniu from Vântul de Jos, Vaida-Voevod from Ighiu and Făgăraş, and Cicio-Pop from Világos. See Seton-Watson, *Corruption and Reform in Hungary*, pp. 113-126, 136, and his *Racial Problems in Hungary*, for a catalog of Romanians imprisoned during election campaigns, including the above-mentioned nationalists, pp. 448-453.

70. Although Trumbić increased the claim, it fell far short of that originally advanced by Pašić on September 21, 1914. The Serbs at that time claimed a wire belt across southern Hungary, the entire Banat, and a fortified bridgehead for Belgrade *(Mezhdunarodnye Otnosheniia,* VI, 1, p. 17).

71. The minutes of this session are in *U.S. Foreign Relations, PPC* III, pp. 822-830; and Miller, *Diary*, XIV, pp. 132-153. Orlando's remark is in Steed, *Through Thirty Years*, II, p. 277. For secondary accounts, see Lloyd George, *Memoirs of the Peace Conference*, pp. 619-621; Georges I. Brătianu, *Origines*, pp. 303-304; Cădere, pp. 287-288; Kiriţescu, III, p. 517; Lederer, p. 232; and *The New York Times*, February 1, 1919. Seton-Watson (*A History*, p. 540) erred in dating this session to be February 8. He probably found that date in Temperley, IV, p. 226.

72. Documents of the Italian Foreign Ministry relating to Conference sessions after January 17 have not yet been published. When materials bearing on the Conference are released, the alleged collaboration between Italy and Romania may be proved or disproved.

73. This view is upheld by Lederer, p. ii.

74. Nicolson, p. 254. Nicolson considered Mişu moderate and "western" in contrast to the "oriental" Brătianu.

75. Memorandum, Johnson to House, January 31, House Papers.

76. See p. 146 for the Romanian occupation of Debreczen.

77. Among Drăghicescu's polemics are *Les roumains,* claiming spiritual communion between 38 million "Latino-Slavs" oppressed by the Magyars (p. 239); "La lutte sociale et politique en Transylvanie," *La Revue,* May 15, 1918, reprint, comparing Transylvania to Alsace-Lorraine (p. 13); *La Transylvanie,* upholding the 1916 Alliance (p. 110); and *Les roumains de Serbie,* claiming one-sixth of Serbia's population was Romanian and demanding minority rights for them (pp. 17, 28).

78. Memorandum, Seymour to House, January 31, House Papers. Robert Howard Lord of Harvard University, the expert on Polish affairs, urged that the Romanians be told confidentially that the Banat dispute could be settled only by the Peace Conference and not on the basis of the 1916 Alliance (Lord to Lansing, January 28, House Papers).

79. David Hunter Miller, *The Drafting of the Covenant*, I, p. 80.

80. Nicolson, p. 254, calling him, at this point, a "silly ass. He is very verbose, and unconvincing, and Balkan."

81. According to Ulysses Grant-Smith, who was counselor of the American Embassy in Vienna in 1915 and who became American commissioner to Hungary in December 1919, military supplies from Germany were shipped through Romania to Turkey in 1915. In his letter to *The New York Times,* February 25, 1958, Grant-Smith cited his trip to Berlin in March 1915, where he spoke with Wilhelm von Stumm, liaison officer between the Foreign Ministry and the General Staff, who revealed that the Straits were almost forced by the Allies but for Germany's ability to furnish the Turks with needed ammunition which "we were able only after a fortnight to get... through via Romania."

82. Brătianu concealed the fact that the Crown Council of March 3, 1918 decided to make peace when it was learned the Bolsheviks had signed the Treaty of Brest-Litovsk. He also failed to note that the Ukrainians had signed their peace a month earlier (February 9), and he did not reiterate his objections made at the time to a retreat through southern Russia.

83. His claims are described in *La Roumanie devant le congrès de la paix: ses revendication territoriales.* The frontiers claimed included all of these comitats in Crişana: Szilágy, Csanád, Satu Mare, Bihor, and Arad; and sections of these comitats in Crişana: Békés and Ugócsa. Crişana is the region east of the Trianon frontier of Hungary and west of the border of Transylvania. Romanian claims to Crişana are outlined in *La Roumanie devant le congrès de la paix: le territoire revendiqué par les roumains au nord-ouest de la Transylvanie proprement dite.*

84. Lloyd George cited the analogy of Scotland's union with England achieved only after certain conditions imposed by the Scots had been carried out by England.

85. Károlyi claimed the Szecklers of Transylvania opposed incorporation (*Memoirs*, p. 155). For reports of Szeckler hostility, see *The Hungarian Peace Negotiations,* I, p. 340. These Szecklers (or "Székely," Magyar for "frontiersmen") are of obscure origin, alleged to be remnants of Attila's Huns. Seton-Watson said they settled in Transylvania in the 11th century (*Roumania and the Great War,* p. 34); he corrected this to the "12th century" in *A History,* p. 20. Magyar and Romanian ethnologists agreed the Szecklers were probably of Magyar origin

(Macartney, *National States and National Minorities*, p. 522). But Iorga tried to prove they were pure Romanians (Macartney, *Hungary and her Successors*, p. 286). For an impartial treatment, see Kann, I, pp. 306-307.

86. Brătianu was prepared to forget other claims if the Allies yielded. He cited the presence of 500,000 Romanians in the Ukraine, 100,000 in Bulgaria, 300,000 in Serbia, and several thousand called Macedo-Romanians in Macedonia. The last group inhabited the region around the Pindus Mountains. There is no general agreement on their origin. Some consider them descendants of Pompey's troops defeated by Caesar at Pharsalia in 48 B.C., hence the alternate name "Tarshilotes." Since 1879 the Romanian government had furnished subsidies for these peoples whose language is akin to Romanian. In 1903, when he was foreign minister, Brătianu professed interest in their fate, and was responsible for a rupture of diplomatic relations with Greece in 1905, caused by ill-treatment of these tribes by the Athens government. When the Peace Conference considered the question of minority rights, the Macedo-Romanians sent a delegation to Paris to request guarantees. See the official brochure *Les Macedo-Rumanes devant le congrès de la paix.*

87. The minutes of the February 1 session are in *U.S. Foreign Relations, PPC,* III, pp. 840-855; and Miller, *Diary,* XIV, pp. 162-182. According to two historians, Orlando's reservations were based solely on his determination to uphold Romanian claims and to protect the secret treaties. See Binkley, p. 530, and Marston, p. 115.

Lansing had proposed to Wilson on January 31 that all territorial questions, including the Banat dispute, should be considered as a whole and not as separate issues between states. He opposed creation of territorial commissions to treat isolated and unrelated problems. Wilson overruled him *(U.S. Foreign Relations, PPC,* XI, pp. 66-67).

88. Available documentary evidence does not substantiate Clemenceau's assertion. He may have been referring to the Council's decision of January 12 to assign two seats to Romania. Balfour expressed doubts at that time about renewing every article of the Alliance. Sonnino did not challenge Balfour's opinion, but proposed, instead, the postponement of discussions regarding the validity of the Alliance. The subject was never raised again in the Council.

89. Baker *(Woodrow Wilson and World Settlement,* I, pp. 186-187) said Orlando "took alarm." Steed *(Through Thirty Years,* II, p. 273) quoted an unnamed Romanian delegate who revealed that Italy and Romania had made a compact to stand or fall on the maintenance of the secret treaties.

90. For secondary accounts of this session, see Almond and Lutz, pp. 546-548, on Brătianus claim to Bucovina; Deák, pp. 32-34, for the injustice of Romanian claims; and Lederer, pp. 253-272, for the Serbian side.

91. Nicolson, p. 126.

92. Jules Laroche, *Au Quai d'Orsay avec Briand et Poincaré, 1913-1926*, p. 34.

93. Lloyd George, *War Memoirs,* I, pp. 313-314, and II, p. 546.

94. Nicolson, pp. 134-135, 255.

95. Marghiloman, IV, p. 229.

96. *Daily Review of the Foreign Press,* V, February 1919, p. 313.

97. "The Question of the Banat," *The New Europe,* X, No. 122, pp. 97-103.

98. Général Mordacq, *Le ministère Clemenceau: journal d'un témoin,* III, p. 110. According to available evidence, Clemenceau never granted anything more than a brief interview to Brătianu. The only known interview Wilson ever granted to Brătianu occurred on April 17, and it lasted a mere fifteen minutes. See Edith Bolling Wilson, *My Memoir,* p. 254; and Dillon, p. 111.

Chapter III

THE DELIMITATION OF
ROMANIA'S FRONTIERS

*"The crescent moon of the Romanian map waxed to full by
the incorporation of Transylvania."*

— Winston Churchill[1]

The Romanian Territorial Commission

The Supreme Council appointed eight experts on February 3 to
serve on "The Commission for the Study of Territorial Questions
Relating to Romania." Those named were Sir Eyre Crowe and Allen
W.A. Leeper for Britain, André Tardieu and Jules Laroche for France,
Giacomo de Martino and Count Vannutelli-Rey for Italy, and Clive
Day and Charles Seymour for the United States.[2] Official statements of
Romanian and Serbian claims were distributed at their first meeting, on
February 8. The French and Italian members wished to include the
promises of the 1916 Alliance, but the Americans and British insisted
the Supreme Council first determine its validity. Since the Council
never officially complied, differences of opinion were encouraged
rather than dispelled by the Council's failure to rule on the status of the
Alliance.

The American experts brought to the Commission a thorough plan
for territorial rectifications, the result of prodigious studies by a group
of scholars known as the "Inquiry," assembled by Colonel House in
1917.[3] Clive Day and his associates had at first urged preservation of
the Habsburg Monarchy and the creation of a Balkan federation as the
most salutary solution to Eastern European problems. These
recommendations coincided with the original Fourteen Points. Not until
Wilson came to view dismemberment of Austria-Hungary as a more

practical solution did the specialists begin to advocate a retracing of the map.[4] In October 1918, Day recommended giving Romania regions of Austria-Hungary populated by Romanian majorities if Romania guaranteed minority rights. He favored partition of the Banat and proposed that Romania retrocede southern Dobrodgea since it contained more Bulgarians than Romanians.[5] Charles Seymour substantiated Day's proposals by rectifying the Hungarian census of 1910 to prove that Romanians greatly outnumbered Magyars in most regions claimed by Romania. The Inquiry's recommendations, presented to Wilson in January 1919, called for granting Transylvania to Romania, except for the predominantly Magyar cities of Satu Mare [Szatmár-Németi in Hungarian], Oradea, and Arad; the partition of the Banat on an ethnic basis with due consideration to economic and political criteria; the award to Romania of ethnically Romanian sections of Crişana and Bucovina; retrocession of southern Dobrodgea; international control over the Danube and the railways traversing Hungary; award of all Bessarabia to Romania; and strong consideration of questions relating to the economic interests of East Central Europe as a whole. These proposals clearly indicated that the United States intended to ignore the 1916 Alliance. No reference to that pact can be found in the Inquiry's proposals. The Inquiry apparently disregarded it, the Department of State had communicated only perfunctory phrases to Bucharest, and Wilson had deliberately shut his eyes to its existence.[6]

The British equivalent of the Inquiry was the Department of Political Intelligence of the Foreign Office, headed by Sir William George Tyrrell.[7] This group produced the famous *Peace Handbooks,* edited by George Walter Prothero.[8] The British, like the Americans, at first supported the integrity of the Habsburg Monarchy and the idea of creating a Balkan federation. These aims were indicated by Lloyd George in his address of January 5, 1918. But British aims, like those of the United States, were revised during 1918, and, by August, the Foreign Office proposed dismemberment of the Habsburg Monarchy.[9] This was evident in proposals submitted to Lloyd George on August 2, 1918, recommending that Romania should solve the question of her national union, retrocede a part of southern Dobrodgea to Bulgaria, offer Hungary an outlet to the Black Sea via the Danube, and join an economic federation of East Central European states. The British intimated that a gradual exchange of populations might reduce tensions, and urged that each state guarantee minority rights.[10] These proposals were defined more specifically in the fall of 1918, at which time the Foreign Office recommended that Romania get all Transylvania, that the Banat be partitioned with Romania acquiring a more favorable frontier than Serbia, that Bucovina be divided between Romania and a Ruthenian state, and that an international control commission be created to supervise Danube traffic.[11]   In December the British delegation adjusted its program to coincide more closely with that of the Americans. Quoting Wilson's words "we must be just toward those to whom we should wish not to be just" — the British proposed treating Magyars according to the same principles applied to Romanians, since Britain "assumes a disinterested and impartial position as mediator and in this we hope to have the cordial cooperation of the United States." Final decisions on frontiers were to be left to the Peace Conference, but if interested states could first arrive at agreements among themselves, the Conference could merely ratify their settlements. If no arrangements could be achieved, the Conference should be empowered to determine settlements, by force of arms if necessary. No reference to the 1916 Alliance was made in the British recommendations.[12]

The French government assembled a group in December 1918 to formulate a peace program. The Comité d'Études produced a comprehensive plan for frontier settlements, which was edited by André Tardieu and Emmanuel De Martonne, an expert on the ethnography of East Central Europe.[13] De Martonne, secretary of the Comité, drafted the recommendations for Romania. He proposed two solutions to the Banat dispute, favorable to Serbia and Romania, respectively. In regard to Transylvania and Crişana, De Martonne was most favorable to the Romanians, insisting that if Romania acquired districts inhabited by Magyar majorities she should guarantee minority rights. He assigned all Bessarabia to Romania on the basis of a Romanian majority of 72 per cent and because of Romanian heroism (a factor not considered by his American and British colleagues):

> Romania never officially raised her voice to claim Bessarabia; she entered the war to realize her national unity without saying a word about Bessarabia. Bessarabia was given to Romania at a time when she was conquered, held by the throat by the enemy and forced to sign a shameful peace, at a time when it seemed that she had to renounce forever Transylvania for which she had raised her standard.

The French program differed radically from the American and British in regard to southern Dobrodgea. De Martonne insisted Romania recover it and even acquire an extra slice from Bulgaria to permit development of more efficient ports. He denied the Romanians were in a minority; they were, instead, 55 per cent of the total population. In regard to Bucovina, De Martonne proposed sending a commission to trace a suitable frontier.[14]

The Award of Bessarabia

The Commission awarded Bessarabia to Romania on the basis of historical, economic, and ethnic considerations, despite the suspicions of American, British, and Italian experts regarding the Sfat vote. Crowe convinced the others to disregard it:

> Romania would probably receive much of what she asked for, but ethnical and national considerations should be put forward as justifying such an arrangement, rather than considerations based on the military situation of Romania or on her provisional occupation of territory.[15]

When Brătianu testified before the Commission on February 28, he was asked about the vote. He called the Sfat a legally constituted assembly recognized by the Russian Provisional Government. Admitting that Romanians formed only 72 per cent of the population, the Premier assured the experts that the aliens were not too unhappy with the occupation and that the impending agrarian reform would calm those who looked to Bolshevism for help and would placate the large landowners, who preferred Russian rule, by indemnifying them for losses. After all, Brătianu declared, Bessarabians of all nationalities owed their very lives to Romania's occupation. These assurances did not deter the Commission from recommending that Romania guarantee minority rights.[16]

The Question of Bucovina: First Phase

The British, reversing their original plan to divide Bucovina between Romania and a Ruthenian state, joined the French and Italians to recommend awarding the entire province to Romania. Crowe believed that 300,000 Ruthenians would benefit by their incorporation into Romania even though they were Slavic. By yielding the entire province, he asserted, Romania would secure an easily defensible frontier. The Italians believed this award would compensate for the loss of 100,000 Romanians living east of the Dniester River. The Italian position, tantamount to awarding regions as compensation for the loss of territories elsewhere, was not acceptable to the Americans, who insisted upon partition. Seymour outlined a defensible frontier to permit the union of Ruthenians with their co-nationals in a Ruthenian state, or in a proposed free state of Eastern Galicia. Opposed by the others, the American experts then raised objections to reliance upon the acts of union of the national assemblies because those plebiscites apparently violated the Supreme Council's proclamation of January 25 prohibiting unauthorized seizures of territory.[17]

Discussion of Bucovina was interrupted on February 11 when Clemenceau instructed the Commission to examine the Romanian-Hungarian frontier at once. Reports of Romanian attempts to seize purely Magyar territory had arrived in Paris, and Brătianu was already seeking permission to occupy land beyond the line of the 1916 Alliance so that he could halt so-called Magyar provocations.[18] Clemenceau desired the tracing of a frontier before acceding to Brătianu's request.

Tardieu, chairman of the Commission, relied implicitly upon the validity of the 1916 Alliance, a conviction he shared with the Italians. In fact, the Italians had become most philanthropic, proposing on February 11 to award Romania a frontier along the Tisa River even though Brătianu had never claimed so much purely Magyar territory. Vannutelli-Rey admitted his line did not represent the best ethnic frontier, but it was Romania, not Hungary, who was the allied state.[19] The French did not go as far, recommending that two predominantly Magyar cities, Satu Mare and Oradea, be awarded to Romania because both were vital railway centers necessary for Romanian prosperity. The Americans wished to leave Hungary with lateral railway lines and the two cities, and they rejected a frontier based upon economic criteria exclusively. When the French cited the strategic value of the railways to the Romanians, the Americans refused to be moved, adding that they did "not feel that the Commission, in its decisions, should try to establish equalities where nature has created inequalities."

At this point, the true intentions of the French became known. Tardieu disclosed that the French General Staff was demanding the inclusion of the two cities and the railway line connecting them in Romania so that she would have a defensible frontier in the event of renewed hostilities. Laroche added:

it is not sufficient to give nations the privilege of living in peace. It is necessary to keep them from dying and to put them in a position to resist aggression.

When the Americans suggested that Romania construct her own railway lines parallel to those left in Hungary, the British joined the French and Italian experts to oppose them. It was clear that no railway connections between the northern and southern sections of Transylvania would exist if the line were withheld from Romania. If Satu Mare, Oradea, and Arad (cities through which the disputed line operated) were not given to Romania, the situation would be ludicrous. Trains would cross and recross international frontiers in going from one city to the next. The Americans insisted, nevertheless, that Romania construct new lines so that the best ethnic frontier could be created. The dispute was assigned to a panel of railway experts.

The Commission agreed unanimously to deny Romania the predominantly Magyar comitat of Békés and most of the Magyar comitat of Csanád. This decision violated the 1916 Alliance which had promised all Csanád to Romania.[20] The loss of most of Csanád deprived Romania of the mouth of the Mureş River, the chief waterway of Transylvania. Furthermore, Csanád lay directly north of Torontál, the Banat comitat claimed by Romania and Serbia. The most unfavorable aspect of this recommendation was the decision to deny Romania a frontier with Hungary along the entire length of the Tisa River from Szeged in the south to Vásáros-Namény in the north.

Within a week of the Commission's decision, Romanian troops were advancing westward in a move to snatch all territory east of the Tisa. D'Esperey's failure to trace a precise line of demarcation between Romanian and Hungarian forces and the Council's disinclination to amend the armistice in Romania's favor gave Brătianu an opportunity to march without any prohibition to the contrary. The French military mission in Budapest instructed the Hungarian government not to resist Romanian troops who were "only going in to protect Romanian peasants." At the same time, Czech and Serbian troops were also advancing into Hungary.[21]

These developments were discussed by the Commission on February 17. Laroche explained that d'Esperey lacked authority to halt the Romanian advance because the Bucharest government, which was not a signatory to the armistice, refused to recognize the supremacy of the Allied High Command over East Central Europe or over a "matter which they claim to be their private affair." He proposed sending an inter-Allied army to Hungary to prevent an outbreak of hostilities or presenting a démarche in Bucharest reminding Romania of the Council's proclamation of January 25. By this date the Romanians had reached a line running from Maramureş-Sighet in the north to a point in the south approximately 100 miles east of the Tisa.[22] The Commission requested the Council to establish a neutral zone in eastern Hungary to separate Magyar and Romanian troops. Romania would be prohibited from advancing west of the railway line from Satu Mare via Oradea to Arad. Romanian troops could advance to within ten kilometers (6¼ miles) of each city, but could not occupy them. This line almost coincided with the frontier recommended by the Americans. Hungary would be prohibited from moving troops east of a line running ten kilometers west of Vásáros-Namény, the confluence of the two Körös (Criş) rivers, and Algyö (directly north of Szeged) on the Tisa. This line was about sixty miles west of the frontier of the 1916 Alliance.[23]

News of the Romanian advance reached the Council the same day (February 17). Winston Churchill, Secretary of State for War, urged the sending of allied troops to East Central Europe to protect the small states from the inroads of Bolshevism.[24] Lansing, acting chief of the American delegation while Wilson was home from February 15 to March 17, opposed this plan, but the French approved it. The French General Staff proposed sending into Hungary several Romanian divisions "now doing nothing in Bessarabia and Romania" to suppress rising Bolshevism.[25] General Alby, Chief of the French General Staff, testified on February 19 about Marshal Foch's plan to rescue the French contingent at Odessa from the advancing Red Army and to assemble an army of Czechs, Poles, Romanians, Serbs, and some Allied troops to move into Hungary and the Ukraine to halt the spread of Bolshevism.[26] According to the Foch scheme, Romanian troops would occupy the cities of Satu Mare, Oradea, and Carei (Nagy-Károly in Hungarian) and the railway lines connecting these cities. Romanian troops could occupy the railway centers until Allied reinforcements arrived. When asked if a Romanian occupation of the railway centers would predetermine the frontier settlement, Alby replied that

> everything should be done to make sure that the occupation does not prejudice the decisions of the Peace Conference any more than the occupation of the bridgeheads on the right bank of the Rhine by French troops signified the eventual transfer to France of those bridgeheads.

After American hesitations and objections were overcome, the Commission submitted the proposal for a neutral zone to the Council.[27] The Council took up the neutral zone on February 21, during the absence of the Allied leaders. Wilson, Lloyd George, and Orlando were home, and Clemenceau was recovering from a bullet wound inflicted by an anarchist on February 19. Pichon presided at the session attended by Lansing, Day, Crowe, Balfour, Sonnino, and Tardieu. Tardieu explained that d'Esperey did not fix in the armistice a precise line of occupation between Romanian and Hungarian troops because Romania had not yet re-entered the war;[28] Hungarian troops had remained east of the Tisa where, according to Brătianu, they were mistreating Romanian peasants; Romanian troops, in response to peasant appeals, had advanced toward the Tisa and were presently occupying territory promised in the 1916 Alliance. Having admitted that Romanian troops had advanced into regions under consideration by the Commission, Tardieu explained this as a prudent move designed to prevent a resumption of war and to stop "the spread of Bolshevism prevalent in Hungary."[29] He asked that military advisers establish the neutral zone and decide whose troops should patrol it. The Council submitted his plan to the military advisers at Versailles, a body headed by General Belin of the French army.[30]

It should be noted that the decision to refer the plan to the military advisers was reached during the absence of the "Big Four." When those leaders first learned of it, they opposed the plan. But by the middle of March they were persuaded by the French Ministry of War and the Quai d'Orsay to permit the implementation of the plan bearing the title "Foch."[31]

The advent of Bolshevism into Central Europe was soon to dictate many Council decisions. The Commission had already been influenced by the warnings of Tardieu and Alby to recommend action to contain Bolshevism. The recommendation that Romania assume control over the railway lines and move unimpeded into Hungary proper facilitated the creation of a grandiose scheme to assemble an inter-Allied army to eliminate Magyar radicalism and then move against Soviet Russia. Such were the implications of Tardieu's presentation of the Foch plan.[32]

The difficulty of determining the Romanian-Hungarian frontier was compounded by the intrusion of this new issue. If the American recommendations were adopted, Romania would be denied a defensible frontier. But for the deteriorating situation in Hungary, this settlement would have probably been imposed in February. The United States was obliged, however, to give moral, material, and possibly military support to protect the East Central European states from the menace of advancing Bolshevism. The Americans, therefore, found themselves ensnared in a predicament. If they dictated a territorial settlement based on impartial examination of both Hungarian and Romanian statistics, an idealistic scheme associated with the Wilsonian principle of self-determination, the small states allied with the Allied Powers would undoubtedly turn against Wilson and his cherished League of Nations. But if the Americans yielded to the pressures of the realistic Quai d'Orsay and to the appeals of the Romanians, Czechs, and Serbs, the claims of those small states would be satisfied, while the lofty idealism represented by Wilson would be dealt a mortal blow.[33]

The Question of the Romanian-Hungarian Frontier: Second Phase

Brătianu and Vaida-Voevod testified before the Commission on February 22. The Premier demanded the mouths of the Mureş, located in Csanád, and Tisa rivers, canals linking those waterways with the Danube, and the railway lines under discussion. Romania, he added, must obtain an uninterrupted railway link with Czechoslovakia and Poland even if the promises of the Alliance had to be increased. He spoke of his plan to teach the Magyars of Transylvania that the Romanians were now the masters:

> The Romanian Government must first impose its wishes on them, to convince them of the final nature of.... victory.

Bolshevik agents from Budapest were allegedly distributing anti-Romanian leaflets among Szecklers, Saxon Germans, and Magyars, and some of these documents bore "the seal of the Hungarian War Ministry." Once this situation was corrected, he assured the experts, Romania would apply very liberal policies in regard to minority rights.

Brătianu increased his claim to Hungarian territory in another sector by demanding the northeast corner of Maramureş so that Romania would secure a longer frontier with Czechoslovakia. This cession would place the railway line from Satu Mare to the Slovakian frontier entirely within Romania, instead of traversing Hungary before reaching Csap in Slovakia.[34] The French supported these new demands for reasons that became apparent on February 24 when General LeRond of the General Staff was sent to the Supreme Council by Marshal Foch to explain his plan to transport General Haller's Polish army in France to Poland across the railway lines claimed by Brătianu. These lines could also be used by an inter-Allied army going from Serbia, via Hungary, to Poland. The next day (February 25) Foch spoke to the Council about the danger of a Russo-German rapprochement. Referring to Napoleon's failure to establish sufficient supply depots and adequate lines of communication in 1812, Foch outlined his plan to erase Bolshevism by amassing an abundance of both before moving into Russia. He proposed to employ Polish, Czech, Finnish, Greek, "White" Russian, Serbian, and Romanian troops to eradicate all traces of Bolshevik sympathy in East Central Europe and to advance against Russia. To this mammoth army would be added a token force of Allied troops. Poland would be the home base of the crusade that could reach that country via the Baltic and the railways traversing Hungary and Slovakia. Therefore, Foch insisted, it was essential to give control of those railway lines to Romania, the nearest allied state.[35]

This bold scheme was discussed by the military advisers on the same day. General Coandă testified that Romania was prepared to join the campaign. General Henrys, commander of the French Army in the East, and General Charpy, Chief of Staff to d'Esperey (Supreme Allied Commander in the East) were present to support Coandă's request to control the railway lines to forestall Magyar attempts to attack Romanians east of the Tisa. The military advisers approved the Foch plan, which the Marshal presented to the Council on February 26. Foch said his operation would not affect the final disposition of occupied territories, and it should be considered as a temporary measure to insure peace. The only serious objection came from Balfour who disliked a reference to the 1916 Alliance because "there had been a great deal of discussion as to whether this Treaty had or had not been abrogated by the agreement between Romania and the enemy." It was agreed to drop the reference. The Council, in the absence of the "Big Four," approved the first part of the Foch plan, namely, to establish a neutral zone between Romania and Hungary. Romania would be allowed temporary occupation of the railway centers of Satu Mare, Oradea, Arad, Carei, and Salonta (Nagy-Szalonta in Hungarian). Hungary would withdraw troops behind a line five kilometers (3.1 miles) west of the frontier promised Romania in the 1916 Alliance. The southern limit of the zone would run along the Mureş River. Available French troops would occupy Szeged (at the confluence of the Tisa and Mureş rivers) and supervise the Romanian occupation of Arad. General

Berthelot would furnish two Romanian battalions for the holding of Arad.[36]

By approving the neutral zone, the Allied Powers condoned Romanian occupation of a line representing a suitable ethnic frontier. This line, however, fell short by 45 miles of the frontier promised in the Alliance, an arrangement, as will be seen, which did not satisfy Brătianu. In permitting occupation of this line, the Allies assumed it to be a temporary expedient, with the Romanians withdrawing after the permanent boundary was delimited, or when threats to Romania were dispelled. Few observers, however, anticipated a Romanian evacuation of territory assigned to Hungary. General Tasker H. Bliss, a keen prophet, predicted Foch's scheme would upset the Peace Conference.[37] Yet Bliss voted with the other military advisers for the neutral zone and for requesting Romania to participate in the first stage of the scheme, namely, to check growing Magyar Bolshevism. The French had been given virtual *carte blanche* to carry out their plans. Not only had the military phase of the operation been condoned by the leaderless Supreme Council, but also Colonel House unwittingly enabled the French to gain control over the political phase of the campaign. He recommended on February 27 the creation of the Central Territorial Commission to coordinate the work of various commissions appointed to delimit frontiers. André Tardieu was named chairman of this new body. Every territorial commission was now in the hands of French chairmen.[38] As chairman, Tardieu could now exert considerable influence to revise recommendations of the commissions in favor of the designs of the Quai d'Orsay and the Ministry of War.

News of the Council's decisions encouraged the Romanians to take further steps. Troop concentrations were made along the Mureş River. The Consiliu Dirigent announced on February 22 that all Magyar officials in territory occupied by the Romanian army must take oaths of allegiance to King Ferdinand or forfeit their jobs and pension rights. All Magyar legal officers were ordered to learn the Romanian language in one year; lawyers were given six months. In Sibiu (formerly Hermannstadt), provincial capital of Transylvania, officers of a Transylvanian corps assembled to cooperate with the Romanian army took an oath of allegiance to the Alba Iulia resolution. The official organ of the Consiliul Dirigent began to appear in Romanian, instead of in the Transylvanian dialect.[39] Reports came from Bucharest and Sibiu about the instability of Károlyi's government and Romanian mobilization of an army to march on Budapest. In an apparent effort to account for imminent intervention in Hungary, Romanian newspapers contained stories of atrocities committed by Magyars against Romanian peasants.[40] The British military mission in Budapest warned Károlyi that if Bolshevism were not stamped out, the Allies would permit Romania, Czechoslovakia, and Serbia to occupy all of Hungary.[41]

When the Americans complained of French intercessions on behalf of the Romanians, Tardieu reassured them of Romania's honest intentions. This solid Romanophile, who once told Saint-Aulaire it was iniquitous for the Council to fail to take a definitive stand for the 1916 Alliance, could now look forward to dictating the work of the Commission without fear of opposition since the Council had just approved the initial step of the Foch plan.[42] In fact, the original recommendations of the Commission regarding the neutral zone (February 17) were overruled by the French General Staff, which now permitted the Romanians to occupy the railway centers. The Supreme Council had even approved Romania's occupation of the centers.[43]

Brătianu's moves during the first week of March appeared to be a direct consequence of the French plans. He requested (March 5) the right to occupy the comitats of Arad, Bihor, Satu Mare, Csanád, and Szilágy in their entirety so as to gain control of the railway lines. A major proportion of these comitats lay in the proposed neutral zone, whose delimitation Brătianu refused to respect. He insisted upon occupation of the comitats as essential for defense, and he wished to seize war matériel left in eastern Hungary by the Germans, and recover railway and a mass of other equipment which, he contended, the Magyars had removed from Transylvania.[44] To support his demands, the Premier began publishing a propaganda weekly, *Bulletin d'informations roumaines,* accusing Hungary of terrorizing Romanians east of the Tisa and warning the Allies about the threat of Bolshevism.

Envious of the lavish receptions accorded in Paris to such heroes of resistance as King Albert of Belgium, Prince-Regent Alexander of Serbia, Emir Feisal, and others, Brătianu agreed to a scheme outlined by Saint-Aulaire, who shared with his superiors at the Quai d'Orsay much enthusiasm for the Foch plan. Saint-Aulaire urged that Queen Marie come to Paris to plead the Romanian case. She arrived on March 5, was given the royal suite at the Hotel Ritz, and proceeded to "try her philters" on Clemenceau and other Allied leaders.[45]

Brătianu instructed Marie as to how to treat certain influential persons. She met Clemenceau on March 7, and heard him speak about his grievances against Romania, "to which he sticks like a leech," and his refusal to exonerate Romania for a separate peace made before the

"Boche" was defeated. Marie explained the circumstances confronting Romania in 1918, caused by "Allies who went Bolshevik." Clemenceau reminded her of the Serbs, who were likewise encircled and defeated, but who never sought separate peace. He spoke of Serbia's justifiable claim to the western Banat, which, he said, the British also supported. Marie replied the British did not understand Balkan geography, a shortcoming she proposed to remedy when she visited her relatives in England. She had come to Paris to modify his intransigence, the Queen insisted, and would succeed in this just as she had succeeded in securing Romania's intervention. Their meeting closed with Clemenceau's curt characterization of Brătianu, "with his lamenting voice," as a very disagreeable politician.[46]

Marie met with Colonel House on March 8. He found her to be one of the most delightful personalities of all the royal women he had ever met.[47] Marie met Herbert Hoover, Chief of the American Relief Administration and representative on the Supreme Economic Council, and found him to be less congenial than House because "he had no desire to be charmed." She then met Briand, who promised to promote Romanian aspirations. Balfour gave a dinner in her honor at which he told of Britain's determination to draft a peace designed to eliminate any possible difficulties between Romania and Serbia.[48] The Queen lunched with Wilson on April 11. The President reportedly directed the conversation toward the League of Nations. His determination not to be cajoled prompted Marie to make the following observations:

> He is a born preacher and might be a highly cultivated clergyman. He is very convinced of always being right. He very sanctimoniously preached to me how we should treat our minorities. He struck me as being rather too fond of the sound of his own voice. I mildly suggested to him that he was evidently acquainted with these difficulties because of the Negro and Japanese questions in the United States. Upon this he bared his rather long teeth in a polite smile, drew up his eyebrows, and declared that he was not aware that there was a Japanese question in America.[49]

Wilson promised to speak personally with Brătianu, but Marie did not think the Premier would get very far because he could not speak English.[50]

The Queen received encouragement from French generals Foch, Petain, and Henrys, who promised to furnish Romania with war matériel, and from Poincaré who hailed her at a ceremony in the Sorbonne as leader of the Romanians who were on the Danube "as we are at Strasbourg — guardians of Latin civilization."[51]

Marie's solicitations failed to elicit the desired responses. The French press was hardly receptive to her bidding if its labelling of her as "The Business Queen" may be taken as an indication. Ionescu shared the opinion held by many Allied statesmen when he reminded them that in a constitutional monarchy like Romania, the King, and still less the Queen, was not responsible for determining national policy.[52] As events turned out during the third week of March, it was clear that the "Big Four," who had returned to the Supreme Council, were about to determine policy for Romania.

The Crisis in Hungary

Although the Foreign Ministers, substituting for the "Big Four," earlier had approved establishment of the neutral zone, it was subsequently decided to refer the matter to the heads of government when they returned to the Council. Foch outlined his plan to the "Big Four" on March 17, and requested acceptance of Romanian assistance "without delay and without hesitation on account of... the proximity of Romania to the theater of operations." Lloyd George, Orlando, and Wilson opposed the crusade against Bolshevism. The Prime Minister termed it a move "solely to perpetuate a great mischief" even after Foch warned of Bolshevik plans to invade Romania from the Ukraine and Hungary. The Council rejected his aggressive plan, but offered military assistance to the small powers if they became threatened by a Bolshevik attack. To lessen the risk of hostilities between Romania and Hungary, the Council reaffirmed the order establishing the neutral zone.[53]

The order imposing the zone was transmitted to Károlyi on March 20 by Lieutenant Colonel Vyx of the Allied military mission in Budapest. Károlyi vainly protested against what he accurately predicted would be the permanent loss of predominantly Magyar territory. The ultimatum produced a government crisis resulting in resignation of the Károlyi cabinet and its replacement by a coalition of left-socialists and communists, the latter led by Béla Kun, a native of Cluj (Kolozsvár in Hungarian).[54] No effort is made here to provide a treatment of the 133 days of the Soviet Republic of Hungary. This interlude has been the subject of several studies, most of which tend to obscure rather than clarify the crisis. Of principal interest here is the role of Romania. The communist seizure of power threatened to block Romania's acquisition of territory. A Romanian crusade against Magyar Bolshevism could be coupled with a land-grab similar to the occupation and subsequent annexation of Bessarabia, or to Japanese intervention in Siberia. No one in Paris could dispute Brătianu's argument that Romania was the only power in East Central Europe capable of restoring order in Hungary.[55] Béla Kun was as determined as Károlyi to retain an undivided Hungary. This intention and his dream of imposing a communist system on the country produced a serious crisis. As soon as news of the coup in Budapest was known, King Ferdinand summoned a Crown Council to discuss the deteriorating situation. Proposals were raised to install a war cabinet in Bucharest under General Văitoianu, Brătianu's minister of war. It was decided instead to send Văitoianu, who had recently cleared Bessarabia of Bolshevik sympathizers, to Paris to acquaint the Allies with the crisis.[56] The Allied envoys joined the growing anti-Kun movement by advising the Supreme Council about Magyar Bolshevik provocations.[57]

One direct result of the crisis was the decision of March 25 to reduce the size of the Supreme Council to the four heads of government. On that day the Council of Four was born to treat primary issues while the Council of Foreign Ministers, which began sessions on March 27, dealt with less important items.[58] The Big Four summoned General Alby on March 25 to explain why d'Esperey had reportedly ordered the Romanians to attack the Magyar Bolsheviks.[59] Alby denied such an order had been issued, but he produced a note from the Romanian government requesting supplies for an invasion of Hungary and an advance into the Ukraine if the Allies so ordered. The French General Staff favored sending the needed equipment.

Wilson was not unduly alarmed; he acknowledged the inefficacy of the neutral zone to prevent hostilities, but still rejected Foch's plan for an anti-Bolshevik campaign. Referring to both Magyar and Russian brands of communism, the President said

> this confirms my belief which is to leave Russia to the Bolsheviks; they cook in their own juice until circumstances make the Russians wiser.

Clemenceau assured him the zone did not correspond to a final frontier and observed that Hungary, not Romania, was the enemy state. Foch again stressed the need to strengthen Romania as a bulwark against Bolshevism, and this time he convinced the Council to send military supplies to Romania. Foch was even asked to prepare a plan for helping Romania to resist Bolshevism.[60]

Wilson's apathy may be attributed to reports of the Coolidge Mission in Vienna and Budapest, whose observers noted that Romanian troops were antagonizing Magyars in regions not yet officially awarded to Romania. They urged Wilson to have the Romanians evacuate Crişana.[61] Coolidge, an admirer of the Magyars, recommended leniency for Hungary, permitting her to retain the Szeckler regions of Transylvania, and tracing a frontier leaving Maramureş to Hungary. Those sections of the Banat inhabited by Swabian Germans should remain in Hungary, too.[62]

Coolidge came to Paris at the end of March to report his findings. He was accompanied by Captain Nicholas Roosevelt who had been in Budapest when Vyx presented the ultimatum to Károlyi. Roosevelt had visited Bucharest and met with cabinet ministers Constantinescu, Cicio-Pop, and Văitoianu, as well as Chief of Staff Constantin Prezan. They told him of Romania's determination to halt mistreatment of Romanians east of the Tisa. Roosevelt noted that the army was mobilized to march to the Hungarian side of the neutral zone. In a talk with Prezan on March 12, Roosevelt learned that the Romanians knew of the plan to erect the neutral zone before official word of it was released. Prezan intimated that the Allies would condone Romanian acquisition of Hungarian territory in view of the Council's order to Hungary to retreat west of the zone.[63] Roosevelt advised the American delegation that the Romanians would attack if the Allies did not send troops to quell Bolshevism in Hungary. His warning was repeated by Philip Marshall Brown, Professor of International Relations at Princeton University, who was in Budapest in March and April as a member of the Coolidge Mission. Brown believed Magyars of all political persuasions would welcome American or British troops, but would fight those of the other allies. He predicted all Hungary would support Béla Kun if he resisted dismemberment.[64]

These observations led the American delegation to advise Wilson to oppose formation of a crusade against Hungary. General Bliss urged Wilson to remain aloof from the crisis. The zone, previously approved by Bliss, lay within ethnically Magyar territory and afforded Romania an opportunity to advance into central Hungary. If the Council insisted on maintaining the zone as a deterrent to hostilities, Bliss advised, it should be moved eastward into purely Romanian territory. If the Council refused, the Allies would find themselves in a war of tremendous magnitude involving Russia who would come to Kun's assistance. The result would be a conflict fought by American troops alone because the Allies, weary of war, would leave the arena to the Americans. Bliss proposed a disavowal of the decision establishing the zone, and urged that orders be issued to d'Esperey and Romania to desist from taking any action. Hungary, he recommended, should be assured her treaty would be concluded on the basis of the Fourteen Points and Wilson's subsequent speeches. Bliss accused Foch, the Quai d'Orsay, and the Ministry of War of hatching a plot to involve the United States in making France supreme over East Central Europe.[65]

These warnings apparently convinced Wilson for he soon disclosed strong opposition to intervention in Hungary. Lloyd George and Clemenceau also rejected the scheme to create a *cordon sanitaire* between Bolshevism and Western Europe.[66] When Orlando cited the menace of Bolshevism to Italy, the Allied Power closest to Hungary, the others rebuffed his suggestion for the Allies to occupy Budapest. Moreover, Lloyd George did not think the Allies should suppress Bolshevism in Hungary because

> there are few countries which need a revolution so much. I have had today a conversation with someone who visited Hungary and who knows it well. He told me that it is a country which had the worst land system in Europe. The peasants are oppressed as in the Middle Ages, and the rights of noblemen still exist.

Wilson concurred and proposed fixing national frontiers and opening all doors to commerce to stop the spread of Bolshevism.[67]

Instead of suppressing the Bolshevik movement by force, the Council decided on March 29 to send a mission to Budapest to discuss with Béla Kun his proposal to accept the Fourteen Points as the basis for peace. Jan Christiaan Smuts of the Union of South Africa was selected to lead the mission. At the last moment Pichon raised objections to negotiations with Kun, "the friend and accomplice of Lenin," who was attempting to regain territory "already detached" from Hungary. Lansing opposed this view by pointing out that the French-sponsored neutral zone had thrown Hungary into the arms of Bolsheviks and that the limits of the zone corresponded to the frontier of the 1916 Alliance, "which no government could accept as a satisfactory frontier." Pichon stood firm in insisting the Allies were bound to Romania by that alliance, whose line had been traced by Britain, France, Italy, and Russia, but not the United States. He noted that "we have traced a line which we believe just. Shall we disavow Romania? This would be an unpardonable mistake." It was clear the Quai d'Orsay was determined to uphold Romanian claims.[68]

Support by the Quai d'Orsay of Romanian claims did not stem from altruism. The French hoped to secure Romanian support for the "White" Russian armies operating in southern Russia where French occupation of Odessa could be maintained despite the Council's decision to evacuate that seaport.[69] But Pichon failed to convert the Council, nor was he able to convince Clemenceau, his superior, who was a moderate nationalist by comparison with the more unyielding elements of the Quai d'Orsay and the Ministry of War.[70] The Allied leaders, influenced by Wilson's disdain for the neutral zone, agreed to tell Béla Kun that Hungary's frontiers would be determined by the Peace Conference and that the zone, which would remain in effect, did not indicate the final territorial settlement.[71]

Brătianu, who had less interest in the Ukraine than in Hungary, joined the efforts of the Quai d'Orsay by appealing to the Council on April 3.

He asked that Kun be forced to evacuate behind the neutral zone and demobilize immediately so that Romania could "successfully make resistance to the East." Brătianu apparently feared Russian Bolshevism less than the French. He knew that a series of incidents had wrecked Lenin's hopes of assisting Kun. Admiral Kolchak, leading the "White" Russian forces, had advanced into the Volga region, compelling the Red Army to reenforce its concentrations in the east by withdrawing troops from the Ukraine, which it had recently occupied. The Red campaign against General Denikin in the Ukraine proved unsuccessful in driving the "Whites" out of the Don and Kuban regions. It would be necessary for the Red Army to throw back the "Whites" before advancing toward Hungary.[72]

Brătianu's propaganda against the Kun régime would have been foolhardy had the Red Army been approaching the Romanian frontier. His provocative verbal campaign against Hungary was carried on to obtain official authorization and support for Romanian occupation of the entire neutral zone and the ultimate incorporation of the territory he claimed. By stirring up panic about the Bolshevik terror, Brătianu could proclaim it his duty to the Allied Powers to march on Budapest and oust the Kun régime. At the same time he could annex the claimed territory.

The official organ of the Romanian delegation, *Bulletin d'informations roumaines*, contained rumors of an imminent Hungarian attack upon Romanian positions. Making no distinction between Károlyi and Kun, the journal alleged that Christian G. Rakovskii, exiled leader of the Romanian socialists, had received from Károlyi, to whose government Lenin had accredited him as an envoy, permission to organize an anti-Romanian regiment of Magyar troops. In exchange, Rakovskii would get Bessarabia for a Sovietized Romania and Károlyi would recover Transylvania. Rakovskii's scheme could now be implemented with the assistance of the more reliable and willing Béla Kun.[73]

Brătianu's efforts to arouse anti-Magyar feelings in Paris were bolstered by news of an invasion launched by Kun against Slovakia on March 28. The attack was interpreted as an attempt to make contact with the Red Army. While his forces, ostensibly fighting to regain Slovakia, were engaged with the Czechs, Béla Kun met with Smuts during the first week in April. Smuts advised him that the neutral zone was temporary and did not predetermine the final frontier. Kun insisted the zone be moved further to the east, but Smuts rejected his demand, since it would permit Magyar troops to occupy territory claimed by Romania. Kun retaliated by refusing to respect the Council's order for him to accept the zone, and he demanded the Romanians be compelled to withdraw east of the Mureş River.[74]

Smuts returned to Paris on April 12 to advise adoption of a wait-and-see attitude, since he expected Kun to be replaced shortly by a group of right-socialists.[75] The Smuts mission helped to create in Budapest the impression that the Allies had recognized the Kun government. This assumption was echoed in Moscow, where Zinoviev appealed to the world proletariat to aid Hungary, whose Bolshevik government had been recognized by the West.[76] At the same time, Soviet foreign commissar Chicherin warned Romania that an attack upon Hungary would be considered an attack upon Russia.[77] The press in Paris and London called upon the Allies to rebut these statements by intervening in Hungary and ousting Béla Kun.

Brătianu interpreted the Smuts mission in much the same way as the Bolsheviks. He feared the Council would invite Kun to send a peace delegation to Paris and, worst of all, accede to his denunciation of the territorial promises in the 1916 Alliance. That fear which had gripped Brătianu in the summer of 1916 when he demanded guarantees Hungary would not be able to save herself by making a separate peace was about to materialize. General d'Esperey increased Brătianu's anxiety when he reported after a visit to Budapest on April 6 that Kun proposed to recover territory occupied by Romanian troops.[78]

On April 10, Brătianu notified Vice-Premier Pherekyde in Bucharest to resist a Hungarian attack if it came.[79] General Prezan interpreted this notice as an official disregard of the neutral zone, and he ordered the army to advance to the Tisa.[80] At approximately the same moment (April 10), Kun's forces attacked Romanian positions before Prezan could move, threw them back, and were then compelled to retreat. The Romanian offensive got under way on April 16, passed the Hungarian side of the neutral zone on April 18, and crossed the Tisa at Szolnok on May 1.

When summoned later to explain his invasion of Hungary, Brătianu told the Council that operations had been designed to drive the Magyars behind the frontier promised him in the 1916 Alliance. The armistice had not permitted him to occupy that frontier. This "omission" had given Károlyi and Kun the opportunity to devastate Romanian-inhabited comitats. When the neutral zone was established, contended Brătianu, Romanian troops moved to occupy their side of the zone, but the Magyars counterattacked. Then the Romanians advanced and stopped on the Tisa.[81]

Brătianu's explanation on June 10 came too late. When told by the Council of the delimitation of Romania's frontiers by the Commission, whose report was submitted to the Council on April 6, four days before the outbreak of hostilities, the Premier declared his ignorance of the Commission's findings and added, "I only know the line which represents our claims."[82] If apprised of the report on April 6, it is very doubtful he would have respected the frontier laid down by the experts.

The Frontier With Hungary

The Commission completed its report on April 6, after two months of discussions. Instead of taking up the report immediately, and thus possibly affecting the events of April, the Big Four referred it to the Council of Foreign Ministers, whose members delayed examination of the thirty-one page document until May 8, the day after the German delegation received its treaty. The Commission's recommendations were the last of all frontier proposals to be approved since they did not affect Germany. All other territorial commissions had long since submitted their reports. By the time the Big Four decided to examine the report on Romania, the political situation in East Central Europe had undergone such violent changes as to endanger the stability of the proposed frontier between Hungary and Romania. Romania had certainly rejected the Council's proclamation of January 25, and Béla

Kun was no less culpable. But the Allied Powers, by failing to publicize or act upon the Commission's recommendations in April, when Romanians and Hungarians were battling, were also guilty; the Council was now faced with the task of forcing an allied state, Romania, to respect the frontier with an enemy state when it was finally approved.

An analysis of the minutes of the Commission's sessions shows that the Americans had to submit to serious compromises.[83] The railway centers of Arad, Satu Mare, Oradea, and Carei, left in Hungary by the Americans, were assigned to Romania at the insistence of the British and French. The British conceded these cities were predominantly Magyar centers, but economic criteria prevailed over the ethnic in the British recommendations. The French agreed with the British finding that Romania could hardly construct parallel lines in the tangled cross-hills of the region, but their argument was based principally upon strategic criteria, since Romania required unbroken lines for defense purposes.[84] The Italians at first recommended a strictly ethnic frontier, but after their government began to experience disappointment over Wilson's criticism of Italy's exorbitant claims, de Martino and Vannutelli-Rey insisted on upholding the 1916 Alliance. When this tactic, employed to defend secret treaties, failed to win support of the others, the Italians tried to sabotage proceedings by increasing territory awarded to Romania whenever the others sought to reduce it.[85]

Italy's obstructionist tactics, shown in one case by insistence on giving two railways in northeastern Hungary to Romania to link her with Poland, and in another by the demand that ethnic character of a comitat, rather than predominant national character of cities in that comitat, should be the basis for awards, forced de Martino and Vannutelli-Rey into the minority quite consistently. Although it is not yet possible to prove the general opinion that Italy and Romania had an understanding to stand or fall on the fulfillment of their respective treaties, actions of the Italian experts indicate the probable existence of some kind of accord. The Italians at first recommended, like the Americans, the tracing of frontiers according to balanced ethnic and economic criteria, but in the end they disavowed this stand and insisted on inserting their minority reservations in the final report. These reservations stated that any railway line essential to the economy or strategy of a state must be contained in its entirety in a state even if it traversed regions inhabited by a predominantly alien population. According to their data, from 225,000 to 360,000 Magyars would be added to Romania if the railway link with Poland were incorporated. The award of this large element, opposed by the Americans, was considered by the Italians of minor relevance in view of the need to provide Romania with a direct link to Poland.[86]

The Commission completed its work after a last effort by the Italians to establish an unbroken railway system from Italy, through Romania and Czechoslovakia, into Poland to carry grains of East Central Europe back to Italy, and to provide Italy with railway communication into Hungary in case of an outbreak of hostilities between Hungary and the Serbs.[87] The Americans succeeded in having the railway from Arad to Satu Mare severed from the former city to Salonta on the argument the region traversed from Arad to Salonta was in the majority Magyar. The line from Arad to Salonta was left in Hungary. At the suggestion of the Americans, whose proposals wrecked the Italian scheme, the Commission recommended that Romania construct an alternate line parallel to the railway left in Hungary. The Americans also won out in having a minor railway line from Nagy-Károly to Csap in Slovakia severed, leaving the longer section in Hungary. Romania could also build an alternate line there to make up for loss of an unbroken route.

Although the Americans won on two points, the frontier recommendations were, in the main, compatible with major French demands for a strategic boundary. Two railway lines, both running north and south, were severed, but this disadvantage could be compensated for by the utilization of the rivers and canals as avenues of transport for troops of Foch's anti-Bolshevik crusade. This was not a setback for the French because the Commission included in its recommendations the following statement: Romania should be given outlets for Transylvania via the waterways and railways, and the railway spurs to be constructed by Romania should link her with rail systems of adjoining allied states; but until such time, as Romania could complete the projects, the Allies should supervise railway lines in eastern Hungary and Transylvania to assure unrestricted transit across frontiers.[88]

The Central Territorial Commission approved the frontier on April 15. Italian member Salvago Raggi withdrew his country's insistence that Romania secure a direct railway link with Poland after other members agreed to decrease Serbia's share of the Banat and give Romania a small section of additional territory there. The Italians, anxious about the threat the south Slavs presented to their security, considered any diminution of Serbian territorial awards to be in the best interests of Italy.[89]

The process of delimiting the Romanian-Hungarian frontier was thus completed despite conflicting French and Italian aims. Eleven of the fifteen comitats comprising Transylvania and Crişana were assigned to Romania. All Transylvania was awarded, but the new frontier fell short of that promised in the 1916 Alliance and it violated ethnic principles because several predominantly Magyar urban centers were transferred to Romania. This gift should have satisfied Brătianu because he had justified his claims to the Alliance line on the basis of historic, strategic, and economic criteria-bases accepted by the experts. If the Commission had not used his criteria and if the political situation had been stable in 1919, ethnic principles, which the Allies ostensibly favored, would have triumphed and the frontier would have been pushed further east.[90]

The Serbian-Romanian Frontier

Conflicting claims of Romania and Serbia to the Banat of Timişoara posed a very difficult problem.[91] Neither claim could be justified on ethnic grounds. The Banat comprised an area of 11,000 square miles, with a population of about 1½ million, of which about 600,000 were Romanians, 385,000 Swabian Germans, 358,000 Serbs, and 240,000 Magyars. When the Commission examined the dispute, the Americans favored partition and the British concurred, but the French insisted Romania be compensated for partition by securing Allied recognition of the union of Bessarabia. The Italians, on the other hand, wanted to give the entire Banat to Romania, since the 1916 Alliance, "whose values the Allies are compelled fully to recognize," had promised it. Faced with opposition, the Italians retreated and agreed to partition if Romania were compensated in Bessarabia.[92]

Brătianu testified before the Commission on February 22 as a result of the Commission's admission that it could not agree on a suitable partition. The Premier did not refute the population statistics, but instead injected new demands and threats. If the Serbs crossed the Danube to obtain their allotment of the Banat, he warned, the "latent irredentism of Romanians living in the Timok valley of Serbia would be aroused," and it would be uncontrollable. When Tardieu asked why he was so adamantly opposed to an artificial frontier with Serbia when he was requesting one with Hungary, an enemy state, Brătianu replied that his race of Latins was entirely surrounded by Slavs except on the

Magyar side. The possession of a very strong natural boundary with Slavic states, the Danube and Dniester rivers, was a strategic necessity to Romania. Serbia's claim to a bridgehead to protect Belgrade was, in his estimation, for attack, not defense purposes. Romania, he asserted, would grant minority rights to Serbs who wished to remain in the Banat and, if requested, he would sign a treaty to that effect "if the principle of such guarantees were adopted by the general treaty of peace for other peoples." He compared the Banat dispute to a "tooth which had to be extracted," after which Serbia would have friendly relations with Romania, "of whom she has need and who, moreover, has already been of great assistance to her." Brătianu absolutely refused to consider a plebiscite.[93]

The Serbs rebutted Brătianu's arguments on February 25. Jovan Cvijić, the noted ethnographer, reported Romania's maps to be concocted fantasies concealing the true ethnic character of the Banat. He denied the Romanian character of the Timok valley, claiming that the Serbs of that valley had found refuge in Wallachia in the 14th century, adopted and preserved the Romanian language, and returned to the Timok when Serbia was liberated from the Turks.[94] Pašić remarked, "They would rather die than be united with Romania. Their fusion with the Serbian nation is an accomplished fact." Vesnić reiterated the charge he made to the Council on January 31, namely, Serbia should not be treated like Romania, a state that had swerved from its loyalty and signed a separate peace. Romania, not Serbia, was able to select the precise moment to intervene after negotiating a bargain promising her territories that rightfully belonged to Serbia. Vesnić said that

> if the Great Powers proposed to consider Romania as an ally, Serbia would be extremely surprised at such a decision and could not accept it. In any case, she could not recognize any value in the Treaty of Alliance on which Romania based her claims to the Banat. That treaty was concluded without Serbia's knowledge and without her having given a mandate to the Russian Government to represent her, as has been alleged without foundation. Moreover, it was annulled on the day Romania negotiated with the enemy.

He repeated a request made to the Council on February 18 to hold a plebiscite to determine the partition line. General Pecić then argued for the bridgehead to protect Belgrade.[95]

Serbia and Romania, however, did not wait for a delimitation. Serbian troops were reenforced in the western half of the Banat and officers announced to the inhabitants that they would soon be united with Serbia. Observers of the Coolidge Mission reported Romania's reaction to Serbian moves had created a critical situation. Romania was massing troops along the Mureş River, which formed the boundary between the Banat and Hungary. Moreover, American agents in Budapest sent word about French detachments at Arad, Szeged, and Timişoara, preparing to assist Serbian and Romanian troops in occupying all Hungary as soon as the Banat dispute was settled. Unable to coordinate Serbian and Romanian troops, glaring at each other across the Mureş, the French traced a demarcation line, warning both to remain in their positions.[96]

This crisis was intensified during the last week in February when Brătianu threatened to resign and permit Bolsheviks to seize Romania if he did not get the entire Banat.[97] The Commission encountered a railway problem in the Banat similar to that of Crişana. On March 18, after three weeks of debate, the experts traced a partition calculated to please neither side. Romania was denied her claim to the entire Banat; only two-thirds was awarded, two major railway lines were severed, no access was given to the Tisa (or, for that matter, anywhere along that river north to its confluence with the Someş in Crişana), and she lost about 75,000 Romanians to Serbia. The Commission may not have acknowledged Brătianu's claim, but it did consider his ethnic criteria. The experts referred to the need to balance the number of Serbs and Romanians assigned to each state. It was hoped that both states would reach an understanding regarding the treatment of their respective minorities; 65,000 Serbs were due to be incorporated into Romania. American insistence upon a favorable ethnic frontier was made clear in the assignment to Hungary of the confluence of the Mureş and Tisa rivers (in the comitat of Csanád) near Szeged, also left in Hungary. The vital riverport of Szeged was a predominantly Magyar center. Railway lines traversing the Banat were to be operated by the Allies until Romania and Serbia could construct substitute lines crossing their assigned territories.

The partition was not without definite strategic factors. The French included a recommendation that both states link their railway lines with the system converging upon Salonika, and they reserved for the French General Staff the right to delimit the frontier on the spot. This would be a difficult task for it would be necessary to force Serbia to withdraw her troops from sections assigned to Romania. Moreover, the recommendations rejected Brătianu's thesis of the indivisibility of the Banat and, consequently, dealt another blow to the 1916 Alliance.[98]

The Question of Bucovina: Second Phase

Bucovina presented less difficulty than the Banat. For that reason its disposition was postponed until after frontiers with Hungary and Serbia were determined. When time arrived to discuss Bucovina, the experts realized that the prospect of an independent Eastern Galicia, to which ethnically Ruthenian sections of Bucovina could be attached, appeared very remote. The British and French overcame American opposition to granting the entire province to Romania on the basis of the Cernăuţi resolution, but the Americans still held out for a possible Ruthenian state. They forced the Commission to detach the basin of the Ceremoş River, whose economic interests lay in the direction of Galicia. This rectification, the Americans noted, involved a strip inhabited by about 85,000 Ruthenians and only 300 Romanians and left to Romania a relative majority in that portion of Bucovina assigned to her. This delimitation could not be enforced, however, because Romania, when informed of the partition of Bucovina, refused to accept it, preferring, instead, a common boundary with Poland in Eastern Galicia.[99]

The Question of Maramureş

The comitat of Maramureş contained a Ruthenian majority, but its capital, Maramureş-Sighet (located at the confluence of the Vizo and upper Tisa rivers), was inhabited by a Romanian majority. The capital and its environs had been promised in the 1916 Alliance at a time when it seemed Russia would acquire the rest of Maramureş. The Tisa would have formed a natural and fairly accurate ethnic frontier between Ruthenians and Romanians. But with Russia's defection and the concurrent upsurge of nationalist sentiment among Ukrainians of Eastern Galicia and northern Bucovina complicating the final award, Brătianu took advantage of the turmoil by claiming more than had been promised him. He asked for the railway line from Maramureş-Sighet to Kolomea in Eastern Galicia so that Romania would have direct contact with Poland, whom he expected to incorporate Eastern Galicia.[100]

Brătianu's claim to ethnically Ruthenian territory conflicted with that of the Czechs who wanted all Maramureş north of the Tisa, with the exception of Maramureş-Sighet. If the Czechs were satisfied, Brătianu would lose his railway link or common frontier with Poland. The Italians supported his claim, but the other experts wished to uphold the Czechs.[101] The Commission on Czech-Slovak Territorial Questions had already recommended giving Maramureş north of the Tisa to the Czechs because the Ruthenians could best look for protection and exercise of their autonomy from their fellow-Slav Czechs. It was proposed that Czechoslovakia grant Romania right of railway access across Maramureş in order to reach the systems of Eastern Galicia and Poland.[102]

This recommendation denied Brătianu the northern environs of Maramureş-Sighet, the capital assigned to Romania. He opposed this arrangement because the railway lines would depend upon Czech good will. The Commission deemed it advisable to compensate Brătianu for this denial to avert possible conflict with the Czechs. After much discussion the experts arrived at an extremely complex solution. One-third of Maramureş and its capital would go to Romania because of the ethnic criterion, but the railway lines connecting the capital with junctions in the rest of Maramureş would go to Czechoslovakia. To give the capital railway access to the south into Transylvania without the need to traverse either Czech or Hungarian soil, the Commission recommended the construction by Romania of a substitute line operating entirely within her borders.[103] This arrangement was a victory for the Americans in their effort to permit Hungary to retain almost one-third of the comitat of Satu Mare, located directly southeast of Maramureş. The railway line from Satu Mare to Csap in Slovakia was thus required to traverse Hungary. This American proposal may have been offered to hinder Foch's aim of securing control of all railways running north to south.[104] Nevertheless, the Supreme Council faced the perplexing problem of disentangling the Romanian, Polish, and Czech troops occupying Maramureş.

Indecision on southern Dobrodgea

The Americans introduced a recommendation on March 3 to trace an ethnic frontier between Romania and Bulgaria in Dobrodgea. Their line represented a compromise between frontiers of the Treaty of Berlin (1878) and the Treaty of Bucharest (1913). In this manner about

38,000 Bulgarians, instead of 135,000, would remain in Romania. The British were disinclined to revise pre-war treaties, but were willing to approve frontier revisions if Bulgaria and Romania reached an understanding. The French at first agreed that the proposed line would rectify past errors, but later disapproved of the plan which would require an allied state to cede territory to an enemy.[105]

Having failed to secure adoption of their proposal, the American experts included a defense of their position in the final report. They acknowledged, along with the other experts, that the Commission was not empowered to propose cession to an enemy state of territory forming *de facto* and *de jure* an integral part of an allied state. But if Romania admitted of her own accord the possibility of retroceding part of southern Dobrodgea, the Commission, except the French members, recommended a new boundary insuring a defensible line to both states and restoring to Bulgaria regions in which the Romanian population was a very insignificant minority compared with Bulgarian elements whose economic interests linked them to the south.[106] This unresolved question was to provoke serious complications.

Unfinished Business

When the Commission completed its work and submitted its report to the Central Territorial Commission on April 6, the least difficult phase of the frontier settlements was finished. The Council had yet to approve the report and enforce the frontiers on Romania, not on Hungary or Serbia. Many factors, meanwhile, combined to weaken the Commission's proposals. These included the Council's insistence that the experts reach unanimous decisions, a ruling that was not carried out; failure to provide the Commission with specific instructions, at the same time denying it authority to treat purely political questions (a denial not observed by the French and Italians); Orlando's refusal to submit his claims to a territorial commission, which strengthened Brătianu's argument that the Allies were not treating all states equitably; and, above all, the illusion entertained by the British and American experts that the Big Four would overrule unsatisfactory compromises reached with their French and Italian colleagues.

Whether Romania's frontiers would have been arranged differently if a Romanian expert had served on the Commission is a purely academic question. One may easily agree with Seymour's observation:

No honest student of European conditions, however, can be blind to the new dangers which have been created. It is undeniable that a considerable stretch of territory has been Balkanized.... The decision was probably inevitable. No one will call it satisfactory.[107]

NOTES

1. *The World Crisis, V: The Aftermath*, p. 227.

2. Crowe (1864-1925) was Assistant Under-Secretary for Foreign Affairs. Laroche had been recalled as First Secretary of the Embassy in Rome to serve as Chief of the European Section of the Quai d'Orsay. Giacomo de Martino (1868-1957) had been ambassador to Berlin, Constantinople, Berne, and, since 1911, Secretary-General of the Foreign Ministry and later Under-Secretary for Foreign Affairs. Vannutelli-Rey was Counselor of the Embassy in Paris. Day and Seymour, members of the faculty of Yale University, had served in the Inquiry; neither had had diplomatic experience. The minutes (procès-verbaux) of sessions of the Commission used in this study are in The New York Public Library in photostatic copy with no pagination.

3. The specialists on Austria-Hungary and the Balkans were Clive Day (Chairman of the Department of Economics at Yale), Charles Seymour (Professor of History at Yale), Will S. Monroe (Professor of History at New Jersey State Normal School, Montelair), Douglas W. Johnson (Professor of Geography at Columbia), Mark Jefferson (Professor of Geography at Michigan State Normal School), Allen A. Young (Professor of Economics at Cornell), and Albert Lybyer (Professor of History, University of Michigan). These scholars formed one of seventeen divisions of the Inquiry, which began its work in a closely guarded room of The New York Public Library, and then moved to the American Geographical Society (Harry Lydenberg, *History of The New York Public Library*, p. 435).

André Tardieu, who was French High Commissioner to the United States in 1917, acquainted the Inquiry with French views. See his *Devant l'obstacle*, pp. 216-241.

4. *U.S. Foreign Relations, PPC*, I, pp. 29, 33, 45, 47, 52, 74; and in manuscript, *Epitome of Boundaries*, House Papers. The National Archives contain the bulk of the Inquiry's data. A catalog has been issued: H. Stephen Helton (ed.), "Records of the American Commission to Negotiate Peace," *Preliminary Inventories*, No. 89. For general studies of the work of the Inquiry, see Shotwell, pp. 7-11, 16-17; Seymour, *House Papers*, III, pp. 170-172, and his *Woodrow Wilson and the War*, pp. 260-261; Mamatey, pp. 173-185; and The National Archives, *Handbook of Federal World War Agencies*, p. 271.

5. Day's revisions are in "Boundaries in the Balkans, October 18, 1918," *House Papers*. Lansing approved them and dispatched the report to Paris for House's attention (*U.S. Foreign Relations, 1918*, Suppl. 1, I, p. 409).

6. The recommendations are in "Outline of Tentative Report and Recommendations prepared by the Intelligence Section with Instructions for President Wilson and the Plenipotentiaries, January 21, 1919," compiled by David Hunter Miller and Allen A. Young (Miller, *Diary*, IV, pp. 219, 233-235, 245, 253, 273). The plan to restore southern Dobrodgea is discussed in Seymour, *House Papers* , III, calling the Treaty of Bucharest (1913) arbitrary in character, pp. 333-334; and Robert Lansing, *The Peace Negotiations*, pp. 194, 197.

Support of the American program was elicited in the fall of 1918 when the Department of State published *Texts of the Roumanian Peace*, containing the Peace of Bucharest and articles by experts. One written by noted geographer Ellen C. Semple supported Romanian claims to Bessarabia and urged restoration of southern Dobrodgea to Bulgaria.

7. In August 1916, Tyrrell proposed dismemberment of the Habsburg Monarchy *(The History of the "Times,")* p. 260). He was then secretary to Sir Edward Grey.

8. Prothero was chief of the Historical Section. He recommended in 1917 that Hungary be forced to yield 3 million Romanians living west of the Carpathians (*A Lasting Peace,* pp. 34, 37).

9. The experts responsible for these proposals were David Mitrany, formerly of the London School of Economics, whom Prothero rated above Seton-Watson as an authority on Romania; Captain Harold W.V. Temperley, formerly Tutor in History at Cambridge and lecturer at Harvard in 1911-12; Arnold Toynbee, considered then a Balkan expert; and Allen Leeper. See Memorandum, Johnson to House, May 1, 1918, House Papers.

10. The text of the complete report is in Miller, *Diary*, XIX, pp. 273-280. These recommendations coincided greatly with those advanced by Seton-Watson in his *Roumania and the Great War*. He did not serve in the Department of Political Intelligence because his criticism of Grey's policy regarding the secret treaties resulted in his being drafted into the Army Medical Corps as a private. He was finally released after the Cabinet was prodded by certain influential persons. See Steed, *Through Thirty Years,* II, pp. 129-130; and Seton-Watson, *Masaryk in England*, p. 87.

11. These recommendations have been collated from the following *Peace Handbooks*: No. 1 "Austria-Hungary," No. 5 "Bukovina," No. 6 "Transylvania and the Banat," No. 7 "Hungarian Ruthenia," No. 15 "History of the Eastern Question," No. 23 "Romania," and No. 51 "Bessarabia." Prothero, in his same preface to all 162 of the *Peace Handbooks,* wrote that they were used by the British delegation to determine the peace settlement. All were published in 1920.

12. H. M. Government, Peace Terms: Confidential, unpublished manuscript in The New York Public Library; Lloyd George, *Memoirs of the Peace Conference*, II, pp. 588-591.

Nicolson noted in his diary that Romania had committed herself to the admission that the Peace of Bucharest was valid, although still unratified, when she declared war on Germany on grounds that Germany had violated that peace. "This was for them a most unfortunate admission" (pp. 134-135).

Douglas Johnson was sent to London in May 1918 to acquaint the British with work of the Inquiry. For studies of collaboration on war aims, see Seymour, *House Papers*, III and IV, passim; Arthur C. Murray, *At Close Quarters;* and Arthur Willert, *The Road to Safety*; Stanley Morison, "Personality and Diplomacy in Anglo-American Relations, 1917," in Pares and Taylor, pp. 431-474; and James Duane Squires, *British Propaganda at Home and in the United States from 1914 to 1917.* The British program stood closer to the American than to the French. For more on this, see G.P. Gooch, *Studies in Diplomacy and Statecraft*, p. 163.

13. The Comité included twenty-seven professors and five corresponding members (Alma Luckau, *The German Delegation at the Paris Peace Conference*, p. 27). Among them were Lavisse, Aulard, Bourgeois, Denis, Diehl, Haumant, and Seignobos.

The text of the Comité's recommendations was published in 1919 as *Travaux du Comité d'études*, 2 vols. Clemenceau relied heavily upon Tardieu's skill, judgment, and organizing ability (Bruun, p. 184).

14. *Travaux du Comité d'études, II: Questions européennes*, pp. 556-577 (on the Banat), pp. 581-603 (on Transylvania), pp. 627-661 (on Bessarabia and southern Dobrodgea).

De Martonne was well qualified to discuss Romania. His study of the topography and ethnography of the Carpathian region had earned for him a doctorate at the Sorbonne in 1902. He was a frequent visitor to Romania before the war. Among his numerous publications on behalf of Romanian aspirations are "Les conditions d'une intervention roumaine," *Revue de Paris*, XXII (1915), pp. 430-448; speech on March 19, 1915 proposing that Romania get Transylvania, southern Bucovina, and the eastern Banat, in *Les Annales des Nationalités*, IV (1915), p. 88; and *La Dobrodgea: Esquisse historique, géographique, ethnographique et statistique.*

15. Minutes, February 8.

16. *Ibid.*, February 22. The anti-Romanian attitude of the landowners was propagandized in numerous pamphlets by Alexander Krupenskii, leader of the Bessarabian Council of Nobility, and Alexander Schmidt, former Mayor of Chişinău. They deposited many polemics with the Peace Conference.

17. *Ibid.*, February 8. Brătianu's claim to all of Bucovina is in *La Roumanie devant le congrès de la paix: ses revendications territoriales*, pp. 15-17. Literature

supporting this claim may be seen in Iorga, *Les roumains au-delà du Dniester;* Drăghicescu, *Les roumains d'Ukraine;* Iancu I. Nistor, *Românii și Rutenii în Bucovina,* alleging the Ruthenians to be recent immigrants; Constantin Lacea, *La Bucovine;* and Basile Vitencu, *La situation ethnographique en Bucovine.*

Ruthenian propaganda challenging Romania's claim may be seen in Myron Korduba, *Le territoire et la population de l'Ukraine;* and *Notes présentées par la délégation de la république ukrainienne à la conférence de la paix,* p. 22.

Imperial Russian claims to the entire province, based on ethnographic data, may be seen in G. I. Tanfil'ev, *Galitsiia i Bukovina,* claiming 305,000 Russians, not Ruthenians, inhabited Bucovina (p. 39).

18. Miller, *Diary,* V, pp. 246-247.

19. If Romania annexed territory as far west as the Tisa, she would acquire purely Magyar comitats of Békés, Hajdu, and Szabolcs. The other experts did not take Italy's magnanimity seriously and, in the end, the three comitats in their entirety were left in Hungary.

20. Minutes, February 11.

21. Deák, p. 12.

22. The French Ministry of War and the Quai d'Orsay have been accused of encouraging the Romanians to advance in accordance with plans of Marshal Foch to erect a barrier against Bolshevism in the East. See Baker, *Woodrow Wilson and World Settlement,* II, p. 29; and Macartney, *A History of Hungary, 1929-1945,* I, p. 22. French generals in the East wished to extend their area of occupation into the Danubian plain for a march on Vienna and Budapest (Harriet G. Wanklyn, *The Eastern Marchlands of Europe,* p. 281, note 29).

23. Minutes, February 17.

24. *U.S. Foreign Relations, 1919: Russia,* pp. 68-69; and E. H. Carr, *The Bolshevik Revolution, 1917-1923,* III, p. 111.

25. *U.S. Foreign Relations, PPC,* IV, pp. 12, 22-28.

26. B.H. Liddell Hart, *Foch: The Man of Orléans,* pp. 417-418. The Red Army took Kiev on February 6, 1919. France's decision to evacuate Odessa was due to the infiltration of Bolshevik agents into the ranks (William H. Chamberlin, *The Russian Revolution, 1917-1921,* 11, p. 167).

27. Minutes, February 19.

28. This statement was an oversight on Tardieu's part. He was obviously referring to the Belgrade armistice of November 13, signed three days after Romania's declaration of war on Germany.

29. French preoccupation with the terror of Bolshevism requires explanation at this point. In December 1917 the British and French agreed to create spheres of influence in the East, the former taking the Caucasus, the latter Bessarabia, the Ukraine, and the Crimea. Both sent occupation troops. The French were less successful since troops could be spared for the occupation of Odessa only. As for Bessarabia, the French enlisted Romanian aid and both states were confronted in 1919 with the threat of a Bolshevik attack, the French at Odessa and the Romanians in Bessarabia and Transylvania. In Budapest, meanwhile, Magyar prisoners of war returning from Russia had formed a Communist Party which tried to seize power in February 1919. See Fischer, II, p. 836; and Chamberlin, II, p. 154.

30. *U.S. Foreign Relations, PPC*, IV, pp. 59-61. The French feared that if the Bolsheviks seized Hungary, the road would be wide open for the implantation in Central Europe of communist states. This anxiety accounts for the scheme devised by Foch and supported by the Quai d'Orsay and Generals d'Esperey and Berthelot to nip Magyar radicalism in the bud. The Romanians, who had much to lose if the Bolsheviks seized Hungary, apparently were willing to help. See Baker, *Woodrow Wilson and World Settlement,* III, p. 241; Lloyd George, *Memoirs of the Peace Conference,* I, p. 248; and Seymour, *House Papers,* IV, pp. 332-334.

31. For the opposition of Wilson and House to the plan, see Seymour, *House Papers,* IV, p. 348; for that of Clemenceau, *ibid.,* IV, pp. 332-334; and for Lloyd George's, *ibid.,* IV, p. 348. Wilson's disapproval is also cited in Arthur Walworth, *Woodrow Wilson, II: World Prophet,* p. 251. The British General Staff opposed it (C.E. Callwell, *Field-Marshal Sir Henry Wilson,* II, p. 31).

32. The Foch plan was interpreted by the Soviet government as an assumption by the Allies of a massive war against Bolshevism. See Fischer, I, pp. 166-167, 170-171; Shtein, passim; and V. P. Potemkin (ed.), *Istoria Diplomaţiei, III: 1919-1939,* pp. 12-54.

33. American inexperience in the intricate workings of European diplomacy may be observed in the discussions on February 18. De Martonne, General LeRond, and Charles Seymour dealt with the disputed railways. LeRond insisted upon an effective strategic frontier for Romania regardless of ethnic considerations. Seymour could only repeat that, in acquiring the railway, Romania would incorporate an additional 300,000 Magyars. When the French added that this railway would link Romanian and Czech systems, a very desirable condition in view of the worsening situation in Hungary, Seymour repeated his objection (Minutes, February 18).

34. Minutes, February 22. Brătianu called on Colonel House the previous day to "soften up" American objections. House suspected the Romanians were looking upon him as a savior (Diary, MSS, XV, p. 62, House Papers).

35. *U.S. Foreign Relations, PPC,* IV, pp. 105-107, 120-126; Baker, *Woodrow Wilson and World Settlement,* III, p. 242; and Lloyd George, *Memoirs,* I, pp. 242-243.
Reports reached Paris that Romania, Czechoslovakia, and Poland had agreed to partition the Ukraine. Romania would acquire Galicia south of the Dniester. See Henri Austruy, "La frontière polono-roumaine," *La Nouvelle Revue,* XL (1919), pp. 289-304; and Charles Upson Clark, *United Roumania,* p. 225.

36. *U.S. Foreign Relations, PPC,* IV, pp. 145-147, 157-158; Miller, *Diary,* XVII, p. 72; Baker, *Woodrow Wilson and World Settlement,* II, p. 29, and III, pp. 241-242; and Temperley, IV, p. 228. The Allied military advisers served on the Supreme War Council at Versailles. Its members were generals Belin, Sackville-West, Cavallero, and Bliss.

37. Frederick Palmer, *Bliss, Peacemaker,* p. 378. Seymour recognized the injustice of the neutral zone at the time, but he recalled years later that the blame should not have been cast upon the Commission which was not competent to deal with military matters (Deák, p.59, note 76).

38. Tardieu was also chairman of these commissions: Belgian and Danish Affairs, and Saar Valley and Alsace-Lorraine. Jules Cambon was chairman of these: Czech Territorial Commission, Polish Affairs, and Greek and Albanian Affairs.
For the creation of the Central Territorial Commission, see *U.S. Foreign Relations, PPC,* IV, pp. 160-161; Miller, *Diary,* XV, p. 102, and XVII, pp. 80-81; and Lapradelle, *La paix de Versailles,* I, p. 298. The appointees were Tardieu, Salvago Raggi (formerly Governor of Eritrea and envoy to Berlin and Paris), Crowe, Otchiai (Japanese envoy to The Hague), and Sidney E. Mezes, House's brother-in-law.

39. Briefs Nos. 1255, 1571, 1572, and Reports Nos. 101, 102, 106, 107, 108, American Commission to Negotiate Peace, Parker T. Moon Papers, Columbia University Library. See also *Daily Review of the Foreign Press, Allied Press Supplement,* V, p. 531;, and Vopicka, p. 295.

40. *Daily Review of the Foreign Press, Allied Press Supplement,* V, pp. 478, 505, 531. *România* (Bucharest) on March 1 reported that Magyar police had entered Maniu's home at Bădăceu, arrested his mother, sister, and niece, bound them and then took them to prison.

41. *U.S. Foreign Relations, PPC,* XI, p. 65.

42. Minutes, February 28; Miller, *Diary*, XVII, p. 95. The Allies, Tardieu told Saint-Aulaire, were responsible for the failure of the Salonika offensive and, therefore, broke the 1916 Alliance (Saint-Aulaire, *Confession,* p. 485).

43. Tardieu was very close to the General Staff. He had served as civil counselor to Joffre and Foch from 1914 to 1916. In February 1916 Briand asked him to become envoy to Romania. His appointment was blocked by Radical Socialists and Socialists (Louis Aubert, *André Tardieu, 1876-1945,* pp. 15-18).

44. Bulletin No. 351, March 6, American Commission to Negotiate Peace, House Papers.

45. Saint-Aulaire, *Confession,* pp. 485-486. It is no wonder that this shrewd diplomat could write, in later years, excellent biographies of Richelieu and Talleyrand.

46. Queen Marie, "My Mission, I: In Paris," *The Cornhill Magazine,* CLX (1939), pp. 437-438, 445-446; Mordacq, III, p. 161. When Marie demanded the entire Banat, Clemenceau retorted that the Romanians wanted the lion's share of the province. To this Marie replied, "That is just why I came to see his first cousin, the Tiger." Clemenceau then remarked, "A tiger never had a child by a lioness" (Saint-Aulaire, *Confession,* p. 485).

47. House, *Diary,* MSS, XV, p. 8, House Papers. They met in the sitting-room of the Ritz suite of Vance McCormick, Chairman of the U.S. Trade Board and a delegate (Diaries of Vance C. McCormick, MSS, United Nations Library). See also Joseph C. Grew, Letters, I, March 8, MSS, Houghton Library, Harvard University; and Stephen Bonsal, *Suitors and Suppliants,* pp. 173-174.

48. Queen Marie, "My Mission, I: In Paris," and "II: At Buckingham Palace," pp. 448-451, 578-603.

49. *Ibid.,* "III: Paris Again," pp. 729-732. Harold Nicolson shared Marie's opinion. He described Wilson as an idealist and "what was more dangerous, a consummate master of English prose. He shared with Robespierre the hallucination that there existed some mystic bond between himself and the People — all people including the Romanians. If he could only penetrate the fog-barrier of governments, politicians, and convey the sweetness and light of his revelation to the ordinary peasant in the Banat, then reason, amity, and concord would spread... He had a gift of giving commonplace ideas the resonance and authority of biblical sentences. Like all phraseologists, he became mesmerized by the strength and neatness of the phrases that he devised" *(The Evolution of Diplomatic Method,* pp. 84-85).
Clemenceau thought of Wilson in a similar way. He once told Wickham Steed that "Wilson is intractable, believing himself to be the first man who for

2,000 years had known anything about peace on earth" *(Through Thirty Years,* II, p. 310).

50. Wilson did meet privately with Brătianu on April 17 (Edith Bolling Wilson, pp. 257-260).

51. *La Roumanie,* No. 66, April 17, 1919; Nicolson, *Peacemaking,* p. 291. Marie gave a dinner for the generals on March 31.

52. *La Roumanie,* No. 61, March 13, 1919.

53. *U.S. Foreign Relations, PPC,* IV, pp. 379-385; G. A. Riddell, *Lord Riddell's Intimate Diary,* p. 35. Foch complained that Wilson forced Clemenceau to kill the plan (Callwell, II, p. 180).

54. The presentation of the ultimatum was described by Captain Nicholas Roosevelt, member of the Coolidge Mission, who witnessed the scene *(U.S. Foreign Relations, PPC,* XII, pp. 413-419). Károlyi blamed the French exclusively *(Memoirs,* pp. 147-161), as did Jászi *(Revolution and Counter-Revolution in Hungary,* pp. 92-101). Jules Cambon rebutted these arguments by claiming Károlyi brazenly offered military aid against Kun if Hungary's territorial integrity were respected. See Cambon, "La Roumanie et la question agraire en Transylvanie," *Revue des Deux Mondes,* XLI-XLII (1927), pp. 618-619; and Geneviève Tabouis, *Jules Cambon par l'un des siens,* p. 342.

55. Károlyi's memoirs and Jászi's study are vital for an understanding of this crisis. Other essential works include Macartney, *Hungary and her Successors,* pp. 109-110, 278; Deák, pp. 57-59; and Hugh Seton-Watson, *From Lenin to Malenkov,* pp. 58-64. Macartney has accused the French of ousting Károlyi in the hope of securing Romania's support by yielding parts of Hungary, which Károlyi refused to give up *(A History of Hungary,* I, p. 22).
Ionescu accused Károlyi of willingly handing over the government to the Bolsheviks *(La Roumanie,* No. 65, April 10). Admiral Horthy echoed the same charge years later in his *Ein Leben für Ungarn,* p. 113.

56. Marghiloman, IV, pp. 258-261; and Iorga, *Memorii,* II, p. 173.

57. Vopicka, pp. 300-302.

58. For organizational changes, see *U.S. Foreign Relations, PPC,* III, p. 468; Marston, p. 165; and Temperley, I, pp. 263-266.

59. D'Esperey's order is in Marghiloman, IV, pp. 250-251. According to press accounts, he ordered the Romanians to advance to the eastern limit of the zone *(Daily Review of the Foreign Press, Allied Press Supplement,* V, p. 531).

60. Paul Mantoux, *Les délibérations du conseil des quatre*, I, pp. 18-23; and Miller, *Diary*, XVII, pp. 281-282.

61. Brief No. 1317, Moon Papers. Cited in Harold J. Coolidge and Robert H. Lord, *Archibald Cary Coolidge: Life and Letters*, pp. 210-212.

62. *U.S. Foreign Relations, PPC*, XII, pp. 272-276, 401-404.

63. *Ibid.*, XII, pp. 404-410; Brief No. 1791, Moon Papers; and Nicholas Roosevelt, *A Front Row Seat*, p. 103.

64. *U.S. Foreign Relations, PPC*, XII, pp. 419-421; Miller, *Diary*, VII, pp. 259-261; and letter from Nicholas Roosevelt to the author, August 8, 1956. For more on Brown's observations, see his "Foreign Relations of the Budapest Soviets in 1919: A Personal Narrative," *The Hungarian Quarterly*, III (1937), pp. 59-69. Brown suspected Kun was being guided directly by Lenin (Author's interview of Professor Brown, Williamstown, Massachusetts, September 10, 1958).

65. The text of this memorandum is in Baker, *Woodrow Wilson and World Settlement*, III, pp. 238-245. Bliss singled out General Berthelot as an agent of the Quai d'Orsay and accused Britain of being in league with France. Nicholas Roosevelt pardoned Bliss for his approval of the zone because the General did not realize the dangers involved (*A Front Row Seat*, p. 105). Bliss may have secured new information in March. His staff of cryptographers had succeeded in decoding Kun's cipher. See Herbert O. Yardley, *The Secret Service in America: The American Black Chamber*, pp. 161, 172.

66. Mantoux, I, pp. 52-57.

67. *Ibid.*

68. *U.S. Foreign Relations, PPC*, V, pp. 17-18; Mantoux, I, p. 99.

69. Macartney (*A History of Hungary*, I, p. 22) upholds this opinion. The Council disregarded an appeal from d'Esperey on April 4. He had pleaded for munitions for the Romanians because of the advance of the Red Army (Miller, *Diary*, XVII, pp. 518-519). The French evacuated Odessa on April 2; the Red Army took the city on April 6 (Azan, p. 245).

70. This view is given by Paul Birdsall, "The Second Decade of Peace Conference History," *Journal of Modern History*, XI (1939), p. 366.

71. *U.S. Foreign Relations, PPC*, V, p. 18; Mantoux, I, pp. 103-104.

72. Lenin ordered troops sent to Hungary in March, but had to recall them immediately because of Denikin's counterattack in the Ukraine. See Fischer, I, pp.

194-196; and Theodore H. Von Laue, "Soviet Diplomacy: G. V. Chicherin, People's Commissar for Foreign Affairs, 1918-1930," in Gordon A. Craig and Felix Gilbert (eds.), *The Diplomats, 1919-1939*, p. 238.

73. *Bulletin d'informations roumaines*, March 25 and April 9.

74. *U.S. Foreign Relations, PPC*, V, pp. 39-42, 59-61; and Mantoux, I, pp. 166, 179. Smuts led a sizeable caravan to Budapest: Leeper, Nicolson, Colonel Stephen Bonsal (House's interpreter who spoke Magyar), and Brigadier General Christopher Birdwood Thomson (the British attaché who had signed the military convention with Romania in August 1916).

75. Mantoux, I, p. 179. For accounts of this mission, see Thomson, pp. 110-111; Nicolson, *Peacemaking*, pp. 292-304; and Bonsal, *Unfinished Business*, pp. 75-143.

76. Calliope G. Caldis, *The Council of Four as a Joint Emergency Authority*, p. 110.

77. Alfred L.P. Dennis, *The Foreign Policies of Soviet Russia*, pp. 171-172.

78. Caldis, p. 114; Azan, p. 250; and Deák, p. 79.

79. Marghiloman, IV, p. 292.

80. *U.S. Foreign Relations, PPC*, VI, pp. 282-283; and Mantoux, II, pp. 369-370.

81. Mantoux, II, p. 370.

82. *Ibid.*

83. Day and Seymour were quick to acquire the art of give-and-take in international politics. It would seem that they could not induce Wilson to uphold his promise to the American delegation uttered on board the "George Washington" on December 10, 1918. The President advised his experts at that time to feel free to come straight to him with anything affecting a critical decision. "Tell me what's right and I'll fight for it," promised Wilson (Walworth, II, p. 219).

84. British experts gave way despite Lloyd George's famous "Fontainebleau Memorandum" of March 25 in which he criticized the assignment of a large Magyar element to Romania. He said ethnic criteria, rather than economic or strategic, should have precedence in determining the frontier (Lloyd George, *Memoirs*, I, pp. 267-269).

85. Crowe was not inclined to dispute Italian motives. He once suggested that, in order to secure a better line of communication for Romania, it would be better to sacrifice a few hundred thousand Magyars than to alienate Romania from the Allied camp (Lapradelle, *La paix de Versailles*, IX/1, p. 348).

86. Minutes, March 10 and 11. For more on the Italian proposals, see Attilio Tamaro, "Romania e Polonia di fronte agli Slavi," *Politica*, XIII (1922), pp. 70-91.

87. Minutes, March 11. See also Franco Vellani-Dionisi, *Il problema territorials transilvano*, pp. 68-69. Francesco Nitti, Orlando's successor, later criticized the dismemberment of Hungary in his *The Wreck of Europe* (Indianapolis: Bobbs-Merrill, 1922), pp. 165-166.

88. Conference on the Preliminaries of Peace, *Report No. 1 with Annexes*, presented to the Supreme Council by the Commission, April 6.

89. Central Territorial Commission, Procés-Verbaux, MSS, Nos. 10-13, April 9, 10, 12, 15, The National Archives.

90. Of the approximately 36,000 square miles of Transylvania and the adjacent comitats claimed by Romania, about 32,000 square miles were awarded. Of the 2½ million Romanians in this region, Romania would incorporate 2,300,000. If Brătianu's claim had been satisfied, Romania would have acquired over 2 million Magyars; the award gave her 1½ million.

91. My use of the name "Serbia" in this study is not intended to deny the existence of the Kingdom of Serbs-Croats-Slovenes (Yugoslavia). I have followed the practice of the Peace Conference in referring to that succession state as "Serbia."

92. Minutes, February 13. Crowe remarked that if the Banat dispute had been between Hungary and Romania, he would uphold the latter's claim to the entire province because Hungary was an enemy state. Original British recommendations were quite harsh. If both Serbs and Romanians became intransigent over partition, the British proposed, the northwest corner of the Banat, inhabited by a Magyar majority, should be given to Hungary, the Serbs warned of Romanian irredentism in the Timok valley, and the Romanians advised of a plan to restore southern Dobrodgea to Bulgaria. A copy of this British program is in the House Papers.

93. Minutes, February 22. For praise of Brătianu's presentation, see George I. Brătianu, *Origines*, p. 306. A critical view is in Deák, p. 47. Brătianu's alienation of the Serbs is criticized in Tilea, p. 139.

94. Cvijić had considerable reputation as an expert on Balkan ethnography. His influential study, *Le péninsule balkanique: géographie humaine*, was a

reference guide at the peace conference. De Martonne had been advised by Cvijić in preparing French recommendations. Cvijić convinced him of the value of religious statistics in correcting Hungarian censuses (Transcript of conversation between Cvijić and Johnson, May 26, 1918, The National Archives).

Cvijić had apparently disavowed his pre-war opinion that the Danube would be a satisfactory frontier with Romania (Lederer, p. 364).

95. Minutes, February 25; and *U.S. Foreign Relations, PPC,* IV, p. 47. Vesnić had changed his views since 1915 when he wrote in *Les Annales des Nationalités* (under the pseudonym "P. P. de Sokolovich") that the Serbs "are the neighbors and friends of the Romanians who, with the south Slavs and Italians, will form an unbreakable barrier to new German pushes toward the East" (IV, No. 3). He admired Ionescu's conciliatory policy toward the Banat and an alliance with Serbia ("Les rapports serbo-roumains", *Revue des Sciences Politiques,* XXXVII [1917], p. 390).

Pecić served with the Serbian force under General Zhivković in Dobrodgea in the fall of 1916. That group was composed of deserters from Austro-Hungarian armies who refused to fight for Romania after the 1916 Alliance, giving the entire Banat to Romania, became known (Temperley, IV, pp. 184-185).

96. Briefs Nos. 1255, 1572, and Reports Nos. 101-108, Moon Papers.

97. Minutes, February 28 and March 7; and Miller, *Diary*, XVII, p.95. De Martonne joined the Commission on March 7.

98. Minutes, March 18. The partition is detailed in *Report No. 1.* Serbia received two-thirds of what she claimed. See the official Serbian brochure, *Delimitation between the Serbs and the Roumanians*, deposited with the peace conference.

99. *Report No.1*; Temperley, IV, p. 228. Bucovina was a crazy-quilt of nationalities. In addition to Romanians and Ruthenians, the province contained Jews, Germans, Hutzuli (considered to be remnants of the Scythians), Magyars, Poles, Lipovans, Armenians, and Gypsies.

100. Minutes, February 22. The Ukrainian nationalists held a conference in Lemberg (Lvov) on October 18, 1918, constituted an assembly demanding the union of all Ukrainians (Ruthenians), and protested the proposed allotment of Maramureş to Romania (Memorandum from Sydorenko, chairman of the Ukrainian Delegation, to Clemenceau, February 21, 1919, in Miller, *Diary*, XVII, p. 161).

101. Minutes, March 11.

102. Beneš claimed Maramureş in his testimony before the Supreme Council on February 5. He hoped for a common frontier with Romania *(U.S. Foreign Relations, PPC,* III, p. 886). For recommendations of the Czech Commission

(Jules Cambon, Laroche, LeRond, Raggi, Crowe, Nicolson, Seymour, Allen W. Dulles, and Johnson), see Lapradelle, *La paix de Versailles,* IX/1, p. 151; and Miller, *Diary*, XVII, p. 94.

103. *Report No. 1.*

104. For a British defense of the Commission's decision, see Harold W.V. Temperley, "How the Hungarian Frontiers Were Drawn," *Foreign Affairs,* VI (1928), pp. 432-447. He wrote that "the argument about violation of racial or ethnic principles is really misleading. No one denied that violation at the time. What the Allies said was that in this case economic necessity was a more compelling force than ethnic justice" (p. 440).

105. Minutes, March 3 and 10.

106. *Report No. 1.*

107. Edward M. House and Charles Seymour (eds.), *What Really Happened at Paris,* pp. 106-107.

Chapter IV

BRĂTIANU'S OPPOSITION TO
THE FRONTIERS

"What a damned fool!"

— Lloyd George, May 31[1]

The Delay in Approving the New Frontiers

Recommendations of the Commission, approved by the Central Territorial Commission, were submitted to the Council of Foreign Ministers on May 8, one month after the experts had completed their work. Lansing blocked unanimous acceptance of the report by objecting to the award of Bessarabia, even though the American experts had favored it. He insisted upon making no changes in Russian territory without the consent of a recognized Russian government, and he repeated Wilson's observation earlier in the day in regard to a possible recognition of the "White" régime of Kolchak as the legally qualified government to represent Russia at the peace conference. Kolchak wished to preserve the territorial integrity of Russia, but was willing to permit a plebiscite in Bessarabia to determine whether its inhabitants preferred Russian or Romanian rule. It was clear that a *modus vivendi* with Kolchak would jeopardize Romania's occupation of the province.[2] Lansing insisted that "the Peace Conference cannot adjudicate on territory belonging to a state with whom the Powers represented were not at war."[3]

Lansing criticized the Commission's disregard of the true ethnic boundary between Hungary and Romania. Tardieu explained an ethnic line would sever railway communications essential for Romania's economy and defense. Lansing's retort was that in every case "the decision seemed to have been given against the Hungarians." But after

Tardieu reminded him that Romania, not Hungary, was an allied state, Lansing agreed to support the Commission's recommendations. Balfour refused to examine the recommendations in detail and so he proposed immediate acceptance. Sonnino and Pichon concurred and the frontier between Hungary and Romania was approved without reservations. It was decided to postpone discussion of Romania's other frontiers until a later date.[4]

Four days later (May 12) the Council of Four hastily concurred in the approval of the Romanian-Hungarian frontier. Sonnino, substituting for Orlando, at first revived objections of his experts to lack of direct railway connection between Romania and Poland, but he was overruled by the impatience of Clemenceau, Lloyd George, and Wilson to dispense with a re-examination of the recommendations.[5] The Council ruled that all of Romania's frontiers be approved by June 2, the day the Austrian delegation was due to arrive in Paris to receive its treaty.

The Foreign Ministers next undertook an examination of the recommendations for Bucovina and southern Dobrodgea (May 14). Lansing and the American experts did not attend that session. Henry White substituted for Lansing, and since he was unfamiliar with American opinions, Laroche was not corrected when he explained the Commission did not feel competent to deal with "the ancient frontier" between Romania and Bulgaria.[6] When Sonnino inquired if that was the unanimous view of the experts, Laroche replied affirmatively, thus misrepresenting American proposals for a rectification of the boundary. He also concealed another American view, already accepted by the Commission, when he asked the ministers to approve a common Polish-Romanian frontier in Bucovina. Laroche convinced the ministers that the creation of a free Ruthenian state in Eastern Galicia was unlikely. Thus the American recommendation to deny Romania a portion of the northern Bucovina was overruled by the Foreign Ministers.[7]

Discussion of southern Dobrodgea was continued on May 16 when Clive Day accompanied Henry White to the Council of Foreign Ministers. Both raised the question of retrocession, but Tardieu insisted "it was difficult to ask an allied country after a victorious war to yield to an enemy state territory which it had possessed before the war." The two Americans still urged consideration of the proposed American line. Balfour and Pichon suggested an appeal be made to Romania to offer a modification in the interests of peace, but Sonnino saw little hope that Brătianu would negotiate with Bulgaria. Tardieu revealed that Brătianu might have yielded if Bulgaria, in turn, had ceded territory in Macedonia to Serbia, who would have surrendered the entire Banat. But such a swap was now impossible, stated Tardieu. Pichon moved to adopt the present frontier, but Sonnino suggested the American proposal "be leaked out unofficially" so that a less pointed intimation induce Brătianu to negotiate on his own initiative.[8]

Tardieu opposed Sonnino's stratagem as taking unfair advantage of Romania, whose "frontier in Bessarabia had been left undecided by reason of Mr. Lansing's remark that this frontier could not be decided in the absence of Russia," and whose Banat boundary was still unsettled. After Sonnino proposed that the Council of Four settle the question of recognizing Kolchak, the Foreign Ministers agreed to postpone further discussions of Romania's frontier.[9]

Although the Foreign Ministers failed to adopt Sonnino's stratagem, it appears the Romanians became cognizant of it. Newspapers in Bucharest reported on May 17 that the Conference proposed to have Pichon act as mediator of boundary disputes between Romania, Bulgaria, and Serbia, and that Trumbić was ready to yield in the Banat in exchange for satisfaction in Fiume and a close alliance with Romania.[10] L'Independance Roumaine, official organ of the National Liberal Party, condemned Allied suggestions that Romania yield to Bulgaria.[11] At the same time, Brătianu again threatened to resign if the Allies continued to treat him disdainfully.[12] These reactions to a possible compromise did not deter the Allies from reviving a similar barter proposal at a later date.

The month of May elapsed before the Allies realized the consequences of their failure to inform Brătianu that his frontier with Hungary had been approved by the Council of Four on May 12. By adhering to their rule to divulge official decisions only at plenary sessions, the Allies neglected to disclose the nature of the new frontier. This inexcusable reticence strengthened Brătianu's subsequent argument that he did not know in May the nature of his boundary and, for that reason, intended to stake out his own.

Brătianu's Independent Course of Action

The Romanian army encamped on the western bank of the Tisa about eighty miles from Budapest increased tension to alarming proportions. The inter-Allied Commission on Repatriation of Prisoners of War, operating in Hungary, reported that an all-out war between Romania and Hungary was imminent. Observers visiting Bucharest noted Romania was requisitioning all available food, clothing, medicines, shoes, and transportation equipment, and recruiting Romanians of Transylvania for a full-scale war on Hungary. Posters in Hungary showed the pre-war Kingdom cut into several parts, each representing a lost province. Every poster carried the admonition "Nem! Nem! Soha!" ("No! No! Never!"). Anti-Romanian propaganda printed in Budapest was being distributed to Romanian prisoners of war as trains carrying them from Germany crossed Hungary into Romania.[13]

Rumors reached Paris of a Romanian effort to organize an anti-communist régime at Arad. A counter-revolutionary government of Magyar "Whites" allegedly included Count Gyula Károlyi, Count Paul Teleki, Admiral Nicholas Horthy, and Count Stephen Bethlen.[14] These rumors were confirmed by agents of the American Relief Administration, who also cited Italy's malefactions in simultaneously releasing Romanian prisoners of war for return home to serve in an anti-Hungarian campaign, and selling munitions to Béla Kun so that he would attack Serbia.[15]

General d'Esperey warned Clemenceau of the deteriorating situation and of his inability to restrain the disputatious states.[16] His warning coincided with Kun's appeal to the workers of Romania to sabotage the planned invasion of Hungary. Romania retaliated by publicizing a message from Brătianu indicating that the Allies had requested him to take appropriate measures against Magyar communism. The Bucharest press explained that since "the Allies are preparing to occupy and bring order into Germany," it was only logical that the East Central European states should do likewise in Hungary to "spare the Great Powers the burden of a further occupation."[17] Romanian police announced the capture of a courier carrying Lenin's plan for a joint Russo-Magyar invasion of Romania and the establishment of a Bolshevik régime in Bucharest.[18]

If doubts about the gravity of the situation existed in Paris, the reaction of Russia to Romanian provocations should have dispelled them. Chicherin warned Romania to terminate her anti-communist activities in Bessarabia and on the Tisa. Rakovskii, leader of the Ukrainian Bolsheviks, likewise issued a warning.[19] Warnings were also directed at Poland whose delegate, Roman Dmowski, had referred to Romania as the only allied state in East Central Europe willing to assist Poland in suppressing Bolshevism.[20] The Council of Four apparently expected that a Polish-Romanian accord to block Kun's attempt to secure a breakthrough to the Ukraine would be concluded. Reports of the French sending large quantities of ammunition to the Poles and Romanians, and the formal request of the two states to purchase stocks of war matériel in Germany, intensified the anxiety of the Allied leaders.[21] When Brătianu sought permission from Colonel House to recruit a legion of Romanian-Americans to assist in stemming the Bolshevik tide, House replied (May 5) that "the time was not opportune for such an act. " [22]

Impatient at Allied indecision, Brătianu served an armistice ultimatum upon Béla Kun on May 6, demanding that he demobilize, surrender all war matériel, yield railway equipment, return prisoners of war, provide hostages, and desist from further provocations.[23] When Kun refused to comply, the Romanians advanced beyond Szolnok and the Czechs joined the march toward Budapest by moving their troops to within thirty miles of the capital. The French military mission in Vienna ordered Kun to resign or face the consequence of an occupation of Budapest by Romanian and Czech troops.[24]

Romania's issuance of armistice terms and the apparent intention to march on Budapest, with the approval of the French General Staff, violated the terms and limits of the neutral zone. Brătianu was preempting the privilege of dictating a new truce to Hungary. The press in Bucharest clamored for an occupation of all Hungary. Ioan Duca, a member of Brătianu's cabinet, was quoted as saying that mere treaties could not promise permanent peace. Marghiloman said Romania had nothing to fear from Hungary because the "Romanians were much more numerous than Magyars." An editorial called upon Brătianu to

> follow the example of Italy. Did Italy wait for the Conference's decision before claiming Fiume? Did the Serbs wait before settling in the Banat? The Romanian army should enter Hungary and the Banat whatever the consequences. Enough of diplomatic lamentations! The I.O.U. signed by the Allies in 1916 shall be taken to Hungary and the Banat on the point of a bayonet, not in a diplomatic pouch.[25]

Another article appearing in a pro-Ionescu newspaper called for the formation of a war government to defend the maximum claims:

> Brătianu understood that the only way to prevent the thwarting of Romania's integral claims was to create accomplished

facts. Consequently, he gave his cabinet certain required instructions. If his conduct in Paris meets with absolute opposition there, he should withdraw from the Conference and from the cabinet. It will be for a national government to solve the problem.[26]

Iorga published the recommendations of the Territorial Commission, which were quite accurate, in an effort to rouse opinion against denial of Romania's maximum claims.[27]

Brătianu released his angry impatience in an interview given on May 16 to a Paris newspaper. He castigated the Allies for refusing to admit him to equal membership in the Supreme Council, reviewed the "miserable record" of broken promises, cited the looting of his home in Bucharest and the burning of his estate at Predeal by the Germans, attacked the Allied plan to present his reparations bill to a commission rather than to the enemy directly, and accused the Allies of ingratitude in refusing to admit that "without our armies, Moscow and Budapest would have joined hands and reached Vienna." He demanded Romania be compensated for "having saved Salonika, decongested Verdun, and stopped Bolshevism," and be permitted to restore order "in the middle of the convulsed East." He concluded that "it seems... that the Big Four do not have a clear conception, since neither financially nor geographically will the treaty of peace bring us our due rewards."[28]

Provocations continued in Romania. The royal family visited the headquarters of General Mărdărescu, commander of the army in eastern Hungary, and toured the front as far south as Békés-Csaba.[29] This trip coincided with a statement attributed to d'Esperey, who visited Mărdărescu on May 19, announcing he had "come to lead the Romanians... and expected to be in Budapest in two or three weeks."[30] A week later, in Bucharest, General Berthelot was honored with a gala banquet as he prepared to return home, and he was hailed as making possible Romania's position equal to that of the Great Powers.[31]

These developments presaging a march on Budapest came to the attention of the Big Four on May 19. Wilson had been informed by the Coolidge Mission that Romania had served the armistice ultimatum on Kun, that Romanian officers expected "to go on to Budapest to get rid of a bad neighbor," and that they were delaying only because of lack of arms. Coolidge appealed for the dispatch of an inter-Allied army to Budapest to thwart Romanian plans.[32] Wilson advised the Council that Romania's actions were unwarranted because the question of "whether or not Kun's regime might yet benefit the Magyars" still remained. He believed Kun was exercising a moderating influence, but the "advance of the Romanians... has tied his hands by making it impossible to meet with the more moderate elements and, when the Romanians stopped, the result of that temporary victory... had been a renewal of terrorism." Wilson expected Kun was ready to obey the orders of the Allies.[33] Clemenceau refused to order French troops, the only available Allied force in Hungary, to occupy Budapest without accompanying British, American, and Italian soldiers. He was prepared to accept Romania's offer to assist the French if the Allies refused to cooperate, and he noted that Wilson's proposal was the same as that offered by d'Esperey, who had for months wanted to occupy Budapest, a request which had always been denied. Wilson feared the presence of Romanians in Budapest would rouse hostility and so he promised provisionally to provide American troops rather than authorize the Romanians to move on Budapest.[34]

As a stop-gap measure the Council of Four instructed the Supreme Economic Council to cease shipments of food to Romania if her aggressive policies continued.[35] The French General Staff advised against this measure which would weaken the only allied state capable of stopping the spread of Bolshevism. This opinion was shared by the Allied military advisers, with whom General Bliss agreed that Romania must have defense resources. The military advisers proposed that Romania's military activities be supervised, but she should not be required to disarm or demobilize. It was recommended that Romania be authorized to maintain a well-equipped army of 60,000 on active duty.[36]

Wilson suggested (May 23) acceptance of the advice of the military advisers, but Lloyd George disagreed because Romania would be allowed to have a large army while other allied states were demobilizing. He feared Romania might turn on other small powers. As a result of the Council's indecision, based on the belief Romania would not dare to move on Budapest, the Foreign Ministers were not furnished the lead they had requested before continuing their examination of the frontiers. Pursuing a contradictory policy, the Big Four at one moment appeared ready to penalize Romania and, at another, make possible her advance toward Budapest. Brătianu's wailing about the Bolshevik menace seemed to have drowned out the cries of the Magyars over the loss of their lands.[37]

Brătianu Defies the Council

The Council of Foreign Ministers resumed examination of the frontiers on May 23. After discussing the boundary in Bucovina, the Ministers agreed to accept the American recommendation which called for the award of a strip in the north to the Allied Powers for future disposition. In the absence of an independent Ruthenian state, which could absorb the strip, the Allies would have to supervise it until the final award. Romania stood to lose 18 per cent of Bucovina if this decision were maintained.[38]

The Ministers then turned to the Banat dispute. Lansing revived the question of a swap, this time intimating that Romania retrocede southern Dobrodgea in exchange for satisfaction in the Banat. The French again objected, but Lansing could not be swayed. He stubbornly refused to approve the Commission's recommendations until Romania indicated a willingness to concede something to Bulgaria. After considerable debate, Lansing yielded and accepted the Banat partition in exchange for an understanding that the Dobrodgea question be examined at a later date.[39]

Lansing's obstructionism was attributable to his determination to revise certain recommendations so as to make American opinions dominant in the final report to the Big Four. The American experts had anticipated the Commission's proposals would be carefully scrutinized by higher authorities. But Lansing's colleagues, who were less interested in Bulgaria than in other enemy states and anxious to treat more important problems, questioned his motives, wondering if the lavish educational and philanthropic benefits conferred on Bulgaria by American missionary organizations had influenced him. The American position in regard to southern Dobrodgea was likened to Germany's successful bid to Bulgaria in September 1915, by which Sofia was lured into war with an offer of recovering the region as well as getting territory from Serbia.[40] The French consistently opposed any scheme which could establish the precedent of having an allied state yield territory to any enemy in order to obtain land in another area.[41]

Sonnino's solution of urging Brătianu to negotiate with Bulgaria would have fallen on deaf ears because the Premier had just rebuffed all compromises with Serbia, an allied state. It is conjectural if Brătianu ever really offered a rectification of his frontier with Bulgaria in view of his declaration as far back as 1908 that Romania must acquire a defensible frontier with Bulgaria, entailing the incorporation of southern Dobrodgea.[42]

Lansing's intransigence delayed a final decision on all of Romania's frontiers. This caused a critical postponement of the Big Four's approval of the new boundaries. A general understanding had been reached in Paris to approve delimitations only insofar as they affected each treaty. The German treaty had already been presented to the Germans on May 7. Austria's treaty was completed insofar as her new frontiers were concerned. In regard to Romania, most of her new territories would be outlined in the treaty for Hungary. Since there did not appear any immediate likelihood of presenting a treaty to Béla Kun, the Big Four were not in any hurry to examine Hungary's new frontiers until a recognized government was established in Budapest. Their failure to approve the recommendations and publicize them enabled Brătianu to challenge the Council's authority to delimit frontiers, since the Big Four did not and apparently could not enforce them.[43]

An opportunity to express his indignation came to Brătianu on May 29 at the seventh plenary session called to hear Clemenceau describe the Austrian treaty. The famous "revolt of the small powers" occurred at this gathering.[44] When asked by Clemenceau to approve the treaty by acclamation, since the Austrian delegation was due to receive it on June 2, Brătianu, acting as spokesman of the small powers, demanded the right to examine the treaty before voting for adoption.[45] He requested the right

> to ascertain what they [the terms] are and to examine them before concurring in them, for, as in the case of the text communicated to the Germans, an oral statement necessarily cannot make everything sufficiently clear. Even now, if the text were read out, we should need time for reflection in order to be in a position to study the effects on each of our states.[46]

The Big Four permitted the disgruntled small powers forty-eight hours in which to study the treaty.

When the plenary session reconvened on May 31, Brătianu presented several amendments to the treaty. He asserted that since Romania was defending Europe against Bolshevism "in a war which had not yet approached its end," he could not accept a frontier in Bucovina denying him a common boundary with the Poles in Eastern Galicia. His most vigorous attack, however, was on an article requiring Romania to accept in advance the principle of a treaty for the protection of minorities in Romania. Article 60 stated that Romania would sign a minority treaty with the Allied Powers according to which she would undertake to provide specific guarantees to non-Romanians in the Kingdom and annexed territories. Brătianu challenged the authority of the Supreme Council to interfere in his domestic affairs.[47] He considered the imposition of such a treaty as dangerous a precedent as the denial of Romania's right to her maximum claims. Romania, he declared, would consent to any principle in the Covenant of the League of Nations designed to protect minorities in all member states, but he refused to accept any special arrangement to which other allied states were not bound.[48]

Responding to Brătianu's charge that the Council had acted in bad faith, Clemenceau warned him that "we are unable to guarantee any portions of territory other than those which we have ourselves assigned, and... it is impossible for us to guarantee others."[49] The French leader acquainted Brătianu with the Allied decision to impose a minority treaty because Romania had failed to carry out similar provisions in the Treaty of Berlin (1878). He tried to convince Brătianu of the Allied intention to draft a treaty which would not interfere with Romania's internal affairs, but he blundered in remarking that "in the matter of minorities, everyone's history had not been quite the same."[50] This insinuation was an undeniable reference to the ill-treatment of Jews in Romania, and it led Brătianu to accuse the Allies of segregating nations into classes differing in sovereignty. He refused to abide by this distinction because Romania, although willing to accept advice, would not tolerate any intervention in her internal affairs.

The delegates of Poland, Serbia, and Czechoslovakia voiced less opposition to the minority treaty system. Each state was due to receive such a treaty, but none interpreted it as foreign intervention. Brătianu, therefore, stood alone in his criticism of the proposed treaty.[51]

In an effort to calm Brătianu, Wilson advised him, in an address that is still quoted, that the Allies did not intend to play an arbitrary role or exercise any undue influence in the matter of minority rights. Military action by the Allies had won for the small powers their independence and additions of territory, whose distribution was being made "according to the racial and ethnographical character of the people inhabiting them." The Allies were now required to safeguard territorial adjustments even though small states were questioning their authority to do so. It would be impossible for the Allies, "who were friends, not dictators," to guarantee territorial settlements which were not right and in which disturbing elements remained to threaten peace.

Oppression of minorities, more than any other factor, would cause serious unrest. The Allies were therefore obliged to demand just and adequate guarantees for maltreated peoples. Wilson insisted there was no distinction between non-Romanians within the Kingdom and those in the new territories when the question of minority rights arose. He asserted he could not return home to report to the American people that the peace settlement was not permanent just because certain allied states refused to abide by the treaties. No state, he warned, could expect the United States to send armies back to Europe to enforce the settlement. For that reason the peace must be permanent.[52] Since Brătianu was seeking the Council's sanction, for great additions of territory which "come to Romania by the common victory of arms," the Allies were therefore entitled to demand certain guarantees from Romania before approving those additions. Any dream of small states to revise territorial settlements after the Peace Conference adjourned was held to be a dangerous idea. Wilson appealed for general acceptance of the Council's decisions; he said he would find them acceptable if he were the delegate of a small power.

Brătianu prefaced his response with a reference to the "eminent personality of the American President whose words and advice had a specially authoritative character," but whose analysis of the situation was inaccurate.[53] He reminded Wilson that the Conference, by virtue of its acceptance of the League Covenant, had conferred equality of rights upon both great and small powers. Romania's representative on the League Commission, of which Wilson was chairman, had proposed insertion of a clause requiring member states to guarantee rights to their minorities. Wilson, Brătianu asserted, could corroborate that if he wished to acknowledge that "certain Great Powers" had compelled him to exclude such an article from the Covenant.[54] Since the Great Powers, including Italy, would not be required to abide by any general minority guarantees in the Covenant and, since no Great Power would be asked to submit to a minority treaty, Romania refused to be treated differently. He also noted that Germany, an enemy state, had not been compelled to accept a minority treaty.[55]

After paying tribute to the lofty principles inspiring the Big Four, Brătianu intimated that, since they would not hold political office forever, their successors might deviate from present policy and perhaps pursue less honorable interests. Wilson's assertion that American troops would not return to enforce peace placed Romania in an isolated position, compelling her "to provide with her own troops for the defense of not only her own frontiers, but also of a cause which is a matter of concern for the whole of Central Europe." If Romania accepted a minority treaty, she "would no longer preserve... the independence... enjoyed in the past for the settlement of her domestic concerns."[56]

Brătianu's defiance failed to net the desired results. The Big Four rejected his demand for changes in the Austrian treaty. Lloyd George could not comprehend Brătianu's ingratitude when the Allies were about to double the extent of Romanian territory, and he agreed with Clemenceau's observation that Romania's performance in the war was not responsible for her recent growth, and that part of Romania would have been lost forever if the Central Powers had won. Brătianu did not hear these remarks because the Big Four had adjourned the plenary session after his last statement. Nor did he learn that day (May 31) of the Council's decision to prohibit him from occupying Budapest. Clemenceau was instructed to inform him of this injunction.[57]

The Council Tries to Restrain Brătianu

After deciding to forbid his seizure of Budapest, the Big Four anticipated Brătianu would demand specific assurances that the Allies would prevent Béla Kun from recovering territories assigned to Romania. They agreed to discuss this with Brătianu and delegates of other small powers who feared Kun might regain lost lands. Wilson believed the small powers were "out for fighting and for what they could get," and he wished to frustrate a joint campaign against Hungary by requiring the small powers to disarm and demobilize. Clemenceau pointed out that the small powers could not be expected to do so as long as Kun remained in power.[58]

Wilson's project was discussed with the small power delegates on June 5. Brătianu learned he had to accept 60,000 as the maximum number of troops he could have on active duty as of January 1, 1921. He again inveighed against the Council's disregard of the principle of equality of nations, could not be convinced the Hungarian crisis would be resolved by that date, and reminded the Council that Romania was faced with the problem of defending frontiers which had not yet been traced. "It is very well to disarm the gendarmes, but on condition of having previously disarmed the brigands," was his reference to the threat of Bolshevism on Romania's frontiers with Russia and Hungary. He denied plans to march on Budapest.[59]

The small powers rejected all disarmament and demobilization proposals. Obtaining no guarantee they would not march on Budapest and with no available Allied forces to stop them, the Big Four resorted to the only possible alternative. They decided to warn Béla Kun to cease his aggressive acts, hoping he would obey and thus assist in solving the crisis. Orlando was asked to consult with Brătianu to make sure he desisted from provoking Hungary. The Italian leader reported back that Brătianu acted like a madman when told to comply and threatened to resign rather than submit to interference by the Allies in his private business.[60]

Brătianu's warnings did not deter the Council from accepting at face value Kun's reply that he would restrain his troops if those of Romania were held back. The Allies decided that Romania, not Hungary, was guilty of direct aggression. On June 9 Wilson and Lloyd George accused Brătianu of provoking the Magyars into rallying around Kun because the communist leader had promised them recovery of lost lands. Lloyd George reported many "aristocratic officers" of the Royal Hungarian Army had enlisted in Kun's defense of Hungarian integrity against Romania, whose Premier had "merely snapped his fingers" at the Council's injunction. He urged cessation of all military supplies to Romania, which, he revealed, Britain had already suspended, and called for just treatment of the Magyars "who were only defending their country." The Prime Minister believed the "greatest part of our difficulties comes from states which are our friends and who refuse to follow instructions." Romania had always asked the Allies to come to her aid, but she was now a "brigand looking for a chance to steal territory."[61] Wilson was convinced the Romanians would never evacuate any territory they had occupied. Both proposed dismissing Romania from the Peace Conference, but Clemenceau and Orlando convinced them to permit Brătianu to explain his case before taking such action.

Brătianu appeared before the Council on June 10.[62] Wilson outlined the Council's position in a tone far different from the soothing words he had uttered at the plenary session. The Allies, he said, were troubled by the military situation in Hungary where, according to Béla Kun, Romanian troops were encroaching upon territory inhabited by Magyar majorities. Romania had violated the limits of the neutral zone, and provocations had enabled Kun to seize power and gain the sympathy of the upper classes. By occupying territory left in Hungary by the Territorial Commission, Brătianu was jeopardizing a fair partition of the Habsburg Monarchy.

The Premier replied that Wilson was "not correctly informed about the role of the Romanian army or about Hungarian provocations." The armistice had left in Hungary most of the Romanian-inhabited regions which he claimed, Károlyi had incited a movement to devastate those regions, Magyar Bolsheviks had assisted Károlyi in this project, Romania had respected the neutral zone until Kun attacked on April 10 and compelled the Romanians to retaliate, and there was "a battle and the Romanians stopped on the Tisa," which was the "only decent military line of defense." Béla Kun seized power with Károlyi's connivance when Romania was willing to march on Budapest to restore order "in a sentiment of solidarity with the Allies," but the Allies were creating the impression that Hungary was not an enemy state and the Magyars not a defeated people. Peace between Hungary and Romania, he predicted, would be unattainable if the Allies treated the Magyars as friends.

In response to questions about his military operations, Brătianu said he had halted the advance "and we have not moved since," in deference to the injunction issued by the Council on May 31. But he warned of his intention to permit the Bolshevik movement to ferment freely in Budapest if the Allies preferred that to an all-out elimination of Hungarian radicalism. He would keep his troops on the Tisa and continue to occupy the city of Debreczen, which he admitted was purely Magyar, because its inhabitants had greeted Romanian soldiers as liberators. He revealed that King Ferdinand, who recently inspected the region, had "everywhere received the thanks of representatives of all social classes which felicitated the Romanians for having delivered them from anarchy." When asked about rumors of his having sponsored the formation of an anti-communist regime at Szeged, Brătianu replied he had been approached by individuals for this purpose, but had rebuffed their advances.[63]

At this point Lloyd George asked if he had received official word about the frontiers assigned to Romania. Brătianu said he knew nothing about them; to him the armistice line and the boundaries of the 1916 Alliance were all that mattered. He admitted having read press accounts of the Commission's recommendations, but he had received no notice from the Council.[64] This confession of ignorance did not convince Lloyd George who warned him to evacuate purely Magyar territory, including Debreczen, if he did not wish to see a strengthening of Bolshevism in Hungary. Brătianu claimed his troops were in Debreczen by right of strategic necessity. Replying to Lloyd George's charge that Károlyi had not sponsored the rise of Kun, the Premier rejoined that "there were answers to some questions that we know better than you because we are nearer." He accused the German army of sowing seeds of Bolshevism in its retreat across Hungary, told how Rakovskii masterminded the Bolshevik coup d'état in Budapest to link Hungary with Russia, with Romania as the doormat, and accused the German Social Democrats of financing the whole plot.[65]

Wilson discounted these wild accusations by crediting the spread of Bolshevism to discontent among inhabitants of all enemy states. He called for a removal of this dissatisfaction by using methods instituted in the United States where the anarchistic activities of the Industrial Workers of the World were subdued by legislative redress of labor grievances. When worker discontent was eased, sabotage activities of that organization ceased. Wilson apologized to Brătianu for the failure to inform him of the Commission's recommendations, but his regrets were followed by these strong words:

> Whatever the strategic reasons, the Romanian armies do not have the right today to be on the Tisa. That is contrary to the armistice terms and the state of things now is a provocation against Hungary.... So long as the Romanian troops remained on the Tisa they were helping to create Bolshevism in Hungary, even more than propaganda would.... I was convinced that it was necessary to fix the frontiers and to respect them. Otherwise, we will not have reached a solution. When we convince the Hungarians that the frontier, once fixed, will not be violated, Bolshevism will be weakened and will approach its end.... The Romanian army does not have the right to be on purely Hungarian ground.... If I were Hungarian, and I am happy not to be, I would be the first to take up arms for the defense of my country.

Wilson's remonstrance forced Brătianu to retreat into promising to evacuate eastern Hungary after Kun's aggressive policies ceased. He pointed out that the occupied territory should not be confused with the regions he claimed, that his troops were on the Tisa for security reasons just as the Allies had temporarily occupied the Rhineland for the same reason, and that the Magyars must be convinced they were a defeated nation.

After Brătianu withdrew, the Council decided to send an ultimatum to Hungary requiring observance of the new frontiers and to instruct Brătianu to evacuate his troops east of the new frontier. Kun was to make the first move lest the impression be given that allied states were retreating in the face of opposition. Brătianu was then recalled to the room to hear Wilson's plan which had been accepted:

> We wish to be in complete accord with you in view of a practical solution and here are our conclusions. The armistice lines and the temporary conventions have not been satisfactory. We are going to ask our Ministers of Foreign Affairs to receive you as soon as possible and to arrive at a definitive decision on the frontier... between Hungary and Romania.... As soon as this is done... we hope that you will respect this frontier and withdraw your troops behind it. On that will depend the assistance that the Powers will give you.

Brătianu considered this solution reasonable, but "he preferred to see how its execution could be guaranteed."[66]

After having informed Brătianu of their objections to his activities, the Allies should have realized they possessed no power to enforce their plan to restrain Romania. Wilson's project contained no indication of an Allied army intervening in the crisis. Thus the restraining order was as useless as the neutral zone had been and as futile as the injunction of May 31 was in stopping Brătianu. It was certainly clear to Brătianu that the Allies lacked military strength to intervene and impose the frontier if his reaction to their veto of his march on Budapest, as reported by Saint-Aulaire, may be cited as evidence, namely, he put the prohibition in his pocket and meditated, "and now we will enter Budapest."[67]

The Council considered Brătianu's "intransigent temper and voracious appetite" sufficient cause to take preventive action.[68] Such a reaction was reasonable, but the Allied leaders unwittingly permitted their intense disgust with Brătianu to obscure a valid reason for his latest tergiversation. They did not see that negotiations with Kun had aroused in him the old fear which beset him during the drafting of the 1916 Alliance. That Hungary might secure a separate peace and, consequently, retain her territorial integrity were fears that still haunted Brătianu. He considered the war between Romania and Hungary, begun on August 27, 1916, still in progress because his government was not a signatory to the Belgrade armistice. Romania did not declare war on Hungary for the second time in November 1918, as she did on Germany for the first time on November 10, 1918. Brătianu was determined to carry out his Alliance obligation to march on Budapest and as far as Timişoara. The Belgrade armistice and ensuing injunctions had temporarily frustrated his plans. He once told the Big Four of his disdain for d'Esperey who failed to consider Romania's interests when negotiating that truce. D'Esperey was, in his opinion, an officer who knew almost nothing about the military and political situations in East Central Europe.[69]

Brătianu had failed to impose his own armistice on Hungary. Allied interference, more than Kun's reaction to his proposed truce of May 6, had emboldened Brătianu's defiance to the Council's pro-Magyar, and hence anti-Romanian, policy. As long as Kun's proclamations spoke of the Allied intention to recognize his government and, consequently, restore Hungary's lost provinces, boastings which the Council did nothing to refute, Brătianu could not share the conviction of the Allies that Kun's provocations would cease if Hungary were not molested.[70]

The Big Four Approve Romania's Frontiers

As Wilson promised, the Foreign Ministers presented Brătianu with the report of the Commission on June 11. The Premier raised strong objections to what he termed a wholesale disavowal of the 1916 Alliance, demanded to see the minutes of the Commission's sessions so that he could find some justification for the recommendations, and deemed it necessary for his government to decide upon acceptance or rejection since the Allies had obviously repudiated the Alliance to which Romania was still committed.[71]

When urged by the Ministers to withdraw his demand for ample time to consult Bucharest, a delay which could have serious consequences, Brătianu refused to accede. His specific criticisms of the frontier with Hungary included the tracing of a line east of the one in the Alliance, retention by Hungary of railway lines and junctions essential for Romanian defenses, the prospect of Romanian trains required to traverse Hungary before reaching Czechoslovakia, and the failure to trace a common Romanian-Czechoslovakian frontier deemed necessary to cut Hungary's contacts with Russia.[72]

The Ministers instructed Tardieu to furnish Brătianu with a synopsis of the minutes in the hope he would comply at once. In return for the privilege to learn why Romania had been treated unfavorably, the Premier promised to secure a decision from Bucharest within a week if the Allies would consider the frontier to be only temporary. Lansing opposed Brătianu's device of increasing demands whenever he was compelled to concede a point. He informed Brătianu that the Big

Four had approved the frontier with Hungary on May 12 and their decision could not be revised unless deemed advisable. Brătianu was quick to grasp Lansing's unguarded admission that the Allies were not infallible. He called upon the Big Four to hear his demand for frontier rectifications.

This challenge disturbed the Ministers, who then divulged quite tactlessly in Brătianu's presence that they had not been authorized to discuss changes with him. By disclosing their inferiority to the Big Four, the Ministers furnished Brătianu with the required expedient. He demanded a delay of at least twelve days to permit him to return home for consultations with his government. If he were denied this privilege, which did not differ from the intention of the Ministers to secure authorization from their superiors, he would be compelled to reserve his decision on all frontiers.[73]

Lansing convinced his colleagues that Brătianu's argument was merely a ruse to delay delimitation since the Premier had no "superiors" in Bucharest. The Ministers recommended an immediate delimitation despite Brătianu's objections. The Council of Four adopted this recommendation. None of the Big Four recalled that precisely one month earlier (on May 12) the Romanian-Hungarian frontier had been approved by them. Clemenceau remembered only after Pichon reminded him. The Allied leaders regretted their oversight in failing to notify Brătianu on May 12, even though Clemenceau suspected him of having known about it for some time. Pichon explained this shortcoming as the result of a decision reached in January to disclose territorial settlements only at plenary sessions. Since the draft treaty for Hungary was not yet completed and since the prospect of inviting a respectable delegation from Budapest still appeared remote, the territorial provisions of that treaty had not been publicized.[74]

The Foreign Ministers also urged the Council to approve immediately Romania's frontiers in the Banat and Bucovina. But Tardieu interceded for Brătianu to postpone the actual delimitation until the Premier could consult with his cabinet. This was agreed to by the Ministers on condition that no alterations would be made in the frontiers if the Romanians rejected them. This decision was reached after it was learned that Mişu, not Brătianu, would leave for Bucharest to inform the government of the proposed frontier with Hungary.[75]

On the same day (June 12) Brătianu's subterfuge led Wilson and Lloyd George to insist upon prompt approval and delimitation of Romania's frontiers, which the Premier had to accept or face expulsion from the Peace Conference. Lloyd George appealed for an end to empty warnings, and he called for effective imposition of the Council's orders. He was even willing to invite Béla Kun to send a delegation to Paris to explain his side of the case.[76] Clemenceau urged caution and leniency because he anticipated Brătianu "would scream" about the indefensible frontier and refuse to retire behind it. He admitted that most of the trouble was being incited by Brătianu, but the Romanian leader had presented a logical argument for a temporary frontier. Instead of treating Hungary less harshly than Romania, Clemenceau urged, it would be prudent to send a mission to Budapest to determine whether Brătianu's arguments were valid and to discuss with Kun the possibility of a new armistice.[77]

Wilson and Lloyd George were won over, but they still demanded a firm attitude. It was decided to submit a strong note to Brătianu, ordering him to cease aggressive acts, withdraw his troops behind the "permanent frontiers adopted by the Peace Conference," and observe the frontiers if he expected to sign the Hungarian treaty. Wilson proposed warning Brătianu of Allied non-recognition of his frontier with Hungary as long as he challenged the Council and demanded concurrently that the Allies sanction what he was doing. "Romania cannot expect the Allies to fight for a boundary they did not believe to be right." If Brătianu rejected these terms, Wilson added, Romania should be deprived of her allied status.[78]

Balfour was instructed to draft a note "in a tone rude enough vis-à-vis Hungary, but in a more friendly tone with regard to the Romanians."[79] He presented it to the Council on June 13 with an explanation indicating he had disavowed his earlier approval of the frontier in the Council of Foreign Ministers. Balfour defended Brătianu's argument about the indefensibility of the frontier, citing the severing of railway lines as an utterly impractical method to perpetuate peace, the unavailability of Allied troops to supervise their operation, and the sensitive problem of synchronizing withdrawals of Romanian and Hungarian troops from areas where they had no right to be. If the Romanians withdrew first, noted Balfour, Hungary might recover territory east of the Tisa assigned to Romania; if the Hungarians evacuated first, the Romanians, who appeared to be the more serious offenders, might not withdraw from their positions.

The Council found a solution; two notes would be dispatched, one to Kun and one to Brătianu, reminding both of the Council's proclamation of January 25, ordering both to respect the boundary experts about to be sent to delimit the frontier, and announcing that the delimitation would be binding "until the peace was finally declared."[80]

This final statement created an impression that a frontier revision might be considered after the signing of Hungary's treaty. Brătianu was ordered to withdraw after Kun evacuated Slovakia, an operation to be completed by June 18. Kun was required to give assurances he would not molest or pursue the withdrawing Romanians. If Kun failed to comply, the Allies assured Brătianu, Budapest would be occupied by Allied troops.[81] The frontier corresponded to that approved by the Big Four on May 12, and it ultimately became the line in the Treaty of Trianon for Hungary.

The notes and details of the frontier were released to the press on June 14. News reached Bucharest newspapers on June 16.[82] At the same time Mişu arrived home to report to a Crown Council convened to discuss acceptance or rejection. One participant noted he was the bearer of bad news.[83] Maniu vowed to break with any government willing to accept a frontier that cancelled the maximum claims. The Crown Council rejected the frontier and reportedly upheld Brătianu's plan to hold out for fulfillment.[84]

Béla Kun also rejected the note and the frontier, but he was ready to evacuate his troops if Romania did likewise. He urged the calling of a conference in Vienna of states about to receive sections of the Habsburg Monarchy so that he could discuss with them questions of liquidating that empire and evacuating disputed areas. This reply so captivated Lloyd George that he proposed convening such a gathering in Paris. But Wilson and Sonnino feared it would create the impression the Allies were arranging a "Prinkipo" for Béla Kun.[85] The Council instructed General Bliss, considered the most qualified expert on the situation, to report on possible Allied occupation of Hungary.[86]

Bliss replied on June 20 that Kun had withdrawn his troops from Slovakia, but was now moving them toward Romanian positions along the Tisa. The Romanians had not yet moved behind the new frontier. Bliss recommended this solution: both armies should evacuate simultaneously at a precise time designated by the Council. He could not furnish any plan for sending Allied troops to intervene.[87]

Marshal Foch hastened to intercede for the Romanians on June 25. He objected to Bliss's plan because, according to the Belgrade armistice, the Romanians should not evacuate the Tisa until Hungary disarmed. Foch relied upon Romanian intentions to "abide scrupulously" by the orders of the Allies if permitted to remain on the Tisa to protect newly-acquired territories from Magyar counterattacks designed to recover them. Romania's withdrawal should be timed with Hungarian disarmament, Foch insisted, not with Kun's promise to evacuate.[88] When asked, Foch failed to come up with a plan for an Allied force to march into Hungary and enforce the Council's orders.

By the middle of June Foch's original plan to assemble a crusade against Bolshevism had been discarded because of the strong opposition of the Allied leaders. Foch had planned not only to check Bolshevism, but also to compel Germany to sign her treaty. His anti-Bolshevik objective remained for the small powers of East Central Europe to carry out. But his anti-German aim was about to be achieved, for Germany was due to sign the treaty on June 28. Since it had been Germany which commanded the attention of the Allied leaders, the chief purpose for which the Peace Conference had been convened was about to be accomplished. The impending signing caused a flurry of excitement during the final week of June. Lloyd George, Wilson, and Orlando (who resigned as premier on June 20) were scheduled to leave Paris as soon as Germany signed.

The Council did manage to find time on June 21 to approve Romania's frontiers in Bucovina and the Banat, and to uphold American recommendations to postpone award of the strip in northern Bucovina until the fate of a Ruthenian state was decided. Romania's annexation of Bessarabia and the question of southern Dobrodgea were assigned to the Foreign Ministers for settlement since they were empowered by the Big Four to continue the work of the Peace Conference as the "Council of the Heads of Delegations."[89] Having approved the frontiers, the Big Four again committed a serious blunder in failing to notify Brătianu of their action.

Messages from Béla Kun concerning new Romanian provocations led Wilson to believe that he was entitled to diplomatic recognition in view of his readiness to obey the June 13 note. Kun requested authority to resist the Romanians. Lloyd George hesitated to endorse Kun's regime even though it appeared to be more representative than former Magyar governments. Pressed for time, the Council again turned to Bliss for a report on the accuracy of Kun's accusations.[90]

The final meeting of the Big Four occurred immediately after the signing of the Treaty of Versailles on June 28. The last item on the agenda was an examination of Bliss's report confessing his inability to determine whether Romania or Hungary had renewed hostilities.[91] No one suggested asking Brătianu about it while he was so close at hand. He, too, had just signed the treaty.

Brătianu Departs From Paris

The first topic taken up by the Council of Heads of Delegations on July 1 concerned Romania. Clemenceau, chairman of the body, proposed priority treatment for the Banat, southern Dobrodgea, Bessarabia, and the northern boundary of Bucovina. He was reminded the Council of Four had approved the Banat partition on June 21 (a settlement communicated to Serbia and Romania on June 27) and Bucovina boundary (not yet disclosed to Romania). Clemenceau apologized for his memory lapse and ordered the Bucovina settlement communicated to Romania. He dismissed a proposal of Tommaso Tittoni, the new Italian foreign minister, to reopen the question of Romanian frontiers.[92]

The Council next considered the fate of Bessarabia. Brătianu's claim was being contested by the Russian Political Conference, a group of exile ministers of the Imperial and Provisional governments, representing Kolchak.[93] Brătianu and Vassili Maklakov (envoy of the Provisional Government to Paris in 1917) were invited to appear separately on July 2. Pichon and Balfour, whose governments were aiding Kolchak, wished to permit an airing of "White" Russian claims.[94] Lansing was still disinclined to adjudicate a dispute between "two friendly powers," since he was authorized to deal with treaties for enemy states only. But he was willing to approve any settlement reached by Brătianu and the "Whites."[95]

Maklakov had the distinction of being the only Russian of any political persuasion permitted to appear before the Peace Conference. Taking advantage of this, he denied the Allied right to dispose of territory belonging to Russia without the consent of her people. He described how Romania had coerced Bessarabians into voting for union by means of a fraudulent plebiscite, which he compared to German schemes in Latvia and Lithuania whose inhabitants had voted for incorporation into Germany. The Sfatul Țării, he pointed out, could claim to represent only four districts with Romanian majorities, and even then it appeared incongruous that the Sfat, established by members of the Petrograd Soviet, would vote for union with a monarchy, since they had just broken away from one. He predicted serious unrest in Bessarabia if Romania tried to assimilate a territory not promised in the 1916 Alliance.[96]

Brătianu was questioned about the Sfat vote even though Tittoni believed its accuracy was incontestable.[97] The Premier insisted the vote expressed the desire of the inhabitants, that it was held in "full freedom," and that although the Sfat was really a revolutionary body, it did request the Romanian army to restore order. The agrarian reform, introduced by the Sfat and subsequently ratified by the Romanian parliament on December 22, 1918, required peasants to pay for their land, but the landlords, mostly Russian, were grumbling about expropriation even though they were promised compensations.[98]

Brătianu refused to permit a plebiscite, proposed by Lansing, because he anticipated the choice would be between Bolshevism and peace. To offer such a choice to inhabitants of a province bordering Soviet Russia would result in endless tumult, especially if Romania were required, as a result of the plebiscite, to evacuate Bessarabia. Brătianu also rejected Lansing's suggestion that a plebiscite be held two years hence because he was convinced revolutionary agitation would take place in the interim and result in an unfavorable vote. If Russia recovered the province, he warned, she would be in a position to revive Tsarist aims to establish Russian hegemony in the Balkans and obtain the Straits. Brătianu also rejected any compromise with the "Whites," insisting that "Russia owes to Romania a great debt as being largely responsible for Romania's misfortunes. The circumstances clearly pointed to the best way in which Russia could discharge that debt. It would be by the cession of Bessarabia." Brătianu categorically refused to permit a plebiscite at any time.[99]

The Council reserved a decision on Bessarabia and postponed discussion of southern Dobrodgea until after Hungary's treaty was drafted. These regions deserved less attention than the question of Hungary. But to Brătianu, these territories, which he felt the Allies had no right to touch, were integral parts of the Kingdom of Romania. He had not entered the war to recover Bessarabia or retain southern Dobrodgea.

For five months Brătianu had stubbornly resisted attempts to diminish his newly-acquired territories. He did not subscribe to principles of the so-called "new diplomacy," whereby territorial settlements would be based on a judicious examination of the claims of both sides. It was galling for him to learn that Britain, France, and Italy, who only three years before joined with Russia to promise territories without any concern for the attitude of enemy states and with little thought for Serbia, should now uphold Wilson's ideal of a settlement based on mediation of conflicting claims of both enemy and allied states. His inability to appreciate the new method caused him profound disillusionment, especially when he suffered such setbacks as the recommendations of the Commission, the Council's concern for

Hungary, partition of the Banat, and intimations that Romania negotiate with Bulgaria over southern Dobrodgea and with the "Whites" regarding Bessarabia. These developments, perhaps more than the warnings of the Supreme Council, proved the Allies had no intention of honoring the 1916 Alliance. Added to these disappointments was the disagreeable prospect of Romania being required to sign a treaty for the protection of her minorities.

Brătianu may have been discouraged and demoralized, but he was not yet admitting defeat. He announced he was going home to resign because he could not accept any diminution of the promises in the Alliance and because he would not sign a minority treaty as long as the Allied Powers and three enemy states (Germany, Austria, and Hungary) were not required to sign similar treaties.[100] He appointed Mişu his successor on July 3, departed from Paris the next day, and arrived in Bucharest on July 7.[101] Rumors circulated that Ferdinand was considering the appointment of a coalition government willing to yield to the Allies so that anticipated censure would be shared by many party leaders, instead of by one only.[102] This scheme to find willing leaders appeared very difficult to carry out in view of press hostility in Bucharest. Various party organs were accusing the Allies of completely repudiating the Alliance, of relegating Romania's claims to the scrutiny of inferior delegates who styled themselves experts, and of failing to fulfil promises made by the predecessors of the Big Four. No party in Romania was willing to yield.[103]

Romania's censored press should, of course, be studied with care, but attacks upon the Allies were not entirely irresponsible if the explanation given by Woodrow Wilson to the Senate on July 10, 1919, may be taken as evidence of the Council's undue preoccupation with problems related to the interests of the Great Powers, rather than with disputes among the small powers.
Wilson explained that

> great populations bounded by sympathy and actual kin to Romania were also linked against their will to the conglomerate Austro-Hungarian Monarchy, or to other alien sovereignties, and it was part of the task of peace to make a new Romania.... No natural frontiers could be found for these new fields of adjustment and redemption. It was necessary to look constantly forward to other related tasks.[104]

NOTES

1. As whispered to Clemenceau (Aldrovandi Marescotti, *Guerra diplomatica*, p. 453).

2. *U.S. Foreign Relations, PPC*, V, pp. 497-498; Mantoux, II, pp. 5-8.

3. *U.S. Foreign Relations, PPC*, IV, pp. 672-673.

4. *Ibid.*, IV, p. 674.

5. *Ibid.*, IV, pp. 503-504, and V, p. 620.

6. White (1850-1927) had been ambassador to Italy, 1905-07, and to France, 1907-09. The only Republican appointed to the delegation by Wilson, White was a close friend of Henry Cabot Lodge, whom he told in January 1919 about the need for the Allies to strengthen Romania as a barrier to Bolshevism *(U.S. Foreign Relations, PPC*, II, p. 711).

7. *U.S. Foreign Relations, PPC*, IV, pp. 705-706.

8. Tardieu's observation was based on a story circulating in Paris that Brătianu had once spoken about ceding southern Dobrodgea to secure a favorable treaty from the Central Powers in 1918, and that he had revived this idea at the Conference to obtain the entire Banat. He was allegedly prepared to sacrifice southern Dobrodgea if Bulgaria, in return, yielded territory in Macedonia to Serbia, who would then disclaim part of the Banat. This scheme is given in Tilea, pp. 139-140; and G. P. Genov, *Bulgaria and Treaty of Neuilly*, pp. 27-28.

9. *U.S. Foreign Relations, PPC*, IV, pp. 718-719.

10. *Daily Review of the Foreign Press*, Allied Press Supplement, V, June 18, quoting newspapers of May 17, p. 285.

11. *Ibid.*, citing issue of May 26, p. 318.

12. *The New York Times*, May 16, 1919.

13. Report of U.S. Commissioner George H. Harries to General Bliss, Berlin, May 1, House Papers.

14. *Daily Review of the Foreign Press, Allied Press Supplement*, V, May 8 and 28, p. 345. Gyula was Mihály Károlyi's cousin whom the latter called a "fascist" *(Memoirs*, p. 150).

15. Herbert C. Hoover, *Memoirs*, I: *Years of Adventure, 1874-1920*, p. 399.

16. Miller, *Diary*, XVII, pp. 517-518.

17. *Daily Review of the Foreign Press, Allied Press Supplement*, V, pp. 221, 254.

18. *Ibid.*, V, p. 254; and William F. A. Rattigan (British chargé d'affaires at Bucharest), *Diversions of a Diplomat*, p. 212.

19. *L'Ukraine Soviétiste*, p. 62. Brătianu accused Lenin and Rakovskii of arranging a mutual assistance pact with Kun *(Bulletin d'informations roumaines*, No. 3, April 9).

20. Miller, *Diary*, X, pp. 337-341. "The Poles had an enormous desire for a common border with Romania versus Russia" (Temperley, *A History*, VI, p. 269).

21. *U.S. Foreign Relations, PPC*, V, p. 59. The Polish-Romanian accord is cited in *Daily Review of the Foreign Press, Allied Press Supplement*, V, p. 399; and Austruy, p. 293.

22. House to Stoica, May 5, House Papers.

23. *Times*, London, May 6 and 26, 1919.

24. *Ibid.*, May 26; and *Daily Review of the Foreign Press, Allied Press Supplement*, V, pp. 241-242. Romanian and Czech troops met at Munkacs on April 29 (Iorga, *Memorii*, II, p. 194).

25. *Daily Review of the Foreign Press, Allied Press Supplement*, V, pp. 285, 318.

26. *Ibid.*, V, p. 345.

27. Iorga, *Memorii*, II, p. 192.

28. *La Roumanie*, No. 71, May 22, quoting *Le Journal* of May 16.

29. *Daily Review of the Foreign Press, Allied Press Supplement*, V, p. 345. Also cited in Iorga, *Memorii*, II, p. 208, and Marghiloman, IV, pp. 323, 325.

Maniu conducted Prince Carol on a tour of Alba Iulia to see the site of the national assembly (*Bulletin d'informations roumaines*, June 3).

30. *Times*, London, May 22, 1919.

31. *Daily Review of the Foreign Press, Allied Press Supplement*, V, p. 221. Also in Iorga, *Memorii*, II, p. 197.

32. *U.S. Foreign Relations, PPC*, XII, pp. 455-458, 465-466; and Brown, "Foreign Relations of the Budapest Soviets," p. 67.

33. *U.S. Foreign Relations, PPC*, V, p. 706; Mantoux, II, pp. 109-110.

34. Mantoux, II, p. 110.

35. *U.S. Foreign Relations, PPC*, X, pp. 268-269.

36. Mantoux, II, pp. 152-153.

37. *U.S. Foreign Relations, PPC*, V, pp. 877-881. Lloyd George compared Romania's latest deeds to her wartime record. He said that if Romania "had remained neutral, the war might have been shortened by two years" (*Ibid.*, V, pp. 830-831).

38. *Ibid.*, IV, pp. 748-749; Miller, *Diary*, XVI, pp. 345-348.

39. *U.S. Foreign Relations, PPC*, IV, pp. 749-751.

40. Lansing had proposed to Wilson on September 21, 1918, that the frontier in Dobrodgea be rectified in Bulgaria's favor (Lansing, p. 194; and *The Lansing Papers*, II, p. 157). House backed Lansing's efforts (*U.S. Foreign Relations, PPC*, XI, pp. 575-577). For Bulgarian praise of Lansing's efforts, see Theodor I. Geshkoff, *Balkan Union*, pp. 54-56; Joseph V. Poppov, *La Dobroudja et les relations bulgaro-roumaines*, pp. 113-115; and Ivan Slivensky, *La Bulgarie depuis le traité de Berlin*, pp. 136-137.
Nicolson believed the United States had taken it upon herself to represent Bulgaria at the conference (*Peacemaking*, p. 347).

41. Robert H. Lord and Charles H. Haskins, American territorial experts, upheld the Allied right to correct injustices of pre-war treaties. See their *Some Problems of the Peace Conference*, pp. 264-265, 275-277.

42. Brătianu's statement is in Trandafir Djuvara, *Cent projets de partage de la Turquie*, p. 574.

43. Ionescu published in *La Roumanie* (May 15) a description of the new frontiers. Seton-Watson analyzed in detail the Banat partition in *The New Europe* (May 8).

44. *The New York Times,* May 30, 1919.

45. Lloyd George, *Memoirs,* II, p. 883.

46. *U.S. Foreign Relations, PPC,* III, pp. 391-393; Miller, *Diary,* XX, p. 188.

47. Foreign intervention in Romanian affairs was not a new issue. As early as 1868 the Romanian government had issued a memorandum opposing intervention in its affairs. See text in Jacques Fouques Duparc, *La protection des minorités de race, de langue, et de religion* (Paris: Librairie Dalloz, 1922), p. 102.

48. A treatment of the minority question affecting Romania is beyond the scope of this study. However, those developments arising from the drafting of Romania's minority treaty which relate to the topic herein will be cited to clarify certain issues. An account of the drafting of the minority treaty may be found in Oscar I. Janowsky, *The Jews and Minority Rights, 1898-1919,* pp. 369-378.

49. *U.S. Foreign Relations, PPC,* III, pp. 398-399.

50. Nicolson recorded that "this reference to Romania's treatment of the Jews causes Brătianu to blush to the roots of his hair. He recovers himself, shrugs his shoulders, resumes his seat. On sitting down he continues to shrug his shoulders like a vain and self-conscious schoolboy" *(Peacemaking,* p. 354).

51. Paderewski of Poland promised to provide minority rights in accordance with stipulations made by the League of Nations. Kramář of Czechoslovakia agreed to accept the friendly counsel of the Allies. Trumbić condescended to provide guarantees to minorities inhabiting newly-acquired regions, but he refused to accept provisions for Serbia which never had a minority problem.

52. Wilson's assertion that he would not send troops back to Europe has been subjected to conflicting interpretations. Joseph Turmulty, an intimate associate, was responsible for the story that Wilson promised Brătianu he would send troops to defend Romanian frontiers (Tumulty, *Woodrow Wilson as I Know Him,* p. 360). Dillon *(The Inside Story of the Peace Conference,* p. 501) and Clark *(United Roumania,* p. 244) said Wilson promised such aid. Seymour denied it (House and Seymour, pp. 452-453). This confusion may have been caused by the impending conclusion of the famous Treaty of Guarantees by which Britain and the United States agreed to send military assistance to France in case of an unprovoked German attack.

53. This description is reminiscent of a remark of Jusserand, French envoy in Washington, to General Bliss: "Had Wilson lived a couple of centuries ago, he would have been the greatest tyrant in the world because he does not seem to have the slightest conception that he can ever be wrong" (Palmer, p. 400).

54. Brătianu's assertion was true. For an account of Wilson's intention to insert such an article, see Miller, *The Drafting of the Covenant*, II, p. 105.

55. Lloyd George whispered to Clemenceau that Brătianu did not seem to understand that "Jews are persecuted in Romania, not in Italy" or in other Allied states (Aldrovandi Marescotti, *Guerra diplomatica*, p. 453).

56. The minutes of this plenary session are in *U.S. Foreign Relations, PPC*, III, pp. 394-410; and Almond and Lutz, pp. 563-572. An abridged version is in Lloyd George, *Memoirs*, II, pp. 822-893. A Romanian-language transcript is in Mircea Djuvara, *Trebuie oare să semnăm tractatul cu Austria?*

57. *U.S. Foreign Relations, PPC*, VI, p. 133; Mantoux, II, pp. 261-262.

58. *U.S. Foreign Relations, PPC*, VI, pp. 184-185.

59. *Ibid.*, VI, pp. 202-209; Mantoux, II, pp. 313-316, 319; Aldrovandi Marescotti, *Nuovi ricordi*, pp. 37-38; and Baker, *Woodrow Wilson and World Settlement*, I, p. 406. Brătianu did not reveal that Romanian and Polish troops had effected their desired juncture at Stanislau in Eastern Galicia *(U.S. Foreign Relations, PPC*, VI, p. 599).

60. *U.S. Foreign Relations, PPC*, VI, pp. 221-222, 233-234, 246-247; Mantoux, II, pp. 331-332, 335. Lloyd George was pleased to learn of Brătianu's intention to resign because it would enable Ionescu, known for his "western point of view" to assume control of the government. Clemenceau discounted Brătianu's threat because he had "eluded all his previous engagements."

61. *U.S. Foreign Relations, PPC*, VI, 255-261; Mantoux, II, pp. 349-352. Kun's reply is in the *Times*, London, June 11.

62. Lloyd George invited Mişu to attend with Brătianu because he was considered more conciliatory than the Premier (Mantoux, II, p. 352).

63. This was a reference to the "Whites" led by Gyula Károlyi. A news report stated the "Whites" had been interned by the Romanian army at Arad and then "set free unconditionally" (*Daily Review of the Foreign Press, Allied Press Supplement*, V, p. 345). Mihály Károlyi accused his cousin of betraying Hungary to the Romanians (*Memoirs*, pp. 171-172).

64. Brătianu could have read quite accurate accounts of the Commission's recommendations in *Le Temps* (May 24), *La Roumanie*, No. 72 (May 29), and in the Bucharest *Epoca* (Marghiloman's newspaper) of June 5.

65. Brătianu's propaganda organ, *Bulletin d'informations roumaines* (April 9), alleged that Rakovskii had been sent to Budapest by Lenin. It is interesting to note in this regard that the American envoy at Berne warned House in December 1918 that Rakovskii, "a friend and co-worker of Lenin," was urging Károlyi to stir up trouble in Transylvania (*U.S. Foreign Relations, PPC*, II, p. 396).

66. *U.S. Foreign Relations, PPC*, VI, pp. 281-289; Mantoux, II, pp. 368-375; and Aldrovandi Marescotti, *Nuovi ricordi*, pp. 59-60.

67. Saint-Aulaire, "Un grand latin — Jean Brătiano," p. 17.

68. This quotation is from Seton-Watson, *A History*, p. 545.

69. Mantoux, II, p. 369.

70. Temperley claimed that the Council's cease-and-desist order to Brătianu gave Kun time to build up his army and an opportunity to spread throughout Hungary the idea that Allies were on his side against Romania (*A History*, I, p. 355).

71. Brătianu was accompanied by Vaida-Voevod and Colonel Toma Dimitrescu. Beneš and Kramář were present to receive the report on Czechoslovakia's frontiers. Members of the Romanian Territorial Commission also attended.

72. Beneš and Kramář supported Brătianu's claim to a common frontier. Romanian and Czech troops effected a juncture at Csap on May 1 (Temperley, *A History*, I, p. 354).

73. *U.S. Foreign Relations, PPC*, IV, pp. 803-813.

74. *Ibid.*, VI, pp. 318-321; Mantoux, II, pp. 387-390.

75. *U.S. Foreign Relations, PPC*, IV, pp. 821-824.

76. *U.S. Foreign Relations, PPC*, VI, p. 351. Orlando was absent on June 12. Sonnino did not substitute for him. That the Italians, who were having troubles of their own, were not present may explain in part the rigidity of Wilson and Lloyd George which Orlando could not mollify.

77. *Ibid.*, VI, p. 352. Clemenceau had apparently preempted the position usually assumed by Orlando.

78. *Ibid.,* VI, p. 352; Mantoux, II, pp. 396-398.

79. It should be noted that Romania was not the exclusive object of the Council's attention at this time. In addition to Hungary and Romania, the Czechs were subjected to demands they cease fighting the Magyars who had occupied parts of Slovakia.

80. De Martonne was already surveying the new frontier. He was warmly welcomed in Bucharest on June 13 when he addressed the Senate and disclosed the nature of the boundary (Iorga, *Memorii,* II, pp. 212-216).

81. *U.S. Foreign Relations, PPC,* VI, pp. 399-400, 411-412, 416-417; Mantoux, II, pp. 415-416. Components of the army to be sent to Budapest were not disclosed in the note.

82. *Times,* London, June 14; *Daily Review of the Foreign Press, Allied Press Supplement,* V, p. 398; and Iorga, *Memorii,* II, pp. 215-216.

83. Marghiloman, IV, p. 327.

84. *Ibid.,* IV, p. 334; and Iorga, *Memorii,* II, p. 223.

85. "Prinkipo" referred to a plan introduced on January 6, 1919 by Lloyd George to summon different factions at war in Russia to a conference on that island in the Sea of Marmora for the purpose of arranging a truce and exchanging views leading to eventual peace. The Soviet Government accepted provisionally, but the "Whites," encouraged by the French, rejected the invitation *(U.S. Foreign Relations, PPC,* III, pp. 581-584, 643-646; and Carr, *The Bolshevik Revolution,* III, pp. 110-111).

86. *U.S. Foreign Relations, PPC,* VI, pp. 513-514, 518-519; Mantoux, II, p. 440.

87. *U.S. Foreign Relations, PPC,* VI, pp. 550-551, 552-553; Mantoux, II, p. 465.

88. Deák, pp. 95-96.

89. *U.S. Foreign Relations, PPC,* VI, p. 587. Wilson, Clemenceau, Sonnino, Balfour, and Makino approved the frontiers. Lloyd George, absent in London, explained years later that he had not been cognizant of the reasons by which the frontiers were determined (*The Daily Mail,* London, September 8, 1927).

90. *U.S. Foreign Relations, PPC,* VI, pp. 701, 706-707; Mantoux, II, p. 525. Bliss described his assignment as "a nice job to unload on a peaceful, peace-loving, and somewhat tired old man" (Palmer, p. 399).

91. *U.S. Foreign Relations, PPC,* VI, pp. 756, 758; Mantoux, II, p. 567.

92. *U.S. Foreign Relations, PPC,* VII, pp. 1-5. Minutes of the sessions of the new Council are also in E. L. Woodward and Rohan Butler (eds.), *Documents on British Foreign Policy,* First Series, I, 1919.

The new Council was composed of first plenipotentiaries Clemenceau, Lansing, Balfour, and Tittoni and their alternates, Pichon, White, Crowe, and de Martino, respectively. Scialoja soon replaced de Martino. Japanese delegates Chinda and Makino attended, but took little part in discussions unrelated to their interests.

Tittoni (1855-1931) had been Foreign Minister, 1903-05 and 1906-09, envoy to London, 1905--06, and Paris, 1910-16. He was now foreign minister in Nitti's cabinet.

93. The Russian Political Conference included Serge Sazonov (whose knowledge of Brătianu's tactics qualified him as an expert), Chaikovskii, L'vov, Maklakov, and Miliukov. General Shcherbachev was chairman of its Military and Naval Committee. For its challenge to Romanian claims, see Paul Miliukov, *The Case for Bessarabia.*

94. Kolchak proposed, in reply to an Allied request he recognize the authority of the Peace Conference to determine the fate of the "Romanian part of Bessarabia," that a Russian constituent assembly be entitled to decide the question. If Romania objected, the League of Nations should settle the dispute. Kolchak's correspondence is in *U.S. Foreign Relations, PPC,* VI, pp. 15, 21-23, 72-75, 158, 326, 348, 356. The Council of Four agreed to his formula on June 12 *(Ibid.,* VI, p. 356).

The British were supporting "White" general Denikin, represented in Bucharest by Poklevskii, former Russian envoy to Romania. Poklevskii was trying to secure, with the help of British chargé Rattigan, military supplies left in Romania by Shcherbachev. Rattigan urged Balfour to obtain Brătianu's release of the materials (*Documents on British Foreign Policy,* First Series, III, pp. 408-409).

95. Lansing had been approached by Boris Bakhmet'ev, former Russian envoy in Washington and now chairman of the Political Committee of the Russian Political Conference. See Walworth, II, for Bakhmet'ev's influence on American policy, pp. 137, 145-146, 159.

96. Maklakov had considerable influence at the Quai d'Orsay. Sazonov was likewise influential in London. See Fischer, I, pp. 159-160; and Kennan, pp. 137-138, 309.

97. Tittoni trusted Brătianu's claim that the Sfat vote was a true expression of self-determination ("La Bessarabia, la Romania, e l'Italia," P. 271). He once proposed to Sazonov (May 1915) that Russia cede Bessarabia to lure Romania into the war (Poincaré, VI, pp. 187, 211).

98. For landowner discontent, see Krupenskii, "The Bessarabian Parliament," in Miliukov, pp. 47-51.

99. *U.S. Foreign Relations, PPC,* VII, pp. 10-13. Brătianu was accompanied by Mişu, Diamandy, and Ioan Pelivan (Director of Justice in Bessarabia).

100. *Le Matin,* Paris, July 4. Austria was required to insure minority rights to her non-German inhabitants (Articles 62-69 of the Treaty of St. Germain), but these stipulations were not contained in a separate treaty. The same requirements were due to be imposed on Hungary (Articles 54-60 of the Treaty of Trianon).

101. Iorga, *Memorii,* II, p. 225.

102. *Documents on British Foreign Policy,* First Series, VI, pp. 21-22. Brătianu circulated this story at a dinner on July 2 (Joseph C. Grew, Letters, July 2, Houghton Library).

103. *Daily Review of the Foreign Press, Allied Press Supplement,* V, pp. 398-399.

104. Baker and Dodd, *The Public Papers of Woodrow Wilson: War and Peace,* I, p. 542. Lloyd George subscribed to this view (*Memoirs,* II, p. 599).

Chapter V

BRĂTIANU'S DEFIANCE: JULY-OCTOBER

*"This is the first time that I learn the Conference has a
tête-à-tête with the Hungarians, because for a several
week interval it has alternately manifested to us its desire
to win the good graces of Kun and its desire to fight and
destroy him. I intend to be at Budapest the collaborator
of the Allies and not to be treated as an enemy or a
conquered state."*

— Ioan I.C. Brătianu
8 August 1919[1]

The Allies Oscillate

The Council of Heads of Delegations completed its major business
in July, when Germany was about to ratify the Treaty of Versailles and
Austria agreed to sign her treaty within two months. The opportunity
then arose to consider Hungary's treaty, which was the most critical
issue for Romania. Conclusion of peace with Hungary entailed Allied
recognition of a Hungarian government and the frontier with Romania
insofar as that treaty concerned the Romanians. If the Allies submitted
a treaty to Béla Kun, Romania would be threatened by a recognized
communist régime in the west. If Romania refused to sign the treaty,
she might run the risk of retaliation by Béla Kun, who could
conceivably rely upon Allied guarantees of Hungary's territorial
integrity. The prospect of Soviet Russia assisting Kun in recovering
lost lands was no less terrifying than an Allied sanction of Kun's
efforts to regain areas assigned to Hungary but still occupied by the
Romanians.

Two choices confronted Brătianu in the summer of 1919.

He could either accept the June 13 order to evacuate eastern Hungary, thereby submitting to reduced territorial gains, but perhaps securing Allied recognition of the union of Bessarabia and retention of southern Dobrodgea; or he could defy the Allies, occupy Budapest, oust the communist regime, and impose on a puppet government his own treaty, recognizing a frontier which would coincide with or exceed the line promised in the 1916 Alliance.

The second choice was apparently adopted, for Brătianu reportedly announced upon arrival in Bucharest on July 7 that he must carry out in Hungary what the Allies were not willing to do, namely, exterminate Bolshevism, install a new government willing to accept a treaty, and compel Hungary to accept a frontier corresponding to the promise of the Alliance.[2] Brătianu's challenge was in response to Romanian anxiety over the Allied correspondence with Kun. Exchange of messages between Paris and Budapest was interpreted as evidence of the Council's readiness to negotiate a peace with Bolshevism.[3]

Brătianu was evidently unaware of American opposition to negotiations with Kun. The United States preferred to send an inter-Allied army composed of other than American troops to Budapest to supervise the installation of a moderate government, which would be invited to sign a treaty. The Americans, influenced by Coolidge's reports, believed that neither Kun nor the "Whites" represented the political thinking of the majority of Magyars, and they recommended the ouster of Kun because he was being urged by Lenin to secure a temporary truce or peace to get "breathing space."[4] The Italians feared the Hungarian revolution would be attractive to less aggressive socialists in other countries because, unlike the upheaval in Russia, it had been quietly successful. The British believed Kun threatened the small states and, as a result, they had a convincing argument on which to base their belligerent attitudes. Balfour noted that Romania could not be expected to withdraw from the Tisa while Kun was still armed, and he proposed employing Romanian, Czech, Serbian, and French (but not British) troops to intimidate Kun into demobilizing. Clemenceau likened the crisis to the La Fontaine fable about "a gathering of rats who decided to hang a bell around a cat's neck." He admitted the impossibility of sending French troops to Budapest because the French Chamber of Deputies was resolutely opposed to intervention and because the army would be reduced to peacetime proportions by October. Tittoni's position was similar because the Italian parliament was also opposed to military intervention, but he intimated the

Romanians might be willing to undertake operations since "they seemed considerably dissatisfied with the Peace Conference."

When Balfour reminded Clemenceau of the grandiose plan conceived by Marshal Foch, the French premier replied that Foch and d'Esperey "were eager to march; they have plans more ambitious than that of Napoleon's march on Moscow." He preferred to let the Hungarian crisis run its own course, but Lansing rejected temporizing. Bliss dismissed his suspicions about Romania when he recommended adoption of Balfour's scheme to eject Kun by using troops of the small powers. His proposal was referred to the military advisers for an opinion.[5]

The report of the military advisers (July 9) recommended that the Romanians be authorized to remain on the Tisa because of Kun's threats. As for inter-Allied occupation of Budapest, the advisers reported the capital to be a "veritable fortress," which could be seized only by an army of 100,000 well-equipped troops. Since the Allies could not furnish such a large force, 84,000 Romanian troops on the Tisa could serve a useful purpose. The advisers nominated d'Esperey to command Romanian forces, as well as other troops if made available, in an occupation of all Hungary.[6]

This report, bearing the signature of Bliss in addition to those of the French, British, and Italian advisers, was certainly an acknowledgment of the efficacy of the Foch plan to exterminate Bolshevism in Hungary. Balfour admired the plan so much that he proposed immediate adoption, not only to intimidate Kun, but also to warn Bulgaria that the Allies would not be too weak to deal with her if she refused to sign her treaty. Clemenceau and Lansing reserved their decisions until the opinions of the small powers could be ascertained.[7]

Two days later, on July 11, Mişu, Vaida-Voevod, and delegates of Serbia and Czechoslovakia appeared before the Council. Foch was present to expatiate on his plan, which now was about to materialize if in abbreviated form only. He expected the Romanians to be the chief contributors of troops because they were maintaining seven divisions on active duty. Mişu added that two army corps were being mobilized in Transylvania, two divisions were being assembled and equipped with Allied military supplies, and four divisions were stationed in Bessarabia. He announced Romania "had a willing spirit" to occupy Budapest.[8] The Serbs and Czechs were unwilling to join the campaign because of threats to their security in other quarters.[9] Neither the British nor the Italians could provide any troops, and Lansing refused to offer American forces.[10]

As a consequence of their backtracking and indecision, the Allies inadvertently served notice on the Romanians that they were too weak to intervene in Hungary. This unintentional exhibition of impotence indicated to the Romanians that the Allies were either unwilling or unable to carry out the terms of the June 13 note, which, it will be recalled, spoke of an inter-Allied force moving on Budapest if the Council's orders were not obeyed. Furthermore, the Allies could not convince the Czechs or Serbs to participate because neither had any claims to Hungarian territory not already awarded by the Peace Conference.

Romania thus stood alone in her determination to fulfill what was tantamount to an Allied invitation to march. This calculation was not challenged when Mişu reported that Romania intended to keep her forces on the Tisa until Hungary was disarmed and demobilized.[11] Brătianu issued the same challenge to the June 13 note when he told Rattigan, the British chargé, that he would keep Romania on a war footing even if the Allies ceased to supply arms or tried to interfere with his plan to eject Kun. The Allies had no authority to demand a retreat which could not be protected, protested Brătianu, because Romania's national existence was at stake. He repeated what Balfour had told him prior to departing from Paris, namely, the Allies must guarantee safe evacuation of Hungary and permit the Romanians to hold another defense line against Magyar Bolsheviks who had outfitted themselves with supplies left in Hungary by the Germans.[12]

Balfour's concern for Romania may be understood in the light of British interests in East Central Europe. Britain was still trying to obtain Brătianu's release of the war matériel left in Romania by Shcherbachev's army.[13] When Brătianu repeatedly insisted upon his need to use those supplies, the British countered with efforts to ease his anxiety. Another factor playing a vital role in British policy was the question of petroleum rights in Romania. During July talks were in progress regarding an Anglo-French scheme to win Brătianu over to permitting British and French concerns to develop the oil industry, which had been partially destroyed in 1916. A trilateral agreement was drafted granting Britain and France the right to purchase German holdings in Romania and providing Romania with an equal voice in the administration of joint Anglo-French companies. This agreement had not yet been approved by Brătianu.[14]

Balfour's attitude left the Americans alone in their insistence Romania comply with previous orders. Balfour debated with Henry White over the accuracy of reports coming from Budapest about

Romanian provocations. He doubted the reliability of a note from his own military attaché in Budapest reporting Romanian preparations for an offensive, and was even willing to believe rumors that Magyars living east of the Tisa were fearful lest a Romanian withdrawal leave them "to the tender mercies of Béla Kun."[15] Kun's description of the devastation perpetrated by the Romanians failed to dissuade Balfour. The communist leader had advised the Allies

> that the devastations of General Hindenburg in the invaded departments of northern France are perfect oases when compared to the conditions brought about by the savagery of the Romanian troops in the economic life of the comitats they have occupied.[16]

Balfour dismissed Kun as a liar and called upon him to disarm and demobilize before the Romanians evacuated.[17]

The Council again considered the question of occupying Budapest. On July 17 the delegates of Romania, Serbia, and Czechoslovakia appeared with Marshal Foch before the Council. This time the Serbs and Czechs agreed to furnish troops, but the Serbs were still hesitant because of the issues of Fiume, Macedonia, and the Banat. Foch outlined his plan to send 25,000 French troops to assist the Romanians, Czechs, and Serbs in installing an acceptable government in Budapest. All that he required now was British and American supplies for the campaign. Balfour questioned the wisdom of setting up an Allied-sponsored regime because it would entail making peace with a puppet government. Tittoni preferred to deal with the "Whites" to give the campaign an aura of liberation from Bolshevism.[18]

The Romanians and Czechs pointed out, in opposition to Tittoni's scheme, that Magyar officers had remained loyal to Kun because he was letting them fight for recovery of lost lands. Beneš saw no hope of "seducing those officers," and he scorned prior arrangements with the "Whites." Vaida-Voevod pleaded to deprive the "Whites" and Kun of a pretext to act as defenders of Hungary since most Magyars opposed a regime led by either faction. The Allies, after occupying Budapest, should proclaim that the Magyars were free to choose their own government, recommended Vaida-Voevod, and the Allies should consult those Romanians, Serbs, and Slovaks who had been Hungarian subjects to ascertain "the devices of the Magyar political parties," and to obtain their cooperation regarding occupation policies.[19]

Bliss was disturbed by this new eagerness to march. Perceiving a resumption of total war and, consequently, the inevitability of American involvement, Bliss retracted his prior recommendation to occupy Budapest. When pressed to furnish American troops, he sought refuge in Wilson's statement to the small powers on May 31. If Americans were sent to Hungary, he noted, they would not be defending the peace; they would be upholding Romania's violation of the Belgrade armistice. Balfour insisted that Hungary, not Romania, had violated the armistice. But Bliss retorted that

> the Romanians had crossed the line in spite of General d'Esperey. He tried to stop them on another line further west, but without avail. Discussions in Paris led to the establishment of the neutral zone approximately representing the Treaty of 1916 line. Even this had not stopped the Romanians... The Romanians should stay on their present line, as all the trouble had been caused by their advance. The Romanians should not cross the line from Arad to Nagy-Várad [Oradea] to Szatmár-Németi [Satu Mare].... The neutral zone was of no advantage because there were not enough Allied troops to guard it.[20]

Bliss was sure Kun had reconstituted Hungary's army after the unwarranted Romanian invasion, and he believed the French unit at Arad could keep order without the assistance of the small powers. Balfour reminded him that Romania had not signed the Belgrade armistice, nor was she a belligerent on the day (November 13) it was signed; thus Romania could not violate an armistice to which she was not a signatory. Bliss replied that no expert in military affairs could deny an armistice entailed a laying down of arms by both sides to permit civil authorities to make peace. Directing his words to the Romanians, Bliss charged that an armistice which bound one side and not the other was an absurdity in view of the fact that the Romanian army had gone into Hungary for purposes of conquest.[21]

The small power delegates interrupted the debate to ask for a waiver of legal complexities and for issuance of orders to march. But Clemenceau postponed a decision, giving the small powers some significant advice. He told them a state of war with Hungary still existed; therefore there was no question of a new war.[22]

Clemenceau's observation coincided with the argument used by Brătianu for some time in defense of his retaliation to Hungarian provocations. The consequence of this open hearing was, for the Romanians, the second time within a week that the Allies expressed their inability to send their own troops to Budapest. Brătianu's calculations about Allied weakness were substantiated on July 17, when d'Esperey, "on instructions from Paris," ordered Kun to resign and permit the Magyars to elect their own government. A refusal would result in the occupation of Budapest by troops whose nationalities were not disclosed.[23]

The Americans devised a plan to have d'Esperey send a French police force into Hungary to maintain order but not to occupy Budapest. Thus the Romanians would no longer have an excuse to pacify Hungary. The Council, however, rejected this plan, insisting instead that Kun comply with the June 13 note before the Romanians withdrew. Clemenceau revived the idea of sending a military mission of four Allied officers to determine who was guilty of transgressing orders. He discounted Foch's report that Kun would soon attack the Romanian positions along the Tisa.[24]

Foch's warning was correct, though. Béla Kun did attack the Romanians on July 20, explaining his move to "make the will of the Entente respected by the Romanians." The Allies decided to act in the only way possible, short of authorizing the small powers to repulse the attack, namely, to send the mission and instruct d'Esperey to retaliate if the Magyars attacked the French at Arad.[25]

Béla Kun was making a desperate effort to seize the grain harvest in Crişana to feed Budapest, which had suffered because of the economic blockade imposed on Hungary since the armistice. He caught the Romanians off-guard, forcing them to withdraw from the Tisa. After a week of combat, the Romanians regained lost ground, and by August 4 were in Budapest. Kun fled to Austria and the communist regime toppled.[26]

It was clear that the Allies had failed to exert their authority in East Central Europe. The Council had done more to encourage Romania's advance than it had to prevent it. While the Allies continued to show irresolution, Brătianu took the bit between his teeth and evicted the Bolsheviks from Hungary.[27] Romania's attitude was only natural, although some of her methods, prior to and after Kun's attack, carried the policy of reprisals too far. Had Romania been defeated by Kun, it is doubtful if any assistance would have been forthcoming from the Allies, since they had shown themselves utterly powerless to deal with Kun. From August until the adjournment of the Peace Conference on January 21, 1920, the Allies would have to coerce Romania, a recalcitrant ally, rather than Hungary, an enemy state, into respecting the impaired authority of the Peace Conference.

The Schism

Romania's swift victory was celebrated in Sibiu when Brătianu addressed the Consiliul Dirigent with these words:

Today the Romanian soldiers on the Tisa and beyond it assured the frontiers of Romania and protected European civilization against the destructive wave of Bolshevism.[28]

The King and Brătianu visited the army near Budapest and then went to Timişoara, which was occupied as soon as the Serbs evacuated the city. This high-tide of Romanian prestige silenced the opposition of those in Bucharest who had been criticizing Brătianu's aggressive policy. Averescu had appealed to Ferdinand to appoint a government willing to compromise with the Allies. Ionescu did not condone the invasion of Hungary; he described Brătianu as behaving "like a girl of ten, who announced her intention to become a 'cocotte', that is, she might wait six or seven years before announcing her dishonor."[29] As in the past, though, Brătianu enjoyed much popularity and the envy of his political opponents whenever he achieved triumphs. Now that he had implemented his policy toward Hungary, the opposition parties could not condemn him without simultaneously advocating a restoration of the status quo ante. Neither Averescu nor Ionescu had sufficient strength to oppose the Premier.

Victory in Hungary would not have occurred had the threat of an attack upon Romania by the Russians not been dispelled beforehand. Brătianu anticipated the inability of the Red Army to move against Romania because it was engaged in repulsing a Polish advance on Minsk, which was seized on August 8.[30] The anti-Bolshevik Ukrainian nationalist Simon Petliura was attacking the Bolsheviks holding Kiev. Brătianu encouraged Petliura in the hope the situation in the Ukraine would become so entangled as to thwart any Red Army attempt to recover Bessarabia.[31] The only effort Soviet Russia could make to assist Hungary was to issue ineffectual warnings. Soviet resistance to the Poles, Petliura, and Denikin began to crumble. Denikin took Kiev on August 2 and cleared the Ukraine of the Red Army by the end of the month.[32]

Denikin's success was due in part to British support.[33] But this British aid and support of the "Whites" carried serious consequences for Brătianu. If the "Whites" distracted the Red Army's attention from Hungary, as did happen, Romania would have a free hand. But if the "Whites" eventually crushed Russian Bolshevism, they would inevitably pursue the same objective as the Reds, namely, the recovery of Bessarabia. This predicament was temporarily solved when Brătianu took the calculated risk of benefiting from "White" victories to eject Kun. Whether the "Whites" would triumph over Bolshevism or vice versa was a question he could face later. In any event, Brătianu gave no comfort to Denikin who continued to appeal for the supplies left in Romania by Shcherbachev.[34]

The turmoil in Russia was assuredly favorable for the implementation of Brătianu's policies, but an even more promising situation existed in East Central Europe, where Britain maintained only 40 troops, Italy had one battalion, and the French 15,000 men.[35] It was clear the Allies could not interpose sufficient troops to stop the Romanian advance.

The Allies, meanwhile, debated over a new government for Hungary. For a while they considered supporting a scheme of William Böhm (Vilmós Bem), Kun's envoy to Vienna and formerly Minister of War in Károlyi's cabinet. Böhm, a moderate socialist, had approached the Allied military mission in Vienna with a project to set up a temporary socialist dictatorship, summon a constituent assembly, and finally establish a democratic republic. His plan elicited American interest, but the other Allies distrusted him. The project was abandoned in favor of Clemenceau's appeal to the Magyars to overthrow the communists in return for an end to the economic blockade, evacuation of Romanian troops as soon as a new government willing to obey the Allies was set up, and prevention of further aggression against Hungary by Romania, Serbia, and Czechoslovakia.[36] The Magyars carried out Clemenceau's proposal by establishing a moderate socialist government led by Gyula Peidl, a former member of Károlyi's cabinet. This new régime requested a revision of the Belgrade armistice on the basis of Clemenceau's three points.[37] Before the Allies could respond, Brătianu carried out his plan to serve a second armistice ultimatum. He demanded that Peidl submit to immediate disarmament and demobilization, control by Romania of all means of communication and transportation, recognition of the Romanian occupation as fulfillment of Allied instructions to liberate Hungary, creation of a government free of ministers who had served in the cabinets of Károlyi and Kun, and surveillance of the new government by Romanians who knew "thoroughly not only all the twists of the Hungarian intellect," but also all Hungarian politicians.[38] Brătianu communicated a copy of this ultimatum to the Allies in the expectation they would acclaim his success in ousting Kun.[39]

After condemning the high-handed treatment of Peidl, Clemenceau declared he would never subscribe to the terms if he were a Magyar. Balfour finally admitted Romania was violating the Belgrade armistice. Even Foch confessed the Romanians had gone too far. But Pichon and Tittoni believed Brătianu had a right to impose the terms because Hungary had precipitated the brief war. Their argument prevailed and it was decided fatefully to permit Romania to maintain troops in their present positions until Peidl carried out the terms of the Belgrade armistice and the note of June 13.[40]

Peidl pleaded for an evacuation of Romanian forces, who had poured into Budapest and were beginning a looting expedition which was to last four months. When he requested the Council to receive a peace delegation, the Allies, wishing to make sure the communists would not return, did not reply. It was decided to revive the project of dispatching a military mission to Budapest.[41] After having failed to prevent a Romanian occupation, the Allies could only try to regulate it now.[42]

The Americans were the strongest advocates of a mission. A change in American plenipotentiaries had occurred on July 28 when Under Secretary of State Frank Lyon Polk arrived in Paris. He was the first delegate to call the Council's attention to reports of looting, cutting of Budapest's communications with the outside, and disregard of the Council's instructions to the Romanians.[43] Tittoni insisted, on the contrary, that the Romanians had been invited to take Budapest, and Foch assumed Brătianu proposed to resolve the crisis because of Allied vacillations.[44] Clemenceau snapped that if Brătianu tried to solve the Council's problems, then the Council would settle its own without Brătianu. Despite opposition from Tittoni, Foch, and Pichon, the others agreed to dispatch a mission of four generals after Polk and Balfour acceded to Clemenceau's proposal not to cut off economic and military assistance to Romania since she "was actually helping the Allied cause."

In a note sent to Bucharest on August 5, Brătianu was advised of the military mission's task to assist Peidl in carrying out provisions of the Belgrade armistice and the June 13 note. He was asked to comply with mission instructions, refrain from looting, and abide by the Allied decision to make peace with Hungary. The penalty for non-compliance was so vague as to render the note useless. Romania was told that any incident might ruin prospects of a swift peace in East Central Europe, that she would not be forgiven if a calamity resulted from any unconsidered action, and that she would not be entitled to Allied good will if she took any steps to prejudice her status as an allied state.[45]

That same day (August 5) four generals were chosen to go to Budapest to assure Hungary's compliance with the Belgrade armistice and subsequent instructions, establish a working relationship with the Peidl government, discuss with Romanian officers a peaceful occupation to be terminated as soon as practicable, and advise Romania and Hungary their common frontier had already been delimited. Hungary was permitted to maintain a small army on active duty to insure order, but she was required to hand over German supplies to the mission. Romania was to permit the mission to determine the strength and distribution of her forces. If the generals considered it necessary, Romania would be required to withdraw superfluous troops.[46]

By virtue of the mission's instructions and the request to Romania to cooperate with the generals, not only was the occupation of Budapest sanctioned, but also Romania's proclamation to the Magyars of July 31 was upheld. That proclamation, attached to Brătianu's armistice ultimatum, depicted Romania as the agent of the Allies in liberating Hungary. It promised "the Allied armies" (a term applying to Romanian forces) would not interfere in Hungary's internal affairs and would be withdrawn as soon as order had been restored "in conformity with provisions to this end by the peace treaty."[47] A scrutiny of this last phrase indicates the Romanians had no intention of leaving Hungary until peace was signed.

The military mission, instructed to proceed immediately to Budapest, was armed only with the written authority of the Peace Conference to carry out the delicate task of maintaining a fragile truce by convincing the Romanians, instead of the Magyars, to cooperate. The four generals, who were not accompanied by any armed escorts, were Major General Harry Hill Bandholtz (United States), Brigadier General Reginald St. George Gorton (Britain), General Jean Cesar Graziani (France), and General Ernesto Mombelli (Italy).[48]

By overruling the objections of Pichon, Tittoni, and Foch, who insisted Romania's actions were fully justified, and by accepting Clemenceau's compromise to treat Romania less harshly than the Americans wished, the Council anticipated Brătianu would comply with the latest instructions. The Allied leaders had not yet been convinced that Brătianu would disregard their instructions. The Romanian Premier not only refused to heed the terms of the August 5 note, but even reasserted his independence of action when the Romanian High Command in Budapest submitted a new ultimatum to Peidl on August 5 requiring Hungary to submit within five hours to a harsh economic arrangement. In terms reminiscent of the economic provisions of the Peace of Bucharest, Brătianu demanded the surrender of all military equipment, 50 per cent of railway rolling stock, 600 automobiles and trucks, 30 per cent of cattle and other domesticated animals, 30 per cent of all agricultural machinery, 35,000 wagon loads of grain, 50 per cent of all river boats and all river craft seized by Magyar troops in Wallachia during the war, and sufficient coal to operate railways under Romanian supervision. Hungary was also required to release soldiers of the Romanian army who had deserted during the war, yield Romanians who were prisoners of war and hostages, and pay the costs of the present Romanian occupation. If Hungary rejected these terms, the Romanians threatened to seize the foregoing items, and possibly more, in retaliation for the "inhumane treatment" meted out to their country by the Central Powers. The occupation would endure until every condition was fulfilled.[49]

This second, unauthorized submission of an ultimatum in the same week aroused the wrath of Frank Polk, who showed the note to Mişu on August 6, warning him it was tantamount to a separate peace which the Allies would not tolerate. Mişu replied that the measures were dictated by military demands because Romania had not been treated fairly in regard to reparations. He claimed the same right for Romania which Belgium had, namely, a seat on the Reparations Commission. Polk rejected this demand and urged the Council to dispatch a note to Brătianu warning him not to impose an armistice or economic terms without permission of the Allies.[50]

That day (August 6) Mişu and Vaida-Voevod were summoned to the Council to explain Romania's actions. They could not understand Allied objections to Romanian seizure of property rightfully belonging to Romanian peasants. Mişu deemed it essential to acquire this property before the Magyars could remove Romanian identification marks. All property taken that was later found to belong to Hungarian citizens would be returned "without a murmur." In the meantime, goods seized would be as safe in Romanian as in Magyar hands. Clemenceau was not convinced; he read a note warning Brătianu of the illegality of actions taken in Hungary, where Romania was disregarding the rights of other allied states to reparations from Hungary. He reiterated the

Allied intention to consider Romania an outcast ally if she continued to defy orders. When Mişu politely promised to forward this note to Brătianu, Clemenceau excoriated him, demanding immediate compliance with what he termed the final decision of the Allies. Balfour interceded to soothe the ruffled Romanians, confessing that no one disputed the fact that Magyars had mistreated Romanians, but he did not think grievances permitted Romania to seize goods which rightfully belonged to Czechs, Serbs, Slovaks, and others who were inhabitants of the former Kingdom of Hungary. The two Romanian delegates replied it was necessary to adopt those means to obtain what was rightfully Romania's because the Allies had rarely allowed her to present claims to reparations.

Vaida-Voevod pointed out that the Allies should declare the Belgrade armistice non-existent because Hungary refused to obey it, while Romania "always accepted" the Council's instructions, and because the Magyars had attacked Romania, "thereby annulling that armistice." Now that Hungary had been conquered and occupied, it was the sincere desire of the Romanians to become friends of the Magyars, and the Allies should assist Romania in pacifying Hungary. He pleaded for a modification of the latest note to Brătianu by adding this sentence: "Romania could still rely upon the Allies' good will." Every note sent to Bucharest had been printed in the Magyar press and interpreted as censure of Romania, Vaida-Voevod asserted, but if a kind word were inserted in the present note, it would encourage Brătianu to comply.

Pichon and Tittoni again supported the Romanians, and they won Clemenceau to their views. The Council agreed to insert the following phrase to conciliate Brătianu: "The Supreme Council whilst fully recognizing the just claims of Romania and her devotion to the common cause..." The note of August 6 was then dispatched.[51] The new note, like previous communications designed to counteract Brătianu's moves, arrived too late. The Peidl government was ousted on August 6 when it rejected Brătianu's economic terms.[52] Rumors of a Romanian plot to install a puppet regime under the nominal leadership of Archduke Joseph Habsburg were confirmed when he was appointed.[53]

Frank Polk demanded an immediate end to Romanian interference in Hungary's affairs lest Bolshevism be encouraged and Lenin be enabled to use this latest example of Romanian misconduct to terrify the Russians into believing the Allies would restore the Romanovs if Bolshevism were wiped out. He produced a memorandum drafted by

John Foster Dulles, American expert on reparations, that pointed out how the allied states, due to receive reparations from Hungary, would find nothing left for them if Romania alone were allowed to seize goods, thereby denying the principle of solidarity established by the Treaty of Versailles. By terms of an agreement to which all Allied and Associated Powers, including Romania, were signatory, each was due to receive reparations in proportion to damages sustained regardless of which enemy state had inflicted the damage. If Romania collected the indemnity she thought due her, nothing but dispute, recrimination, and serious trouble would ensue.[54]

Polk urged termination of military assistance to Romania and her expulsion from the Allied camp. Even pro-Romanian Pichon admitted Brătianu had committed an unjustifiable act in setting up a reactionary régime with a Habsburg as provisional governor.[55] Tittoni likewise abandoned his defense of Romania and criticized a report that King Ferdinand was about to enter Budapest at the head of a victory parade.[56] But Balfour cautioned against tossing Romania out of the Allied camp lest a serious quarrel within the Peace Conference be publicized. Clemenceau adamantly refused to keep the crisis silent. He stipulated in no uncertain terms that

> he would rather leave his place in the Supreme Council. The Romanians had always behaved like this and deserved to be told that if they continued they would be regarded as having broken the Alliance. They were in conflict with the Conference and they must suffer for it.

Polk concurred, adding that, when Romania wanted money from the United States, she would declare herself an ally, but "she could not be an ally for financial purposes only." The Council decided to send another note warning of a diplomatic rupture if Romania failed to comply with previous instructions.[57]

The third note sent since the Romanians occupied Budapest was, like the others, rendered less forceful by the inclusion of a paragraph calculated to appease Brătianu. He was requested to show solidarity with the Allies by "immediately destroying" the impression of Romania intending to separate herself from the Allied camp. The Premier was asked to prove publicly that he was ready to execute in good faith the policy of the Council. In other words, Romania was still permitted to act in concert with the Allies in dealing with the Hungarian crisis because the Council was obviously unable to act there alone.[58]

This dispatch, sent on August 7, may not have reached Brătianu before he forwarded a note to Paris on August 9. His message did not reach the Council until August 14.[59] In the interim, reports of the military mission in Budapest began to arrive in Paris. Direful stories of depredations and atrocities perpetrated by Romanians were catalogued in dispatches transmitted jointly by the four generals. A treatment of that four-month episode cannot be given extensive coverage here; only those developments affecting decisions at higher levels will be cited.[60] The first such event was the arrival in Budapest of Constantin Diamandy, whom Brătianu appointed as High Commissioner of Occupied Hungary to cooperate with the mission on an equal level.[61] Diamandy refused to acknowledge the mission's authority, but he was prepared to reach decisions in common with the generals. He overruled the mission's objections to the looting and denied the accusation that Romania had served an ultimatum on Archduke Joseph to yield the entire Banat and the comitat of Békés, and join Romania in an anti-Slav union.[62]

Since it was generally believed the Archduke had been imposed on Hungary by Romania, the Allies found themselves in the incongruous situation of asserting their authority against Romania, an allied state, while concurrently permitting the mission to deal with a puppet regime under a Habsburg, whose ejection both Czechoslovakia and Serbia demanded.[63] The four generals believed, however, the Archduke was willing to work with them against the Romanians. His cabinet was headed by Stephen Friedrich, formerly a member of Károlyi's government, who soon indicated a readiness to work for any side promising Hungary the greatest benefits.[64]

Balfour noted the paradox of supporting a Habsburg, whom the Romanians had installed, while simultaneously challenging Romania's authority to establish a government in Budapest. Moreover, he expected the Czechs and Serbs to take action compelling the Archduke to retire from office. Clemenceau, accepting Diamandy's denial of Romanian complicity in installing the Archduke, objected to a proposal to recognize the Habsburg régime in return for a promise to comply with Council orders. To do so, he pointed out, entailed disavowal of Allied commitments to Czechoslovakia and Serbia to forestall a Habsburg restoration. His argument prevailed and it was agreed to force the Archduke to resign, but permit his cabinet to remain in office.[65]

The Council learned on August 13 of Brătianu's latest set of demands on Hungary — cession of the entire Banat, the comitat of

Békés, and all territory east of the Tisa.[66] This new ultimatum aroused Clemenceau's wrath to fever pitch; he wailed

> that France had lost thousands of cattle and had recovered less than 100,000 head from Germany. France submitted to the Supreme Council's decisions. The victory of the Allies had found Romania bound by the Peace of Bucharest, in other words, at the feet of Germany as a result.... Romania was doubling her territory. She now grabs goods belonging to the Allies as a whole. If France and Italy behaved like this, there would be no peace. France and Italy obtained far less than their demands and far less than they had lost.[67]

Clemenceau and Polk urged the Council to publicize the first open defiance of Allied authority and to deny Transylvania and part of the Banat to Romania if resistance continued. But Balfour wished to postpone such drastic measures, and Tittoni did not think Romania's misconduct justified giving any more of the Banat to Serbia.

Brătianu's reply of August 9 reached the Council the next day (August 14). Acknowledging the latest note from Paris, the Premier expressed surprise over undeserved reproaches and accusations heaped upon him. He insisted upon his right as an ally to submit a new armistice to Hungary because the Belgrade truce was no longer in existence and because the Allies had invited him to cooperate in the campaign against Hungary. The success of that operation gave him a new title to claims which included the right to collaborate with the mission in restoring order and establishing an acceptable government in Budapest, the maintenance of his troops in Budapest until the crisis was resolved, requisition of war matériel and other goods left by the retreating Germans, and operation of Hungarian railways in the interests of security. Brătianu denied having evicted Peidl or installing the Archduke. As for the charge he had disregarded orders to refrain from occupying Budapest, Brătianu denied having received the order before Romanian troops entered the city. He insisted he was rendering great service to the work of peace and, for that reason

> it would be difficult to conceive that the rights should be denied to Romania when other allied armies were able, without any obstacle on the part of the Conference, to completely drain and exhaust occupied territories which should

have been, according to the peace, turned over not to a former enemy, but to an ally.[68]

This response convinced the Council of Brătianu's intention to act in accord with the Allies. The Allied statesmen assumed Brătianu would never risk a rupture with the Peace Conference. This naïve underestimation of his resolve to act independently in Hungary, where his actions could not be controlled by the mission, was a fatal blunder on the part of statesmen who, it must be admitted, had not experienced the give-and-take negotiations with Brătianu during the war years. The Council members failed to see that despite all their notes to the contrary, Brătianu was determined to carry out the 1916 guarantee giving him an open road to Budapest. Thus the Council decided to notify the Premier of its satisfaction with his reply and to request him to respect the authority of the mission. In a note to Brătianu on August 14, the Allies indicated their readiness to discuss controversial points raised by the Premier after he complied with orders.[69]

In seeking an explanation of the Allied attitude, it would seem that they feared a revival of communism in Hungary. Their anxiety led them to consider the Romanian occupation preferable to the chaos which could ensue from a resurgence of radicalism. But they planned to compel Romania's evacuation as soon as the mission equipped a native Hungarian constabulary to replace Romanian troops as guardians of peace. Another explanation of the Council's anxiety lay in the presence at Szeged of the "shadow cabinet" of "Whites," steadily growing in strength and prestige. It was apparent the "Whites" had become a divisive force threatening to incite civil war.

Admiral Nicholas Horthy, Minister of War and commander of the "White" army, visited Romanian headquarters in Budapest to warn against an advance west of the Danube.[70] Horthy's order set off rumors, attributed to Friedrich, that only by an alliance with Romania could the Budapest régime defend Hungary against machinations of "Whites" intent on reviving feudal Hungary.[71] These stories, as well as the Council's earlier instructions, prompted the mission to force the Archduke to resign on August 23. Friedrich remained premier despite Romanian protests. He soon defied the Romanians by scheduling elections for the end of September in the hope a government acceptable to the Allies would be established. Romanian protests indicated the Archduke, not Friedrich, was the puppet.[72]

The situation in Hungary had become so entangled by mid-August that the Allies were led to believe the best course of action was to permit the crisis to run its course. Rather than provoke Brătianu any further, the Council considered it wiser to let the occupation continue lest civil war break out between the fractious elements in Hungary where Romania was at least maintaining a fragile peace.

The Clerk Mission

Reaction in Bucharest to Brătianu's successful defiance of the Allies encouraged him to still further feats. In interviews with the British chargé, Brătianu revealed a wish for a close association with Hungary and Poland to counteract any Czech-Serb alliance designed to make Romania their satellite. He accused Prague and Belgrade of plotting to force him to yield Bessarabia to Russia. For that reason, he had to protect Romania against the Slavs because the League of Nations, whose failure he prophesied, was too utopian for small states to trust. When asked about rumors of his plan to annex Hungary, Brătianu called the stories "mere moonshine." Such reports were circulated by Averescu and Ionescu, who would "wreck the country in two months" if either gained office. He claimed to have irrefutable evidence Averescu had planned as early as September 1916 to sign a separate peace with the Central Powers.[73] Brătianu boasted about the Allied inability to dislodge his troops from Hungary, and reiterated a willingness to cooperate with the Allies in establishing a "good government" there; in his opinion such a régime must not be "aggressively chauvinistic in its attitude toward its neighbors."[74] It was clear Brătianu would never consent to evacuate Hungary until a régime willing to submit to his maximum demands was established in Budapest.

In the meantime requisitioning and intimidating continued in Budapest, were relaxed whenever the Allies reacted sternly to news from the mission about provocations, and then resumed after apologies were made to allay the distress of the Allies and their representatives in Budapest. As evidence of Allied irresolution, the episode about children's medical supplies seized by the Romanians may be cited. Herbert Hoover reported Romanian troops had entered a children's hospital and confiscated its medical supplies. Instead of retaliating in a manner to indicate their wrath, the Allies could only send another note instructing Brătianu to recognize the reparations principle and respect the mission's authority in regard to requisitioning.[75] In fact, the Allies still threatened to end shipments of military supplies and relief if their authority was not respected. Earlier decisions to terminate such assistance had evidently never been carried out. The Allies finally did agree to place an embargo on shipments at the end of August.[76]

Brătianu's defiance aroused American suspicions that he was being encouraged by the French and Italian foreign ministries; otherwise, as Polk intimated, he would never have dared to defy the Council alone. Polk accused the French and Italians on September 2 of supporting Brătianu's obstructive tactics and his "propensity for deceit." Philippe Berthelot, who frequently assumed Clemenceau's duties as plenipotentiary while the Premier was steering ratification of the Versailles Treaty through the Chamber of Deputies, denied the charge and advised Polk that violent language used in the notes had prompted Brătianu to repudiate them.[77]

This explanation did not satisfy Polk or Balfour. Both accused Brătianu of outright prevarication for saying at one moment he had not seen the notes and asserting at another his distaste for their language. Polk offered, for the first and only time, to send ships from American squadrons stationed at Fiume and Smyrna into the Black Sea to serve notice upon Brătianu that the Allies were serious. Balfour was prepared to have British vessels do the same. But Clemenceau and Tittoni did not favor such strong demonstrations to force Brătianu into yielding.[78]

Clemenceau's retreat was due to his professed fear of the pro-Romanian press of Paris, which, "by concocting a story that the Allies were preparing to fight the Romanians," could inspire increased opposition to him in the Chamber.[79] His argument was based on his pledge to parliamentary critics that France would extract satisfactory terms from Germany. Since the Treaty of Versailles did not contain the extremely harsh provisions demanded by Poincaré, Foch, and other vigorous nationalists, Clemenceau was obliged to explain that this shortcoming was compensated for by the Treaty of Guarantees with Britain and the United States, signed June 28, which assured France military assistance in the event of an unprovoked German attack.[80] But Clemenceau, suspecting for some time that Wilson would not obtain Senate ratification of the guarantee treaty in view of the President's reluctance to fight for it during public debates in August, already had given free rein to the Quai d'Orsay to revive the traditional policy of erecting an alliance system encircling Germany.[81] Since Russia was no longer available as an ally, the small states in East Central Europe could fill the vacuum. Fear of Germany and measures to thwart her revenge explain the ensuing moves by the Quai d'Orsay to cultivate the friendship of Romania and other small powers located south and east of Germany.[82]

The Americans detected a deviation in French policy which, by its very nature, entailed a course independent of, and hence contrary to, the unanimous decisions of the Council. Although occasional references to unauthorized acts of the Quai d'Orsay had been made in the past by Coolidge, Bliss, White, and Hoover, not until September did the Americans realize the danger of these activities insofar as Allied policy toward Romania was concerned.[83] The Americans, and especially Wilson, could not or refused to believe that France was actuated by considerations of national security, balance of power, and potential markets. This myopia precluded Wilson's adoption of tactics assuring the French of American readiness to recognize these considerations. Those who succeeded Wilson as first plenipotentiaries (Lansing, White, and Polk) also failed to understand French motives.

Polk was the first delegate to defy the Quai d'Orsay, but he apparently could not comprehend the basis of its decision to placate Brătianu. He went so far as to request Lansing to approve moving Council sessions to quarters other than those in the Quai because "permanent French Foreign Office personnel were creating in Romania the impression that the British and American policies were antagonistic to their own."[84] Although Lansing rejected the request, he did summon the French ambassador on September 29 to express objections to the pro-Romanian attitudes of the Quai d'Orsay and Saint-Aulaire, who was implementing French policy in Bucharest.[85] Saint-Aulaire's activities were also condemned by Polk, who accused the French envoy of deliberately delaying the delivery of notes to Brătianu and forwarding of the Premier's replies to Paris. Polk's evidence came from Henry Schoenfeld, American chargé in Bucharest, who reported on September 2 that Saint-Aulaire was placing blame upon the United States for the Allied attitude and persuading Brătianu that France could not modify American hostility toward Romania. Schoenfeld revealed that, according to Brătianu, France could do nothing because of Hoover's bitter animosity toward Romania.[86] Dispatches from Bucharest told how Saint-Aulaire was encouraging Brătianu to prolong the occupation of Hungary until he had acquired more rolling stock and assuring him that the Council's notes would have been more moderate had the Quai d'Orsay drafted all of them.[87]

Intercessions by Saint-Aulaire emboldened Brătianu's defiance. He denied (September 4) having received the notes of August 14, 23, and 25 (regarding cessation of requisitioning, termination of shipments of Allied supplies, and warning of a possible rupture with the Allies, respectively). But Brătianu was obviously aware of the contents of these notes in view of his assertions that the "pernicious and dangerous" Allied attitude failed to consider the services Romania had rendered in eliminating Magyar Bolshevism. He declared his intention to evacuate Hungary, but only as far as the Tisa, rather than play the Entente policeman." The withdrawal, he asserted, would be carried out after Hungary was disarmed, required railway equipment was requisitioned, and Romanian economic interests assured. Brătianu declined "all responsibility for the chaotic state into which the evacuation will plunge this region of Europe, disrupted by the Bolsheviks and monarchical reactionaries."[88]

Brătianu's inadvertent admission describing the notes while denying he had received them did not escape Polk and Balfour, who believed his complaint of ignorance was "well-nigh incredible." They said it was an elaborate scheme to ignore the Council's wishes.[89] Polk wanted to recall the mission because its authority was being flouted, but Clemenceau again succeeded in winning him over to less drastic steps. The French leader proposed sending an official emissary to Bucharest to hand a stern message to Brătianu personally. In suggesting this, Clemenceau confirmed Polk's charge that some Allied envoys in Bucharest were subverting Council policy. The Council accepted the plan and, on Balfour's nomination, instructed Sir George Russell Clerk (private secretary to Under Secretary for Foreign Affairs Curzon) to undertake the mission.[90]

The note conveyed by Clerk contained the strongest language yet used: Romania had deliberately resolved to defy the Allies by following an independent and unauthorized course in Hungary; Romania may have had a legal right to defend herself, but she had no right to occupy unassigned regions of Hungary or oust Béla Kun without Allied approval; Romania was violating the Belgrade armistice and the principle of reparations by systematically stripping Hungary "of every species of movable wealth, alive or dead, which seems worth the labor of transportation," the total of which would be deducted from her bill of claims; and Romania had willfully ignored remonstrances to a point where it was questionable whether she was still entitled to the appellation "Allied Power," since the five Great Powers were the ones "who mainly won the war," and who had sufficient evidence to deny Romania all privileges.

Brătianu was requested to reply affirmatively to the following queries: (1) is Romania prepared to evacuate Hungary on a day to be set by the Council? (2) is Romania ready to cease all requisitioning immediately? (3) is Romania prepared to surrender goods already seized? and (4) is Romania willing to cooperate faithfully with the Allies and under their direction in restoring order in Hungary so that a responsible government could be installed to negotiate peace? The note concluded with a charge that no responsible Romanian statesman would wish to sever relations with the Allies.[91]

This latest message (September 5) could hardly be called an ultimatum because only the second question required immediate compliance, while the others indicated obedience at unspecified dates. Three statements in the note, moreover, rendered its impact harmless. The first stated the Allies acknowledged Romania's right to occupy the Tisa for defense purposes while Kun represented a threat. The second denied the validity of Romania's claim to occupy the Tisa since Kun was gone, but permitted her troops to remain in Hungary until a specific date was set for evacuation. And the third assured Brătianu that Romania would be reinstated as a fully privileged allied state if he signified a willingness to comply with the four questions. Furthermore, the note, like previous communications, was conspicuous for the absence of an indication the Allies would send their troops to enforce compliance.[92] The Americans were skeptical about the success of Clerk's mission. Polk wished to warn Brătianu of a diminution of Romania's territorial awards if he continued to resist, but the American delegation convinced him to abandon the idea because of opposition already shown to similar schemes by the French, British, and Italians.[93] Then, by coincidence, General Bandholtz undertook a journey to Bucharest to acquaint himself with the reasons for Brătianu's obduracy.[94] Arriving in the Romanian capital on September 9, three days before Clerk was expected, Bandholtz met with Brătianu, who told him America was too far away to have any knowledge of Romania, that the requisitioning was fully justified, and that the war had equalized all nations which had participated in it as allies. The Premier called the visit of Smuts to Budapest "an appeasement mission." Reconstructing history, he lied to Bandholtz in saying Germany had promised all territories acquired by Romania since the war, but that did not deter him from joining the Allies, to whom he was now rendering a service in pacifying Hungary. He promised to evacuate as soon as he felt secure, and he assured Bandholtz his word would be binding upon his successors. Expecting to resign shortly to avoid signing the minority treaty, Brătianu asserted his successor would be entirely under his control.

Brătianu permitted Bandholtz to read the reply he was preparing to send to the Council. It contained the already familiar charges, including his reiteration that the Allies had asked him to occupy Budapest and that he would treat Hungary as a conquered state in a manner no different from that of the Allies in regions they had occupied, namely, "by draining them dry." He categorically refused to sign the treaty with Austria unless his demands were completely satisfied.[95]

The Americans, apprised by Bandholtz of the reception Clerk could expect, were convinced of Brătianu's determination to resist despite Council warnings. Ever since his arrival in Budapest, Bandholtz had been asserting the French were encouraging Romanian resistance. His accusation was confirmed in Bucharest where he learned non-receipt of the Council's notes was considered a diplomatic joke. He advised Polk of French plans to dominate Romania by throwing blame for the Council's policy upon the United States and by securing commercial advantages in Romania.[96]

As soon as Clerk arrived in Bucharest (September 12), he became aware of French intrigues when he met with the four Allied envoys. After examining the latest note, Saint-Aulaire, supported by Italian envoy Martin Franklin, expressed grave concern about the proposed evacuation of Hungary. The French minister was convinced an immediate withdrawal would produce anarchy, with the result that the Allies would be obliged to request the Romanians to return. He insisted, as Brătianu had for months, that the Allies had asked Romania to occupy Budapest, and then proceeded to describe the note Brătianu had shown Bandholtz on September 9. It was received in Paris on September 11.[97]

Brătianu greeted Clerk on September 12 with news of his government's resignation. In his letter to the King, Brătianu explained he was quitting because the 1916 Alliance had been brought into disrepute and because the "Supreme Council, which replaced the Peace Conference of the Allies," imposed on Romania conditions he could not accept.[98] The fall of the Liberal government did not entail any shift in policy because a new cabinet was not formed for some time. When one was finally appointed on September 29 under Văitoianu, Brătianu's minister of war, it was dominated by Brătianu even though he did not serve in it. He was authorized by the King to control affairs during an "interregnum" that observers compared to the period in November-December 1918, when Brătianu installed Coandă, whom he controlled. Technically, therefore, no legal government existed from September 12 to 29, a circumstance Brătianu utilized in his negotiations with Clerk and the Council. He repeatedly claimed his decisions would have to be referred to the next government for approval because he held no official position. Thus he procrastinated while citing his lack of authority.[99]

When presented the collection of notes by the monocled Council emissary on September 16, Brătianu brushed them aside, declaring every message to be unjust and untrue. He confessed to Clerk he was completely responsible for the occupation of Budapest, admitting that

> when the last Hungarian advance failed and became a retreat, he ordered the Romanian army not to stop until Budapest was taken.... This was done in the general interests of peace and security, although unauthorized. He did not hesitate to take Budapest rather than refer to Paris and risk refusal such as he had experienced.[100]

Brătianu revealed he had issued orders for the immediate evacuation of Hungary, and he was ready to permit agents of the Reparations Commission to make inventories of goods not seized as legal requisitions. If a Romanian expert were named to that commission, he would permit the Allies to deduct the value of those goods from Romania's share of Hungarian reparations. As to charges of interference in Hungary's affairs, Brătianu accused Friedrich of hostility in arranging elections for September 28, which he was determined to regulate lest an inimical government be established.[101]

At their meeting on September 20, Brătianu assured Clerk all confiscations of Hungarian private property had ceased. In return, he asked the Allies to reject any regime in Hungary which he considered unfriendly. He again demanded an alteration of the frontier so that Romania could obtain the mouth of the Mureş River (located in the comitat of Csanád), the railway line from Satu Mare to Oradea, and the railway junction of Békés-Csaba. If the Allies rejected these terms, he warned that he or his successor would treat Hungary alone, and again threatened to evacuate Hungary at once and permit the communists to regain power.[102]

Clerk deduced the crisis as being intentionally prolonged in the hope the Allies would ultimately capitulate. Brătianu was whipping up an inflammatory press campaign against partition of the Banat, the minority treaty, and Allied policy in general.[103] He intended to wreck the chances of any successor government willing to compromise, especially after learning of British approaches to Ionescu and Maniu about forming a conciliatory government. Neither the Conservative

Democrats nor the Transylvanian Nationalists, nor Averescu and Marghiloman, who were also consulted, had the strength to form a government without the support of the other, and none had the courage to defy Brătianu, who had much influence over the King. All opposition leaders agreed with Brătianu on at least one point, namely, acceptance of Allied demands entailed political suicide. Formation of an anti-Liberal bloc could not materialize because Ionescu refused to meet with either Averescu or Marghiloman, whom he considered traitors, and Maniu rejected dealings with any of the others lest his party's collaboration with Brătianu be jeopardized.[104]

While Clerk was in Bucharest, Brătianu further compounded the crisis by arranging on September 23 for the nomination of Corneliu Manolescu-Râmniceanu, President of the Court of Cassation, to form a new government.[105] This was a ruse to prove to the Allies that the Liberals enjoyed mass support, for Manolescu held out an olive branch to the opposition parties, asking them to join a coalition with the Liberals. When no one responded, Manolescu advised the Allied envoys the public demanded a continuation of the Liberal regime which promised him to secure fulfillment of Romanian aspirations.[106]

When Clerk was about to leave on September 28, two important announcements were made. Elections were scheduled for the first week in November, and a new government under Văitoianu would assume office the next day. Clerk met with Văitoianu and Brătianu on September 29 in a final effort, only to come away with the realization that the new government was a continuation of Brătianu's régime in another form. This conclusion was evident when Văitoianu assured him of his determination to pursue Brătianu's policy. On his return to Paris, Clerk stopped in Budapest to meet with the mission, whose information indicated Romania had not ceased requisitioning. Clerk became convinced that the crisis could be resolved if the Friedrich government were dismissed, the Romanians forced to withdraw, and a swift peace with Hungary were concluded.[107] His recommendations and the methods to be employed depended for their success upon Văitoianu's attitude, not upon the situation in Budapest. When Clerk arrived in Paris on October 10, the turmoil in Hungary had not ended, nor was there any indication Romania was prepared to comply with the notes he had delivered to Brătianu.

The Văitoianu Government

The new cabinet in Bucharest, consisting of seven generals, was called a neutralist, non-party regime appointed to solve difficulties with the Allies and hold elections in a free and impartial atmosphere.[108] This description did not convince opposition leaders who called Văitoianu a puppet of Brătianu installed for purposes of delaying elections and keeping the army mobilized so that soldiers could not return home to vote.[109]

Văitoianu was not the statesman the British had in mind. He was not only a loyal trouble-shooter for Brătianu, renowned for his "corrupt and oppressive administration of Bessarabia," but also a non-entity with no diplomatic experience.[110] His ten-week ministry was not considered to be anything but a Brătianu régime in military disguise. This belief was strengthened by Văitoianu's frequent assertions, whenever pressed for a definite answer, that he must consult his cabinet before responding. Since his government was composed of non-entities like himself, with the possible exception of Foreign Minister Mişu, the conclusion was that Brătianu made the decisions.

Those acquainted with Brătianu's tactics could recall how he habitually resigned whenever confronted with fateful decisions, or threatened to quit if his policies encountered determined opposition. His first threat had occurred in December 1910, when King Carol opposed his aggressive policy in maintaining the balance of power in the Balkans. Carol dismissed Brătianu and appointed Titu Maiorescu to head a Conservative government that went ahead to fulfill the Liberal policy. Brătianu did not permit Carol to repeat this in following years, nor did he ever allow Ferdinand to interfere in government affairs. During his negotiations with both sides during the war, Brătianu always gave notice of an intention to quit if either side rejected his demands. To the Germans this signified subsequent appointment of a pro-Allied government; to the Allies his resignation entailed summoning of either a neutralist or pro-German régime.

It will be recalled that Brătianu did not quit until he was faced with the critical question of separate peace. Then he promoted the candidacy of Averescu, who refused to be obedient and, consequently, was dismissed. Marghiloman then carried to completion the inauspicious task of obtaining peace, as a result of which his political career and the reputation of the Conservatives were ruined. The Coandă government held office only until Brătianu, who had the King appoint it, was invited to the Peace Conference. Finally, in September 1919, the cycle was completed with Văitoianu performing the same duties Averescu, Marghiloman, and Coandă did before him, namely, serving as *locum tenens* for Brătianu and acting as scapegoat for altercations Brătianu preferred to avoid.

Brătianu had no intention of relinquishing the coveted position as molder of Romania's destiny. He needed to emerge victorious in the coming, long overdue elections, not because defeat entailed any diminution of his power, but for the purpose of winning popular vindication of his policies. The elections would be the first held according to the electoral reform of June 1917, which provided for universal manhood suffrage, proportional representation, and compulsory voting.[111] Brătianu anticipated the voters of Transylvania, who were recently granted an agrarian reform by the Consiliul Dirigent (September 12, 1919), would favor Liberals instead of Transylvanian Nationalists because the peasants there were enjoying the harvest of goods from Hungary while awaiting ratification of the reform by the Liberal parliament. An agrarian reform for Bucovina was announced on September 7, but needed ratification. The reform for Bessarabia had been ratified in December 1918. By emphasizing the inevitable restoration of the new provinces to their former rulers (Magyars, Austrians, and Russians), which would allegedly result if Romania yielded to the Allies, Brătianu undermined the election campaign of his opponents. In stressing opposition to the minority treaty, he expected to soothe the anxieties of voters in the Old Kingdom who were destined to be outnumbered by the peoples of the new provinces. To assuage these and other concocted fears, Brătianu skillfully aroused the belief that benefits conferred on or promised to the Romanians would not be carried to completion if the Liberals lost. Rattigan, the British chargé, strove to convince Brătianu of the harmless nature of the minority treaty, but his efforts failed. He advised the Foreign Office that "it must be remembered that there is much of the naughty child in the Romanian character. Conscious he is doing wrong and frightened at the impending punishment, he becomes almost impossible to deal with."[112]

Six weeks remained before the elections. Brătianu had to resist the Allies until then. His determination did not pass unnoticed by Clerk, who reported to the Council on October 10 that the Romanian statesman was playing for time so that the "Allied waters would become sufficiently troubled for him to catch many excellent fish." Clerk urged that Brătianu be advised the Allies were not divided over issues such as the treaty for Turkey, the Fiume dispute between Italy and Serbia, and the policy toward Romania. As long as the Allies remained indecisive, Clerk asserted, Brătianu would be able to reinforce his position against that of opposition leaders who were reportedly interested in yielding to Allied demands.

Clerk presented the Council with an evaluation of the crisis prepared by Allen Leeper, who had accompanied him to Bucharest. Leeper wrote a masterly appraisal based on interviews with Brătianu and his opponents. Brătianu's objectives were known to all, but Leeper uncovered new devices by which he proposed to succeed. Brătianu planned to nationalize the petroleum and other essential industries to place the Liberals in full control of the economy and to thwart efforts already made by the Americans, British, and French to regain their oil holdings or secure new ones. By pitting one Allied Power against the other in the question of petroleum concessions, Brătianu hoped to emerge the victor.[113]

Leeper noted that Brătianu anticipated the disintegration of the Allies into the Great Power combinations as had existed before the war. This would enable Romania to form an alliance with Poland and arrange a rapprochement with a Hungarian puppet government to thwart a revival of Russian influence in East Central Europe and to unite thereby a solid bloc of powers against Czechoslovakia and Serbia.[114] According to Leeper, Brătianu was depending upon French and Italian military assistance, British indifference, and American disengagement from European affairs. He had called the League of Nations an Anglo-American weapon to exploit small states and an organization of no value to France or Italy. The censored press in Bucharest was filled with articles about differences of opinions among the Allies, the inevitability of a breach between the British and French, and an end to Anglo-American friendship because their economic interests were vitally opposed to each other. Leeper attributed this propaganda to French press and publicity agencies, which were inspiring Brătianu, "probably with the approval of" the Quai d'Orsay, to resist.[115] This observation was borne out by a statement of Saint-Aulaire to Rattigan on October 10, according to which the French envoy admitted he had sharply criticized American policy toward Romania.[116]

No less guilty of upsetting the Allied stand was Italy and her envoy, Martin Franklin. The Italians had, as their major objective, the isolation of the new south Slav kingdom. This aim naturally appealed to Brătianu, who also stood to lose territory if south Slav claims were realized. He was therefore receptive to Italy's approaches in the spring and summer of 1919, but his counter-demands (support of Romania's maximum claims, plans to erect a Romanian-Hungarian-Polish bloc, and need of military assistance) were shunned by the Italians, who then made overtures to Hungary in August 1919 to secure aid in return for a promise to evict Romanian occupation forces. When Hungary rejected this scheme, the Italians again turned to Romania only to encounter Brătianu's anger at learning the Italians had supported the plan to retrocede southern Dobrodgea.[117] Leeper noted, in light of these and other revelations, how delighted Brătianu was by the imminent break in Allied ranks due to Italy's involvement in the dispute over Fiume.

The Allied statesmen were only too well aware of the split in their ranks. For that reason, none but the Americans desired to adopt Leeper's recommendation of an unequivocal ultimatum ordering Romania to comply or lose her ties to the Allies and her membership in the League of Nations. This stern proposal would have upset French, Italian, and, to a lesser degree, long-range British plans for Romania. The French and Italian delegates were more interested in the alternative suggested by British diplomats to keep Romania in the Allied camp. This was a scheme to encourage Ferdinand to summon Averescu, Ionescu, or Maniu to form a government of Brătianu's opponents. Clerk had described them as more conciliatory than Brătianu; all they requested was a firm Allied promise permitting Romania to discuss minor changes in the minority treaty, which none wished to accept in its present form. Clerk and Leeper believed a cordial invitation to Văitoianu to discuss the minority treaty, a bid which they believed he would not spurn, would deprive Brătianu of his argument that only those Romanians contemplating political suicide would dare sign the treaty. Leeper was convinced Brătianu would resist until the last moment, but would never break with the Allies. If Ferdinand and the wavering opposition leaders were promised a satisfactory revision of the minority treaty, the King would dismiss Brătianu and summon a coalition to sign rather than risk a rupture with the Allies.[118]

The Council was influenced by Clerk and Leeper and by the intercession of the French, who wanted to concede even more. In their note to Văitoianu of October 11, the Allies extended an invitation to the Romanian delegation in Paris to examine the minority treaty and present amendments after Văitoianu agreed to accept the principle of the treaty. Romania was also extended the privilege, suggested by Loucheur of the Reparations Commission, of naming a representative with full powers to a sub-commission about to make an inventory of goods requisitioned in Hungary. An evacuation of Hungary was still urged, but to a lesser degree because a Hungarian police force had not yet been organized. No specific date was set for the evacuation to begin. The only item in the latest note indicating any firmness was the statement about the frontier not being subject to change. That reiteration of previous notices was included at American insistence. The Americans also secured adoption of a new procedure intended to show Allied unity, namely, the note would be handed to Văitoianu by the four Allied envoys jointly. Polk wanted to release the note to the press, but Clemenceau convinced him to await Văitoianu's reply.[119]

The note was received in Bucharest within a week, an unusually short period in view of the fact that previous messages regularly required at least three weeks to travel from the Quai d'Orsay to the Romanian capital. Văitoianu, away on a vacation, did not receive it until October 20 when three of the four envoys delivered it. Italian minister Franklin abstained from joining his colleagues because he had no instructions from Rome.[120] This display of dissension, criticized by Clerk, Leeper, and the Americans, rendered nugatory the notes intended impact upon Văitoianu. Not only had the Italians wrecked the Council's plan, but they also went further to demonstrate their independent action by sending a battleship to Constanţa on October 24, and a company of troops, accompanied by a band, to Bucharest to celebrate the first anniversary of the battle of Vittorio Veneto.[121] Perhaps because of these Italian gestures, Văitoianu did not reply until one month later. No one could dispute Brătianu's oft-repeated charge that a schism existed in Allied ranks.

In Paris, meanwhile, Polk was growing increasingly impatient over Văitoianu's delay and the continued disregard of orders of the mission in Budapest. He insisted on Romania's evacuation before a Hungarian police force was effectively established. General Bliss cursed the French and Romanians in the same breath, and he urged Polk to deny Romania every benefit of the peace treaties and to warn his colleagues that the United States opposed any break-up of the Peace Conference brought on by the independent action of one or more powers. Bliss recommended that

if the Council permits the dissolution of the Allied and Associated Powers.... the United States regards itself as dissolved from any association it has entered into until the obligations of that association are admitted to be binding on all.[122]

The Americans then drafted a plan, approved by Lansing, by which the allied states could sign protocols recognizing Hungary's cession of territory to her neighbors. Actual signing of a peace with Hungary, which had been drafted and was ready to be submitted to a responsible government, could take place after the Peace Conference, but, in the meantime, the frontier settlement could be concluded. The Americans believed Romania would not hesitate to sign such a protocol, but the scheme was rejected by the Council in favor of awaiting Văitoianu's reply.[123]

Polk would not be discouraged. He summoned Mişu, who was about to return home to his new post of foreign minister, and asked point-blank if Văitoianu was not actually carrying out Brătianu's policy of confronting the Allies with a *fait accompli* in every case. Polk referred to reports of elections to be held in the new provinces not yet awarded by treaty. Mişu replied that Văitoianu was fulfilling the wishes of the new provinces to participate in the elections.[124]

American attitudes were attributable in part to the impatience of the delegation to complete its assignment in Paris and return home. Treaties with Germany and Austria had been signed, the one for Bulgaria was ready for signing, and the Turkish treaty was almost completed. The treaty for Hungary, also completed, could not be signed on account of Romanian intransigence, which Polk was determined to overcome before leaving Paris. The Romanians were equally determined to prolong the crisis in the hope the Americans would withdraw from the Conference and thus render the reduced Council less hostile. Romania's calculation need not have been contingent upon American disengagement from European affairs because delegates of the United States were yielding to the appeasing methods of other representatives for the sake of a common Allied policy.

American failure to engineer a rigidly consistent Allied attitude toward Romania has been amply demonstrated in the foregoing "battle of the notes." Initial inflexibility and subsequent tractability of the Americans may be noted in debates over the award of southern Dobrodgea, the Bucovina strip, and Bessarabia. It will be recalled that those regions had not yet been officially awarded to Romania. Unlike territories Romania was to acquire from Hungary, these regions were still subject to review because of American insistence they be withheld until Romania began to act in good faith.

When the British, French, and Italians considered it essential to award the regions to Romania to secure her compliance, the

Americans, about to lose their trump cards, stalled by offering alternative plans. Polk tried to push through the insertion of a clause in the Bulgarian treaty giving the Allies the right to examine Romania's title to southern Dobrodgea and inviting her to rectify the boundary by retroceding those areas in which Romanians formed a minority. He believed Romania would not resist this proposal, advanced by the Americans months before and even suggested by Sonnino at one time, if it were tied to this condition — since Romania "stood a good chance of receiving considerable accessions of territory in Transylvania and Bucovina, perhaps her acquisition of these could be made contingent upon her yielding in Dobrodgea.[125]

The French still scorned any cession of allied territory to an enemy state, and the British agreed. Balfour recalled

> that the Supreme Council decided that Romania, as an allied power, cannot be asked to yield any territory to Bulgaria. The decision was never cancelled. The Supreme Council, however, had not concealed its feeling that Romania ought to yield a piece which was clearly not Romanian. Strained relations with Romania would not... justify a change in this policy. If the Powers were to go to war with Romania, the situation would doubtless be altered.[126]

Confronted by this authoritative report, the Americans could not recommend a resort to war to force Romania into yielding in Dobrodgea, nor would they have wished to propose use of force to correct Romanian behavior. From the original American proposal to retrocede all of southern Dobrodgea to the second plan to restore part of that region, the Americans now lost everything because nothing was included in the Bulgarian treaty regarding a cession of any territory.

The status of Bucovina was provided for in the Treaty with Austria, which Romania had not yet signed. Article 59 required Austria to renounce title to Bucovina and recognize the right of the Allies to award the province to another power or powers. The privilege of the Allies to delimit boundaries of Bucovina or assign the entire province was seized upon by the Americans, who proposed to withhold it until Romania behaved. This recommendation was in addition to the proposal approved by the Foreign Ministers to detach the northern strip and award it to a Ruthenian state. But the prospect in October of a Ruthenian state emerging had vanished. The Americans could devise no effective plan to deny Bucovina to Romania, nor did their delimitation of its northern boundary become permanent.[127]

Bessarabia alone remained for American use to thwart Romania's growth in retaliation for her obstinacy. That province, in contrast to other territories, was technically the property of an allied state, Russia, in view of support given to the "Whites" by the British and French. The Big Four, it will be recalled, had agreed to uphold Kolchak's wish for a plebiscite in Bessarabia. The Americans held tenaciously to this promise and refused to participate in the dismemberment of Russian territory.

Other statesmen on the Council deferred to Polk's insistence, since he did not raise the issue of awarding the province to Romania on condition of good behavior. Romania was allowed to occupy Bessarabia until the Allies decided its future status. The British and French preferred a Romanian occupation to a Bolshevik or "White" one. When the time arrived to assign the province, the problem raised by rival claims had vanished. The "Whites" were no longer supported by the British and French, the Americans had returned home, and Romania had, in the opinion of the Allies, reformed.

Frank Polk refused to admit defeat in the face of frustrations administered to his plans. He would not retreat, even though, as he described the situation to Bandholtz on October 17, "there was a hard battle here as the French and Italians are very tender toward the feelings of the Romanians, and the British, while backing us up, are not desirous of drawing too much of the ill will of Romania."[128] One member of the American delegation could find some amusement in the crisis:

> Dead are the Fourteen Points of Wilson,
> Romania straps her stilts on,
> Struts and stalks like a flaming peacock
> (Worthy a sketch by Stephen Leacock).

> She loots the stores of Budapest,
> Sacks the lot and leaves the rest.
> And kills the scheme of reparations
> Framed by all the Allied nations.

> Promises by Bratiano
> Soft as music played piano

Are wafted on the winds, but Clerk
Smells something sinister and dark.

'I think I understand Romania,
Well, Sir George, we won't detain yuh,'
And Bandholtz and his men are able
Only to cable... cable... cable.[129]

NOTES

1. Georges I. Brătianu, *Origines*, p. 318.

2. Iorga, *Memorii*, II, p. 226.

3. According to Deák (p. 98), the Allied statesmen were of the general opinion that Kun was justified in repelling Romania's aggressive moves.

4. Lenin's alleged instructions are described in Bulletin No. 484, American Commission to Negotiate Peace, Moon Papers. Herbert Hoover obtained this information from agents in the American Relief Administration who considered Kun an economic threat because he was now "overflowing his frontiers." To Hoover, the "Whites" were no less reprehensible because "they were extreme reactionaries having no notable intellectual capacity and were currently debating about the resumption of the right of dueling... (*U.S. Foreign Relations, PPC,* XI, p. 259; and Hoover, *Memoirs,* I, pp. 398-410).

5. *U.S. Foreign Relations, PPC,* VII, pp. 20-28. Jules Cambon wrote later that Bliss's proposal authorized Romania to march on Budapest ("La Roumanie et la question agraire en Transylvanie," p. 619).

6. *U.S. Foreign Relations, PPC,* VII, pp. 67-71. About 16,000 French troops would be made available.

7. *Ibid.,* VII, pp. 60-62.

8. Mişu's mention of Allied supplies indicated that the earlier decision of the Big Four to terminate assistance had apparently failed to reach the stage of implementation.

9. Vesnić offered one division, but he could not donate more because he feared "the house would be burglarized" if Serbia's frontiers were left unprotected.

10. *U.S. Foreign Relations, PPC,* VII, pp. 103-108. This was Lansing's last day in Paris. He left for home on July 12. Henry White replaced him as chief plenipotentiary.

11. *Documents on British Foreign Policy,* VI, pp. 82-83.

12. *Ibid.,* III, p. 408.

13. *Ibid.*

14. *Ibid.,* IV, pp. 1100-1104. Brătianu signed the agreement on July 29, thus vindicating Balfour's moves during that month. For American hostility to the oil agreement, see Baker, *Woodrow Wilson and World Settlement*, II, pp. 422-423. The accord had its origin in a pact signed by the British and French on April 18, 1919, to exploit jointly the oilfields in Romania and the Middle East (Temperley, *A History*, VI, pp. 182-183).

15. *Documents on British Foreign Policy*, I, p. 88, and VI, pp. 76-77.

16. *U.S. Foreign Relations, PPC*, VII, p. 120-121, 125-127.

17. *Ibid.,* VII, pp. 127, 129-130, 139-140.

18. A sympathetic appraisal of the "Whites" is provided by Deák (pp. 101-102) who, as a native Hungarian, found it awkward to treat Béla Kun antagonistically because the communist, like the "Whites," was defending Hungary's territorial integrity.

19. *U.S. Foreign Relations, PPC*, VII, pp. 177-181, 187-190.

20. Bliss said Hungary did not oppose the Belgrade armistice or the advance of French and Serbian troops. The first trouble began when the Romanians moved. When d'Esperey protested, the Romanians replied their advance had been authorized by Károlyi. This was a lie, Bliss said, in quoting d'Esperey.

21. *U.S. Foreign Relations, PPC,* VII, pp. 181-182. Balfour failed to mention that Romania had become a belligerent on November 10, when she declared war on Germany.

22. Bliss recorded in his diary: "They have talked for days about sending an Allied army to Hungary, and we are going to talk again about it this afternoon at the Quai. They are quite enthusiastic about it until it comes to the question of what nation or nations is to furnish the troops and foot the bills. Each one in turn says the United States must do it because we got into war so late that we had only a relatively small number of men killed and that we must keep on fighting until our butcher's bill is as big as theirs. Then the United States delegates say, 'Nothing doing, unless Congress orders it.' Then they all look blankly at each other until a bright idea occurs to someone who proposes that they send a telegram to Kun calling him a liar and a thief — at which they brighten up immensely, order the telegram sent, and then pass on to something equally inane and futile" (Palmer, p. 409).

23. Temperley, *A History,* I, p. 356.

24. *U.S. Foreign Relations, PPC*, VII, pp. 198-200, 208, and XI, pp. 312-322; *Documents on British Foreign Policy*, I, pp. 130-131.

25. *U.S. Foreign Relations, PPC*, VII, pp. 236, 248-249; Miller, *Diary*, XX, p. 353.

26. The British military attaché in Vienna had warned the Romanians of an imminent attack (*Documents on British Foreign Policy*, VI, p. 110). According to Károlyi, Kun's chief of staff betrayed the plan to the "Whites," who gave it to the Romanians (*Memoirs*, p. 172).

The Romanians outnumbered Hungarian troops by two to one. About 170,000 Romanians counterattacked 84,000 Magyars (C. Kormos, *Romania*, p. 72).

27. The victory was celebrated with speeches in praise of Brătianu at a session of the Romanian parliament on July 28 (*Monitorul Oficial*, No. 39, July 28; Iorga, *Memorii*, II, p. 236-237).

28. George I. Brătianu, *Origines*, pp. 316-317. See also Iorga, *Memorii*, II, p. 238. The brief campaign is treated as a justifiable defensive action in Kirițescu, III, pp. 473-504; Clark, *United Roumania*, pp. 192-203. The Magyar view is in Deák, pp. 103-104. Brief accounts are in Seton-Watson, *A History*, p. 545; and Temperley, *A History*, I, pp. 356-357.

29. *Documents on British Foreign Policy*, VI, pp. 21-22, 61-63, 87-88,137-138.

30. Count Skrzinski, Polish Under Secretary for Foreign Affairs, visited Bucharest on July 6 and noted that his country and Romania were working together to secure a common frontier to withstand the "Jewish Bolsheviks" (*Documents on British Foreign Policy*, VI, pp. 33-34).

31. *Ibid.*, III, pp. 585-586. Petliura sent a mission to Bucharest in January 1919 to secure assistance (Letter from Vopicka to Robert H. Lord, January 9, 1919, Moon Papers). See Iorga, *Memorii*, II, p. 193, for activities of the Petliura mission.

32. *Times*, London, August 5. Odessa fell to Denikin on August 27.

No Red Army troops were available in July and August to move against Romania (Von Lane, p. 238). Rakovskii reminisced years later that the Soviet government in the summer of 1919 feared the Allies would arm the Romanians, Poles, Petliura, Denikin, and Kolchak to drive Bolshevism out of Russia (Louis Fischer, *Men and Politics*, p. 132).

33. Sazonov, Kolchak's foreign minister, played a prominent role in bringing Denikin to the attention of Winston Churchill who, in turn, furnished Denikin with

supplies for 250,000 men *(The Manchester Guardian,* May 21, 1919). The British were still backing Poklevskii's request that Brătianu release Russian arms to Denikin. It was very unlikely that Brătianu would materially assist Denikin who, it was alleged, dreamed of carving an empire for himself out of southern Russia, including Bessarabia (Fischer, *The Soviets in World Affairs,* I, pp. 198-199, 201, 203; and Rattigan, p. 213).

34. Brătianu always referred Poklevskii and Rattigan to Văitoianu, his minister of war, whenever the subject of arms was raised. Văitoianu had recently completed a thorough job of purging Bessarabia of Bolshevik sympathizers; he was not disposed to assist another group intent upon recovering that province *(Documents on British Foreign Policy,* III, p. 408).

35. Miller, *Diary,* XX, p. 378. Foch revealed these figures on August 4.

36. *U.S. Foreign Relations, PPC,* VII, pp. 304-308, 310-311, 317-322. Clemenceau hoped to see Hungary encircled by a ring of hostile states. Böhm had a very cheekered career. He was a typewriter salesman before the war, a lieutenant in the Hungarian army, and Károlyi's minister of war. No admirer of Kun, but willing to serve as his envoy to Vienna, Böhm reportedly accepted a bribe from Basil Zaharoff, the munitions magnate, to work against Kun. The Romanians did not trust him, accusing him of stirring up the Saxon Germans. Böhm reappeared in Hungary in 1946 when he was named envoy to Sweden. See Macartney, "Hungary since 1918," *The Slavonic and East European Review,* VII (1929), p. 581; Guiles Davenport, *Zaharoff: High Priest of War,* p. 261; and *Bulletin d'informations roumaines,* April 12, 1919.

Böhm had apparently enchanted Coolidge whom he met in Vienna. Coolidge convinced Hoover of his capabilities. See *U.S. Foreign Relations, PPC,* VII, pp. 236, 253-256, and XII, p. 446; Hoover, *Memoirs,* I, p. 399. For Böhm's account, see his *Két forradalom Tüzében.*

37. *U.S. Foreign Relations, PPC,* VII, pp. 516-517.

38. Deák, pp. 473-476.

39. Rattigan shared Brătianu's opinion that the Allies should congratulate him for routing Kun. He wrote on August 10 that the Allies had asked Romania's cooperation in the advance on Budapest because they did not regard the Belgrade armistice as still in effect *(Documents on British Foreign Policy,* VI, p. 139).

40. *U.S. Foreign Relations, PPC,* VII, pp. 480-483, 490-491, 529. The Americans wanted to deal more harshly with Romania (Hoover, *The Ordeal of Woodrow Wilson,* pp. 137-138).

41. *U.S. Foreign Relations, PPC,* VII, pp. 510, 516-517.

42. The Italian military mission in Budapest, acting on behalf of the Allies, played an agonizing game of hide-and-seek with the Romanian officers in an effort to forestall the occupation. See Kaas and Lazarovics, *Bolshevism in Hungary*, pp. 306-307.

43. Polk (1871-1943) had served as Counselor to the Department of State, 1915-19. Not until September 3 did Lansing empower him to agree to Council decisions without prior referral to Washington *(U.S. Foreign Relations, PPC,* XI, p. 640). Henry White did not have that privilege.

Polk warned Mişu on August 4 that if any incident occurred in Budapest to arouse American opinion against Romania, the consequence would be an end to American aid *(U.S. Foreign Relations, PPC,* VII, p. 509).

44. The views of Pichon, Tittoni, and Foch were shared by influential newspapers and journals. Pertinax wrote in *L'Echo de Paris* (August 10) that the Allies had proven themselves incapable of protecting the Romanians "in their hour of danger." Auguste Gauvain of *Le Journal des Débats* (August 11) advised the Allies to forget about the Romanians, who could take care of themselves. *The New York Herald* (August 10) said the Allies should not stop Romania from inflicting deserved punishment on Hungary. *The New York Times* (August 14) reported the Romanians had entered Budapest with the expressed permission of the Allies. Seton-Watson wrote that "not unnaturally the Romanians, having fewer illusions about Hungary than did the Big Four, were disinclined to obey.... The Allies feared western labor would side with Kun.... Romania's military action was a whiff of grapeshot... and the Romanians took the bit between their teeth to rectify the unjust armistice and to halt western amateurism and Habsburg intrigue" *(The New Europe,* XII, pp. 98-99).

45. *U.S. Foreign Relations, PPC,* VII, pp. 504-511, 517-518; Deák, p. 110. The note was cited in the *Times,* London, August 6.

46. *U.S. Foreign Relations, PPC,* VII, pp. 528-532, 541-543.

47. The text of the proclamation is in Deák, p. 476. Brătianu's claim to be the Allied agent can be understood in the light of the lack of Allied troops. The four Allied Powers could not provide replacements for the Romanian troops. Tittoni did offer one company, Balfour mentioned sending a gunboat up the Danube, Clemenceau said he would consider Foch's wish to send a company, and Polk had nothing to offer *(U.S. Foreign Relations, PPC,* VII, pp. 532-533). According to Clemenceau, only three brigades remained of the Army of the Orient *(Ibid.,* VII, p. 348).

48. Bandholtz, nominated by Bliss, was Provost Marshal General of the American Expeditionary Force. Gorton was chief of the British military mission in Hungary; he was already in Budapest. Graziani was Berthelot's successor as

adviser to the Romanian General Staff. Mombelli was chief of the Italian military mission in Bulgaria.

49. *U.S. Foreign Relations, PPC*, VII, pp. 567-569; *Documents on British Foreign Policy*, VI, pp. 129-130.

50. *U.S. Foreign Relations, PPC*, VII, p. 548.

51. *Ibid.*, VII, pp. 551-555. The note was published in the *Times*, London, August 9.

52. *U.S. Foreign Relations, PPC*, VII, p. 605; Deák, p. 113.

53. The Archduke, a distant relative of Emperor Charles, commanded the Austro-Hungarian army at Mărăşeşti and was, for a time, considered by the Central Powers as a suitable candidate for the Romanian throne if Ferdinand were evicted (Seton-Watson, *A History*, pp. 502, 506). According to the Archduke's memoirs, Marghiloman, Maiorescu, and Prince Barbu Ştirbei (Brătianu's brother-in-law) offered him the throne on July 10, 1917, but he preferred to remain in his native Hungary. See the *Central European Observer* (Prague), IX (February 1931), pp. 127-128, quoting Vol. V of *A Világháború Amilyennek én Láttam*, p. 128. During October and November, 1918, Joseph acted as "homo regius" in Budapest (Temperley, *A History*, IV, p. 115).

54. *U.S. Foreign Relations, PPC*, VII, pp. 603-606, 613-615; and XI, p. 387.

55. *Ibid.*, VII, p. 605. Polk reported the Archduke had appeared in Budapest, accompanied by two Romanian brigades, and installed as provisional governor. Joseph told Allied officers of his intention to form a government according to Allied instructions.

56. Rattigan reported from Bucharest that the King and Queen drove through the streets of the Romanian capital on August 5 and were given an ovation (*Documents on British Foreign Policy*, VI, p. 129). This accounted for the confusion between "Bucharest" and "Budapest" in *The New York Times*, August 9, stating Ferdinand was in Budapest. As far as is known, he never went to Budapest.

57. *U.S. Foreign Relations, PPC*, VII, pp. 606-607, 616-617. Tardieu asked Clemenceau if he was referring to the 1916 Alliance which "had been abrogated by the Peace of Bucharest." If so, Tardieu suggested, Brătianu should be told that the Conference was "a definite thing while the 1916 Alliance was a vague thing."

58. Clemenceau sent a copy of this note to Saint-Aulaire.

59. The Quai d'Orsay transmitted all notes to Bucharest in the most inexpeditious manner. See Deák, p. 123, note 74.

60. The mission's reports are in *U.S. Foreign Relations, PPC*, XII, "The Bandholtz Mission," pp. 635-735. See also Major General Harry Hill Bandholtz, *An Undiplomatic Diary.*

61. Brătianu informed Rattigan of his intention to send Diamandy to make sure the Magyars were not mistreated. He explained Romania wished to impose an armistice on Hungary because the Allies regarded the Belgrade truce as ineffective. He termed the looting "legal requisitioning" (*Documents on British Foreign Policy,* VI, pp. 137-139).

62. *U.S. Foreign Relations, PPC*, VII, pp. 677-678.

63. *Ibid.*, VII, pp. 677-679. Protests by Beneš and Pašić are in Deák, pp. 483-487; and the *Times*, London, August 14.

64. Seton-Watson asserted Romania sponsored the Archduke in the hope of annexing Hungary (*The New Europe*, XIV, No. 157, P. 10).

65. *U.S. Foreign Relations, PPC*, VII, pp. 679-681. This decision made possible Friedrich's control of the government. According to Jászi, Friedrich was an ultra-reactionary (*Revolution and Counter-Revolution in Hungary*, p. 156). For an analysis of his questionable tactics, see M. W. Fodor, *Plot and Counter-Plot in Central Europe,* pp. 151-155, 180.

66. *U.S. Foreign Relations, PPC*, VII, pp. 678-679. The latest demands were presented by Ioan Erdélyi, a member of the Consiliu Dirigent. Victor Antonescu tried to persuade the Quai d'Orsay the terms were justifiable (*Ibid.*, VII, p. 681).

67. *Ibid.*, VII, pp. 679-682. Wilson instructed Polk on August 12 to request a diminution of Romania's territorial awards if she continued to resist (*Ibid.*, VII, p. 682).

Balfour's reservations may have been inspired by Rattigan's intercession. In a note of August 10, the British chargé cited the following points in defense of Romanian actions: (1) the Council prohibited Romania from occupying Budapest after the city had been taken; (2) the Allies "had asked Romanian cooperation in the Allied advance on Budapest"; (3) the Romanians had acted in self-defense; (4) charges of brutality were being propagated by Magyar newspapers; (5) Hungarian troops did not wear uniforms and could not be distinguished from civilians; and (6) the Habsburg régime was not installed by Brătianu (*Documents on British Foreign Policy,* VI, pp. 138-140).

68. *U.S. Foreign Relations, PPC*, VII, pp. 689-691; Deák, pp. 479-481; and the *Times*, London, August 16. Brătianu's note bore a striking similarity to that of Rattigan's of August 10.

69. *U.S. Foreign Relations, PPC*, VII, pp. 683-686, 691-692; *Documents on British Foreign Policy*, I, pp. 416-417. The August 14 note was drafted by Philippe Berthelot.

70. Horthy, p. 103; and Owen Rutter, *Regent of Hungary*, p. 204. Horthy commanded an army of 8,000 in unoccupied western Hungary.

71. *U.S. Foreign Relations, PPC*, VII, p. 804, and XII, p. 658.

72. Hoover credited himself with initiating the move to oust the Archduke (*The Ordeal of Woodrow Wilson*, pp. 139-140).
Romanian protests were also directed against Friedrich's appointment of "White" Count Paul Teleki, the noted geographer, to prepare materials for peace negotiations with the Allies (Bandholtz, pp. 30-33). Other Romanian outcries are in *U.S. Foreign Relations, PPC*, VII, pp. 694-695, 707-708.

73. *Documents on British Foreign Policy*, VI, pp. 170-174. Ionescu told Rattigan the charges against Averescu were true (*Ibid.*, VI, p. 152).

74. *Ibid.*, VI, pp. 195-197.

75. *U.S. Foreign Relations, PPC*, VII, pp. 774-778, 811-813, 819-822; and Hoover, *The Ordeal of Woodrow Wilson*, pp. 138-139. Wilson expressed anxiety over Romania's disregard of the authority of the Conference. He feared Germany would be encouraged to resist fulfilling the terms of the Versailles treaty (*U.S. Foreign Relations, PPC*, XI, pp. 634-635).

76. *U.S. Foreign Relations, PPC*, VII, pp. 836-838, 857. Supplies were finally halted as of September 20 (*Ibid.*, X, p. 561). By that late date the Romanians had obtained in Hungary enough rolling stock to wage an effective campaign against any Magyar resistance. See General G.D. Mărdărescu, *Campania pentru desrobirea Ardealului și ocuparea Budapestei*, p. 10.

77. Berthelot (1866-1934), son of a foreign minister, was the most capable and well-informed official at the Quai, of which he had been the *eminence grise* since 1914, when he was named Director of the Diplomatic Cabinet until elevated in 1919 to Director of Political and Commercial Affairs. He was responsible for French responses in July 1914 when Poincaré and Viviani were in St. Petersburg, and for Briand's moves in securing Romanian intervention in 1916. In 1918 he urged representation at the Conference for the small powers whose interests he subsequently championed as member of the New States Committee appointed to draft the minority treaties. He succeeded in removing objectionable articles, not

because he thought them unjustifiable, but because he was working assiduously to enlist Romania in that system eventually known as the *cordon sanitaire*. Clemenceau trusted him and shared with him skepticism about the League and the Treaty of Guarantees (Laroche, pp. 30, 34, 62-63, 95-96).

78. *U.S. Foreign Relations, PPC*, VIII, pp. 57-60, 77-79.

79. Clemenceau cited the influence in press circles of Robert de Flers, a dramatist who had served in Bucharest as Saint-Aulaire's cultural attaché. His articles attacked French harshness toward Romania. See his *La petite table* (p. 208) accusing France of capitulating to American and British designs on Romania.

Pichon regularly informed the Paris press about the work of the Council and told correspondents what to stress and what to omit (G. Bernard Noble, *Policies and Opinions at Paris, 1919*, p. 310).

80. For a study of the Treaty of Guarantees, see Louis A. R. Yates, *The United States and French Security, 1917-1921*. This treaty showed that Clemeceau did not place much trust in the League. He had given up much in the Versailles treaty in exchange for American assurances that began to vanish in July and August.

81. In presenting the treaty to the Senate on July 29, Wilson stressed it would be a temporary arrangement. He told the Foreign Relations Committee on August 10 it was less important than the Treaty of Versailles. The uproar which ensued presaged defeat for the guarantee treaty.

82. According to Hugh Seton-Watson (*Eastern Europe between the Wars*, p. 362), the chief purpose of the 1919 peace settlement in Eastern Europe was to create a *cordon sanitaire* of new states between the two dangerous great powers, Germany and Russia. This observation may be compared to Clemenceau's statement of March 31, 1919: "Can the Peace Conference, without committing an injustice, sacrifice [the new states]... by imposing on them unacceptable frontiers? [The] policy of France is resolutely to aid these young peoples.... If one is obliged in giving [them] frontiers without which they cannot live, it is to be regretted and it must be done with moderation, but it cannot be avoided" (Baker, *Woodrow Wilson and World Settlement*, III, pp. 250-251).

83. Bliss had called General Berthelot an agent of the Quai (Baker, *Woodrow Wilson and World Settlement*, III, p. 244). White wrote to Senator Lodge on August 31 that the French had encouraged the Romanians to march into Hungary (Allan Nevins, *Henry White: Thirty Years of American Diplomacy*, p. 460). Hoover, perhaps the American most disliked by Brătianu, proposed to counter French influence in Romania by offering American loans and relief. This wish and negotiations that followed, involving alleged petroleum concessions to Standard Oil of New Jersey, were unsuccessful, but Brătianu manipulated them for anti-American and anti-Jewish propaganda purposes. See Baker, *Woodrow Wilson and*

World Settlement, II, p. 422; Bonsal, *Suitors and Suppliants*, pp. 170-171; Georges I. Brătianu, *Origines*, p. 320; Dillon, pp. 237-238; Hoover, *Memoirs*, I, pp. 407-408; Seton-Watson, *A History*, p. 543; Joseph C. Grew, Diary, I, November 1, 1919, Houghton Library; and House, Diary, XV, April 26, 1919, p. 175, House Papers.

84. *U.S. Foreign Relations, PPC*, XI, pp. 642-643.

85. *Ibid.*, XI, p. 436. Briand had named Saint-Aulaire at the suggestion of Philippe Berthelot after Tardieu's nomination had been challenged by the Radicals and Socialists. Like other diplomats accredited to Romania, he soon developed a strong admiration for the Romanians, and became the most prestigious of Allied envoys, all of whom were champions of Romanian aspirations. Even Poklevskii shared their enthusiasm.

86. *Documents on British Foreign Policy*, VI, pp. 203-204, 210. Rattigan substantiated Schoenfeld's observations.

87. *Ibid.*, VI, pp. 236-237.

88. *U.S. Foreign Relations, PPC*, VIII, p. 110-111. A message from Saint-Aulaire, containing the text of Brătianu's notes, was received in Paris on August 30. Polk received a stern letter from Queen Marie on September 4 in which she spoke of Romania being treated like an enemy while Hungary was treated like a friend, of how the United States "goes out of her way to try and punish her for having been loyal and true. I would cite you no army which has never looted. Please remember that every man in our army is a peasant" (*Ibid.*, VIII, p. 99; and in the Frank Lyon Polk Papers, Yale University Library. Cited by Hoover, *Memoirs*, I, p. 404, and *The Ordeal of Woodrow Wilson*, p. 140).

89. *U.S. Foreign Relations, PPC*, VIII, pp. 99-100. Polk quoted a statement of Constantinescu, Brătianu's Minister of Finance, to an American officer: "Romania intended to stay in Budapest, Romania intends to settle and manage her own affairs in her own way, and Romania received an insulting letter from the Council and answered it in the most suitable way by ignoring it. Romania had nothing to fear from the Allies who did not intend to follow up threats by effective action" (*Ibid.*, VIII, p. 99; Polk Papers).

90. *Ibid.*, VIII, pp. 77-79, 101. Polk consented to this mission if Clerk were not empowered to haggle with Brătianu.
    Clerk had been Director of the Oriental (East European) Department of the Foreign Office, 1913-18, and had just been designated the first British envoy to Czechoslovakia. He was reputed to be one of the most enlightened of higher Foreign Office officials and sympathetic to the cause of small powers (Seton-Watson, *The New Europe*, XII, No. 152, p. 210).

91. *U.S. Foreign Relations*, PPC, VIII, pp. 111-114, 124; Miller, *Diary*, XX, pp. 404-407. Balfour drafted the text, it was approved on September 5, and Clerk left Paris on September 7, carrying this note and copies of all previous messages sent to Brătianu.

92. The note's innocuous tone was a consequence of Clemenceau's misgivings about sending a harsh ultimatum. He remarked that he at first refused to accept Brătianu's denial of having seen previous notes, but had later on "come to the conclusion that there might be a certain degree of truth in it... it is hard for the Council to act as though it was absolutely certain that Romania was acting in bad faith in Hungary" (*U.S. Foreign Relations, PPC,* VIII, pp. 98-99).

93. *U.S. Foreign Relations, PPC,* XI, pp. 406-407. Polk, Johnson, and James Brown Scott (the legal adviser) discussed the possibility of withholding Transylvania and refusing to recognize the annexation of Bessarabia.

94. *Ibid.,* XI, p. 426, and XII, p. 674. Bandholtz claimed his trip was neither ordered nor authorized by Polk, but his report won for him a promotion recommended by Polk (*Ibid.*, XII, p. 676).

95. *Ibid.,* XII, pp. 675-676; Bandholtz, pp. 65-79. Queen Marie told Bandholtz that the "Americans could call the requisitioning looting... or any other name. I feel that we are perfectly entitled to do what we want to."

96. *Ibid.,* XII, p. 676. Bliss urged Polk to "make everybody in Europe understand that if they expect further cooperation and assistance from the United States, they must play the game properly, or we will show them at once that we intend to withdraw completely and leave them to their own resources" (Bandholtz, pp. 87-88).

97. *Documents on British Foreign Policy,* VI, pp. 236-237. Brătianu's reply was printed in the Bucharest press on September 11. Prior intimations of his attitude appeared in *The Daily Mail,* September 5, and *The New York Times,* September 6.

98. The text of his resignation is in Minesco, pp. 108-109. Brătianu informed the Council of his refusal to sign the treaty with Austria. Mişu had already advised the Council on September 8 of Romania's specific objections to Article 60 (requiring Romania to accept in advance the principle of a minority treaty). Romania did not sign the Treaty of St. Germain at the ceremony on September 10 (*U.S. Foreign Relations, PPC,* VIII, pp. 152-153; *Documents on British Foreign Policy,* VI, pp. 210-216).

99. George I. Brătianu, *Origines*, p. 322; Marghiloman, IV, pp. 379-380. News of the resignation appeared in the *Times*, London, September 15.

100. *U.S. Foreign Relations*, *PPC*, VIII, p. 334; Miller, *Diary*, XVI, pp. 534-536. Clerk's report was read to the Council on September 23. There was no reaction to Brătianu's confession. It was agreed, at French urgings, to await Clerk's return to Paris. He did not arrive until October 10.
Clerk may have met Brătianu at the inter-Allied Conference in Petrograd, January 1917 (R. H. Bruce Lockhart, *British Agent*, pp. 159, 162).

101. *U.S. Foreign Relations*, *PPC*, VIII, pp. 333-335; Miller, *Diary*, XVI, pp. 534-535.

102. *U.S. Foreign Relations*, *PPC*, VIII, p. 563; *Documents on British Foreign Policy*, I, pp. 885-886, and VI, pp. 236-237.
The Slovaks of Békés-Csaba met on June 13, 1919, to vote for incorporation into Romania (Tilea, p. 68).

103. George I. Brătianu, *Origines*, pp. 319-320.

104. For Rattigan's activities see *Documents on British Foreign Policy*, VI, pp. 21-22, 61-63, 87-89, 137-138, 148-152, 170-174, 208-209, 233-236. Curzon approved of his efforts to promote formation of a new cabinet (*Ibid.*, VI, p. 235). The British were upset by Brătianu's cancellation of the petroleum agreement on August 18 *(Ibid.,* IV, p. 1109).

105. *Ibid.*, VI, pp. 273, 278. Manolescu-Râmniceanu had been Brătianu's emissary to Tittoni, the Italian envoy to Paris in 1914, for purposes of discussing the Italo-Romanian accord completed in September of that year.

106. Tilea, p. 31.

107. *U.S. Foreign Relations*, *PPC*, VIII, pp. 550-570; *Documents on British Foreign Policy*, VI, pp. 271-279. Clerk's stay in Budapest is recounted by Deák, pp. 147-151.

108. Văitoianu assumed the posts of Premier, Minister of the Interior, and ad interim Foreign Minister until Mişu could arrive home to take over the last office. Five nationalists from the new provinces were named ministers without portfolio: Inculeţ (Bessarabia), Nistor (Bucovina), and Cicio-Pop, Goldiş, and Vaida-Voevod (Transylvania). See *Moniteur du petrôle roumain*, XVIII (October 1, 1919), No. 6, p. 196; and *The New York Times,* October 2, 1919.

109. *Documents on British Foreign Policy*, VI, p. 278; Iorga, *Memorii*, II, pp. 265-266.

110. *Documents on British Foreign Policy*, VI, pp. 280-281.

111. Extension of the electoral reform to the new provinces is recounted in Axente, pp. 466-467.

112. *Documents on British Foreign Policy*, VI, p. 281.

113. The question of petroleum concessions and other natural resources was of primary interest to these powers, and Brătianu knew it. He juggled their offers and bid up the price quite skillfully, always tying concessions to a softening of their attitudes. Talks with Americans revealed he would permit Standard Oil of New Jersey to regain its holdings in the Romȃno-Americănă installations if America increased relief assistance and looked favorably upon his demands. Hoover denounced his tactics, calling him "a liar and a horse thief" (Bonsal, *Suitors and Suppliants*, p. 171).

The British and French were told they could regain their holdings if both agreed to furnish the relief the Americans had ceased (*Documents on British Foreign Policy*, IV, pp. 1109-1110).

114. Count Skrzinski, Polish Under-Secretary for Foreign Affairs, told Rattigan in July that it was essential for Poland and Romania to form a strong bloc against Germany and Russia (*Documents on British Foreign Policy*, VI, p. 33).

115. Brătianu told Rattigan on September 2 that Pichon, in a talk with Mişu, expressed French sympathy for Romania's travail, "but could do nothing in view of the animosity of Hoover" (*Documents on British Foreign Policy*, VI, p. 204). Rattigan noted on September 18 that Romanian newspapers, full of praise for France, were edited by journalists trained in Paris (*Ibid.*, VI, p. 243). Polk was sure Antonescu "takes the cue from the Quai d'Orsay" after the two met on October 1 (*U.S. Foreign Relations, PPC*, XI, p. 440).

116. *Documents on British Foreign Policy*, VI, pp. 285-286. Saint-Aulaire returned to Paris on October 11 for an extended leave. His absence from Bucharest did not result in any fundamental change in French policy. Henri Cambon, son of Paul Cambon, was chargé d'affaires. Saint-Aulaire wrote in his memoirs that he went to Paris to fight "with least success the aberrations of the Supreme Council" (*Confession*, p. 487).

117. The available evidence indicating Italian duplicity appears in American and British sources. American officials in Romania kept Wilson and his successors at Paris informed about Italian moves during the crisis over fulfillment of Italy's maximum territorial demands. It was reported on May 21 that Italy and Romania had agreed to take joint action against Hungary, with Italy furnishing Romania relief assistance which the Americans were expected to terminate (Hoover, *Memoirs*, I, pp. 408-409; House Papers). Bandholtz frequently cited Italian attempts to have Romania distract the attention of the Council from Fiume by creating incidents in Hungary. When the Romanians allegedly complied, the Italians became distraught because Romania had "upset the fat into the fire by the

extravagance of her requisitions as it has left Hungary in such a mood that for fifty years she will never think of any alliance with Romania, as a result of which Italy cannot carry out a beautifully conceived scheme to isolate Yugoslavia" *(U.S. Foreign Relations, PPC,* XII, p. 713).

Italy had plans to place the Duke of Genoa on a Hungarian throne *(Documents on British Foreign Policy,* VI, p. 186). Brătianu's indignation over Italian recommendations on southern Dobrodgea is described by Rattigan, *Ibid.,* VI, pp. 87-88.

118. *U.S. Foreign Relations, PPC,* VIII, pp. 550-551, 561-562, 563-566; *Documents on British Foreign Policy,* VI, pp. 271-279. Excerpts from their report are in Deák, pp. 503-504.

119. *U.S. Foreign Relations, PPC,* VIII, pp. 583-586. Polk had summoned Vopicka to Paris to have him explain his excessively pro-Romanian attitude. He was detained because, Polk wrote Bandholtz, he "is far too enthusiastic in his admiration for the Romanians; I may let him go next week, but by that time he will be sufficiently educated not to be too enthusiastic every time the Romanians' name is mentioned" (Letter of October 17, Polk Papers).

120. *Documents on British Foreign Policy,* VI, p. 316.

121. *Ibid.,* VI, p. 317.

122. *U.S. Foreign Relations, PPC,* VIII, pp. 603-604, 709; Polk Papers. The Americans were aroused by a Romanian attempt to loot the National Museum in Budapest. Bandholtz "rode to the rescue" to forestall the thefts *(U.S. Foreign Relations, PPC,* VIII, pp. 678681, and XII, p. 698; Bandholtz, pp. 136-138).

123. *U.S. Foreign Relations, PPC,* XI, pp. 652-653.

124. Polk Papers.

125. *U.S. Foreign Relations, PPC,* VIII, pp. 82-84, 116-118, 125. Tittoni supported the American proposal, but his backing was spurned when it was learned Italy aimed to arm Bulgaria for an attack upon Yugoslavia *(Ibid.,* V, p. 466).

126. *Ibid.,* VIII, p. 84.

127. *Ibid.,* VII, pp. 234-235, 455-456. The Romanians presented on October 10 a claim to additional territory in Maramureş to acquire a longer frontier with Czechoslovakia. They considered it compensation for the loss of Romanian enclaves around Debreczen. The Council rejected this claim because the frontier with Czechoslovakia had been approved on August 7 (Deák, pp. 513-516).

128. Polk Papers. Polk was referring to British opposition to halting assistance to Romania. By the end of October the British were making inquiries about a resumption of aid and the beginning of trade lest they be cut out of commerce "by competition of rivals" *(Documents on British Foreign Policy,* VI, p. 316).

129. Composed by Whitney Shepardson, Secretary of the League of Nations Commission (Joseph C. Grew, Diary, I, 1920, p. 34, Houghton Library).

The reference to Clerk concerned his assignment to proceed on October 16 to Budapest to discuss formation of an acceptable government. This ultimately successful mission is recounted in Deák, pp. 155-170.

Chapter VI

THE COMPROMISE WITH ROMANIA

*"The Conference is in sympathy with your cause, but it
has been hindered by your predecessor for two years."*

— Clemenceau to Vaida-Voevod, 20 January 1920[1]

Continued Stalemate

It was during November that the policies of the four Allied
Powers with regard to Romania came into sharp dispute. The Quai
d'Orsay intervened unremittingly on behalf of Romania for the purpose
of implementing its plan to form a ring of allied states in East Central
Europe. American and British diplomats, although differing on other
issues, strove to diminish French influence in Romania. The Italians,
on the other hand, compounded the crisis by ignoring the Council's
decisions. In retaliation for American, British, and French opposition
to its policy in the Adriatic, the Italian government urged Brătianu to
perpetuate the crisis in Hungary to distract the Council's attention from
Fiume. Rather than accept Italy's biddings in November, Brătianu
characteristically vacillated before naming his price, since Italy was in
no position to sway the Council to a pro-Romanian policy. His
disinclination to take a positive stand led the Italians to solicit the
cooperation of Hungary in an anti-Yugoslav movement.[2]

Italian machinations provoked the Quai d'Orsay into demanding
the dispatch of an inter-Allied army to Hungary. Philippe Berthelot
presented this recommendation to the Council on November 3. He
noted certain unnamed Allied Powers were conspiring with Romania
to place a puppet ruler on a restored Hungarian throne.[3] This attempt
to revert to pre-war conditions threatened the security of the succession
states in East Central Europe, and the Council was asked to intervene.
Berthelot favored inclusion of the Romanian army in the inter-Allied

force despite reproaches against it with regard to requisitions and the "evident abuses of force committed by it." The Romanian army represented to him the only material force capable of preventing reconstruction of a royalist government in Budapest. In order to compel the Romanians to behave, Berthelot proposed having Czech and Serb troops take up positions in Hungary evacuated by Romanian soldiers. The inter-Allied army would withdraw from Hungary when Friedrich retired in favor of democratic elements, and after Horthy's army of "adventurers" was disarmed, free elections were held, and a peace treaty was signed.[4]

Suspicions arose that the Foch plan was being revived in Berthelot's scheme and, instead of formally rejecting it, the Council members accused each other of deliberately prolonging the crisis to achieve gains elsewhere. Polk accused Berthelot of creating an impression in Romania that Council orders were of purely Anglo-American origin. Berthelot charged Tittoni with refusing to join in the delivery of messages to the Romanian government. Crowe urged all sides to join in compelling Brătianu to "stop spreading false versions of the notes sent to him." It was agreed to send still another note to Bucharest indicating the Council's displeasure at learning that Coandă, Mişu's replacement, had arrived in Paris without a reply to the note of October 11. The four Allied envoys were instructed to obtain from Văitoianu a response within the shortest time.[5]

Berthelot's plan was based on recommendations sent by Clerk from Budapest. Clerk believed a too abrupt evacuation would increase the risk of civil war between radical and conservative elements. A native police force had not yet been adequately armed, and the moderate elements were too weak to assume office. Crowe persuaded Polk and Berthelot that the Magyars had a right to form a government of any political conviction, on condition that a Habsburg was not restored. It was agreed to look with favor upon Horthy, rather than Friedrich, as the least objectionable candidate to assume power, since he commanded the only force capable of maintaining order after the Romanians withdrew.[6]

An opportunity to encourage Horthy occurred on November 4, when the Romanians began to withdraw troops from Budapest. The entire capital was evacuated by November 14.[7] The Americans and British believed the Romanians were planning a general withdrawal from Hungary as the result of Allied pressure. While Allied insistence was an indirect cause, a more decisive reason was achievement of the principal purposes for occupying Budapest. The eviction of a communist régime, a purge of radical sympathizers, and a vengeful requisitioning had been carried out most effectively.

Defeat of the Liberals

General Văitoianu, whose government was termed the "new and corrected version of Coandă's ministry," permitted elections to be held during the first week in November.[8] The Liberals, indisputably the strongest party in the Old Kingdom, were ignominiously defeated at the polls. This was the first occasion in Romania's constitutional history when elections were not rigged.[9] As a result, the Transylvanian Nationalists, allied with the Peasant parties of the Old Kingdom and the new provinces, gained a majority of seats in both houses.[10] The new parliament was scheduled to convene on November 20, but the King refused to dismiss Văitoianu and appoint Maniu to head a new cabinet. Ferdinand, "still hypnotized by Brătianu and fearing radical elements among the peasantry," procrastinated for three weeks before bowing to the election results. It may be true, as suggested by several authorities, that the King could not find a government willing to obey orders of the Allies. Brătianu had apparently failed to convince the electorate that Maniu had accepted bribes from Anglo-American sources and that he would capitulate to Council injunctions. Such charges did not detract appreciably from Maniu's popularity, but the Transylvanian leader did not act to demand his appointment.[11]

The Transylvanian Nationalists had not campaigned on a policy of conciliation. Their success may be attributed, in one respect, to promises that long overdue agrarian reforms would be enacted immediately. Although Brătianu could not prevent the success of the Transylvanians at the polls, he did win out in another effort. His press campaign against Allied mistreatment of Romania had so aroused public opinion that Maniu still hesitated, despite his victory, to defer to Council demands. The King, convinced by Brătianu of the risks in yielding to the Allies at the time, decided to retain Văitoianu in office while Romanian troops gradually withdrew from Hungary.[12]

The long-awaited reply to the note of October 11 was received in Paris on November 12. It did not indicate any change in policy despite the election results. Văitoianu agreed to the establishment of a reparations sub-commission on which a Romanian would sit, but he rejected plans to have the commission hear complaints of Hungarian officials because that would subject Romania to treatment hitherto not imposed on other allied states. He did not oppose establishing an acceptable government in Hungary, but he insisted on keeping Romanian troops on the Tisa until a régime agreeable to Romania was constituted in Budapest. Văitoianu still maintained Romania was obeying orders of the mission to postpone a complete evacuation until a new government was set up in Hungary.[13]

This reply elicited from Crowe a sharp denunciation:

> Brătianu was merely dilly-dallying and playing for time, and the measures adopted by him had resulted in deluding the majority of his countrymen into thinking him a great patriot. I feel that if the King and the majority of the Romanians were made clearly to see that a persistence in their present attitude would necessarily mean a breach with the Allied and Associated Powers and Romania's expulsion from the alliance, then Romania would adopt a more compliant attitude. In such an event, the present government would be forced to retire and a ministry would be constituted which would see the wisdom of meeting the Council's just demands and would act accordingly.[14]

Crowe pointed out that a diplomatic rupture was the only alternative because the Council had no available forces to drive the Romanians from Hungary. Clemenceau and Polk agreed with this observation, but the Italians refused to approve a rupture and Berthelot cautioned against any break which could antagonize the Romanian people. Clemenceau retorted that

> he had been long suffering with Romania and had even been reproached for that attitude. Romania had always tried to prolong pourparlers indefinitely, and this must be put an end to.

The French Premier brushed aside remarks made by General Maxime Weygand, Chief of Staff to Foch, who interceded for a delay in the rupture because Văitoianu could not handle foreign affairs in view of the recent elections. Clemenceau insisted "Brătianu was behind the whole matter." Crowe agreed Brătianu had installed Văitoianu "so that precisely that argument could be advanced." Polk pushed for even more drastic action entailing the withdrawal of Transylvania from the list of awards in order to compel Romania's compliance. But the others overruled this scheme because no Allied troops were available to occupy Transylvania, which, the French insisted, should not be restored to Hungary.[15]

The Council decided to dispatch its first true ultimatum containing a time limit in which to reply. Although Berthelot was instructed to draft it, the note he presented on November 13 did not betray his Romanophile views. It bore, instead, the unmistakable imprint of irate Clemenceau, who proposed to hand the ultimatum to the Romanian delegate in Paris rather than follow the slow procedure of telegraphing it to Bucharest. This ultimatum summed up in unequivocal terms the exhaustion of Allied patience. The Romanians were required to evacuate behind the new frontier, sign the Austrian and minority treaties (the privilege of discussing certain changes in the latter treaty was reiterated), and accept the rulings of the reparations sub-commission. The penalty for non-compliance was not only Romania's dismissal from the Allied camp, but also a rupture of diplomatic relations with each Allied Power.

The ultimatum could succeed if the four Allied Powers agreed to carry out the penalties, but Italy refused. De Martino, the Italian delegate, objected to references to Romania's wartime defection and the call for a diplomatic break. Clemenceau rejected any pacification of Brătianu and told de Martino that

> France was abandoned by Romania, which did not prevent France from carrying on the war to an end. Three months before the Bucharest Peace I warned Brătianu that he was committing Romania to a disastrous policy. Brătianu protested that he would never conclude a separate peace — a protest which had not prevented his doing so.[16]

Developments in the afternoon of November 13 led to a revision of the ultimatum and hence a vitiation of a united Allied stand. De Martino, acting contrary to the Council's decision, met privately with Coandă and Antonescu to assure them of Italy's intention of securing a modification of the ultimatum in view of reports Romania was about to evacuate Hungary and Antonescu's promise that Romania would sign the Austrian treaty and renounce claims to additional territory. The two Romanians, assured of Italian support, convinced Clemenceau, when he handed them the ultimatum, that he should delete references to Romania's defection and extend the deadline from six to eight days. The French premier came away believing Romania was prepared at last to provide satisfaction on every point. [17]

Polk and Crowe agreed to the two modifications requested by Clemenceau, but de Martino, urging further amendments to insure Romanian acceptance, refused to subscribe to the ultimatum until he had received instructions from Rome. It was decided to dispatch the ultimatum without Italy's adherence.[18]

Coandă carried the ultimatum to Bucharest. It contained a final appeal "to the wisdom of the Romanian Government and people," requesting compliance "without discussion, reservation, or condition" with previous orders. The note concluded by expressing the Council's deep regret at seeing itself "forced to sever relations with Romania," but it expressed confidence that it had "been patient to the very last degree."[19]

Nine days passed before the ultimatum was handed to Văitoianu by the four Allied envoys on November 24. Italian minister Franklin was authorized at the last minute to join his colleagues in submitting it. During this interval Romanian troops retreated toward the Tisa, thus permitting Horthy to occupy Budapest. Clerk obtained Friedrich's resignation on November 16. A new government, led by moderate democrat Karl Huszár, was installed on November 25. The Allied Powers immediately granted *de facto* recognition to Huszár and invited him to send a peace delegation to Paris.[20]

It became apparent the Huszár government, supported by both "Whites" and right-wing socialists, was not a Romanian puppet régime, nor one subservient to the Allies because it soon reaffirmed a right to regain Transylvania, the Banat, and Maramureş.[21] Also apparent was the Romanian disinclination to tangle with the new government while it was enjoying the armed protection of Horthy's troops and Allied recognition. The Romanians had enabled, by their withdrawal from Budapest, the installation of Huszár, whom they were unwilling to recognize as leader of an acceptable government. For that reason, the Romanians took up positions along the Tisa and reiterated claims to additional Hungarian territory along that river. At this point the crisis developed into one requiring the Allies to prevent an outbreak of hostilities between the "Whites" and Romanians.

The Envoys Conciliate

The improved situation in Hungary did not lead to a revision of Council policy toward Romania. Having granted *de facto* recognition to Huszar's coalition government and inviting him to send a delegation to receive a treaty, the Council was obliged to evict Romanian troops from eastern Hungary, where reports indicated a "Romanizing" campaign was being undertaken by occupation forces.[22]

Efforts to dislodge the Romanians and force them to recognize the frontier were rendered nugatory on November 24, when the Allied envoys presented the ultimatum to Văitoianu. Although he had already received the copy brought from Paris by Coandă, Văitoianu gave no indication that he knew its contents when handed the note by the envoys.[23] He requested an extension of the eight-day deadline so that the new parliament, whose first session was postponed to November 28, could discuss the ultimatum. The American, British, and French diplomats refused to consider an extension, but Franklin wrecked the united stand by announcing Italy's intention to seek an extension until December 15. Since the other envoys were in no sense anti-Romanian, they agreed to seek an extension of at most three days. This unauthorized promise of a revision of the ultimatum, caused by Italy's defection, indicated once again a serious rift among the Allies. It enabled Văitoianu to temporize once more in the hope the Allies would capitulate to demands that the frontier and other issues be decided in Romania's favor.[24]

The Council, meanwhile, also yielded to Romanian demands in regard to the minority treaty. The Council learned on November 25 that Coandă was returning to Paris with a note from King Ferdinand indicating his desire to maintain diplomatic relations with the Allies. At the proposal of French delegate Jules Cambon, the Council agreed to permit Romania to sign the Treaty with Bulgaria on or before December 4 in view of her apparent readiness to comply with the ultimatum. Bulgaria's treaty was scheduled to be signed on November 27; Romania, therefore, was given a week's extension. Furthermore, an opportunity was granted the Romanian delegation to discuss limited changes in the minority treaty.[25]

Romania's success in obtaining an extension of the deadline regarding the Treaty of Bulgaria and an opportunity to discuss the terms of the minority treaty did not derive exclusively from Italy's encouragement or the conciliatory attitude of the Allied envoys. It was rather a result of action taken on November 19 by the United States Senate, when it refused to ratify the Treaty of Versailles unless certain reservations were first inserted. Senate objections to the German treaty, involving reservations to the Covenant of the League of Nations, were interpreted in Bucharest, and in every Allied capital as well, as setting a precedent according to which every Allied Power, big and small, could refuse to sign objectionable treaties.[26]

Heretofore the United States had been the most vigorous opponent of reservations raised by China and Italy regarding unfavorable articles in the German and Austrian treaties, respectively. The American delegation had succeeded in securing British and French support to deny those recalcitrant allies the privilege of signing the treaties with reservations. Now that the Senate was struggling with Wilson to have the German treaty amended, the staunch American position was seriously compromised. It was clear that every Allied Power could claim the same right to revise treaties if Wilson yielded to Senate demands. Moreover, if Wilson rejected the Senate reservations, the United States would not become a party to the treaties and hence would no longer be a member of the Allied and Associated Powers. American retreat from the Peace Conference would mean for Romania the departure of her most implacable opponent.

Wilson decided to reject the reservations, and he ordered the American delegation to withdraw from the Conference. Polk quickly foresaw the consequences of this move while the problem of Romania's behavior remained unsolved. He appealed to Lansing to authorize Hugh Campbell Wallace, American ambassador to France, to replace him on the Council until the Romanian crisis was settled. Polk pointed out that since

> we have been taking a firm and consistent stand from the
> first, our withdrawal would be a great embarrassment to the
> Allies and would be a great benefit to Romania. It would
> hurt our prestige. In view of the fact that it has nothing
> whatever to do with the German treaty, we most urgently
> urge Wallace to be authorized to sit on the Council.[27]

Lansing responded with instructions to expedite settlement of the crisis by December 9, the date on which the American delegation was ordered to leave Paris.[28] Ensuing developments indicate that Polk's impatience to settle the problem led to a hastily concocted appeasement of the refractory Romanian government.

Revision of the Minority Treaty

In the midst of the crisis, the Bulgarians came to Paris to sign the Treaty of Neuilly-sur-Seine on November 27. The Council had invited the Romanians to sign on condition they first initial the Austrian treaty and accept the principle of the minority treaty. Romania rejected these prerequisites, and so no Romanian delegate was present at the ceremony. As a result of the Council's determination to secure Romania's signature to the three treaties, an extension of the grace period was offered. When this privilege was also rejected, the Council agreed to permit the Romanians to discuss amendments to the minority treaty with members of the New States Committee (the group created in May to draft minority treaties). This added privilege was conceded after Romania had complained that the Council had yielded to arguments raised by the Greeks and Serbs in regard to their minority treaties. After having consented to revisions of the Greek and Serbian treaties, the Council relented by instructing the New States Committee to examine Romanian objections in an effort to make the treaty acceptable. It was believed Romania would accept the treaty if Articles 10 and 11, conferring special rights on the Jews, were amended.[29] Moreover, if the minority treaty were revised, Brătianu's opponents would be willing to accept it and thus show the Romanian people that the treaty did not infringe upon the nation's sovereignty. In this manner, the more conciliatory Maniu would find it less difficult to assume office.[30] When the Council's decision was communicated to the Romanian delegation, Antonescu requested further concessions. He asked that Articles 10 and 11 be omitted and the following clause in the treaty's preamble be deleted:

> Considering that, in the Treaty of Berlin, the independence of the Kingdom of Romania had only been recognized conditionally; considering further that the Principal Allied and Associated Powers wished to recognize the independence of the Kingdom of Romania unconditionally in its former and new territories...

Antonescu asked for insertion of a substitute clause affirming Romania had accepted the minority treaty only after discussions and agreement with the Allies "in order to prevent Romanian public opinion from considering the treaty as having been purely and simply imposed" by the Allies.[31]

The British, French, and Italian delegates considered Antonescu's request reasonable. Crowe believed the Council would be able to secure unconditional compliance with the November 15 ultimatum if Antonescu's wishes were granted. Berthelot, a former chairman of the New States Committee, revealed he had voted for Articles 10 and 11 and the preamble to reach a unanimous decision in the Committee, but he had actually opposed their inclusion and now wished to eliminate them. De Martino, also a member of the Committee, thought it would be a mistake to ask special privileges for the Jews in Romania because

> such a way of acting could only end in deepening further the gulf which separated the Jews from the rest of the population, with which, on the contrary, they should make an effort to identify themselves. In Jewish circles, opinion was divided upon the expediency of such privileges. The more uncompromising Jews demanded them, but those of a more liberal tendency did not wish even to hear about them.[32]

Polk did not object to an emendation of the preamble, but he hesitated to concur in eliminating the articles despite the advice of Allen W. Dulles, American member of the Committee, who believed yielding to Romania would not seriously affect the treaty.[33] Romania, Polk insisted, must first reply favorably to the ultimatum before the Council acceded. He did not oppose a scheme devised by his colleagues to notify Romania the Allies would look with favor upon Antonescu's requests if she complied with the ultimatum. The Council agreed to extend the deadline to noon on December 2, at which time Romania must comply with the ultimatum. Antonescu's proposals were referred to the New States Committee.[34]

When this decision reached Bucharest on November 28, Văitoianu refused to be swayed. Instead of yielding to an Allied attempt to facilitate installation of a conciliatory government in Bucharest, the Romanian government sent a letter written by Ferdinand to President Poincaré, King George V, and King Victor Emmanuel III, in which he appealed for their intercession in Conference affairs for the sake of Romania's interests. He criticized Council decisions reached without Romania's concurrence, but to which his government had submitted even though most were contrary to her interests. Allied policy toward Romania had resulted in "a violence inconsistent with our friendly relations and the principle of justice." The King defended his government's actions with the following declaration:

> It is believed that I am creating difficulties, while I only defend a just cause, and the fact that my appeals are not listened to is indirectly favoring the danger which threatens every nation, for the encouragement given to elements of disorder by the Council's attitude has a tendency to lessen

the authority of my Government, who are only guilty of defending the order, honor, and independence of their country. However, it would be natural that the great Allies, whose responsibilities are in proportion to their power, support what represents the best guarantee of order against invading anarchy, as was recently proved in Hungary and on the Dniester. In the name of these principles, I deem it my duty to appeal to you in order to bring your Government to a more friendly and just attitude toward us.[35]

Clemenceau accused Brătianu of forcing his unwitting monarch to request the constitutionally illegal interference of heads of state in affairs in which they had no right to meddle. Brătianu's influence could be seen in this statement by Ferdinand:

In spite of the fact that, from the beginning of operations of the Peace Conference, the Council of Four alone made all the decisions, Romania, in order to prove her fidelity and solidarity, has, however, submitted to the stipulations which were decided upon, unknown to her and against her interests.

The French Premier urged his colleagues to join in denouncing Ferdinand's unwarranted plea to the heads of state, especially since the King had committed a serious act of discourtesy in failing to address copies of his letter to the Emperor of Japan or President Wilson. All except de Martino concurred, but they objected to his wish to withdraw those concessions already agreed upon. After Crowe noted that "perfect ignorance existed in Romania with respect to the attitude of the Council," it was decided to publish the November 15 ultimatum and advise the envoys to leave Bucharest if the Romanian government refused to fulfill the terms.[36]

The Final Warning

The Council's failure to evoke a favorable reply from Văitoianu, in spite of concessions offered in exchange for compliance, did not lead to a stiffening of Allied policy. On the contrary, the Allies agreed to hold open the door for modifications of the minority treaty in the hope Ferdinand would summon the less refractory Maniu to power. By refraining from sending further orders to Văitoianu, whose government did not enjoy popular support in view of the recent elections, the Allies believed Maniu's appointment would be facilitated if Romania were no longer treated with stern remonstrances.

Maniu had appealed in person to the Allied envoys for an end to Council injunctions. In return, he promised to prevent a diplomatic rupture if the King named him Premier and if the Council granted an extension of the deadline so that he could obtain parliamentary support for a modified minority treaty. He feared the influence of the Liberal press, which was denouncing the treaty as an instrument of foreign intervention and was threatening those statesmen who wished to comply with Allied demands. Maniu believed the Liberals would be completely discredited if the Council acceded to his requests. When questioned about his attitude toward Hungary, Maniu proposed to maintain troops on the Tisa until Hungary signed her treaty. Although noting the frontier left Romania defenseless in the event of a Magyar invasion, Maniu proposed to respect the new boundary.[37]

Maniu's accommodating spirit led the envoys to urge the Council to grant further concessions. Although the Transylvanian Nationalist appeared flexible, his attitude was scarcely less intransigent than Brătianu's. He gave no indication of yielding to the Allies without first obtaining adequate assurances of a revision of the minority treaty and revocation of orders to the reparations sub-commission to hear complaints of the Magyars.[38] Ferdinand and Marie expressed genuine fears that the Allies proposed to overthrow their dynasty. This and other unfounded beliefs were being propagated in the Liberal press to the accompaniment of admonitions that the country would fall to the Bolsheviks if Maniu or any political leader yielded to the Allies.[39]

Văitoianu handed his reply to the envoys on November 29. It was like the "ebullition of a bad-tempered and naughty child."[40] Beginning with a sharp denunciation of the tone of the November 15 ultimatum, the note recalled how Romania had entered the war only to be disappointed by Allied failures to assist her while she rendered notable service in forcing the enemy to concentrate troops in the East during the siege of Verdun. Romania would have entered the war when Italy did but for an Allied refusal to guarantee fulfillment of her aspirations. The Allies had imposed on Romania the date of intervention, but they failed to fulfill their part of the bargain to commence the offensive from Salonika and supply Romania with promised war matériel. One sentence in the November 15 ultimatum was vigorously denounced: the reproach that Romania "consented to treat separately with the enemy and to submit to his law" was not called for because the Allied envoys had approved the separate peace. Admitting Allied victory in the war accounted for the territorial growth of many states, the Romanians, by their action against Hungary and stand against the Russian Bolsheviks, preserved the acquisition and prevented the recovery of territories claimed by Romania. Occupation of Budapest was explained as the result of an invitation from the Council to cooperate with other allied armies in subduing Hungary, but Romania was not responsible for the Council's failure to send other troops. In regard to the frontier, Romanian troops were holding positions on the Tisa to insure the new Hungarian government made peace. This action was no different from the stationing of Allied troops in the Rhineland to make sure Germany fulfilled her treaty.[41]

Văitoianu did not close the door to further dealings with the Allies. He accepted the offer to discuss in common a modification of the minority treaty. This concession was tied to his announcement of the impending installation of a new government, representing majority parties in parliament, which would examine and act upon the November 15 ultimatum.

Văitoianu's rejection of the other terms was blamed on Brătianu, whom the envoys charged with rousing public opinion against submission. When Văitoianu signified a readiness to discuss the minority treaty, the stumbling-block causing Maniu to hesitate, the four envoys agreed to seek another extension and a promise of additional modifications of the treaty if he would comply with the ultimatum. Văitoianu then met with his cabinet to discuss the offers. Their decision, to which Brătianu was obviously a party, was rejection of the offers and announcement of Văitoianu's intention to resign. The new government would have responsibility to act upon the ultimatum.[42]

Despite this reaction, the Allied envoys did not retract their offers. They appealed to the Council to display all possible consideration to Maniu, absolving him of all responsibility for Brătianu's intrigues. Such a show of support would make Romanians believe the shortsighted policy of the Liberals would result in a break with the Allies and the eventual relapse of the country into anarchy and Bolshevism.[43] Rattigan pleaded with Queen Marie to have the King appoint Maniu. She promised to do so after hearing the British chargé describe how Romania, if evicted from the Allied camp, would be obliged to maintain a large army at great expense and defend herself against neighbors bent on revenge.[44]

The Council learned of these developments on December 3, when Berthelot presented the envoys' appeal for an extension of the deadline so that Maniu could secure parliamentary support. This plea contained news of an advance by the Red Army against Denikin, who was being forced to retreat from the Western Ukraine and had already evacuated Kiev, destined to fall to Soviet forces on December 12. The envoys feared a weakening of the Romanian state would spark an indigenous Bolshevik movement which would welcome Soviet intervention and occupation of Romania.[45]

Clemenceau believed Brătianu had deliberately provoked the government crisis to gain time, but he proposed to accede to the envoys' appeal by granting an extension of six days. Crowe criticized the envoys for allowing Văitoianu to hope Council decisions were not final; he noted that

> quite possibly the Romanian reply might have been satisfactory if the attitude of the representatives of the Allies had been more firm. His impression is whatever the Council did, Romania was determined not to sign. The representatives of the Allies seemed to think that if the Council granted a further delay, Romania would emancipate herself from Brătianu's influence and would at last see where her true interests lay. He was far from convinced of that. Brătianu was no longer in power and his party no longer held a majority in Parliament; but he remained very powerful. His counsels had certainly prevailed once more.[46]

When Berthelot noted that Vaida-Voevod, the Transylvanian Nationalist, had been elected President of the Chamber of Deputies and had made a speech insisting upon the necessity of strengthening ties with the Allies, Crowe called him "quite unreliable — he was, in fact, nothing more than Brătianu's puppet." The British delegate was aware that difficulties raised by the adverse vote in the United States Senate and the arrogant attitude Germany was assuming made it necessary to accede to the appeal of the envoys in order to lessen chances of an open break with Romania. Italian delegate Vittorio Scialoja, concurring in a remark made by Clemenceau that "the situation in the United States imposed added caution," urged granting a six-day delay even though

> it is quite possible the crisis was a subterfuge. Nevertheless, it is necessary that there be a government at Bucharest to reach a final decision. At a time when enemies of the Allies

seemed to be again lifting their heads, it would be very serious if a breach were made in Allied ranks. If, as he felt sure, Romania finally decided to sign, the prestige of the Peace Conference would be greatly increased.

Clemenceau recommended yielding to the appeal of the envoys because the crisis, due solely to the "perfidy of Brătianu and the intrigues" of his government, was about to terminate with the installation of a new regime. He was prepared to pardon Romania's attitude in view of the unauthorized acts of the envoys. This argument led Polk to concur because, as he put it, there was no course to follow except to support the envoys. The Council then granted Romania an extension of six days until noon, December 8, by which time a favorable reply to the November 15 ultimatum must be received.[47]

The text of the Council's final note to Romania was published on December 4. It began with a declaration that if the Allies had fulfilled their formal notifications, they would have suspended diplomatic relations because Romania had agreed to nothing for many months. Then its tone became rather conciliatory in stating that the Allies, contrary to their prior notices, desired to retain Romania in their camp and hoped this spirit would be appreciated by the new government, whose decision, it was anticipated, would determine Romania's future orientation. The note promised modifications of the minority treaty. Even more significant than the Council's readiness to compromise was an appeal contained in the note, which was in effect directed to the Romanian people. The Allies were summoning the Romanians to repudiate Brătianu's policy and to support the conciliatory program of the Transylvanian Nationalists; thus they were committing the so-called offense that Brătianu had been denouncing for months, namely, intervention in Romania's internal affairs. Brătianu's widely publicized premonitions with regard to this alleged disregard of Romanian sovereignty encouraged the Transylvanian Nationalists, none of whom wished to incur indictment of treason by deferring to foreign demands, to proceed cautiously after Ferdinand summoned them to form a government.[48]

Romania Signs the Treaties

The final note of December 3 played a minor role in the events of the first week of the month. On December 1 and 2, the Allied envoys met with Vaida-Voevod, President of the Chamber, to discuss the impending change in government. Vaida-Voevod was the only Transylvanian Nationalist holding an official position in addition to his post of minister without portfolio in the Văitoianu cabinet, and it was to him that Maniu referred the envoys. Acting as spokesman for the parliamentary majority, Vaida-Voevod reaffirmed Maniu's readiness to comply with the November 15 ultimatum, and went even further by promising to withdraw troops to the new frontier with Hungary before a peace treaty was signed. In return, Vaida-Voevod appealed for assurances Romania would not be penalized for the requisitioning. He revealed the King had charged him with the duty of forming a new government, but he was encountering difficulties in finding ministers willing to yield to the Allies.[49]

Ferdinand's decision to designate Vaida-Voevod surprised the envoys, who expected Maniu would be summoned. Maniu's refusal to form a government became known on December 3, but reasons for his rejection were not revealed. Subsequent events indicated he was unwilling to pursue the policy which the King, still under Brătianu's influence, had requested of him. Ferdinand wanted Maniu to head a national coalition so that the onus of deferring to the ultimatum would be shared by every politician and party. Maniu's devotion to constitutionality and legality deterred him from accepting the summons, which entailed responsibility of obtaining more concessions from the Allies.[50] But Vaida-Voevod was ready to do the bidding of the King, behind whom Brătianu still stood.[51] He had already been privy to the decisions of the Văitoianu government. The King was still reluctant to entrust the government to Transylvanian Nationalists, who were inexperienced in Old Kingdom politics and were considered by some to be socialists in disguise.[52]

Vaida-Voevod consulted all politicians except the Liberals and found they favored complying with the ultimatum. When he told the envoys, they reciprocated by promising to obtain a generous extension of the deadline so that another blow could be dealt to the Liberals. But Vaida-Voevod, whom the envoys relied upon to uphold assurances previously given by Maniu, stunned the diplomats when he declared an extension to be insufficient. He now insisted the minority treaty be eliminated or completely revised in accordance with wishes previously expressed by Brătianu and Văitoianu.[53]

Vaida-Voevod evidently planned to pursue a policy closely associated with Brătianu's. Rather than reject his reassertion of Brătianu's demands, the envoys agreed to intercede once more on Romania's behalf. They appealed to the Council to "let Romania down as gently as possible in order to strike a blow at Brătianu and the Liberals." This plea encouraged rumors of Allied willingness to yield more on the minority treaty and accede to the maximum territorial demands if the new government complied.[54] The envoys did not deny these rumors. On the contrary, they did much to reinforce them when, on December 4 and 5, the British and French ministers assured Vaida-Voevod the Allies would recognize his government, even though it had not yet been constituted, and, what was more significant, the Council would arrange a formula whereby a new régime would not be stigmatized by signing the minority treaty. Rattigan and Henri Cambon plied Vaida-Voevod with these unauthorized assurances, while the Quai d'Orsay offered similar promises to Coandă, the only Romanian delegate still in Paris.[55]

The final note of December 3 had not yet reached Bucharest. But a more important message arrived from Paris to indicate the assurances of the envoys were supported by the Council. The Quai d'Orsay forwarded a draft of the revised minority treaty drawn up by the New States Committee in accordance with Antonescu's requests. This disclosure, arriving before the Council's note, prompted Ferdinand to hasten formation of a new government.[56] It was clear that if the Allies upheld the envoys' assurances, further concessions could certainly be extracted with the assistance of the magnanimous Allied diplomats in Bucharest. When the December 3 note finally reached Bucharest on December 5, its intended effect — to assist the new régime into office — had been rendered useless by the premature action of the Quai d'Orsay.

The new government was officially constituted on December 5. Although described as an anti-Liberal régime reflecting the results of the elections, several ministers were selected from Brătianu's government — Inculeţ of Bessarabia, Nistor of Bucovina, and Popovici from the Banat. Only two Transylvanian Nationalists in addition to Vaida-Voevod were named — Aurel Vlad as Minister of the Interior and Octavian Goga as Minister of Instruction and Cults. The Peasant Party was represented by Ion Mihalache as Minister of Domains and the Social Democrats by Nicolae Lupu. The most surprising appointment, in view of the fact that he had not participated in the elections, was Averescu as Minister of War. The most conspicuous absentee was Maniu, who preferred to remain president of the Consiliul Dirigent.[57]

Suspicion arose that the new cabinet was Brătianu's creation when it failed to reply to the Council's note and when the extension expired at the deadline of noon, December 8. The feeling developed among the envoys that Vaida-Voevod feared Brătianu's wrath if he capitulated. They warned the new Premier that resistance had become senseless, for it entailed complete estrangement from the Allied camp and the isolation of Romania, a situation the Liberals could not conceivably desire in view of the menace of the advancing Red Army.

In Paris, meanwhile, news of Vaida-Voevod's formation of a new government met with no acclaim because Coandă, under instructions from the new premier, requested still another extension of the deadline. Vaida-Voevod now wished to send a new delegation to Paris to discuss changes not only in the minority treaty, but also in the Austrian and Hungarian treaties. Polk balked, refusing to sanction any more treaty modifications. The American delegation was due to leave for home on December 9, the day after Coandă presented the new requests. Although Hugh Campbell Wallace had been authorized to sign the minority and Hungarian treaties after the delegation's departure, the Quai d'Orsay appealed to Polk to defer to Coandă's wishes before leaving Paris.[58]

Polk hesitated to leave before fulfilling Lansing's assignment to reach a settlement of the Romanian crisis.[59] He urged Berthelot to exert pressure on Coandă to sign the three treaties (Austrian, Bulgarian, and minority) at once. Berthelot reported Coandă had been instructed to sign the treaties in order to secure American recognition of a modified minority treaty. But since the text of that treaty, whose revision by the New States Committee had not yet been formally communicated to Bucharest, implied interference in Romanian internal affairs, the new government's acceptance under duress would result in political upheaval in Bucharest.[60]

Berthelot pointed out, in defense of Vaida-Voevod's argument, that if Romania signed the minority treaty, which still contained Articles 10 and 11, the new régime would collapse and be replaced by an obstructive Brătianu government. He urged Polk to uphold the assurances of the four envoys, who had promised to secure elimination of the two articles. Frederic Kammerer (Chief of the Russian Division of the Quai d'Orsay), who was now chairman of the New States Committee, was brought in by Berthelot to convince Polk that the articles were no longer needed because Brătianu had issued a decree-law on May 22, 1919, granting Jews the right to apply for citizenship. Kammerer claimed Romanian Jews preferred this law to the articles, since it provided for their assimilation rather than for the continuation of their alien status implied in the two articles.[61]

Polk raised a new argument at this point by referring to the minority treaty signed by Poland on June 28, which included similar "Jewish articles." He did not think Romania should be treated more favorably than Poland, where Paderewski was encountering difficulties over the same problem. If Romania's treaty did not contain the articles, the Poles would demand a similar revision of their treaty, argued Polk. Berthelot reminded Polk that Romania, unlike Poland, had never permitted pogroms, that she had only refused to grant citizenship to Jews, and that Jews had protested against non-citizenship, not against persecution.[62] Crowe agreed, pointing out that British Jews wished to have the two articles omitted.[63]

Kammerer produced a compromise proposal of the British, French, and Italian members of the New States Committee. Omission of the two articles and substitution of the following clause were recommended:

Lastly, considering that Romania has declared her intention of recognizing as Romanian subjects, with full rights and without any formality, Jews inhabiting all the territories of Romania and unable to claim other nationality...

Faced with his colleagues' determination to capitulate and realizing continued opposition would cause Romania to resist still further, Polk yielded by voting with the Council to delete Articles 10 and 11, substitute Kammerer's clause, and revise the preamble. It was also agreed to insert in the preamble a statement declaring the treaty had been prepared after agreement with the Romanian government.[64]

The New States Committee held its final meeting immediately thereafter to draft the modified treaty so that Polk could sign it before leaving.[65] At seven o'clock in the evening of that day, December 9, Polk, Henry White, and General Bliss signed the revised treaty at the Hotel Crillon while automobiles waited to take them to the railway station.[66] Polk refused to give Coandă the satisfaction of signing the treaty at the same time the Romanian delegate affixed his signature. Coandă had to wait until the next morning, December 10, to learn the Allied Powers had consented to modify the treaty in accordance with Romanian wishes and the Americans had already signed. Coandă then proceeded to sign the Austrian, Bulgarian, and minority treaties without raising any new objections or reviving old ones. He did request one favor which the Council granted — his signing was antedated to

December 9 so as to signify to posterity that Romania had signed the treaty simultaneously with the Allied Powers.[67]

Romania's decision to sign did not produce any elation among the Council members. If they anticipated the Romanians would now carry out the terms of the November 15 or December 3 notes, they were soon to be disappointed. At the moment Coandă was signing, Romanian troops were fortifying the east bank of the Tisa; arresting Magyar officials in the city of Tokaj, which had been shelled by Romanian artillery on November 26; boasting to the military mission that their army was the only force capable of maintaining peace in East Central Europe; and defying orders of the Allied generals in Budapest with the excuse that Romania had signed the treaties and thus was no longer required to obey orders of the Allied Powers.[68]

Reaction in Bucharest was no less disappointing to the Allies. On December 16 and 17 Brătianu delivered a lengthy oration to the Chamber of Deputies, claiming that by modifying the minority treaty the Allies had, in effect, recognized the validity of his decree-law of May 22, 1919. Therefore, he declared, the minority question had been solved without Allied interference. He assured the legislators that while the Alba Iulia and other resolutions were certainly significant, Romania's territorial growth could be attributed in the main to the 1916 Alliance, "sealed with the blood of 800,000 Romanian soldiers and civilians." No one could dispute the fact that his policy of resistance had triumphed. The Allies, not Romania, had capitulated in the end.[69]

The Final Territorial Settlements

In a scramble to settle problems caused by Romanian resistance, the Allied statesmen were concerned more with the occupation of Hungary and the minority treaty than with completion of Romania's territorial settlement. The territorial experts continued to discuss frontiers, while the Council dealt with more pressing issues. Until Bulgaria signed her treaty on November 27, the American experts held out for returning southern Dobrodgea to that enemy state. Romania's hostile attitude angered American experts Douglas Johnson and Isaiah Bowman, who had replaced Day and Seymour. The official Romanian memorandum on southern Dobrodgea fortified the American argument to return the region to Bulgaria, especially when Romania claimed to have entered the second Balkan War

> to end it quickly with the authorization, more or less, of the
> Great Powers.... Romania could have taken the entire
> Dobrodgea in 1913, but she preferred moderation and was
> content with the Quadrilateral.[70]

The American position could not prevail against the determination of the others to leave the region in Romania. Polk was unsuccessful, as has been shown, in inserting an article in the Treaty of Neuilly providing for bilateral talks between Romania and Bulgaria with regard to tracing of the improved frontier. He also failed to secure Council approval of an article in the Romanian minority treaty requiring Bucharest to provide special rights for the Bulgarians of southern Dobrodgea. The Allies overruled Polk, maintaining that Romania, by her acceptance of the principle of the minority treaty, would extend guarantees to her Bulgarian inhabitants without the formality of citing them specifically in the treaty.[71] Thus the campaign waged by the United States to favor the Bulgarians ended in capitulation to the Allied demand that the Romanian question not be aggravated by raising of new issues.[72]

In regard to the Banat of Timişoara, partitioned between Romania and Serbia, the Allies were spared the problem of disentangling the two states from a war that appeared imminent in the summer and fall of 1919. Romania, flushed by success over Béla Kun, reinvigorated claims to the entire Banat while the Serbs were involved with Italy over Fiume and with Austria concerning disposition of the Klagenfurt basin. Anxiety in Belgrade led Prince-Regent Alexander to seek an improvement in relations with Romania. He appealed to the first Romanian envoy to the new Kingdom of Serbs-Croats-Slovenes, Langa Raşcanu, for assurances that Serbs of the Romanian Banat would not be molested in return for a promise to evacuate immediately Serbian troops still occupying sections of the comitat of Timiş awarded to Romania.[73]

Instead of responding to Alexander's approaches, Brătianu increased his claim by demanding the island of Ada-Kaleh, situated in the Danube, which protected the Romanian riverport of Orşova and the Iron Gates. The Territorial Commission had awarded Ada-Kaleh to Romania, but Serbian troops refused to yield it until d'Esperey forced the Serbs to evacuate. This incident intensified animosity between the two states.[74]

The French found themselves refereeing a dispute between two states considered potential members of a new alliance system inspired by the Quai d'Orsay. General de Lobit, commanding the French contingent in the Banat, maintained a precarious peace between the two states.[75] Meanwhile, rumors spread of a Romanian plan to seize the entire province and of Serbian approaches to Hungary for the formation of an anti-Romanian alliance.

The Council ignored a memorandum deposited by the Romanian delegation, according to which Swabian Germans of the Banat had convened a national assembly in the city of Timişoara on August 10 to demand union of the entire province with Romania.[76] A report from Budapest about two Romanian divisions moving toward the Banat failed to excite the Allies, who preferred to debate the frequently raised proposal that Romania yield in Dobrodgea and Bulgaria surrender more territory in Macedonia to Serbia, who, in return, would recognize the loss to Romania of the entire Banat. This triple swap did not appeal to the French, who were invariably opposed to taking territory from an allied state.[77]

The Banat dispute was settled in October 1919 when the Romanians and Serbs, at d'Esperey's urging, agreed provisionally to respect the partition line. Not until 1923, however, did both states sign a protocol recognizing the new frontier.[78] There was a lesson in the Banat dispute. Two allied states, Romania and Serbia, had been so enraged by the imposed partition that their mutual enmity was forgotten temporarily in their common disgust with the Allied Powers. This may not have been an effective method of dictating a territorial settlement, but it had, at least, the virtue of preventing a war.

While the Allies were able to permit the Banat dispute to run its course, they could not settle the Bucovina question in the same manner. It will be recalled that the Council had postponed award of that province until Romania proved her good will by signing the treaties. After Romania complied on December 10, the Council reopened the question. Jules Laroche proposed awarding 82% of Bucovina to Romania, with 18% including the railway from Zaleszcyki to Kolomea going to Poland, since Romania had fulfilled the Council's orders, but Crowe demanded that Romania reply to the November 15 ultimatum before the Allies adopted his proposal. Wallace, the American observer with no authority to participate in discussions, did not revive American reservations. Thus it was easy for Laroche to convince Crowe that the Allies should not confuse the Bucovina question with that of Hungary. He pointed out that Vaida-Voevod's government would be strengthened if the Allies awarded the province, and he noted the improbability of a Ruthenian state, to which the strip detached from northern Bucovina would have been assigned by the Americans. Polish and Romanian troops had already delimited a common frontier, which the Allies, Laroche insisted, were obliged to recognize. Crowe was swayed by this logic and voted on December 18 to award the lion's share of Bucovina to Romania.[79] The Allies thereby assigned Romania more territory in Bucovina than had been promised in the 1916 Alliance. It will be recalled that Russia was due to obtain the northern one-third inhabited by a Ruthenian majority. The small portion of Bucovina left out of Romania was given to Poland, to include an important railway junction on the Polish frontier.

The Ruthenian question played a role in the delimitation of the frontier between Romania and Czechoslovakia. Both Masaryk and Brătianu considered a mutual frontier indispensable for defense.[80] General Prezan, Romanian Chief of Staff, urged establishment of a common boundary to sever more effectively Hungary's ties with Russia.[81] American experts opposed inclusion of a large Ruthenian minority in Romania, but since no Ruthenian state was to be created in the region, the Council overcame American objections and permitted Romania and Czechoslovakia to have a common 112-mile boundary in Maramureş. Both states subsequently signed a collective treaty on frontiers in 1920, according to which two-thirds of Maramureş was given to Czechoslovakia and the rest to Romania. The Romanians did not abandon their claim to more of Maramureş, despite a friendly territorial settlement reached by the two states in 1921. Romanian propagandists strove to inflame an irredentist movement in the region north of the upper Tisa.[82]

The final act of the drama concerned the award of Bessarabia, whose status was discussed by the Council on January 20, 1920, one day before the Peace Conference ended. Allied recognition of Romania's annexation had been delayed because of complex factors involving American reservations about questionable methods Romania used in obtaining Bessarabia, American disinclination to participate in partitioning the Russian Empire, British and French support of the "White" Russians who claimed Bessarabia, and tacit acceptance of an American device to withhold recognition until Romania complied with Council orders. This complicated situation led Vaida-Voevod to appeal for immediate recognition of the union because the Red Army, after seizing Kiev on December 12, was moving rapidly toward the Dniester River. In return for recognition, he promised to furnish Denikin with the war matériel British diplomats had asked Brătianu to yield.[83] Vaida-Voevod even hinted he would be prepared to retrocede part of southern

Dobrodgea if the Allies would recognize the union and promise to assist Romania in the event of a Bolshevik invasion. [84]

The external threat to Romania was as real as difficulties at home where, in December, several pro-Bolshevik riots occurred among Romanian soldiers and sailors.[85] When the Council failed to respond to his appeal, Vaida-Voevod arranged for parliament to meet in extraordinary session on December 29. Deputies from the new provinces, including Bessarabia, presented resolutions for the creation of "Greater Romania." Armed a second time with a unanimous vote, the first having been arranged by Brătianu in January 1919, Vaida-Voevod decided to go to Paris to seek recognition of the union of Bessarabia, the only region not yet awarded.[86]

Arriving in Paris in time to testify before the Conference terminated, Vaida-Voevod met with Clemenceau, Lloyd George, Italian premier Francesco Nitti, and Wallace on January 20. The reception accorded him was scarcely cordial. Clemenceau demanded to know precisely when the Romanians would complete their evacuation of eastern Hungary. Vaida-Voevod pleaded for indulgence because of the critical situation in Hungary where, he claimed, Horthy was organizing a conspiracy against Romania, Serbia, and Czechoslovakia, and planning to invade Romania in the spring.[87] Lloyd George believed Horthy was justified in taking such action because Romanian troops were

> still in Hungarian territory which Romania promised to evacuate. If you were attacked while Romania was still occupying territory which ought to remain Hungarian, what would you have to complain of? The Hungarians will employ all imaginable means in their attempts to drive you from it, and they will be entirely within their rights in so doing.

The Prime Minister accused Vaida-Voevod of adhering to policies associated with Brătianu when he said that

> ever since July we have urgently insisted on evacuation. It was always retarded on account of various difficulties. We are told today it cannot be carried out more quickly for want of means of transport. The Romanian army of occupation has, however, been able to find means of transport to transfer to Romania cattle and agricultural implements

requisitioned by her. These facts may cause new difficulties between Hungary and Romania, and cause Romania to forfeit the sympathies of those who are her best friends, simply on account of resistance Romania has shown so long to the desire expressed by the Council that evacuation be effected without delay. At present, since their agricultural implements have been taken away and Hungarian peasants are deprived of the means of working they may lose patience and bloodshed may ensue. If war broke out again, it would be regrettable, under these conditions, to think that the responsibility would rest with Romania, and that consequently she would not have the sympathy of the Western Powers.[88]

When Vaida-Voevod yielded to this invective by promising to evacuate troops by March 1, 1920, Clemenceau assured him the Allies would assist Romania in the event of a Magyar attack.[89] Lloyd George refused to offer the same guarantee; he preferred to wait until Romania withdrew her troops. Vaida-Voevod insisted his government should not be punished "for the faults of former régimes." At this point Lloyd George suggested a formula whereby Vaida-Voevod could overcome opposition of those in Romania who did not wish to withdraw from Hungary. He proposed a reciprocal arrangement by which the Allies would recognize the union of Bessarabia on condition that Romania first evacuate Hungary. Clemenceau not only agreed to this scheme, but also went further by informing the Romanian premier that he would offer a stronger assurance:

In my name, and I think I can say in the name of France, I can state we are prepared to recognize Romania's right to Bessarabia.[90]

Vaida-Voevod expressed gratitude for the "great concessions" that had been granted and he departed, after promising to evacuate Hungary as soon as possible. The Council decided afterwards to postpone recognition of the union until Hungary was evacuated.[91]

Not until Averescu succeeded Vaida-Voevod in March 1920 did Romania comply with the Council order to withdraw from eastern Hungary. Under the direction of Take Ionescu, Averescu's foreign minister, Romania assumed a conciliatory course by evacuating troops at the end of March.[92] The retreat from Hungary resulted in the drafting of a treaty by the Council of Ambassadors (successor to the Peace Conference) providing for recognition of the union of Bessarabia. The Allies were prepared to grant *de jure* recognition if Romania, in turn, promised to accord minority rights to non-Romanian inhabitants of Bessarabia and respect the delimitation of her frontier with Soviet Russia. These conditions were inserted in the hope that the United States would subscribe to the treaty, but Bainbridge Colby, Lansing's successor, refused to participate in any dismemberment of Russia without the consent of her people.[93]

The Council of Ambassadors postponed signing the treaty until Romania agreed to the peace with Hungary. This condition was fulfilled on June 4, 1920, when Romania joined with other allied states to sign the Treaty of Trianon.[94] It was not until October 28, 1920, that Ionescu agreed to sign the collective treaty on frontiers providing for recognition of common frontiers of those states that had acquired territory from the Habsburg Monarchy.[95] The Council of Ambassadors, in return for Romania's acceptance of her boundaries with Yugoslavia, Czechoslovakia, and Poland, presented to Ionescu on that day the treaty awarding *de jure* recognition of the union of Bessarabia. A new article had been inserted in a vain hope the United States would also sign. It provided that Russia would sign the treaty as soon as a Russian government recognized by the Allies came into office. This provision did not deter Ionescu from accepting the treaty.[96] The foreign minister, long an advocate of cooperation with the Allies, thus secured their recognition of the 466-mile frontier with Soviet Russia, even though he was technically obliged to await the approval of a respectable Russian régime.[97] Such concurrence appeared very remote, in view of the stern Soviet note to the Allies. Chicherin refused to acknowledge the validity of any agreement on Bessarabia reached without the participation of Soviet representatives.[98]

With the Allied Powers formally recognizing Romania's annexation of Bessarabia, and with Romania, in exchange, acknowledging her new frontiers, this account of the creation of "Greater Romania" must end. The dream of sincere and unscrupulous persons to unite all Romanians in one state had come true. Its realization was due only in part to the actions of the Romanian people. "Greater Romania" was, for the most part, the result of the skillful diplomacy of Brătianu, who was supported in the long run by the anti-communist policies of many countries. Brătianu did not solve Romania's problems. He had, instead, intensified them by producing an empire, not a nation. For post-war Romania acquired in addition to a doubling of her territory the insuperable task of assimilating an alien population comprising approximately 30 per cent of the total number of her inhabitants.

NOTES

1. *U.S. Foreign Relations*, *PPC*, IX, p. 916.

2. *Documents on British Foreign Policy*, VI, pp. 321-324. Brătianu told Rattigan on November 1 that he had rebuffed Italian bribes to distract the attention of the Allies. Italian approaches to Friedrich and Horthy were described by Clerk (*Ibid.*, VI, pp. 321, 412-416).

3. The Council learned Italy had proposed Prince Carol as King of Hungary, but Cardinal Primate Csernoch of Hungary rejected him because of his Orthodox faith (*Documents on British Foreign Policy*, VI, pp. 337, 412-416). Carol was fêted at a banquet in Budapest on October 12 at which he boasted about becoming Hungarian king "to show his father he would yet be a king and that there would be no difficulty in handling the situation" (*U.S. Foreign Relations*, *PPC*, XII, p. 704). Bandholtz reported on November 1 that Archduke Joseph still hoped to become King of Hungary and then invade Romania to recover lost lands (*An Undiplomatic Diary*, p. 193).

4. *U.S. Foreign Relations*, *PPC*, VIII, pp. 918-920. Clerk recommended retention of Romanian troops in Hungary until Horthy could gain more strength and assume policing duties currently being carried out by Romanian soldiers (*Documents on British Foreign Policy*, VI, p. 339).

5. *U.S. Foreign Relations*, *PPC*, VIII, pp. 910-912, 920. Polk was disturbed by Bandholtz's report that General Mombelli was "peculiar and erratic" in his efforts to disrupt the work of the mission whenever the need arose to take direct action. Mombelli reportedly flew into gesticulatory arguments in "machine-gun French" to prevent reaching of any decision he deemed detrimental to Romanian interests (*Ibid.*, XII, pp. 680, 687, 713).

6. *U.S. Foreign Relations*, *PPC*, VIII, pp. 936-941, 953-954, 958-959. Three Americans urged Polk to take a lenient attitude. Vopicka relayed a message from Brătianu that he intended to obey the Allies after elections in Romania were held. Brătianu wished to await results of the debate in the United States Senate in regard to ratification of the Treaty of Versailles before determining his future policy (Polk Papers).
Charles Upson Clark told Polk that there was no evidence of looting or anti-Romanian feeling in Budapest. Polk replied that he should not judge "conditions from what one sees out of a railway carriage window (Polk Papers; author's interview of Dr. Clark, North Hatley, Quebec, July 14, 1956). Clark's visit to Budapest is recounted in his *United Roumania*, pp. 206-221.

Henry Schoenfeld, the American chargé in Bucharest, told Polk on November 1 the Allies did not really understand the Romanian character and had treated Romania most tactlessly. He believed the Romanians were like children who should be treated as such to make them behave (Joseph C. Grew, *Diary*, I, November 1, 1919). Schoenfeld's views were shared by Rattigan who urged Crowe on October 18 to "combine firmness with an attitude of friendliness and good will" in dealing with the Romanians (*Documents on British Foreign Policy*, VI, p. 283).

7. *U.S. Foreign Relations, PPC*, IX, p. 9, and XII, pp. 716-717. Văitoianu explained that troops had been kept in Budapest until this time "at the direct request of the Allies" (*Documents on British Foreign Policy*, VI, p. 326).

8. Georges I. Brătianu, *Origines*, p. 322.

9. According to Roberts (*Romania*, p. 91), only two elections in the period 1919-1945 "were at all free and fair, and both produced marked upsets in political life." The first was in November 1919.

10. The Liberals gained only 102 seats in the Chamber and 18 in the Senate. Their failure to secure more may be attributed to the fact that of 568 deputies to be elected, 247 were to come from the Old Kingdom, where the Liberals were strongest, while 321 were to be elected from the new provinces (Marcel Gillard, *Le Roumanie nouvelle*, p. 165). The Transylvanian Nationalists gained 199 seats in the Chamber (Seton-Watson, *A History*, p. 547).

11. Brătianu accused the British of plotting to assure the success of Maniu. This charge was not unfounded, since Rattigan had urged the Foreign Office to support Maniu because he appeared more flexible than Brătianu. Brătianu could not convince Rattigan that Maniu was corrupt (*Documents on British Foreign Policy*, VI, pp. 301-302, 310).

12. For treatments of the campaign and election, see Seton-Watson, *A History*, p. 548, and his preface to an article by George D. Herron, "The New Roumania," *The New Europe*, XII (1919), No. 155, p. 282; Temperley, *A History*, IV, p. 262; André Tibal, *Problèmes politiques contemporains de l'Europe orientale*, Lesson 15, pp. 2-4.

The Conservative Democrats refused to participate in the elections. Ionescu termed them a fraud (Iorga, *Memorii*, II, p. 262). Iorga accused Brătianu of preventing the return of troops from Hungary so they could not vote for their favorite, Averescu. The General, however, refused to stand for election (*Memorii*, II, p. 260).

13. *U.S. Foreign Relations, PPC*, IX, pp. 136-138.

14. Crowe told the Foreign Office about the "bad faith and dishonesty" of Brătianu, "who is perfectly aware that British territorial experts were far more

generous than other experts." He quoted Brătianu's statement — "wait and see what Italy will do if she is not satisfied as regards Fiume" — to show that Fiume was a test case (*Documents on British Foreign Policy*, VI, pp. 370-371).

15. *U.S. Foreign Relations*, PPC, IX, pp. 124-129.

16. *Ibid.*, IX, p. 146.

17. *Ibid.*, IX, pp. 159-160, 176-179.

18. *Ibid.*, IX, p. 179. The ultimatum was dated November 15. When de Martino congratulated Clemenceau for his handling of the two Romanians, the French premier retorted, "It was a result of his association with his Italian colleagues that he had acquired diplomatic skill."
Italy's defense of Romania at this time coincided with a visit to Rome of Prince Barbu Ştirbei, Brătianu's brother-in-law, whom Rattigan said had been sent to arrange a *modus operandi* (*Documents on British Foreign Policy*, VI, pp. 373-374).

19. Two versions of the ultimatum were printed in the documents. The original is in *U.S. Foreign Relations, PPC*, IX, pp. 182-184; the amended version is in *Ibid.*, IX, pp. 154-157. It was agreed to delay publishing the ultimatum until Romania replied.

20. For Clerk's reports on developments in Budapest, see *Documents on British Foreign Policy*, VI, pp. 387-389, 402-405, 411; *U.S. Foreign Relations, PPC*, IX, pp. 394-404; and Deák, pp. 533-534, 536-537.

21. Huszár's claim is in *Daily Review of the Foreign Press, The Political Review*, I-II, No. 1, pp. 27-28. For an analysis of the change in governments, see Deák, pp. 164-166.
Polk wrote to Vopicka that the Romanians had nothing left to do but evacuate all Hungary to lessen the risk of an armed struggle with Horthy (Polk Papers).

22. Reports had reached Paris about Romanian officers requiring Magyar officials to take oaths of allegiance to King Ferdinand. There were rumors of the creation of a Romanian-controlled administration at Debreczen (*U.S. Foreign Relations, PPC*, IX, pp. 139-140, and XII, p. 712; *Documents on British Foreign Policy*, VI, p. 356).

23. Rattigan had apprised Văitoianu of the ultimatum on November 23. He urged the General to yield in return for an unofficial guarantee that certain modifications of the treaties in question would be permitted by the Allies (*Documents on British Foreign Policy*, VI, p. 406).

24. *Ibid.*, VI, p. 412. Italy's duplicity was shown in a statement of a Romanian official on November 26 to the effect that "when you Allies have made a decision, one of them always comes and advises us in contrary sense" (*Ibid.*, VI, p. 434).

25. *U.S. Foreign Relations, PPC,* IX, pp. 329-331. The King had instructed Văitoianu to prevent a rupture with the Allies (Polk Papers). Romania spurned the extension offer by refusing to sign the Treaty of Neuilly on or before December 4.

26. This view was expressed by C. J. Hurst, Legal Adviser to the British delegation (*Documents on British Foreign Policy,* V, p. 1024).

The Senate rejection of the Treaty of Guarantees led the Quai d'Orsay to intensify efforts to secure Romania's friendship. New moves in that direction were the logical outcome of America's repudiation of her commitments to France (Yates, pp. 32, 151).

27. *U.S. Foreign Relations, 1919,* I, p. 25. Clemenceau appealed to Wilson to keep the American delegation in Paris until Romania signed all treaties (Nevins, p. 477).

28. *U.S. Foreign Relations, 1919,* I, p. 26. Polk argued that the Hungarian and Romanian questions would have been settled long ago if the Council had taken a firm stand against Romania in August. He noted the consideration shown to Romania by certain Allied Powers who had encouraged Italy and d'Annunzio to defy the Conference (*Ibid., PPC,* XI, pp. 677-678).

29. *Ibid., PPC,* IX, pp. 223-224, 233-234, 331. Article 10 provided for creation of Jewish educational committees to distribute a proportional share of public funds for Jewish parochial schools. Article 11 was designed to prohibit the Romanian government from compelling Jews to work or appear in law courts on Saturdays, and from holding national elections on the Jewish Sabbath.

30. Maniu told Rattigan on November 26 of his intention to take advantage of the privilege if the Council would permit another extension of the deadline. He believed a revised minority treaty would be acceptable to the new parliament, but hesitated to announce this publicly until a Transylvanian Nationalist government was installed (*Documents on British Foreign Policy,* VI, pp. 417-418).

31. *U.S. Foreign Relations, PPC,* IX, pp. 352-353. Antonescu requested recognition of the decree-law of May 22, 1919 issued by the Romanian government for the naturalization of Jews. This decree was not considered adequate by the New States Committee because it required individual applications by Jews (Miller, *Diary,* XIII, pp. 99-102).

32. *U.S. Foreign Relations, PPC,* IX, p. 353.

33. *Ibid.,* IX, pp. 353-354; Polk Papers. Polk may have hesitated because of pressure exerted on Wilson by American Jewish spokesmen demanding inclusion of the so-called "Jewish Articles." See Charles Reznikoff, *Louis Marshall: Champion of Liberty,* II, pp. 548-549.

34. *U.S. Foreign Relations, PPC,* IX, pp. 368-369. The New States Committee recommended yielding to Antonescu. The Council, however, tabled the Committee's amendments of the treaty until Romania complied with the ultimatum (Miller, *Diary,* XlII, pp. 520, 540-541, 543, 551-552).

35. *U.S. Foreign Relations, PPC,* IX, pp. 376-377.

36. *ibid.,* IX, pp. 370, 376-377. Crowe urged Foreign Secretary Curzon to obtain King George's adherence to a joint protest (*Documents on British Foreign Policy,* VI, pp. 437-438). No remonstrance was ever sent to Bucharest.
Ferdinand's letter may have been written by Brătianu, but the appeal for intercession by heads of Allied states was apparently encouraged by Rattigan's frequent appeals to the King to interfere in government affairs by dismissing Văitoianu and appointing Maniu. Since the prerogative of shuffling cabinets had been used quite often by King Carol, Ferdinand was certainly entitled to do the same. He apparently believed heads of other states had the same privilege.

37. *Documents on British Foreign Policy,* VI, pp. 417-418. Maniu asked Rattigan to visit Transylvania to see the Magyars, who, he claimed, had complete confidence in him. Rattigan planned to go, but he refused to accompany Vopicka, likewise invited, because the American envoy's "knowledge of language is elementary, and neither his judgment nor his experience with men and matters... are such as to justify any confidence in the accuracy of his findings" (*Ibid.,* VI, p. 434).
Vopicka was a wealthy Chicago brewer and prominent contributor to the Democratic Party. "He allegedly neither drank his own beer nor allowed it in his home" (Arthur S. Link, *Wilson: The New Freedom,* p. 106, note 40).

38. *Documents on British Foreign Policy,* VI, pp. 418-419.

39. *Ibid.,* VI, pp. 435-436. According to Rattigan, the Queen learned from Coandă that Clemenceau attached no importance to the maintenance of the monarchy in Romania (*Ibid.,* VI, p. 436).

40. *Ibid.,* VI, p. 443.

41. *Ibid.,* VI, pp. 445-450. Henri Cambon disputed Văitoianu's assertion that Romania's intervention turned the tide at Verdun (*Ibid.,* VI, p. 444). Mişu believed the Allies wished Văitoianu "to bend [his] head for the blow and say how sorry [he was] for all the crimes they had committed" (*Ibid.,* VI, p. 443).

42. *Ibid.*, VI, p. 444.

43. *Ibid.*, VI, p. 445.

44. *U.S. Foreign Relations, PPC,* IX, p. 460.

45. *Ibid.*, IX, p. 466. The text of Văitoianu's reply was not sent to Paris; the envoys merely forwarded a telegram containing his points of view. The Red Army success is reported in the *Times*, London, December 13; and Chamberlin, II, p. 281.

46. *U.S. Foreign Relations, PPC,* IX, p. 460. Crowe complained to Curzon about Rattigan's unauthorized actions (*Documents on British Foreign Policy*, VI, pp. 468-469). Polk was displeased by Vopicka's behavior *(U.S. Foreign Relations, PPC,* IX, p. 460).

47. *U.S. Foreign Relations, PPC,* IX, pp. 460-462. Crowe doubted the efficacy of still another warning because further delay would give Brătianu "a weapon to exploit the favorite theme of weakness and divided counsels" of the Allies *(Documents on British Foreign Policy*, VI, p. 468).

The French decision to thwart Brătianu was based on a plan of the Quai d'Orsay to befriend Maniu and win him over to an alliance. Paris newspapers began to praise the good will of the Council toward Romania. This change was noted by Lord Derby, British ambassador to France, in a note to Curzon on December 14 *(Documents on British Foreign Policy*, VI, p. 512).

48. The text of the final note is in the *Times*, London, December 4, and reprinted in Temperley, *A History*, IV, pp. 517-519.

The Transylvanian Nationalists may have become alarmed by the tumultuous reception given Brătianu by the parliament when it convened on November 28. He was cheered as the liberator of the new provinces (Iorga, *Memorii*, II, p. 268).

49. *Documents on British Foreign Policy*, VI, p. 466.

50. For a character description of Maniu, see Roberts, pp. 135-136. Maniu's incorrigibility in later years was defined as a wish "to sit tight, calmly confident that future history would record that he never did anything a good Christian ought not to do" (Hugh Seton-Watson, *Eastern Europe between the Wars*, p. 212).

51. The envoys may have been unaware of the fact that Vaida-Voevod had been an obedient delegate to the Peace Conference. Brătianu certainly would not have appointed anyone to that post if the candidate opposed policies associated with the Liberals.

52. Iorga once reported that Maniu and Vaida-Voevod were socialists. See his *Histoire des roumains de Transylvanie et de Hongrie*, II, pp. 399-400.

53. *U.S. Foreign Relations, PPC,* IX, p. 508; *Documents on British Foreign Policy,* VI, p. 499-500.

54. *Documents on British Foreign Policy,* VI, p. 496; Vopicka, p. 307.

55. *U.S. Foreign Relations, PPC,* IX, p. 477.

56. Marghiloman, IV, p. 421.

57. *Ibid.,* IV, pp. 427-428. For more on the change of government, see Axente, p. 479; Iorga, *Memorii,* II, pp. 281-282; and Joseph S. Roucek, *Contemporary Roumania and her Problems,* p. 104.
Averescu told Maniu he would support the Transylvanians in accepting Allied demands either morally or by actual inclusion of some of his supporters in the new government on one condition, namely, dissolution of the present parliament after a short session to transact the most urgent business and ratify the treaties (*Documents on British Foreign Policy,* VI, p. 419). When Vaida-Voevod failed to carry out Averescu's terms, the General resigned on December 15.

58. *U.S. Foreign Relations, PPC,* IX, pp. 538-539. Wallace's orders are in *Ibid.,* IX, p. 523, and XI, p. 697.

59. Polk was in a very delicate position. He was demanding Romania's acceptance of a treaty to which the United States might not become a party. Vopicka had pointed out the incongruity of this situation on November 30 when he wrote Polk the American position differed very little from the Romanian (Polk Papers).

60. *U.S. Foreign Relations, PPC,* IX, p. 538; Miller, *Diary,* XVI, pp. 497-498. Polk was dismayed by Coandă's resistance in view of his earlier estimate of the General as a "charming old gentleman who realized it was time" for the Romanians to comply (Polk Papers).

61. The New States Committee had submitted the first draft of a minority treaty to the Council on July 16. The report accompanying the draft stated that the decree-law of May 22 "cannot suffice to reassure all of the racial and religious minorities who are now, as a result of the Allied victory, to be included in Romania" (Miller, *Diary,* XIII, p. 277).

62. Berthelot cited the testimony of the Grand Rabbi of France and the statement of Edmund de Rothschild, the famous financier. Both urged elimination of the two articles because, by the terms, Jews of Romania would be placed outside the body of the nation.

63. For arguments of British Jews against the articles, see Janowsky, pp. 200, 368.

64. *U.S. Foreign Relations, PPC,* IX, pp. 538-540; Miller, *Diary,* XVI, pp. 497-498.

65. Miller, *Diary,* XIII, pp. 554-555.

66. Polk's report of the discharge of his last assignment is in *U.S. Foreign Relations, PPC,* IX, p. 700. The departure of the American delegation is described by Roucek, *Contemporary Roumania,* p. 56.

67. Clemenceau was in London on December 13 and told Lloyd George that Coandă had already signed on the 10th *(Documents on British Foreign Policy,* II, p. 754). The signing was announced in the *Times,* London, December 11.

68. *U.S. Foreign Relations, PPC,* XII, p. 726-730, 731. Bandholtz ceased to be a member of the mission on December 13. He remained in Budapest until February 9, 1920, at which time he returned to Paris on the train carrying the Hungarian delegation.

69. *Monitorul Oficial,* No. 157, December 30, and No. 165, January 1, 1920. The speeches are described in Iorga, *Memorii,* II, pp. 293-294.

70. La Roumanie *devant le congrès de la paix: La Dobroudja méridionale (le Quadrilatère),* pp. 5-6. Discussions of the Central Territorial Commission are in its *Report on Bulgaria,* The National Archives.
A rumor reached Paris in the summer that Brătianu had suggested to Bulgaria she furnish him with two divisions to fight Béla Kun for which he would cede southern Dobrodgea *(Documents on British Foreign Policy,* VI, p. 87). This report intensified American irritation *(U.S. Foreign Relations, PPC,* XI, p. 280).

71. *U.S. Foreign Relations, PPC,* VIII, pp. 805-807, 821-822, 856-857, 874, 901-902, and XI, pp. 406-407, 664. The minority question is treated in Lapradelle, *La paix de Versailles,* X, p. 340.

72. Berthelot's vigorous defense of the sanctity of pre-war treaties could not be overcome by the Americans who insisted upon the right of the Conference to undo treaties that threatened to endanger the peace settlement. For more on Berthelot's success, see Richard D. Challener, "The French Foreign Office: The Era of Philippe Berthelot," in Craig and Gilbert, *The Diplomats,* pp. 65-85.

73. *Documents on British Foreign Policy,* VI, pp. 182-183, 192-193, 209-210, 243-245, 279, 283-284. French envoy Fontenay in Belgrade believed a Serbo-Magyar alliance possible. Percival Dodge, American minister in Belgrade, warned of imminent war (Miller, *Diary,* XX, p. 356).

74. Ada Kaleh was part of the Ottoman Empire until 1716 when it was ceded to Austria, who returned it to Turkey in 1738 and reacquired it by the Treaty of

Berlin in 1878. See J. de Blociszewski, "Ada-Kalé: une île turque annexée par l'Autriche-Hongrie," *Revue Générale de Droit Internationale,* XXI (1914).

75. *U.S. Foreign Relations, PPC,* VII, pp. 455-456, 471-473. Maintenance of peace by the French is discussed in Temperley, *A History,* IV, p. 135; and Tilea, pp. 143-145.

76. *U.S. Foreign Relations, PPC,* VII, p. 327. Their call for union is also in *La Roumanie devant le congrès de la paix: L'Unité du Banat*; and Lapradelle, *La paix de Versailles,* IX/1, pp. 330-337.

77. *U.S. Foreign Relations, PPC,* XII, p. 683. Pichon once told Beneš it was unthinkable to cede the Egerland to Germany when the Czech leader suggested it (S. Harrison Thomson, *Czechoslovakia in European History,* pp, 308-309). The French never took Brătianu's proposals seriously that he would yield southern Dobrodgea in exchange for the entire Banat or Bessarabia. Brătianu had used southern Dobrodgea as a pawn to acquire gains elsewhere. In May 1915 he offered to cede it if Bulgaria yielded Monastir to Serbia and if the Serbs agreed to cession of the entire Banat. After Serbia was defeated, he offered to cede it to Russia if she gave him Bessarabia *(Tsarskaia Rossiia,* pp. 188-190, 207, 211).

78. *U.S. Foreign Relations, PPC,* VIII, p. 540, and XII, p. 709. The protocol is in Daşcovici, *Interesele şi Drepturile României,* pp. 503-512.

79. *U.S. Foreign Relations, PPC,* IX, pp. 596-597. Poland recommended on November 20 the creation of a common Polish-Romanian frontier to eliminate the intervening region of Eastern Galicia *(Ibid.,* IX, pp. 244-247). Although the Allies had ruled Eastern Galicia would be supervised by the League of Nations and its destiny determined after a waiting period of twenty-five years, Poland refused to evacuate the region (Temperley, *A History,* VI, pp. 266-274).

80. *U.S. Foreign Relations, PPC,* XII, p. 404.

81. Tilea, pp. 149-150.

82. Coolidge was a strong defender of Ruthenian independence (*U.S. Foreign Relations, PPC,* XII, pp. 434-436; and Coolidge and Lord, p. 227).
    Recommendations of the Czech Territorial Commission were more favorable to Czechoslovakia than to Romania (Lapradelle, *La paix de Versailles,* IX/1, pp. 151-152).
    The text of the 1920 treaty is in Treaty Series, 1921, Cmd. 1548, No. 20, *Treaty Between the Principal Allied and Associated Powers and Poland, Romania, the Serb-Croat-Slovene State, and the Czechoslovak State Relative to Certain Frontiers of Those States.* Romania signed on October 28, 1920. The 1921 agreement is cited in Macartney, *Hungary and Her Successors,* p. 220.

Romanian claims to additional territory in Maramureş are in Deák, p. 515. Loss of this region was mourned in Romulus Seişanu, *Romania*, p. 97.

83. *Documents on British Foreign Policy*, III, pp. 740-741. For the Red Army campaign, see Chamberlin, II, p. 281; Fischer, *The Soviets in World Affairs*, I, pp. 210-211; and Richard Pipes, *The Formation of the Soviet Union*, pp. 142-143, 148.

According to Shcherbachev, Brătianu had promised to hand over the weapons left in Romania by Russian troops. It was believed the arms would equip forty-three infantry divisions *(U.S. Foreign Relations, PPC,* IX, pp. 342, 42-26).

84. *Documents on British Foreign Policy*, III, pp. 740-741.

85. K. Kushnir-Mikhailovich, "Velikaia Oktiabr'skaia Sotsialisticheskaia Revolutsiia i revolutsionnaia situatsiia v Rumynii v 1917-1921 gg.," *Voprosy Istorii, No.* 11, November, 1957, pp. 78-79.

86. The Council's reaction is in *U.S. Foreign Relations, PPC,* IX, pp. 784, 796-797. The parliamentary session is in Marghiloman, IV, pp, 435-436.

87. Vaida-Voevod asked for "some pity toward the Romanian peasants who were worse off than the Magyar peasants" because German troops "had left only one shirt to each peasant and had taken away even the children's cradles."

88. Lloyd George apparently expected the Allies would act in concert now. This anticipation differed from his denunciation of September 15 that the League of Nations would be condemned to impotence in advance if one nation were permitted to flout the authority of the Peace Conference, the League's progenitor. He singled out the French and Italian governments as being responsible for Romanian resistance *(U.S. Foreign Relations, PPC,* VIII, p. 227).

89. Clemenceau comforted Vaida-Voevod by placing blame for the current state of affairs upon Brătianu, but he advised the premier that "Your position is a false one. You do not carry out certain decisions of the Conference while you ask it to carry out others. I know that you are not personally responsible for this."

90. Clemenceau glanced at Alexandre Millerand, his successor as Premier, who nodded assent.

91. *U.S. Foreign Relations, PPC,* IX, pp. 910-917; *Documents on British Foreign Policy,* II, pp. 932-938.

According to Deák (p. 226, note 137), Vaida-Voevod sought to enlist French support for a continuation of the occupation of eastern Hungary to protect the rear of the Romanian army in the event of an attempt by Soviet Russia to recover Bessarabia. This request was also made of Lloyd George on March 3 *(Documents on British Foreign Policy,* VII, p. 379).

92. For analyses of Vaida-Voevod's dismissal, attributed to Ferdinand's fear he would arrange a *modus vivendi* with Soviet Russia, see Roberts, p. 94; and Hugh Seton-Watson, *Eastern Europe between the Wars*, p. 199. Press accounts of the evacuation of Hungary are in *Daily Review of the Foreign Press, The Political Review*, I-II, No. 19, p. 551.

93. *U.S. Foreign Relations*, 1920, III, pp. 427-430, 432. The treaty was interpreted in Washington as an attempt to force the United States to make legal an *ex parte* judgment on the merits and validity of Romanian claims to Bessarabia.

94. Temperley, *A History*, V, p. 168. The Treaty of Trianon was ratified by the Romanian parliament on July 26, 1920 (*Monitorul Oficial*, No. 136, September 21, 1920).

95. Temperley, *A History*, IV, p. 165. The delay in signing the Bessarabian treaty may have been also due to slow negotiations in 1920 between Britain, France, and Romania culminating in a petroleum agreement. Vaida-Voevod had been approached by Lloyd George with a plan reviving the previous agreement annulled by Brătianu in August 1919. Not until Averescu assumed office did the Romanians agree to an arrangement permitting British and French concerns to purchase the German holdings. This agreement was signed at San Remo on April 25, 1920. See *Documents on British Foreign Policy*, IV, pp. 1117-1118; Temperley, *A History*, VI, pp. 183, 603; and C. C. Rommenhoeller, *La Grande-Roumanie*, p. 388.

96. Ionescu told Lloyd George in London on October 20 that Romania would never be able to secure Russia's approval of the union (*Documents on British Foreign Policy*, VIII, pp. 795-802).

97. The text of the treaty is in *U.S. Foreign Relations*, 1920, III, pp. 427-430. A Romanian-language text is in Dașcovici, *Interesele și Drepturile României*, pp. 29-33.

Jules Cambon, Derby, and Ishii were the Allied signatories. Italy adhered in 1921. The treaty was ratified by Britain in 1921, France in 1924, and Italy in 1927. Japan never ratified and the United States never signed. See Max Beloff, *The Foreign Policy of Soviet Russia*, I, p. 22, note 1; and Malbone W. Graham, "The Legal Status of the Bukovina and Bessarabia," *American Journal of International Law*, XXXVIII (1944), No. 4, pp. 667-673.

Romania ratified the collective treaty on frontiers at the same time as the Bessarabian treaty (May 19, 1922). See *Monitorul Oficial*, No. 100, August 8, 1922.

98. Kliuchnikov and Sabanin (eds.), *Mezhdunarodnaia Politika Noveishego Vremeni v Dogovorakh, Notakh i Deklaratsiakh*, III, 1, p. 69.

A legal interpretation of the Bessarabian dispute is provided by Robert Langer, *Seizure of Territory*, pp. 29-31.

CONCLUSION

Romania emerged from World War I with few, if any, disappointments. A greater Romanian state coming into existence as a geographical entity represented the fulfillment of an idea that only five years earlier had been no more than a dream. From a pre-war area of 53,661 square miles and a population of 7½ million, Romania grew to 113,941 square miles (an area almost equal to the combined territories of the states of Connecticut, New York, New Jersey, Delaware, and Maryland) and a population of about 16 million. These figures show that the denial of bits of territory in the interest of compromise was negligible. Not even the Italians or Greeks, who also challenged the authority of the Peace Conference, entered the post-war era so rich in territorial gains. Romania secured more territory than had been promised in the 1916 Alliance. Although Romania was deprived of 3,618 square miles in Crişana and 3,409 square miles in the Banat, this reduction of her Alliance promise was richly compensated for by the incorporation of 16,988 square miles in Bessarabia and about 1,000 square miles of Bucovina (the latter area consigned to Russia by the Alliance). Reflecting on the troubled years between the signing of the Alliance and the in-gathering of the new provinces, most Romanians had good cause for satisfaction. Basic national aspirations had become a reality, and the obstacles to a "Greater Romania" had been overcome.

How did the unique privilege of more than doubling her size and population come to a state whose leader, perhaps more than any other statesman, tenaciously resisted the efforts of the Allies to renege on their 1916 promises? This is the basic question which pervades the account just presented. Dour, intractable, rigid, possessing a logical mind and clear-cut opinions which never changed, the Romanian Premier, with his insatiable lust for power and vanity, had the most extraordinary talent for diplomatic acrobatics and intrigue; he was a superb actor, a master of timing, and an ingenious dissimulator. One cannot blame his contemporaries for distrusting Brătianu, because they had to judge him by his deeds, not by his explanation of them. His strength lay in the dexterity of his maneuvers, in the manipulations of the ideals of others, and in inventing devices for attaining goals.

Brătianu was a master of that subtle, farsighted, and somewhat disreputable diplomacy which in other times was called "Byzantine." Like his Byzantine forebears, Brătianu was adept in the art of playing nations against each other for his own benefit. The uncertainty in which he left the Great Powers as to the side Romania would eventually join was a masterpiece of political strategy. Vacillation as a diplomatic art was brought to its loftiest height of perfection by Romanian rulers during centuries of precarious existence wedged between Turks, Magyars, and Slavs. Brătianu proved a worthy successor to his predecessors. From 1914 to 1916 he executed one of the most notable acts of political tightrope walking. The Germans assumed he would never fight against them, but feared he might not fight for them. The Allies doubted if he ever would fight for them, but hoped he would not fight against them. At the decisive moment, he threw in with the Allies and the results were catastrophic, but out of the catastrophe Romania emerged with her territory and population doubled, the sixth largest country in Europe, and the dominant state in Southeastern Europe.

Brătianu was a product of the 19th century, standing for the continued validity of Realpolitik in the tradition of Talleyrand and Bismarck. His attitude was compounded of devotion to old yet realistic diplomacy, an incurable aversion to new ideas, and a nationalism resting at home on a government by the narrowest of cliques and in disregard of constitutional government. In the appraisal of an astute observer, Romanian politics had "an ineradicable proclivity for şmecherie (a term of half-admiration for fraudulent actions performed with a degree of poise and dexterity)." Romania's easy victory over Bulgaria in 1913 and her diplomatic success after the Balkan Wars contributed materially to both society and government exaggerating their own importance. Politically and militarily, Brătianu and the Romanians overrated themselves. But this exultation did not blind Brătianu from understanding, as his father had, that Romania lay between the upper and lower grindstones of belligerent diplomacy. He was equally uninfluenced by the promises of Germany, the blandishments of Russia, the pleas of France, and the loans of Britain. For two years he refused to deviate from a policy of more or less impartial neutrality, and awaited what he himself described as "*le moment opportun.*"

From the beginning of the war Brătianu knew the ultimate consequences of ill-timed intervention. Romanian neutrality wavered on two calculations: a wish to arrive in time for the dismemberment of Austria-Hungary and an effort to earn as much as possible at the expense of the belligerents. Brătianu did not share with the other wartime leaders that propensity to offer extravagant promises to their people as to what might be expected to flow from victory. He declared candidly in 1914 that the choice between belligerency and neutrality had to be determined solely by the balance of territorial advantages which were offered by both sides. He could not afford to repeat the mistake made in 1878, when, in return for heavy sacrifices, Romania was deprived of southern Bessarabia and given, as compensation, northern Dobrodgea. The Premier insisted upon advantageous terms clearly specified and adequately guaranteed, and unless they outweighed those which he could secure from one side in return for neutrality, he felt it his duty to reject them.

Brătianu had too sound a judgment to be dazzled by proposals, however spacious, which held out prospects of territorial aggrandizement unless such conquests would satisfy not his greed, but his anxiety. He believed that justice to his people demanded a protection of national security; and this protection could be secured only by strategic frontiers at the expense of another people. To him the war was not a fight for international right and human liberty. His interest in either of these 20th century ideals was indifferent and somewhat scornful. The war was to him a supreme chance for extending boundaries and increasing the security, prestige, and importance of Romania. That is why he abandoned the Central Powers and used his influence to induce Romania to join the Allies. He was shrewd enough to see that the Central Powers would give him nothing for either alliance or neutrality. Deliberate and practical in urging his views, which were not affected by idealistic considerations, Brătianu constantly sought material benefits for his country. It was clearly national interest rather than abstract justice that determined his policy. Certainly Brătianu's position was such that he had a responsibility to see what was done was in Romania's best interests, and he must be judged by that standard. After all, this same policy was pursued by the leaders of both sides during the war. In international relations, there are virtually no absolute values except the existence of the state and the satisfaction of its interests. The state is morally its own excuse for being; it needs no moral justification other than those which it furnishes itself. The only concepts of "good" and "bad" which relate to the international conduct of a state are relative to its success or failure in attaining its objectives. Any policy which succeeds in advancing national interest is a "good" policy; any policy which fails to reach its objective is a "bad" one.

That Brătianu was able to select his own way and his own moment demanded skill. He could not make obvious his preparations for war against the Central Powers, for that would give them time to prepare while it would weaken his position with the Allies. Because the risks of war could not be taken lightly, he tried to obtain concessions from Austria-Hungary by playing the threat of intervention. That policy, characterized by the self-righteous as blackmail, was a sane and sound national policy from the Romanian point of view because Brătianu was taking advantage of circumstances not of his own making. One needs to reflect on the military situation in 1914-1916. Things were not going too well for the Allies. Both sides came to the realization that the adventure upon which they had embarked was beset with greater difficulties and perils than they had fully contemplated, that victory was not so assured as they had at first anticipated, that they must seek and, if necessary, purchase the assistance of an ally. But Brătianu did not require defeats on the battlefield to convince him of these facts. He advised the Crown Council of August 1914, before hostilities commenced, that Romania would await the most favorable bid. As his father's son, he suspected all Russians of treachery and guile and, while holding his neutrality agreement with Russia as a trump card affording him rights without duties and protection without obligation, he was quick to take advantage of every Allied disagreement on Balkan policy and turn it to his gain at Russia's expense. He simultaneously flirted with the Central Powers. Unlike the Great Powers, none of whom planned the war and all of whom muddled into it, Romania deliberately entered it with expressed war aims.

Brătianu shared the belief of other realists that however exalted ideals may be, they can never be achieved without force. He did not succumb to the doctrine preached that much could be gained without intervention. Like Sonnino, he was filled with a nationalistic desire to use to the full this opportunity of creating a greater Romania. The Allies were only too well pleased to secure the adherence of another ally to scrutinize the proposed territorial readjustments which were the conditions of the 1916 bargain. When Lloyd George wrote, "War plays havoc with the refinements of conscience," he was obviously closing his eyes to the secret treaties and paying lip-service to the intrusion of Wilsonian ideals, destined to produce a new era in diplomacy. For it was the American intervention that led to a lack of confidence in the traditional channels and techniques of diplomacy. Brătianu was aware of the naive American assumption that moral force and reason would lead to an orderly and righteous international society. Although Wilson's eloquently expressed ideals swayed many judgments, Brătianu overturned such concepts by first implementing his decisions and then laying down principles to justify them. He spoke of dismembering Austria-Hungary in 1916, long before the Allies adopted this as a war aim. While the Allies had the short range goal of winning the war and the long range goal of fulfilling war aims, Brătianu telescoped the two aims into one. He never shared with the Allies any enthusiasm for their professed idealistic aims and, for that reason, the Allies never secured from him any modicum of support for any enterprise, military or naval, which was not purely and strictly Romanian, however important it might have been for the success of the common Allied cause.

For a casual observer to conclude that Brătianu cheated the Allies is to absolve the Allies of all complicity in meeting his demands. One must note that there existed a certain insincerity in inter-Allied relations, a combination of idealism and opportunism, and a lack of moral strength accompanied by a wavering attitude. That Brătianu asked for a written alliance in the face of these conditions is certainly understandable. He regarded the 1916 Alliance as sacrosanct and rested his case solely upon it. The real basis of the Alliance must be seen as an application of the doctrine of the balance of power. In 1916 the total dismemberment of Austria-Hungary was a very real possibility, but hardly an immediate prospect. By assigning parts of that empire to Romania, the Allies made dismemberment inevitable. When the Allies later realized the dangers of dismemberment, it was too late to stop Brătianu. His unswerving fight to seize promised lands blinded him to Wilsonian principles, and eventually led him afoul of the will of the Peace Conference.

In his naïve belief that he had elevated Romania to a position of equality with the Allies, Brătianu expected a reserved seat on the Supreme Council. His anticipation was somewhat justified in that Romania had been the partner of Great Powers in the Triple Alliance. The 1883 treaty had accorded Romania equal status in negotiating peace treaties. Brătianu's expectation that the 1916 Alliance signed with enemies of the Triplice granted him the same right suffered a severe jolt when the Allies assumed authority for the final disposition of claims of the "small powers with special interests," a label which infuriated Brătianu. The Allies anticipated that Brătianu would accept their decisions cheerfully. Deeply resenting exclusion from the

Council, which angered him more than equivocations over the validity of the 1916 Alliance, Brătianu resumed in Paris his vexatious wartime tactics to resist adverse decisions reached without his participation. He did not like to be dealt with by others as he had dealt with them. In Paris he was astonished to learn how seldom and how reluctantly he had acknowledged the virtue of compromise during his long life in politics. He had never considered a question settled until it was settled his way. For him to have violated the Alliance by making a separate peace was, in Brătianu's estimation, an entirely justifiable act; but for the Allies to betray that sacred compact was contrary to international justice. His exasperating resistance to the dictates of the Allied leaders, all of whom he considered parvenus and unqualified to interfere in Romania's private affairs, and his rejection of compromise involved the Allies in such a tangle of contradictions as to accentuate the rift in their ranks. Perhaps nothing serves as well to illustrate the success of his divide-and-conquer tactics than the failure of the Allied statesmen to repudiate or honor the Alliance publicly. Their disinclination to disavow it was a by-product of the bickerings and rivalries among the peacemakers.

Angered and disappointed, Brătianu accused the Allies of bad faith, but his indignation did not blind him to the fact that the Peace Conference was not omnipotent. The Allies had no means of enforcing their decisions in East Central Europe simply because they had failed to occupy the region in strength after the armistices. War weariness and mutually antagonistic aims hindered inter-Allied occupation, the most effective means of enforcing territorial settlements. What the Allies failed to realize was that the boundaries that involved annexations of territories in East Central Europe were an accomplished fact before the Allies ever adjudicated upon their fairness. The map of the Habsburg Monarchy had been rearranged before the Peace Conference convened. The Conference could only ratify or regulate retracings already carried out by Romania and other states located on the periphery of Austria-Hungary. The political and military situation existing in the winter of 1918-1919 limited the freedom of action of the Allies. By that time the liberation and unification of all Romanians had been proclaimed. Detailed boundaries of the newly-enlarged nation had to be fixed by negotiation, but it could not be denied that "Greater Romania" was already established. The final territorial settlements merely entailed a formal legalization of Romania's new frontiers which war and conquest already had created. To take away what Romania had been promised and had acquired and to return it to Hungary and other states in the interests of permanent peace was anathema to Brătianu.

By taking advantage of dissensions within Allied ranks, Brătianu was able to control the course of events in 1919. His encouragement of disputes among the Allies and his ability to turn resulting imbroglios to his favor show that he was more skilled than any of the Big Four, none of whom had had first-hand acquaintance with his diplomatic dexterity. Whenever the Allies finally made up their minds that they needed his assistance, they were clearly not in a position to haggle over details. When any solution threatened to become complete and decisive, Brătianu's demands became excessive and his counter-thrusts jeopardized the final peace settlement. This pattern, at times verging on the absurd, had become so ingrained that Brătianu could never discard it. Wilsonian principles condemning a continuation of this type of diplomacy won popular lip-service, but Brătianu openly repudiated the "new diplomacy." To him the peace treaties were "Wilsonian garlands around Napoleonic clauses." He referred in December 1919 to the Peace Conference as "a provisional institution above which existed the supreme and permanent interests" of Romania who "was strong by the conscience that it has a high mission."

The infusion of Wilsonian ideals into peacemaking made Romania's position one of particular difficulty and ambiguity, but since Allied statesmen were neither united as to policy nor faithful to their decisions, Brătianu found conditions most favorable for his policy of resistance, delay, and skillful bargaining. He never believed in, nor would he allow himself to be seduced by, the dream of a brave new world emerging under the aegis of the League of Nations. This attitude reflected general European mistrust of a peace based on the Fourteen Points. It was as natural for Brătianu to resent American interference as it was for French, Italian, and Japanese statesmen to thwart Wilson's dreams. One has only to point to the American rejection of French claims to the Rhineland, Italian designs on the eastern Adriatic shore, or Japanese claims to Shantung to demonstrate that Brătianu's claims might not have been satisfied if the Americans had won out completely in Paris. As Sonnino so aptly put it, "The War undoubtedly had had the effect of over-exciting the feeling of nationality.... Perhaps America fostered it by putting the principles so clearly." When the Americans attempted to restrain rampant nationalism by means of abstract formulas, based largely upon the essentials of liberal democracy, their efforts met with least success in East Central Europe where frontiers were so tangled historically and traditionally that no one could with certainty unravel the title to lands on either side.

Added to the complexities produced by American intervention was the complicated relationship between foreign and domestic policy. "Democratic" foreign policy was in its infancy in 1919. Brătianu evinced little or no understanding of its merits. The relationship in Romania between foreign and domestic policy played a far less significant role in the formulation of policies than in the development of British, French, and Italian statesmanship. Unlike other elected statesmen, Brătianu was not really accountable to public opinion for his acts. Moreover, in contrast to the diplomatic tactics of the British, French, and Italians, which shifted with changes in administrations, Romanian policy remained steadfast despite shufflings of cabinets in Bucharest. Brătianu, by virtue of his control of Romanian politics, steered a consistent course to victory without deferring to his opponents at home. By contriving to show that Romania could no longer be expected to remain under constant subjection to the machinations of the Great Powers, who were still trying to use her as a pawn, Brătianu overturned the established concept that smaller European states had only marginal control over their destinies.

Insisting the 1916 Alliance to be valid and binding, Brătianu first tried to secure by negotiations a general recognition of his new frontiers and of Romania as a great power defending European civilization in the East. After learning that the Allies, each of whom had come to Paris with a program of contradictions, no longer considered the Alliance absolutely binding, Brătianu believed the time had come for Romania to stand alone or select such allies as suited her best. When he proceeded alone to implement the Alliance promises, all the misunderstandings and difficulties which arose in the case of Hungary revealed the shocking lack of unity and singularity of approach among the Allied governments. The Allied statesmen failed to reconcile their various views, and the more clumsily they berated or the more loftily they sermonized, the more violently did Brătianu spout defiance. The Allies overlooked the fact that Romania lived in fear of her national life. Not until it was too late did the Big Four, none of whom had negotiated the 1916 Alliance, realize that there was no unity either of military command or political direction in the treatment of the forces of the defunct Habsburg Monarchy as a whole, that the Belgrade armistice had taken little account of the interests of Romania, and that nine months after that armistice Romania had, rightly or wrongly, received no compensation in kind for her material losses sustained during the war. When dealing with Béla Kun, who made no secret of his belligerent aims, the Big Four preferred relying upon Kun's promises instead of restraining him. When plans were finally considered for military operations to force Hungary into line, the campaign was so retarded that in the meantime Romania, the state most directly interested, had already taken independent action.

At that point, in August 1919, the irreconcilability of Allied war aims became evident when the mask of hypocrisy and equivocation was removed. While the Allies at first were involved in a high degree of improvisation and of confusion in the effort to solve the Romanian crisis, *raison d'état* soon seized the Allies and led them to concentrate their energies upon winning Romania's favor by meeting Brătianu halfway. The brief flirtation with ideals was now over. Although not admitted at the time, the wearisome negotiations with Brătianu were conducted in a spirit reflecting the effects of the secret treaties and the pressure of frankly selfish national objectives. Decisions of the Big Four that for a time echoed abstract principles were flouted whenever they interfered with the ambitions of the state against whom judgment was rendered.

France, perhaps more accountable than any other Allied Power for the munificent promises that lured Romania into the war, appears no less responsible than Romania for the course of events. But it should be noted that Europe was the most important of all continents to France. The French, therefore, decided every issue with a keen eye on prospects for stronger friends and weaker enemies. France was not in a position to uphold the peace settlements by her own strength. The alternative to the abortive Treaty of Guarantees was alliances with the East Central European states. France valued Romania's military resources, strategic location, raw materials, and position in the new balance of power. Such an appreciation of Romania was hardly different from the attitude previously shown by states of the Triple Alliance. The Quai d'Orsay appropriated the pre-war German view that Romania signified a market for business and finance, a causeway to the Ottoman Empire which the French expected to carve up, and the base of French power in East Central Europe. Since these aims conflicted with those of Italy, the French moved swiftly to accommodate Brătianu's maximum demands before the Italians could upset the balance of power. Romania ultimately reciprocated by becoming as vigorous an anti-revisionist state as France.

Romania's success was due indirectly to American inexperience in the give-and-take of Realpolitik and the subsequent defection of the

United States from the Peace Conference. American impatience to have done with participation in European affairs gave fresh impetus to French designs, sparked Italian moves toward the same aims, and improved Brătianu's game of chance. Certainly a decisive factor was the American rejection of the peace treaties, an act which rendered the settlement incomplete.

Perhaps as significant as the American default was Russia's absence from the Peace Conference. The collapse of Imperial Russia was an event which had immediately favorable consequences for Romania. If Imperial Russia had been represented, Romania would certainly not have acquired so much non-Romanian territory, and most assuredly not Bessarabia or northern Bucovina. Closely related to Russia's disappearance from the European concert was the very real panic Bolshevism inspired in the West. Brătianu's manipulation of this fear assisted his campaign most effectively. As a result, Romania's increase in size was due as much to Lenin as to the French and Americans.

Grumbling chauvinism and intransigence blinded Brătianu to the fact, which did not become evident until later, that Russia was still his neighbor. He would have been wise to recognize that Romania had been the most favored of allied states in that she had acquired territory from enemy and ally alike. Brătianu should have realized that only by a far-sighted moderation of his territorial claims and respect for the nationalistic tendencies of those non-Romanian peoples whom he incorporated would Romania preserve what she had needed help to win.

BIBLIOGRAPHY

I. BIBLIOGRAPHIES AND REFERENCE GUIDES

Adamescu, Gheorghe. "Dicţionar Istoric-Geografic," Part II of Aurel Candrea, *Dicţionarul Enciclopedic Ilustrat "Cartea Românească."* Bucharest: Cartea Românească, 1931.

Binkley, Robert C. "Ten Years of Peace Conference History," *Journal of Modern History*, I (1929), No. 4, pp. 607-629.

— — —. "New Light on the Paris Peace Conference," *Political Science Quarterly*, XLVI (1931), Nos. 3-4, pp. 335-361, 509-547.

Birdsall, Paul. "The Second Decade of Peace Conference History," *Journal of Modern History*, XI (1939), No. 3, pp. 362-378.

— — —. *Versailles Twenty Years Later.* New York: Reynal and Hitchcock, 1941.

Clark, John (ed.). *Politics and Political Parties in Roumania.* London: International Reference Library, 1936.

Council on Foreign Relations. *Foreign Affairs Bibliography, 1919-1932.* Edited by William Leonard Langer and Hamilton Fish Armstrong. New York: Harper and Bros., 1933.

— — —. *Foreign Affairs Bibliography, 1932-1942.* Edited by Robert Gale Woolbert. New York : Harper and Bros., 1945.

— — —. *Foreign Affairs Bibliography, 1942-1952.* Edited by Henry L. Roberts. New York: Harper and Bros., 1955.

Crăciun, Joachim. "Bibliographie de la Transylvanie roumaine," *Revue de Transylvanie* (Cluj), III (1937), No. 4, pp. 3-366.

Fischer-Galaţi, Stephen A. *Slavic-Romanian Relations in Modern Romanian Historiography.* Mimeographed Series No. 8. New York: Mid-European Studies Center of the National Committee for a Free Europe, 1953.

Ghyka, Matila Costiescu. *A Documented Chronology of Roumanian History from Pre-Historic Times to the Present Day.* Translated from the French by Fernand G. Renier and Anne Cliff. Oxford: Basil Blackwell, 1941.

Great Britain. Foreign Office. Historical Section. *A Select Analytical List of Books concerning the Great War.* Edited by Sir George Walter Prothero. London: H.M. Stationery Office, 1923.

Gregory, Winifred (ed.). *List of the Serial Publications of Foreign Governments, 1815-1931.* New York: H.W. Wilson Co., 1932.

Henry, Paul. "Bibliographie de la Roumanie: Histoire," *Revue Historique* (Paris), No. 176 (July-December, 1935), pp. 486-537; No. 194 (1944), pp. 42-64, 132-150, 233-252.

Hoover Library on War, Revolution, and Peace. *The Hoover War Collection.* Edited by Ephraim Adams. Stanford: Stanford University Press, 1921.

– – –. *A Catalogue of Paris Peace Conference Delegation Propaganda.* Vol. I. Stanford: Stanford University Press, 1926.

– – –. *An Introduction to a Bibliography of the Paris Peace Conference.* Edited by Nina Almond and Ralph Haswell Lutz. Stanford: Stanford University Press, 1935.

– – –. *Special Collections in the Hoover Library on War, Revolution, and Peace.* Edited by Nina Almond and Ralph Haswell Lutz. Stanford: Stanford University Press, 1940.

International Comittee of Historical Sciences, Lausanne. *International Bibliography of Historical Sciences.* Annual since 1926. Paris: International Committee for Philosophy and Humanistic Studies.

Rally, Alexandre, and Rally, Getta A. (eds.). *Bibliographie franco-roumaine.* 2 vols. I: "Les oeuvres françaises des auteurs roumains," and II: "Les oeuvres françaises relatives à la Roumanie." Paris: E. Leroux, 1930.

Ruffini, Mario. "Introduzione bibliografica allo studio della Romania," *L'Europa Orientale* (Rome), XV (May-June, 1935), pp. 236-289.

Romania. Academia Română. *Bulletin de la section historique.* Edited by Nicolae Iorga. Bucharest, 1912-1938.

––––. *L'Institut Social Roumain: XV ans d'activité.* Edited by G. Vlădescu-Racoassa. Bucharest: I.E. Toroutiu, 1933.

––––. *Anglo-Romanian and Romanian-English Bibliography.* Edited by Octav Păduraru. Bucharest: Monitorul Oficial şi Imprimeriile Statului, 1946.

Savadjian, Léon (ed.). *Bibliographie balkanique,* 1920-1938. 8 vols. Paris: Société générale d'imprimerie et d'édition, 1931-1939.

––––. *Encyclopédie balkanique permanente.* Paris: Société générale d'imprimerie at d'édition, 1936.

Société des Nations. Conférence Permanente des Hautes Études Internationales. *Chronique des Evénements Politiques et Économiques dans le Bassin Danubien, 1918-1936: Roumanie.* Paris. Institut International Coopération Intellectuelle, 1938.

Sztachová, Jiřina (ed.). *Mid-Europe: A Selective Bibliography.* New York: Mid-European Studies Center of the National Committee for a Free Europe, 1953.

Taylor, R. P. D. (ed.). *Handbook of Central and East Europe, 1937.* Zűrich: Central European Times Publishing Co., Ltd., 1937.

United States. Department of State. *International Transfers of Territory in Europe.* Edited by Sophia Saucerman. Washington: Govemment Printing Office, 1937.

— — —. Library of Congress. Division of Bibliography. *The Balkans: A Selected List of References.* Vol. IV. *Roumania.* Edited by Helen Field Conover. Washington: The Library of Congress, 1945.

— — —. The National Archives. *Handbook of Federal World War Agencies and their Records,* 1917-1921. Washington: Government Printing Office, 1943.

— — —. The National Archives. "Cartographic Records of the American Commission to Negotiate Peace." *Preliminary Inventories* No. 68. Compiled by James Berton Rhoads. Washington: General Services Administration, 1954.

— — —. The National Archives. "Records of the American Commission to Negotiate Peace." *Preliminary Inventories* No. 89. Compiled by H. Stephen Helton. Washington: General Services Administration, 1955.

Wegerer, Alfred von (ed.). *Bibliographie zur Vorgeschichte des Weltkrieges.* Berlin: Quaderverlag, 1934.

II. Primary Sources: UNPUBLISHED DOCUMENTS

Allied and Associated Powers. Committee for the Study of Territorial Questions Relating to Romania. Minutes (procès-verbaux). Photostatic reproduction of original manuscript is in The New York Public Library.

Great Britain. H. M. Government, Peace Terms: Confidential. Prepared by the Foreign Office for the Prime Minister, December, 1918. Photostatic reproduction of original manuscript is in The New York Public Library.

Grew, Joseph Clark. Secretary-General of the American Delegation. Diary and Letters, 1919-1920. Houghton Library, Harvard University. With the permission of Mr. Grew.

House, Edward Mandell. Diary and correspondence, materials of the Inquiry, and miscellaneous papers. Yale University Library. With the permission of Dr. Charles Seymour, Curator of the House Collection.

McConnick, Vance. Chairman, War Trade Board, and Technical Adviser, Economics Section, American Delegation. Diary, 1919. United Nations Library, New York City.

Mezes, Sidney E. Director of the Division of Territorial, Economic, and Political Intelligence, American Delegation. Correspondence and papers, 1918-1919. Special Collections, Columbia University Library.

Moon, Parker T. Technical Assistant, Division of Territorial, Economic, and Political Intelligence, American Delegation. Bulletins, reports, and miscellaneous papers. International Law Library, Columbia University.

Polk, Frank Lyon. Under-Secretary of State. Correspondence and papers. House Collection, Yale University Library. With the permission of Dr. Charles Seymour, Curator.

United States. The National Archives, Washington, D.C. Repository of the Bulletins of the American Delegation, procès-verbaux of the Supreme Council and the commissions, and dispatches to and from American embassies and legations. Records of the German Foreign Ministry for the period 1914-1918, catalogued on data sheets, do not contain information significant for this study.

III. Primary Sources: PUBLISHED DOCUMENTS ON THE WAR PERIOD

Austria. Ministerium des Äussern. *Österreichisch-Ungarisches Rotbuch: Diplomatische Aktenstücke betreffend die Beziehungen Österreich-Ungarns zu Rumdnien in der Zeit vom 22. Juli 1914 bis 27. August 1916.* Vienna: Manzsche k.u.k. Hof-Verlags- und Universitäts-Buchhandlung, 1916.

———. Ministerium des Äussem. *Österreich-Ungarns Aussenpolitik van der Bosnischen Krise 1908 bis zum Kriegsausbruch 1914.* Vol. VIII. Edited by L. Bittner, A. F. Pribram, H. Srbik, and H. Uebersberger. Vienna: Österreichischer Bundesverlag, 1930.

Cocks, F. Seymour. *The Secret Treaties and Understandings.* London: Union of Democratic Control, 1918.

Daşcovici, Nicolae. *Interesele şi Drepturile României în texte de drept internaţional public.* Iaşi: Tipografia concesionară Alexandru Ţerek, 1936.

Degras, Jane (ed.). *Soviet Documents on Foreign Policy.* Vol. I: *1917-1924.* London: Oxford University Press, 1951.

Dickinson, G. Lowes (ed.). *Documents and Statements Relating to Peace Proposals and War Aims.* London: Allen and Unwin, 1919.

France. Ministère des affaires étrangères. *Conventions d'armistice passées avec la Turquie, la Bulgarie, l'Autriche-Hongrie, et l'Allemagne par les puissances alliées et associées.* Paris: Imprimerie nationale, 1919.

Germany. *Die Deutschen Dokumente zum Kriegsausbruch.* Vol. IV. Edited by Karl Kautsky, Graf Montgelas, and W. Schücking. Charlottenburg: Deutsche Verlagsgesellschaft für Politik und Geschichte, 1919.

———. *Die Grosse Politik der Europäischen Kabinette, 1871-1914.* Vols. XXXIV-XXXIX. Edited by J. Lepsius, A. Mendelssohn-Bartholdy, and F. Thimme. Berlin: Deutsche Verlagsgesellschaft für Politik und Geschichte, 1922-1927.

Golder, Frank Alfred. *Documents of Russian History, 1914-1917.* New York: The Century Co., 1927.

Great Britain. Foreign Office. Cmd. 9105. Misc. No. 18, 1918. *Treaty of Peace Signed at Brest-Litovsk between the Central Powers and the Ukrainian People's Republic.* London: H. M. Stationery Office, 1918.

— — —. Foreign Office. Cmd. 9102. Misc. No. 15, 1918. *Observations by the Allied Ministers at Jassy with regard to Conditions of Peace Imposed upon Roumania by the Central Powers.* London. H. M. Stationery Office, 1918.

Italy. Ministero degli affari esteri. Commissione per la pubblicazione dei documenti diplomatici. *I documenti diplomatici italiani.* 5. Serie: 1914-1918. Vol. I, 2 agosto-16 ottobre 1914. Rome: Istituto poligrafico dello stato, 1954.

Laloy, Émile (ed.). *Les documents secrets des archives du ministère des affaires étrangères de Russie publiés par les bolchévistes.* *Paris:* Bossard, 1920.

Lapradelle, A. de, Eisenmann, L., Mirkine-Guetsévitch, B., and Renouvin, P. (eds.). *Constantinople et les Détroits.* Paris: Les Éditions Internationales, 1930. This is a translation of Vol. I of Evgenii A. Adamov (ed.), *Evropeiskie Derzhavy i Turtsiia vo vremia mirovoi voiny.* Moscow: Narkomindel, 1925.

Marghiloman, Alexandru. *Note Politice, 1897-1924.* Vols. I-III. Bucharest: Institutul de arte grafice "Eminescu," 1927. Courtesy of the University of Michigan Library.

Pribram, Alfred Franžis (ed.). *The Secret Treaties of Austria-Hungary, 1879-1914.* 2 vols. Cambridge: Harvard University Press, 1920-1921.

Romania. Ministère des affaires étrangères. *Constitution de 30 juin/12 iuillet 1866, avec les modifications y introduites en 1879 et 1884.* Bucharest, 1884.

— — —. *Monitorul Oficial,* 1916-1917. Official gazette of the Parliament and Government. Bucharest.

— — —. *Războiul dintre România şi Grupul Puterilor Centrale: Comunicatele Oficiale.* Bucharest: I. Branişteanu, 1923.

———. *Documente secrete din arhivia ministerului de externe din Petrograd.* Iaşi: *Neamul Românesc,* 1918.

Russia. *Sbornik sekretnykh dokumentov iz arkhiva byvshago ministerstva inostrannykh del.* 7 vols. in 1. Petrograd. Tipografiia Komissariata po Inostrannym Delam, 1917.

———. Tsentrarkhiv. *Tsarskaia Rossiia v mirovoi voine.* Vol. I. Edited by M. N. Pokrovskii. Leningrad: Gosudarstvennoe Izdatel'stvo, 1926. Only one volume has been issued.

———. Komissiia pri TsIK SSSR po Izdaniiu Dokumentov Epokhi Imperializma. *Mezhdunarodnye Otnosheniia v Epokhu Imperializma.* Series 3, Vols. VI-X. Moscow-Leningrad: Gosudarstvennoe Izdatel'stvo, 1931-1940.

———. *Mezhdunarodnaia Politika Noveishego Vremeni v Dogovorakh, Notakh i Deklaratsiakh.* Vols. I-III. Edited by I. V. Kliuchnikov and A. Sabanin. Moscow: Narkomindel, 1925-1928.

———. *Sobranie Uzakonenii i Rasporiazhenii Rabochevo i Krestian'- skogo Pravitel'stva RSFSR,* 1917-1918. Moscow: Gosizdat, 1917-1918.

Scott, James Brown (ed.). *Official Statements of War Aims and Peace Proposals.* Washington: Carnegie Endowment for International Peace, 1921.

Stieve, Friedrich (ed.). *Iswolski im Weltkriege.* Berlin: Deutsche Verlagsgesellschaft für Politik und Geschichte, 1925.

Triepel, Heinrich von (ed.). *Nouveau recueil général de traités.* 3ème série. Vol. X. Leipzig: Theodor Weicher, 1921.

United States. Department of State. *Papers Relating to the Foreign Relations of the United States, 1916.* Washington: Government Printing Office, 1929.

———. Department of State. *Papers Relating to the Foreign Relations of the United States, The World War, 1916,* Supplement. Washington: Government Printing Office, 1929.

— — —. Department of State. *Papers Relating to the Foreign Relations of the United States, The World War, 1917, Supplements 1 and 2.* 3 vols. Washington: Government Printing Office, 1931-1932.

— — —. Department of State. *Papers Relating to the Foreign Relations of the United States, The World War, 1918, Supplement 1.* 2 vols. Washington: Government Printing Office, 1933.

— — —. Department of State. *Papers Relating to the Foreign Relations of the United States, Russia, 1918.* 3 vols. Washington: Government Printing Office, 1931-1932.

— — —. Department of State. *Papers Relating to the Foreign Relations of the United States, The Lansing Papers, 1914-1920.* 2 vols. Washington: Government Printing Office, 1940.

— — —. Department of State. *Papers Relating to the Foreign Relations of the United States, The Paris Peace Conference, 1919.* Vols. I-II. Washington: Government Printing Office, 1942.

— — —. Department of State. *Declarations of War and Severances of Diplomatic Relations,* 1914-1918. Washington: Government Printing Office, 1919.

— — —. Department of State. *Texts of the Roumanian Peace.* Washington: Government Printing Office, 1918.

Zeman, Z. A. B. (ed.). *Germany and the Revolution in Russia, 1915-1918.* London: Oxford University Press, 1958.

IV. Primary Sources: PUBLISHED DOCUMENTS ON THE PEACE CONFERENCE

Allied and Associated Powers. Conference on the Preliminaries of Peace. *Report No. 1 with Annexes.* Presented to the Supreme Council of the Allies by the Commission for the Study of Territorial Questions Relating to Romania and Yugoslavia, April 6, 1919.

Baker, Ray Stannard. *Woodrow Wilson and World Settlement*. Vol. III. Garden City: Doubleday, Page, 1923.

———, and Dodd, William E. (eds.). *The Public Papers of Woodrow Wilson: War and Peace*. 2 vols. New York: Harper and Bros., 1927.

———. *Woodrow Wilson: Life and Letters*. Vol. VIII. Garden City: Doubleday, Doran, 1939.

Bulgaria. Ministry of Foreign Affairs. *La question bulgare et les états balkaniques*. Sofia: Imprimerie de l'état, 1919.

Carnegie Endowment for International Peace. *The Treaties of Peace, 1919-1923*. 2 vols. in 1. New York: Carnegie Endowment for International Peace, 1924.

France. *Travaux du Comité d'études*. Vol. II: *Questions européennes*. Paris: Imprimerie nationale, 1919.

Great Britain. Foreign Office. Historical Section. *Peace Handbooks*. Edited by George Walter Prothero. London: H.M. Stationery Office, 1920.

———. *Documents on British Foreign Policy, 1919-1939*. First Series. Vols. I-VIII. Edited by E.L. Woodward, Rohan Butler, and J.P. T. Bury. London: H.M. Stationery Office, 1947-1958.

———. Treaty Series, 1921. Cmd. 1548. No. 20. *Treaty Between the Principal Allied and Associated Powers and Poland, Runmania, the Serb-Croat-Slovene State, and the Czechoslovak State Relative to Certain Frontiers of Those States*. Signed at Sèvres, August 10, 1920. London: H.M. Stationery Office, 1921.

Hungary. Royal Hungarian Ministry of Foreign Affairs. *The Hungarian Peace Negotiations*. 4 vols. Budapest: Victor Hornyánszky, 1920-1922.

Italy. Ministero degli affari esteri. Commissione per la pubblicazione dei documenti diplomatici. *I documenti diplomatici italiani*. 6.

Serie: 1918-1922. Vol. I, 4 novembre 1918-17 gennaio 1919. Rome: Istituto poligrafico dello stato, 1956.

Lapradelle, A. de (ed.). *La paix de Versailles: la documentation internationale.* 12 vols. Paris: Les Éditions Internationales, 1930-1939.

Mantoux, Paul (ed.). *Les délibérations du conseil des quatre (24 mars-28 juin 1919)*: *Notes de l'officier interprète.* 2 vols. Paris: Centre national de la recherche scientifique, 1955.

Miller, David Hunter. *My Diary at the Conference of Paris with Documents.* 21 vols. New York: Appeal Publishing Co., 1924.

Romania. Comitetul de direcţie al "Monitorul Oficial" şi Imprimeriilor Statului. *Monitorul Oficial,* 1832-1932. Bucharest: Imprimeria naţională, 1932.

— — —. *La Roumanie devant le congrès de la paix. : Actes d'union des provinces de Bessarabie, la Bucovine, Transylvanie, Banat, et des régions roumaines de Hongrie avec le Royaume de Roumanie*; II: *Ses revendications territoriales;* III: *La Transylvanie et les territoires roumains de Hongrie;* IV: *Le territoire revendiqué par les roumains au nord-ouest de la Transylvanie proprement dite;* V: *La question du Banat de Temeshvar;* VI: *Le Banat de Temeshvar;* VII: *Le Banat de Temeshvar ne peut pas être partagé;* VIII: La *Dobroudja méridionale (le Quadrilatère);* IX: *Le Danube et les intérêts d'économiques de l'Europe;* X: *La question de la Bessarabie;* XI: *L'Unité du Banat.* Edited by Alexandru Lăpedatu. Paris: Dubois et Bauer, 1919.

United States. Department of State. *Papers Relating to the Foreign Relations of the United States,* 1919. 2 vols. Washington: Government Printing Office, 1934.

— — —. Department of State. *Papers Relating to the Foreign Relations of the United States, Russia,* 1919. Washington: Government Printing Office, 1937.

––––. Department of State. *Papers Relating to the Foreign Relations of the United States, The Paris Peace Conference,* 1919. Vols. III-XII. Washington: Government Printing Office, 1943-1947.

––––. Department of State. *Papers Relating to the Foreign Relations of the United States,* 1920. Vol. III. Washington: Government Printing Office, 1936.

––––. Department of State. *The Treaty of Versailles and After: Annotations of the Text of the Treaty.* Washington: Government Printing Ofiice, 1947.

V. Secondary Sources: MEMOIRS

Bandholtz, Harry Hill, Major General. *An Undiplomatic Diary.* Edited by Fritz-Konrad Krüger. New York: Columbia University Press, 1933.

Beneš, Eduard. *My War Memoirs.* Translated by Paul Selver. Boston and New York: Houghton Mifflin Co., 1928.

Bőhm, Vilmos. *Két forradalom Tüzében. (In the Fires of Two Revolutions).* Budapest: Népszava, 1947.

Buchanan, Sir George. *My Mission to Russia.* 2 vols. Boston: Little, Brown, 1923.

Bülow, Bernhard Fürst von. *Denkwürdigkeiten.* Vol. III. Berlin: Ullstein, 1931.

Burián Yon Rajecz, Graf Stephan. *Drei Jahre aus der Zeit meiner Amtsführung.* Berlin: Ullstein, 1923.

Callimachi, Princess Anne-Marie. *Yesterday Was Mine.* New York: McGraw-Hill, 1949.

Conrad von Hötzendorf, Feldmarschall. *Aus meiner Dienstzeit, 1906-1918.* Vols. III-IV. Vienna-Leipzig-Munich: Rikola Verlag, 1922-1923.

Czernin, Count Ottokar. *In the World* War. London: Cassell, 1919.

Djuvara, Trandafir G. *Mes missions diplomatiques, 1887-1925*. Paris: Félix Alcan, 1930.

Falkenhayn, Erich George von, General. *Der Feldzug der Neunten Armee gegen die Rumänen und Russen, 1916-1917*. 2 vols. Berlin: Mittler, 1920-1921.

Gourko, Basil, General. *Memories and Impressions of War and Revolution in Russia, 1914-1917*. London: John Murray, 1918.

Grey of Fallodon, Viscount. (Sir Edward Grey.) *Twenty-Five Years, 1892-1916*. Vol. II. New York: Frederick A. Stokes, 1925.

Hanssen, Hans Peter. *Diary of a Dying Empire*. Translated by Oscar Osbom Winther ("Indiana University Social Science Series No. 14"). Bloomington: Indiana University Press, 1955.

Hoover, Herbert Clark. *Memoirs*. Vol. I: *Years of Adventure, 1874-1920*. New York: Macmillan, 1951.

Horthy, Nikolaus von, Admiral. *Ein Leben für Ungarn*. Bonn: Athenäum-Verlag, 1953.

Ionescu, Take. *Some Personal Impressions*. London: Nisbet, 1919.

— — —. *Souvenirs*. Paris: Payot, 1919. The same as above, but has text of his address to the Romanian Chamber of Deputies, "The Policy of National Instinct," December 16-17, 1915.

Iorga, Nicolae. *Memorii*. Vols. I-II: *Însemnări zilnice (maiu 1917-mart 1920). Războiul național. Lupta pentru o nouă viață politică. (Daily Notes May 1917-March 1920. The National War. The Struggle for our New Political Life):* Bucharest: Editura națională S. Ciornei, no date.

Károlyi, Mihály. *Memoirs: Faith Without Illusion*. London: Jonathan Cape, 1956.

Lansing, Robert. *The Peace Negotiations: A Personal Narrative.* Boston: Houghton Mifflin Co., 1921.

Laroche, Jules. *Au Quai d'Orsay avec Briand et Poincaré, 1913-1926.* Paris: Hachette, 1957.

Lloyd George, David. *War Memoirs of David Lloyd George,* 6 vols. London: Ivor Nicholson and Watson, 1933-1936.

– – –. *Memoirs of the Peace Conference.* 2 vols. New Haven: Yale University Press, 1939.

Lockhart, R.H. Bruce. *British Agent.* New York: G.P. Putnam's Sons, 1933.

Ludendorff, Erich, General. *The General Staff and its Problems.* Translated by F.A. Holt. Vol. II. London: Hutchinson, 1920.

Marghiloman, Alexandru. *Note Poltice, 1897-1924.* Vol I: 1897-1915; Vol. II: 1916-June 22, 1917; Vol. III: July 18, 1917-July 18, 1918; Vol. IV: July 18, 1918-December 31, 1919; Vol. V: 1920-1924. Bucharest: Institutul de arte grafice "Eminescu," 1927. Courtesy of the University of Michigan Library.

Marie, Queen of Roumania. *The Story of My Life.* New York. Charles Scribner's Sons, 1934. Reminiscences of 1875-1914.

– – –. *Ordeal: The Story of My Life.* New York: Charles Scribner's Sons, 1935. Wartime reminiscences.

Masaryk, Thomas Garrigue. *The Making of a State, Memories and Observations, 1914-1918.* New York: Frederick A. Stokes, 1927.

Morgenthau, Henry, Sr. *All in a Life-Time.* Garden City: Doubleday, Page, 1922.

Napier, H. D., Lieutenant Colonel. *The Experiences of a Military Attaché in the Balkans.* London: Drane's, 1924.

Noulens, Joseph. *Mon ambassade en Russie soviétique, 1917-1919.* Vol. I. Paris: Plon, 1933.

Paléologue, Maurice. *La Russie des tsars pendant la grande guerre.* 3 vols. Vol. I: July 1914-June 1915; Vol. II June 1915-August 1916; Vol. III: August 1916-May 1917. Paris: Plon, 1921-1922.

Poincaré, Raymond. *Au service de la France: neuf années de souvenirs.* Vols. V-VIII. Paris: Plon, 1928-1931.

Rattigan, William Frank Arthur. *Diversions of a Diplomat.* London: Chapman, Hall, 1924.

Riddell, G.A., First Baron. *Lord Riddell's Intimate Diary of the Peace Conference and After, 1918-1923.* New York: Reynal and Hitchcock, 1934.

Roosevelt, Nicholas. *A Front Row Seat.* Norman: University of Oklahoma Press, 1953.

Saint-Aulaire, Comte de. *Confession d'un vieux diplomate.* Paris: Flammarion, 1953.

Sazonov, Serge. *Fateful Years, 1909-1916.* London: Jonathan Cape, 1928. Abridged and translated from his *Vospominaniia.* Paris: Knigoizdatel'stvo E. Sial'skoi, 1927.

Schelking, Eugene de. *Recollections of a Russian Diplomat.* New York: Macmillan, 1918.

Steed, Henry Wickham. *Through Thirty Years, 1892-1922: A Personal Narrative.* 2 vols. Garden City: Doubleday, Page, 1925.

Tardieu, André. *Devant l'obstacle: l'Amérique et nous.* Paris: Émile-Paul Frères, 1927.

Thomson of Cardington, Lord. (Christopher Birdwood Thomson). *Smaranda.* New York: George H. Doran, 1931.

Vopicka, Charles J. *Secrets of the Balkans: Seven Years of a Diplomatist's Life in the Storm Centre of Europe.* Chicago: Rand McNally, 1921.

Wilson, Edith Bolling. *My Memoir.* Indianapolis: Bobbs-Merrill, 1938.

VI. Secondary Sources: BIOGRAPHIES

Aubert, Louis, and Others. *André Tardieu, 1876-1945*. Paris: Plon, 1957.

Azan, Paul, Général. *Franchet d'Esperey*. Paris: Flammarion, 1949.

Bagger, Eugene S. *Eminent Europeans: Studies in Continental Reality*. New York: G.P. Putnam's Sons, 1924.

Baker, Ray Stannard. *Woodrow Wilson and World Settlement*. Vols.I-II. Garden City: Doubleday, Page, 1922.

Beattie, Kim. *Brother, Here's a Man: The Saga of Klondike Boyle*. New York: Macmillan, 1940.

Bréal, Auguste. *Philippe Berthelot*. Paris: Gallimard, 1937.

Briggs, Mitchell Pirie. *George D. Herron and the European Settlement*. University Series. History, Economics, and Political Science. Vol. III. No. 2, Stanford University Publications. Stanford: Stanford University Press, 1932.

Bruun, Geoffrey. *Clemenceanu*. Cambridge: Harvard University Press, 1943.

Callwell, Sir C. E., Major-General. *Field-Marshal Sir Henry Wilson: His Life and Diaries*. Vol. II. London: Cassell, 1927.

Cantacuzino, Sabine. *Din viaţa familiei I.C. Brătianu: Războiul, 1914-1918*. Bucharest: Universul, 1937.

Coolidge, Harold Jefferson, and Lord, Robert Howard. *Archibald Cary Coolidge: Life and Letters*. Boston: Houghton Mifflin Co., 1932.

Davenport, Guiles. *Zaharoff: High Priest of War*. Boston: Lothrop, Lee and Shepard, 1934.

Dugdale, Blanche E. D. *Arthur James Balfour*. Vol. II. London: Hutchinson, 1936.

Easterman, A. L. *King Carol, Hitler, and Lupescu*. London: Victor Gollancz, 1942.

Gay, George. *King Carol of Roumania*. London: Pilot Press, 1941.

Hoven, Baroness Helena von der. *King Carol of Romania*. London: Hutchinson, 1940.

Iancovici, D. *Take Ionesco*. Paris: Payot, 1919.

Liddell Hart, B.H. *Foch: The Man of Orléans*. Boston: Little, Brown, 1932.

Lindenberg, Paul. *König Karl von Rumänien: Ein Lebensbild dargestellt unter Mitarbeit des Königs*. Vol. II. Berlin: Hafen-Verlag. 1923.

Link, Arthur S. *Wilson: The New Freedom*. Princeton: Princeton University Press, 1956.

Martin, William. *Statesmen of the War in Retrospect, 1918-1928*. New York: Minton, Balch, 1928.

Mordacq, Jean Jules Henri, Général. *Le ministère Clemenceau: journal d'un témoin*. Vols. III-IV. Paris: Plon et Nourrit, 1931.

Nevins, Allan. *Henry White: Thirty Years of American Diplomacy*. New York. Harper and Bros., 1930.

Palmer, Frederick. *Bliss, Peacemaker: The Life and Letters of General Tasker Howard Bliss*. New York: Dodd, Mead, 1934.

Pillat, Nicolae. *Silhouettes de ma famille*. Paris: Sirot, 1943. The author was Brătianu's nephew.

Reznikoff, Charles (ed.). *Louis Marshall: Champion of Liberty, 1856-1929*. Vol. II. Philadelphia: The Jewish Publication Society of America, 1957.

Rutter, Owen. *Regent of Hungary*. London: Rich and Cowan, 1939.

Tabouis, Geneviève. *Jules Cambon par l'un des siens.* Paris: Payot, 1938.

Tumulty, Joseph P. *Woodrow Wilson as I Know Him.* Garden City: Doubleday, Page, 1921.

Walworth, Arthur. *Woodrow Wilson.* Vol. II: *World Prophet.* New York: Longmans, Green, 1958.

Wolbe, Eugen. *Ferdinand I: Der Begründer Grossrumäniens.* Locarno, 1938.

Xeni, C. *Take Ionescu.* Bucharest: Universul, 1933.

VII. General Works: THE WAR PERIOD

Abrudeanu, Ion Rusu. *Pacostea Rusească. (Russian Calamity).* Bucharest: Socec, 1920.

Albertini, Luigi. *The Origins of the War of 1914.* Translated by Isabella M. Massey. 3 vols. London: Oxford University Press, 1952-1957.

Averescu, Alexandru, General. *Notițe zilnice din războiu, 1916-1918. (Daily Notes of the War, 1916-1918).* Bucharest: Cultură națională, 1928.

Axente, T. Crișan. *Essai sur le régime représentatif en Roumanie.* Paris: Sirey, 1937.

Balch, Emily Greene. *Approaches to the Great Settlement.* New York: B.W. Huebsch, 1918.

Basilesco, Nicolae. *La Roumanie dans la guerre et dans la paix.* 2 vols. Paris: Félix Alcan, 1919.

Bicknell, Ernest P. *With the Red Cross in Europe, 1917-1922.* Washington: The American National Red Cross, 1938.

Bocu, Sever. *Les légions roumains de Transylvanie.* Paris: Dupont, 1918.

Bourgeois, Émile. *Manuel historique de politique étrangère.* Vol. III. Paris: Belin Frères, 1915.

Brătianu, Georges I. *Origines et formation de l'unité roumaine.* Bucharest: Institut d'histoire universelle "N. Iorga," 1943.

Bujac, Émile. *Campagnes de l'armée roumaine, 1916-1919.* Paris: Charles-Lavauzelle, 1933.

Bunyan, James, and Fisher, Harold H. (eds.). *The Bolshevik Revolution, 1917-1918, Documents and Materials.* Hoover War Library, Publication No. 3. Stanford: Stanford University Press, 1934.

Burián von Rajecz, Count Stephan. *Austria in Dissolution.* New York: George H. Doran, 1925.

Chambers, Frank P. *The War Behind the War, 1914-1918.* London: Faber and Faber, 1939.

Cialdea, Lilio. *La politica estera della Romania nel quarantennio prebellico.* Bologna: Licinio Cappelli, 1933.

Clark, Charles Upson, *Greater Roumania.* New York: Dodd Mead, 1922.

— — —. *Bessarabia, Russia and Roumania on the Black Sea.* New York: Dodd, Mead, 1927.

— — —. *United Roumania.* New York: Dodd, Mead, 1932.

Clopoţel, Ion. *Revoluţia din 1918 şi unirea Ardealului cu România.* Cluj: Societatea de Mâine, 1926.

Cole, George Douglas Howard. *A History of Socialist Thought. Vol. III, Part 2: The Second International, 1889-1914.* London: Macmillan, 1956.

Cosma, Aurel. *La petite entente.* Paris: Jouve, 1926.

Cvijič, Jovan. *La péninsule balkanique: géographic humaine.* Paris: Colin, 1918.

Davison, Henry P. *The American Red Cross in the Great War.* New York: Macmillan, 1920.

Djuvara, Trandafir G. *Cent projets de portage de la Turquie, 1281-1913.* Paris: Félix Alcan, 1914.

Drutzu, Şerban. *Românii în America.* Bucharest: Cartea Românească, 1926.

Fainsod, Merle. *International Socialism and the World War.* Cambridge: Harvard University Press, 1935.

Fay, Sidney Bradshaw. *The Origins of the World War.* Vol. I. New York: Macmillan, 1930.

Fischer, Louis. *The Soviets in World Affairs: A History of Relations Between the Soviet Union and the Rest of the World.* 2 vols. London: Jonathan Cape, 1930.

Forster, Kent. *The Failures of Peace.* Washington: American Council on Public Affairs, 1941.

France. Ministère de la guerre. *Les armées françaises dans la grande guerre.* Vol. I: *La campagne d'orient jusqu'á l'intervention de la Roumanie.* Vol. VIII; *La campagne roumaine, 1916-1918.* Paris: Imprimerie nationale, 1928, 1933-1934.

Galitzi, Christine Avghi. *A Study of Assimilation among the Rumanians in the United States.* New York: Columbia University Press, 1929.

Glaise-Horstenau, Edmund von. *The Collapse of the Austro-Hungarian Empire.* New York: E. P. Dutton, 1930.

Gooch, George Peabody. *Before the War: Studies in Diplomacy.* 2 vols. New York: Longmans, Green, 1936-1938.

― ― ―. *Recent Revelations of European Diplomacy.* 4th ed. London: Longmans, Green, 1940.

― ― ―. *Studies in Diplomacy and Statecraft.* New York: Longmans, Green, 1942.

Gottlieb, W. W. *Studies in Secret Diplomacy during the First World War.* London: Allen and Unwin, 1957.

Gratz, Gustav, and Schüller, Richard. *The Economic Policy of Austria-Hungary during the War in its External Relations.* Carnegie Endowment for International Peace: Division of Economics and History. Economic and Social History of the World War. Translated and Abridged Series. New Haven: Yale University Press, 1928.

Great Britain. Admiralty. Naval Staff. Geographical Section of the Naval Intelligence Division. I. D. 1204. *A Handbook of Roumania.* London: H. M. Stationery Office, 1920.

Howard, Harry Nicholas. *The Partition of Turkey: A Diplomatic History, 1913-1923.* Norman: University of Oklahoma Press, 1931.

Hurst, A. Herşcovici. *Roumania and Great Britain.* London: Hodder and Stoughton, 1916.

Iancovici, D. *La paix de Bucarest.* Paris: Payot, 1918.

Ionescu, Take. *La politique étrangère de la Roumanie.* Bucharest: F. Göbl, 1891.

― ― ―. *The Policy of National Instinct.* Address to the Chamber of Deputies, December 16-17, 1915. London. Sir Joseph Causton and Sons, 1916.

― ― ―. *The Origins of the War.* London: Council for the Study of International Relations, 1917.

Iorga, Nicolae. *Histoire des roumains de Transylvanie et de Hongrie.* 2 vols. 2ème ed. Bucharest: Imprimerie "Gutenberg," J. Göbl successeurs, 1916.

― ― ―. *Relations des roumains avec les alliés.* Iaşi: *Neamul Românesc,* 1917.

― ― ―. *Histoire des relations russo-roumaines.* Iaşi: *Neamul Românesc,* 1917.

― ― ―. *Histoire des roumains de la péninsule des Balkans.* Bucharest: *Neamul Românesc,* 1919.

― ― ―. *Histoire des états balkaniques jusqu'à 1924.* Paris: Camber, 1925.

― ― ―. *A History of Roumania: Land, People, Civilisation.* Translated from the 2nd ed. by Joseph McCabe. London: T. Fisher Unwin, 1925.

Jászi, Oscar. *Revolution and Counter-Revolution in Hungary.* Translated by E. W. Dickes, from *Magyariens Schuld, Ungarns Sühne, Revolution und Gegenrevolution in Ungarn* (Munich 1923). Translated by A. Gas from Magyar original. London: P. S. King and Son, 1924.

― ― ―. *The Dissolution of the Habsburg Monarchy: A Failure in Civic Training.* University of Chicago Studies in the Making of Citizens. Chicago: University of Chicago Press, 1929.

Kabisch, Ernst. *Der Rumänenkrieg, 1916.* Berlin: Schlegel, 1938.

Kann, Robert A. *The Multinational Empire: Nationalism and National Reform in the Habsburg Monarchy, 1848-1918.* 2 vols. New York: Columbia University Press, 1950.

Kennan, George F. *Soviet-American Relations, 1917-1920.* Vol. I: *Russia Leaves the War (November 1917-March 1918).* Vol. II: *The Decision to Intervene (March 1918-July 1918).* Princeton: Princeton University Press, 1956-1958.

Kiriţescu, Constantin. *Istoria războiului pentru întregirea României, 1916-1919. (History of the War for the Unification of Rumania).* 3 vols. Bucharest: Atelierele Cartea Românească, 1925.

———. *La Roumanie dans la guerre mondiale, 1916-1919.* Abridged and translated by L. Barral. Preface by André Tardieu. Paris: Payot, 1934.

Larcher, M. *La grande guerre dans les Balkans.* Paris: Payot, 1929.

Lasswell, Harold D. *Propaganda Technique in the World War.* London: Kegan Paul, Trench, and Trubner, 1938.

Logio, George Clenton. *Bulgaria Past and Present.* Manchester, England: Sherratt and Hughes, 1936.

———. *Rumania: Its History, Politics, and Economics.* Manchester, England: Sherratt and Hughes, 1932.

Lutz, Ralph Haswell. *Fall of the German Empire, 1914-1918.* Hoover War Library Publications. 2 vols. Stanford: Stanford University Press, 1932.

Lydenberg, Harry. *History of The New York Public Library.* New York: The Public Library, 1923.

Macartney, Carlile Aylmer. *National States and National Minorities.* London: Oxford University Press, 1934.

Machray, Robert. *The Little Entente.* New York: Richard R. Smith, 1930.

Magnus, Leonard A. *Roumania's Cause and Ideals.* London: Kegan Paul, 1917.

Mamatey, Victor S. *The United States and East Central Europe, 1914-1918: A Study in Wilsonian Diplomacy and Propaganda.* Princeton: Princeton University Press, 1957.

Marriott, J. A. R. *The Eastern Question: An Historical Study in European Diplomacy.* 3rd ed. Oxford: At the Clarendon Press, 1925.

Maurice, Sir Frederick. *The Armistices of 1918.* London: Oxford University Press, 1943.

May, Ernest H. *The World War and American Isolation, 1914-1917.* Cambridge: Harvard University Press, 1959.

Mélot, Henri. *La mission du Général Pau aux Balkans et en Russie tzariste.* Paris: Payot, 1931.

Minesco, Constantin. *L'action diplomatique de la Roumanie pendant la guerre.* Paris: Société générale de l'imprimerie, 1922.

Mitrany, David. *The Land and Peasant in Rumania: The War and Agrarian Reform, 1917-1921.* Carnegie Endowment for International Peace: Division of Economics and History. Economic and Social History of the World War. New Haven: Yale University Press, 1930.

Moore, Wilbert E. *Economic Demography of Eastern and Southern Europe.* League of Nations Publications, 1945. II. A. 9. New York: Columbia University Press, 1946.

Moroïanu, Georges. *Les luttes des roumains transylvains pour la liberté et l'opinion européenne: épisodes et souvenirs.* Paris: Gamber, 1933.

Mousset, Albert. *La petite entente.* Paris: Bossard, 1923.

Murray, Arthur C., Lieutenant Colonel. *At Close Quarters.* London: John Murray, 1946.

Nicorescu, Paul. *La Roumanie nouvelle.* Bucharest: "Globus," 1924.

Notovich, F. I. *Diplomaticheskaia Bor'ba v gody Pervoi Mirovoi Voiny.* Vol. I. Moscow-Leningrad: Izdatel'stvo Akademii Nauk SSSR, Institut Istorii, 1947.

Nowak, Karl Friedrich. *The Collapse of Central Europe.* London: Kegan Paul, Trench, Trubner, 1924.

Paraschivesco, C. C. *Les finances de guerre de la Roumanie.* Paris: Bailet, 1920.

Pétin, Henri, Général. *Le drame roumain.* Paris: Payot, 1931.

Pingaud, Albert. *Histoire diplomatique de la France pendant la grande guerre*. 3 vols. Paris: Éditions Alsatia, 1938.

Popovici, Andrei. *The Political Status of Bessarabia*. Washington: Ransdell, 1931.

Popovici, Aurele. *Die Vereinigten Staaten von Gross-Österreich*. Leipzig: Elischer, 1906.

Pribram, Alfred Franžis. *Austrian Foreign Policy, 1908-1918*. London: Allen and Unwin, 1923.

Rădulesco, Alexandre-Radu F. *Le contrôle de la constitutionnalité des lois en Roumanie*. Paris: Les Presses Modernes, 1935.

Recouly, Raymond. *Les heures tragiques d'avant-guerre*. Paris: La Renaissance du Livre, 1923.

Renouvin, Pierre. *The Immediate Origins of the War, June 28-August 4, 1914*. Carnegie Endowment for International Peace: Division of Economics and History. Economic and Social History of the World War. New Haven: Yale University Press, 1928.

———. *Les crises du XXème siècle: I. de 1914 à 1929*. Vol. VII of *Histoire des relations internationales*. Edited by Pierre Renouvin. Paris: Hachette, 1957.

Romaşcanu, Gr. *Tezaurul Român de la Moscova*. Bucharest: Cartea Românească, 1934.

Roucek, Joseph S. *Contemporary Roumania and her Problems: A Study in Modern Nationalism*. Stanford Books in World Politics. Stanford: Stanford University Press, 1932.

Rudin, Harry R. *Armistice, 1918*. New Haven: Yale University Press, 1944.

Schlesinger, Rudolf. *Federalism in Central and Eastern Europe*. International Library of Sociology and Social Reconstruction. New York: Oxford University Press, 1945.

Schmitt, Bernadotte Everly. *The Coming of the War, 1914.* 2 vols. New York: Charles Scribner's Sons, 1930.

Seton-Watson, Robert William. *Racial Problems in Hungary.* London: Constable, 1908.

― ― ―. *Corruption and Reform in Hungary.* London: Constable, 1911.

― ― ―. *Roumania and the Great War.* London: Constable, 1915.

― ― ―. *A History of the Roumanians from Roman Times to the Completion of Unity.* Cambridge: At the University Press, 1934.

― ― ―. *Masaryk in England.* Cambridge: At the University Press, 1943.

Seymour, Charles (ed.). *The Intimate Papers of Colonel House.* Vols. I-III. Boston: Houghton Mifflin Co., 1926-1928.

― ― ―. *American Diplomacy during the World War.* Baltimore: Johns Hopkins Press, 1934.

Smith, Clarence Jay. *The Russian Struggle for Power, 1914-1917: A Study of Russian Foreign Policy during the First World War.* New York: Philosophical Library, 1956.

Squires, James Duane. *British Propaganda at Home and in the United States from 1914 to 1917.* Cambridge: Harvard University Press, 1935.

Steed, Henry Wickham. *The Antecedents of Post-War Europe.* Publication of the Graduate Institute of International Studies, No. 6. London: Oxford University Press, 1932.

Sterian, Paul. *La Roumanie et la réparation des dommages de guerre.* Paris: Librairie générale de Droit et de Jurisprudence, 1929.

Stoica, Vasile. *În America pentru cauza românească.* Bucharest: Universul, 1926.

Stuart, Sir Campbell. *Secrets of Crewe House*. London: Hodder and Stoughton, 1920.

Tătăresco, Georges. *Le régime électoral et parlementaire en Roumanie*. Paris: Giard et Brière, 1912.

Taylor, A. J. P. *The Struggle for Mastery in Europe, 1848-1918*. Vol. II of *The Oxford History of Modern Europe*. Oxford: At the Clarendon Press, 1954.

Teleki, Count Paul. *The Evolution of Hungary and its Place in European History*. Institute of Politics, Williams College. New York: Macmillan, 1923.

Terrail, Gabriel. (pseud. "Mermeix"). *Le commandement unique*. Vol. IV of *Fragments d'histoire*, 1914-1919, 2ème partie, *Sarrail et les armées d'orient*. Paris: Paul Ollendorff, 1920.

———. *Les négociations secrètes et les quatres armistices avec pièces justificatives*. Vol. V of *Fragments d'histoire, 1914-1919*. Paris: Paul Ollendorff, 1921.

Thomson, Christopher Birdwood, Brigadier-General. *Old Europe's Suicide*. New York: Thomas Seltzer, 1922.

Times, London. *The History of the "Times": The 150th Anniversary and Beyond, 1912-1948*. Part I, Chapters I-XII, 1912-1920. London: The Office of the *Times*, 1952.

Toscano, Mario. *Il patto di Londra*. Bologna: Nicola Zanichelli, 1934.

L'Ukraine Soviétiste. Recueil des documents d'après les livres rouges ukrainiens. Berlin: Puttkammer und Mühlbrecht, 1922.

Vondráček, Felix J. *The Foreign Policy of Czechoslovakia, 1918-1935*. New York: Columbia University Press, 1937.

Wanklyn, Harriet G. *The Eastern Marchlands of Europe*. London: George Philip, 1941.

Warth, Robert D. *The Allies and the Russian Revolution: From the Downfall of the Monarchy to the Peace of Brest-Litovsk.* Durham: Duke University Press, 1954.

Willert, Arthur. *The Road to Safety.* New York: Frederick A. Praeger, 1953.

VIII. General Works: THE CONFERENCE PERIOD

Albrecht-Carrié, René. *Italy at the Paris Peace Conference.* New York: Columbia University Press, 1938.

Aldrovandi Marescotti, Luigi. *Guerra diplomatica: Ricordi e frammenti di diario, 1914-1919.* Milan: A. Mondadori, 1938.

—— ——. *Nuovi ricordi e frammenti di diario per far séguito a "Guerra diplomatica."* Milan: A. Mondadori, 1938.

Almond, Nina, and Lutz, Ralph Haswell (comps. and eds.). *The Treaty of St. Germain: A Documentary History of its Territorial and Political Clauses; with a Survey of the Documents of the Supreme Council of the Paris Peace Conference.* Hoover War Library Publication No. 5. Stanford: Stanford University Press, 1935.

Bailey, Thomas A. *Wilson and the Peacemakers.* New York: Macmillan, 1947.

Baker, Ray Stannard. *Woodrow Wilson and World Settlement.* Vols. I-II. Garden City: Doubleday, Page, 1922.

Bane, Suda Lorena, and Lutz, Ralph Haswell (comps. and eds.). *Organization of American Relief in Europe, 1918-1919.* Hoover War Library Publication No. 20. Stanford: Stanford University Press, 1943.

Beloff, Max. *The Foreign Policy of Soviet Russia.* Vol. I: 1929-1936. London: Oxford University Press, 1947.

Bonsal, Stephen. *Unfinished Business.* Garden City: Doubleday, Doran, 1944.

— — —. *Suitors and Suppliants: The Little Nations at Versailles*. New York: Prentice-Hall, 1946.

Bowman, Isaiah. *The New World: Problems in Political Geography*. Yonkers-on-Hudson, New York: World Book Co., 1922.

Cabot, John M. *The Racial Conflict in Transylvania: A Discussion of the Conflicting Claims of Rumania and Hungary to Transylvania, the Banat, and the Eastern Section of the Hungarian Plain*. Boston: Beacon Press, 1926.

Caldis, Calliope G. *The Council of Four as a Joint Emergency Authority in the European Crisis at the Paris Peace Conference, 1919*. Geneva: Imprimerie France-Suisse, Ambilly-Annemasse, 1953.

Carnegie, Centre européen de la dotation. *Centenaire Woodrow Wilson, 1856-1956*. Geneva: Atar Arts Graphiques, 1956.

Carr, Edward Hallett. *The Bolshevik Revolution, 1917-1923*. Vol. III. New York: Macmillan, 1953.

Chamberlin, William Henry, *The Russian Revolution, 1917-1921*. Vol. II. New York: Macmillan, 1935.

Churchill, Winston L. S. *The World Crisis*. Vol V: *The Aftermath*. London: Thornton Butterworth, 1929.

Craig, Gordon A., and Gilbert, Felix (eds.). *The Diplomats, 1919-1939*. Princeton: Princeton University Press, 1953.

Deák, Francis. *Hungary at the Paris Peace Conference: The Diplomatic History of the Treaty of Trianon*. New York: Columbia University Press, 1942.

Dennis, Alfred L. P. *The Foreign Policies of Soviet Russia*. New York: E. P. Dutton Co., 1924.

Dillon, E. J. *The Inside Story of the Peace Conference*. New York: Harper and Bros., 1920.

Fischer, Louis. *Men and Politics: An Autobiography*. New York: Duell, Sloan and Pearce, 1941.

Fodor, Marcel W. *Plot and Counter-Plot in Central Europe*. Boston: Houghton Mifflin Co., 1937.

Ceshkoff, Theodor I. *Balkan Union: A Road to Peace in Southeastern Europe*. New York: Columbia University Press, 1940.

Gillard, Marcel. *La Roumanie nouvelle*. Paris: Félix Alcan, 1922.

Graur, Ştefan St. *Les relations entre la Roumanie et l'U.R.S.S. depuis le Traité de Versailles*. Paris: Pedone, 1936.

Haskins, Charles Homer, and Lord, Robert Howard. *Some Problems of the Peace Conference*. Cambridge: Harvard University Press, 1920.

Hoover, Herbert Clark. *The Ordeal of Woodrow Wilson*. New York: McGraw-Hill, 1958.

House, Edward Mandell, and Seymour, Charles (eds.). *What Really Happened at Paris: The Story of the Peace Conference, 1918-1919, by American Delegates*. New York: Charles Scribner's Sons, 1921.

Janowsky, Oscar I. *The Jews and Minority Rights, 1898-1919*. New York: Columbia University Press, 1933.

Kaas, Albert, Baron, and Lazarovics, Fedor de. *Bolshevism in Hungary: The Béla Kun Period*. London: Grant Richards, 1931.

Kormos, C. *Rumania*. British Society for International Under-standing. British Survey Handbooks, No. 2. Cambridge: At the University Press, 1944.

Lamont, Thomas W. *Across World Frontiers*. New York: Harcourt, Brace, 1951.

Langer, Robert. *Seizure of Territory: The Stimson Doctrine and Related Principles in Legal Theory and Diplomatic Practice.* Princeton: Princeton University Press, 1947.

Lansing, Robert. *The Big Four and Others of the Peace Conference.* Boston: Houghton Mifflin Co., 1921.

Laurian, Marius-Auguste. *Le principe des nationalités et l'unité nationale roumaine.* Paris: Jouve, 1923.

Luckau, Alma. *The German Delegation at the Paris Peace Conference.* New York: Columbia University Press, 1941.

Macartney, Carlile Aylmer. *Hungary and her Successors: The Treaty of Trianon and Its Consequences, 1919-1937.* London: Oxford University Press, 1937.

— — —. *A History of Hungary, 1929-1945.* Vol. I. New York: Frederick A. Praeger, 1957.

Mărdărescu, Gheorghe, D., General. *Campania pentru desrobirea Ardealului şi ocuparea Budapestei. (Campaign for the Liberation of Transylvania and Occupation of Budapest).* Bucharest: Cartea Românească, 1921.

Marston, Frank S. *The Peace Conference of 1919: Organization and Procedure.* London: Oxford University Press, 1944.

Miller, David Hunter. *The Drafting of the Covenant.* 2 vols. New York: G. P. Putnam's Sons, 1928.

Mitrany, David. *The Effect of the War in Southeastern Europe.* Carnegie Endowment for International Peace: Division of Economics and History. Economic and Social History of the World War. New Haven: Yale University Press, 1936.

Nicolson, Harold. *Peacemaking, 1919.* London: Constable, 1933.

— — —. *The Evolution of Diplomatic Method.* New York: Macmillan, 1954.

Noble, George Bernard. *Policies and Opinions at Paris, 1919: Wilsonian Diplomacy, the Versailles Peace, and French Public Opinion*. New York: Macmillan, 1935.

Pipes, Richard. *The Formation of the Soviet Union: Communism and Nationalism, 1917-1923*. Cambridge: Harvard University Press, 1954.

Potemkin, V. P., and Others. *Istoria Diplomatii*. Vol. III: *1919-1939*. Moscow-Leningrad: Gosudarstvennoe Izdatel'stvo Politicheskoi Literatury, 1945.

Roberts, Henry L. *Rumania: Political Problems of an Agrarian State*. New Haven: Yale University Press, 1951.

Rommenhoeller, Carol G. *La Grande-Roumanie: sa structure économique, sociale, financière, politique et particulièrement ses richesses*. The Hague: Martinus Nijhoff, 1926.

Romania. Institut Social Român. *Politica externă a României: 19 prelegeri publice*. Bucharest: Cultură națională, 1925. Lectures on foreign policy. See especially "The Principles and the Spirit of the Last Peace Treaties," by Mircea Djuvara (pp. 1-33); "The Problem of the Straits," by Constantin Diamandy (pp. 205-222); "The Problem of the Minorities," by Maniu (pp. 223-243); and "The Problem of the Romanian Boundaries," by Vaida-Voevod (pp. 277-292).

Seton-Watson, Hugh. *Eastern Europe between the Wars, 1918-1941*. Cambridge: At the University Press, 1946.

– – –. *From Lenin to Malenkov: The History of World Communism*. New York: Frederick A. Praeger, 1953.

Seton-Watson, Robert William. *Europe in the Melting-Pot*. London: Macmillan, 1919.

– – –. *Treaty Revision and the Hungarian Frontiers*. London: Eyre and Spottiswoode, 1934.

————. *The Problem of Small Nations and European Anarchy.* Nottingham: University of Nottingham Press, 1939.

Transylvania: A Key-Problem. London: Oxford University Press, 1943.

Seymour, Charles. *Woodrow Wilson and the World War: A Chronicle of our own Times.* Vol. XLVIII of *The Chronicles of America* series. Edited by Allen Johnson. New Haven: Yale University Press, 1921.

————. (ed.). *The Intimate Papers of Colonel House.* Vol. IV. Boston: Houghton Mifflin Co., 1928.

Shotwell, James T. *At the Paris Peace Conference.* New York: Macmffian, 1937.

Shtein, Boris E. *Russkii vopros na parizhskoi mirnoi konferentsii, 1919-1920.* Moscow: Gospolitizdat, 1949.

Sofronie, Georges. *Le principe des nationalités et les traités de paix de 1919/1920.* Bucharest: Universul, 1937.

————. *La position internationale de la Roumanie: étude juridique et diplomatique de ses engagements internationaux.* Institut Social Român. Bucharest: Centre des hautes études internationales, 1938.

Szász, Zsombor de. *The Minorities in Roumanian Transylvania.* London: The Richards Press, 1927.

Tardieu, André. *The Truth about the Treaty.* Indianapolis: Bobbs-Merrill, 1921.

Temperley, Harold William Vazielle (ed.). *A History of the Peace Conference of Paris.* 6 vols. London: Henry Frowde, Hodder and Stoughton, 1920-1924.

Thompson, Charles T. *The Peace Conference Day by Day.* New York: Brentano's, 1920.

Thomson, S. Harrison. *Czechoslovakia in European History.* Princeton: Princeton University Press, 1944.

Tibal, André. *Problèmes politiques contemporains de l'Europe orientale: conférence, novembre 1928-Juin 1929.* Paris: Centre européen de la dotation Carnegie, 1930.

Tilea, Viorel V. *Acţiunea Diplomatică a României, Nov. 1919-Mart. 1920.* Sibiu: Tipografia Poporului, 1925.

Ward, A. W., and Gooch, G. P. (eds.). *The Cambridge History of British Foreign Policy.* Vol. III: 1866-1919. Cambridge: At the University Press, 1923.

Yardley, Herbert O. *The Secret Service in America: The American Black Chamber.* London: Faber and Faber, 1940.

Yates, Louis A. R. *The United States and French Security, 1917-1921.* New York: Twayne Publishers, 1957.

IX. Unpublished Monographs

Lederer, Ivo J. "Yugoslavia and the Paris Peace Settlement: Yugoslav-Italian Relations and the Territorial Settlement, 1918-1920." Ph.D. dissertation, Department of History, Princeton University, 1957.

Mayer, Amo J. "The Politics of Allied War Aims: The Soviet and Russian Impact, March, 1917-January, 1918." 2 vols. Ph.D. dissertation, Department of History, Yale University, 1953.

Nano, Frederic D. "Survey of the Foreign Policy of Romania, 1918-1939." New York: Mid-European Studies Center of the National Committee for a Free Europe, 1950.

Rieber, Alfred. "Russian Policy and Romania — August, 1914 to August, 1916: A Study in War Diplomacy." Essay for A. M., Department of History, and Certificate, Russian Institute, Columbia University, 1954.

Spector, Sherman D. "The Question of Bessarabia in the Political Relations between Russia and Rumania, 1812-1935." Essay for A.M., Department of History, Columbia University, 1951.

X. Controversial Writings of Contemporaries: BOOKS AND PAMPHLETS

Apponyi, Albert; Berzeviczy, Albert; Horváth, Eugene, and Others. *Justice for Hungary: A Review and Criticism of the Effect of the Treaty of Trianon*. London: Longmans, Green, 1928.

Bernstein, Simon. *Les persécutions des juifs en Roumanie*. Copenhagen: Éditions du Bureau de l'organisation sioniste, 1919.

Brătiano, Elise J. *Lettre ouverte à M. William Martin*. Bucharest: Scrisul Românesc, 1929. A rebuttal by Brătianu's widow to the author of *Statesmen of the War in Retrospect*. Reprint of an article in *L'Indépendance Roumaine*, September 22, 1929.

Clark, Charles Upson. *Racial Aspects of Romania's Case*. New York: Caxton Press, 1941.

De Martonne, Emmanuel. *La Dobrodgea: Esquisse historique, géographique, ethnographique et statistique*. Paris: Félix Alcan, 1918.

Djuvara, Mircea. *La guerre roumaine, 1916-1918*. Paris: Berger-Levrault, 1919.

— — —. *Trebuie oare să semnăm Tractatul cu Austria? (Must We Sign the Treaty with Austria?)* Bucharest: Imprimeria Independenţa, 1919.

Drăghicescu, Dimitrie. *Les roumains*. Paris: Bossard, 1918.

— — —. *La Transylvanie: Esquisse historique, géographique, ethnographique et statistique*. Paris: Félix Alcan, 1918.

— — —. *Les roumains de Serbie*. Paris: Dubois et Bauer, 1919.

― ― ―. *Les roumains d'Ukraine.* Paris: Dubois et Bauer, 1919.

― ― ―. *La Bessarabie et le droit des peuples: Esquisse historique, géographique, ethnographique et statistique.* Paris: Félix Alcan, 1919.

Erdélyi, Ion. *Les Magyars peints par eux-mêmes.* Nancy-Paris: Berger-Levrault, 1919.

Flers, Robert de. *Sur les chemins de la guerre (France-Roumanie-Russie).* Paris: Lafitte, 1919.

― ― ―. *La petite table.* Paris: Flammarion, 1920.

Genov, Georgi P. *Bulgaria and the Treaty of Neuilly.* Sofia: Hristo G. Danov, 1935.

Guillemot, Marcel. *L'Unité roumaine.* Paris: Dubois et Bauer, 1919.

Herron, George D. *The Defeat in Victory.* London: Cecil Palmer, 1921.

Ionescu, Toma. *La question roumaine.* 2 vols. Paris: Payot, 1919.

― ― ―. *Les questions roumaines du temps présent.* Paris: Félix Alcan. 1921.

Iorga, Nicolae. *Droits des roumains sur leur territoire national unitaire.* Bucharest: *Neamul Românesc,* 1919.

― ― ―. *Les roumains au-delà du Dniester.* Paris: Gamber, 1925.

Ishirkov, Anastas. *Les bulgares en Dobrodgea.* Berne: Pochon-Jent et Bühler, 1919.

Ivanoff, Jordan. *Les bulgares devant le congrès de la paix.* Berne: Paul Haupt, 1919.

Kapchev, G.I. *Sovremennaia Rumyniia i ee zadachi.* Petrograd: Izdanie Berezovskii, Kommissioner Voenno-Uchebnykh Zavedenii, 1916.

Korduba, Myron. *Le territoire et la population de l'Ukraine*. Berne: Suter, 1919.

Kreppel, J. *Der Friede im Osten*. Vienna: Verlag *Der Tag,* 1918.

Krupenskii, Alexander N. *Mémoire sur la situation de la Bessarabie*. Paris: Lahure, 1919.

Lacea, Constantin. *La Bucovine*. Paris: Dubois et Bauer, 1919.

Lalescu, Traian. *Le problème ethnographique du Banat*. Paris: Paul Dupont, 1919.

Leeper, Allen W. A. *The Justice of Rumania's Cause*. London: Hodder and Stoughton, 1917.

Lupu, Nicolae. *Rumania and the War*. Boston: Richard G. Badger, 1919.

Marie, Queen of Rumania. *My Country*. London: Hodder and Stoughton, 1916.

Markham, Reuben H. *Bulgaria and the Y.M.C.A*. Sofia: Stopansko Razvitic, 1926.

Miliukov, Paul (ed.). *The Case for Bessarabia*. London: Russian Liberation Committee, 1919.

Mitrany, David. *Greater Rumania: A Study in National Ideals*. London: Hodder and Stoughton, 1917.

Negulesco, Gogu. *Rumania's Sacrifice*. New York: The Century Co., 1918.

Nistor, Iancu I. *Românii şi Rutenii în Bucovina*. Bucharest: Socec, 1915.

– – –. *Der Nationale Kampf in der Bukovina*. Bucharest: F. Göbl, 1918.

Pătrășcanu, D.D. *Vinovații, 1916-1918. (Culprits, 1916-1918)*. Bucharest: Ziarul *Lumina*, 1918.

Pavel, Pavel. *Transylvania at the Peace Conference of Paris*. London: Pavel, 1945.

Pelivan, Ion G. *Bessarabia under the Russian Rule*. Paris: Charpentier, 1920.

Petrescu-Comnen, Nicolae. *Notes sur la guerre roumaine, 1916-1917*. Paris: Payot, 1918.

— — —. *Roumania through the Ages*. Paris: Payot, 1919.

— — —. *Roumania: Ethnographic Atlas*. Bucharest: Institut de arte grafice, 1938.

Poppov, Joseph V. *La Dobroudja et les relations bulgaro-roumaines*. Liège: Thone, 1935.

Prothero, George Walter. *A Lasting Peace*. London: Hodder and Stoughton, 1917.

Radonić, Yovan. *The Banat and the Serbo-Roumanian Frontier Problem*. Paris: Ligue des universitaires serbo-croat-slovènes, 1919.

Rakovskii, Khristian G. *Roumanie et Bessarabie*. Paris: Librairie du travail, 1925.

Romania. *Enciclopedia României*. Vol. I. Edited by D. Gusti. Articles on the war and peace, pp. 883-1002. Bucharest: Cartea Românească, 1938.

Romanian National Council, Paris. *Actes et documents concernant la question roumaine*. Paris: Paul Dupont, 1918.

— — —. *Report Presented by the Roumanian Colony to the Commission Charged with Tracing the Map of Territories Inhabited by the Roumanians*. Edited by Aureliu M. Eliescu. Paris: Wellkoff et Roche, 1919.

– – –. *Réponse des universitaires roumains au mémoire des professeurs magyars de l'université de Cluj*. Paris: Wellkoff et Roche, 1919.

Seişanu, Romulus. *Rumania*. Bucharest: Imprimeria naţională, 1939.

Serbian Delegation to the Peace Conference. *Delimitation between the Serbs and the Roumanians in the Banat*. Paris, 1919.

Sirianu, Rusu Mircea. *Le question du Transylvanie et l'unité politique roumaine*. Paris: Jouve, 1916.

Slivensky, Ivan. *La Bulgarie depuis le traité de Berlin et la paix dans les Balkans*. Paris: Jouve, 1927.

Tanfil'ev, G. I. *Galitsiia i Bukovina*. Odessa: Sklad Izdaniia Uranii, 1915.

Thomas, Albert. *La Roumanie et la guerre*. Paris, 1919.

Tsanoff, Vladimii A. (ed.). *Reports and Letters of American Missionaries*. Sofia, 1919.

Ukraine. *Notes présentées par la délégation de la république ukrainienne à la conference de la paix*. Paris: Robinet-Houtain, 1919.

Ullein-Reviczky, Antal. *La nature juridique des clauses territoriales du traité de Trianon*. Paris: Pedone, 1936.

Ursu, Ion. *Pourquoi la Roumanie a fait la guerre*. Paris: Payot, 1918.

Vellani-Dionisi, Franco. *Il problema territoriale transilvano*. Bologna: Nicola Zanichelli, 1932.

Vitencu, Basile. *La situation ethnographique en Bucovine*. Paris: Dubois et Bauer, 1919.

XI. Controversial Writings of Contemporaries:
ARTICLES

Daşcovici, Nicolae. "La question des Détroits et les nationalités du sud-est européen," *Les Annales des Nationalités* (Paris), IV (1915), No. 4, pp. 93-99.

De Martonne, Emmanuel. "Les conditions d'une intervention roumaine," *Revue de Paris*, XXII (May 15, 1915), No. 10, pp. 430-448.

― ― ―. "La Roumanie et son rôle dans l'Europe orientale," *Bulletin de la Société Géographique* (Paris), XXX (1915), No. 4, pp. 328-346.

― ― ―. "What I Have Seen in Bessarabia," *Revue de Paris*, XXVI (November 1919), No. 21, reprint.

― ― ―. "Essai de carte ethnographique des pays roumains," *Annales de Géographie* (Paris), XXIX (March 1920), No. 158, pp. 81-98.

Drăghicescu, Dimitrie. "La lutte sociale et politique en Transylvanie," *La Revue* (Paris), I (May 15, 1918), reprint.

Herre, Paul. "Rumäniens Vertragsverhältnis zum Dreibund," *Historische Zeitschrift* (Munich), CXVIII (1917), Folge 3, pp. 63-75.

Leeper, Allen W. A. "Great Roumania," *La Roumanie* (Paris), No. 30, August 8, 1918.

Lupu, Nicolae. "Rumania in the Mid-European Belt," *Asia* (New York), XVIII (1918), pp. 1036-1043.

Maxwell, William. "Bessarabia had Soviets," *Soviet Russia Today*, August 1940.

Prahovan, Albert. "Take Jonesco anecdotique et intime," *La Revue* (Paris), CXXVII (1918), Nos. 19-20, pp. 85-90.

Steed, Henry Wickham. "A Programme for Peace," reprint of article in *The Edinburgh Review* for the Bohemian National Alliance, 1916.

Tamaro, Attilio. "Romania e Polonia de fronte agli Slavi," *Politica* (Rome), XIII (1922), pp. 70-91.

Tilea, Viorel V. "Romania: The Forming of a Nation," *The Scottish Geographical Magazine* (Edinburgh), LVII (1941), No. 1, pp. 1-9.

Vaida-Voevod, Alexandru. "Slawen, Deutsche, Magyaren, und Rumänen," *Österreichische Rundschau* (Vienna), XXIV (1913), pp. 8-12.

— — — and Drăghicescu, Dimitrie. "Les aspirations nationales des roumains," *La Paix des Peuples* (Paris), I (1919), No. 3, pp. 430-445.

Vesnić, Milenko. (pseud. "P. P. de Sokolovich"), Untitled article. *Les Annales des Nationalités* (Paris), IV (1915), No. 3, reprint.

— — —. "Les rapports serbo-roumains, passé-présent-avenir," *Revue des Sciences Politiques* (Paris), XXXVII (1917), pp. 367-390.

XII. General Articles: THE WAR PERIOD

Adamov, Evgenii A. "Bessarabskii vopros v russko-rumynskikh otnosheniiakh," *Mezhdunarodnaia Zhizn'* (Moscow), II (1927), No. 1, pp. 57-74.

Ancel, Jacques. "La politique de la Roumanie vaincue (mars-novembre, 1918)," *La Revue du Mois* (Paris), XXI (1920), No. 122, pp. 167-189.

Berthelot, Henri, Général. "Sur le front roumain en 1917," *Revue de France* (Paris), IV (1927), pp. 642-664; V (1927), pp. 96-123.

Brătianu, Gheorghe I. "Bismarck şi Ion C. Brătianu," *Revistă Istorică Română* (Bucharest), V-VI (1935-1936), pp. 86-103.

Broussilow, Général (Brusilov, Aleksei A.). "L'Offensive de 1916," *Revue des Deux Mondes*, LI (1929), pp. 370-391, 903-928.

Burks, Richard V. "Romania and the Balkan Crisis of 1875-1878," *Journal of Central European Affairs*, II (1942), No. 2, pp. 119-134.

Cădere, Victor C. "Politica României in marele război, 1914-1924," *Arhivă pentru Știință și Reformă Socială* (Bucharest), VIII (1929), pp. 268-291.

Campbell, John C. "Nicholas Iorga," *The Slavonic and East European Review* (London), XXVI (1947), No. 66, pp. 44-59.

Diamandy, Constantin. "La grande guerre vue du versant oriental," *Revue des Deux Mondes*, XLII (1927), "1912-1914," pp. 781-804; XLIII (1928), "À Constanza," pp. 129-143; XLIX (1929), "Ma mission en Russie, 1914-1918," pp. 794-820; LX (1930), "Ma mission en Russie, octobre 1914-mai 1915," pp. 421-432.

Dudu, Velicu. "Misiunea secretă a unui nobil polon la curtea regelui Carol I" ("Secret Mission of a Polish noble to the Court of Carol I"), *Revistă Istorică Română* (Bucharest), VIII (1938), pp. 185-209.

Duggan, Stephen. "Balkan Diplomacy," *Political Science Quarterly*, XXXII (1917), Nos. 1-2, pp. 36-59, 224-251.

Ebel, Ernst. "Rumänien und die Mittelmächte, 1877-1913," *Historische Studien* (Berlin: Verlag Dr. Emil Ebering), Heft 351, 1939, reprint.

Emets, V. A. "Protivorechiia mezhdu Rossiei i soiuznikami po voprosu o vstuplenii Rumynii v voinu (1915-1916 gg.)," ("Contradictions between Russia and the Allies regarding the Question of the Intervention of Rumania into the War"), *Istoricheskie Zapiski* (Moscow), No. 56 (1956), pp. 52-90.

Fedorov, V. "Russkaia voennaia missiia v Rumynii vo vremia mirovoi voiny," ("The Russian Military Mission in Rumania during the

World War"), *Voprosy Istorii* (Moscow), No. 8 (1947), pp. 94-99.

Fotino, Georges. "La neutralité roumaine: une séance historique au conseil de la couronne, 3 août 1914," *Revue des Deux Mondes,* LVIII (1930), pp. 529-541.

Gheorghiu, I. "Relaţiile romîno-ruse in perioada neutralităţii Romîniei," *Studii şi Referate privind Istoria Romîniei,* II (1954), pp. 1445-1518. Bucharest: Editura Academiei Republicii Populare Romîne, 1954. Paper given at sessions of the Section of Historical, Philological, and Economic-Juridical Science, December 21-24, 1953.

Gottschalk, Egon. "Rumänien und der Dreibund his zur Krise 1914," *Die Kriegsschuldfrage: Berliner Monatshefte für Internationale Aufklärung,* V (1927), pp. 632-665.

Horváth, Eugene. "La correspondence du comte Étienne Tisza," *Revue de Hongrie* (Budapest), XXXVII (1927), No. 3, pp. 193-198.

Ionescu, Take. "La petite entente," *Revue des Balkans* (Paris), III (1921), No. 26, pp. 189-190.

Iorga, Nicolae. "Acte privitoare la istoria marelui război: I. Consiliile de coroană din Februar 1918" ("Acts concerning the history of the Great War: I. The Crown Council of February 1918"), *Revistă Istorică* (Bucharest), XVIII (1932), pp. 193-215.

Johnson, Douglas W. "The Conquest of Rumania," *Geographical Review* (New York), III (1917), No. 6, pp. 438-456.

Kann, Robert A. "Count Ottokar Czernin and Archduke Francis Ferdinand," *Journal of Central European Affairs,* XVI (1956), No. 2, pp. 117-145.

Kasterska, Marya. "Le comte Bohdan Hutten-Czapski et la Roumanie, dans ses mémoires," *Revue Historique du sud-est européen* (Bucharest), XVI (1939), Nos. 1-3, pp. 1-33.

Mamatey, Victor S. "The United States and Bulgaria in World War I," *The American Slavic and East European Review,* XII (1953), No. 2, pp. 236-238.

Miles. "M. Joan J. C. Brătiano: Silhouette de guerre," *Le Correspondant* (Paris), CCXXIX (1916), pp. 36-54.

Mitrany, David. "Rumania: Her History and Politics," in Forbes, N., Toynbee, A. J.Mitrany, D., and Hogarth, D., *The Balkans.* Oxford: At the Clarendon Press, 1915, pp. 251-318.

Morison, Stanley. "Personality and Diplomacy in Anglo-American Relations, 1917," in Pares, Richard, and Taylor, A.J.P. (eds.), *Essays Presented to Sir Lewis Namier.* London: Macmillan, 1956, pp. 431-474.

Munteanu, Eugen, and Necşa, Teodor. "Jefuirea petrolului românesc de către trusturile imperialiste in anii 1917-1923," ("Seizure of Romanian Petroleum by Imperialistic Trusts in the years 1917-1923"), *Studii şi Referate privind Istoria Romîniei,* II (1954), pp. 1549-1586. Bucharest: Editura Academiei Republicii Populare Romîne, 1954. Paper given at sessions of the Section of Historical, Philological, and Economic-Juridical Science, December 21-24, 1953.

Pingaud, Albert, "L'Entente et les balkaniques aux premiers mois de la guerre," *Revue des Deux Mondes,* LIV (1929), pp. 48-83.

— — —. "Études diplomatiques: L'Entente et la Roumanie, 3 mai-2 août 1915," *Revue des Deux Mondes,* LVII (1930), pp. 144-161.

— — —. "La grande guerre et l'alliance franco-russe," *La Revue de France* (Paris), XII (1932), No. 22, pp. 292-315.

Pop, Valeriu. "The Romanian Legion in Italy," *Revue de Transylvanie* (Cluj), III (1936-1937), No. 2, pp. 154-166.

Revue d'Histoire de la Guerre Mondiale (Paris), "L'Intervention roumaine: Extrait des notes d'Alexandre Marghiloman," VI (1928), No. 2, pp. 157-166.

Rosental, Salamon. "Une page d'histoire roumaine: la Roumanie dans la grande guerre," *Revue d'Histoire Diplomatique* (Paris), LI (1936), pp. 415-452.

Roucek, Joseph S. "The Little Entente," *Roumania* (New York), VI (1930), No. 2, pp. 16-20.

Seton-Watson, Hugh. "The Intellectuals and Revolution: Social Forces in Eastern Europe since 1848," in Pares and Taylor (eds.), *Essays Presented to Sir Lewis Namier,* pp. 394-430.

Smedovski, Assen. "La Roumanie et la triple alliance, 1883-1913," *Revue d'histoire diplomatique* (Paris), LII (1937), pp. 39-56.

Sterian, G. "La Roumanie: son passé, ses attachés françaises, les partis politiques," *La Revue Hebdomadaire* (Paris), September 9, 1916.

Taylor, A.J.P. "The War Aims of the Allies in the First World War," in Pares and Taylor (eds.), *Essays Presented to Sir Lewis Namier,* pp. 475-505.

Witte, Jehan de. "Les entretiens du comte Czernin d'après le 'livre rouge austro-hongrois,'" *Revue des Deux Mondes,* XXXIX (1917), pp. 391-413.

XIII. General Articles: THE CONFERENCE PERIOD

Albrecht-Carrié, René. "Versailles Twenty Years After," *Political Science Quarterly,* LV (1940), No. 1, pp. 1-24.

Austruy, Henri. "La frontière polono-roumanie," *La Nouvelle Revue* (Paris), XL (1919), No. 161, pp. 289-304.

Blociszewski, J. de. "Ada-Kalè: une île turque annexée par l'Autriche-Hongrie," *Revue Générale de Droit Internationale* (Paris), XXI, 1914.

Bowman, Isaiah. "The Strategy of Territorial Decisions," *Foreign Affairs* (New York), XXIV (1946), No. 2, pp. 177-194.

Brown, Philip Marshall. "Foreign Relations of the Budapest Soviets in 1919: A Personal Narrative," *The Hungarian Quarterly* (Budapest), III (1937), No. 1, pp. 59-69.

Cambon, Jules. "La Roumanie et la question agraire en Transylvanie," *Revue des Deux Mondes*, XLI-XLII (1927), pp. 614-623.

Challener, Richard D. "The French Foreign Office: The Era of Philippe Berthelot," in Craig, Cordon A., and Gilbert, Felix (eds.), *The Diplomats*, 1919-1939. Princeton: Princeton University Press, 1953, pp. 49-85.

Cox, Frederick J. "The French Peace Plans, 1918-1919," in Cox and Others, *Studies in Modern European History in Honor of Franklin Charles Palm*. New York: Bookman Associates, 1956, pp. 71-104.

Craig, Gordon A. "The British Foreign Office from Grey to Austen Chamberlain," in Craig and Gilbert (eds.), *The Diplomats, 1919-1939*, pp. 15-48.

Gedye, G.E.D. "Ion Brătianu," *Contemporary Review* (London), CXXXIII (1928), pp. 35-38.

Graham, Malbone W. "The Legal Status of the Bukovina and Bessarabia," *American Journal of International Law*, XXXVIII (1944), No. 4, pp. 667-673.

Herron, George D. "The New Roumania," *The New Europe*, XII (1919), No. 155, pp. 282-284.

Kushnir-Mikhailovich, K. "Velikaia Oktiabr'skaia Sotsialisticheskaia Revolutsiia i revolutsionnaia situatsiia v Rumynii v 1917-1921 gg.," *Voprosy Istorii* (Moscow), No. 11 (November 1957), pp. 65-85.

Laue, Theodore H. Von. "Soviet Diplomacy: G.V. Chicherin, People's Commissar for Foreign Affairs, 1918-1930," in Craig and Gilbert (eds.), *The Diplomats, 1919-1939*, pp. 234-248.

Macartney, Carlile Aylmer. "Hungary since 1918," *The Slavonic and East European Review* (London), VII (1929), No. 21, pp. 577-594.

Marie, Queen of Romania. "My Mission: I. In Paris; II. At Buckingham Palace; III. Paris Again," *The Cornhill Magazine* (London), CLX (1939), Nos. 958-960, pp. 433-457, 578-603, 722-752.

Mosely, Philip E. "Transylvania Partitioned," *Foreign Affairs* (New York), XIX (1940), No. 1, pp. 237-244.

Rudéano, Général. "La Roumanie an congrès de la paix," *La Géographie* (Paris), XXXII (1918-1919), No. 5, pp. 291-308.

Saint-Aulaire, Comte de. "La figure véridique d'un grand roi: Ferdinand Ier de Roumanie," *La Revue Hebdomadaire* (Paris), October 1, 1927, pp. 31-51.

– – –. "Un grand latin – Jean Brătiano," *La Revue Hebdomadaire* (Paris), August 4, 1928, pp. 5-26.

Seton-Watson, R.W., Tributes to: A Symposium." *The Slavonic and East European Review* (London), XXX (1952), No. 75, pp. 331-363.

Seton-Watson, Robert William. "The Question of the Banat," *The New Europe,* X (1919), No. 122, pp. 97-103.

– – –. "The Treaty with Austria," *The New Europe,* XII (1919), No. 153, p. 228.

– – –. "The New Frontiers of Hungary," *The New Europe,* XIV (1920), No. 170, pp. 18-22.

Temperley, Harold W. V. "How the Hungarian Frontiers were Drawn," *Foreign Affairs* (New York), VI (1928), No. 3, pp. 432-447.

Tittoni, Tommaso. "La Bessarabia, la Romania, et l'Italia," *Nuova Antologia* (Rome), MCCCXXI (1927), pp. 257-277.

XIV. Newspapers

Great Britain. The War Office. *Daily Review of the Foreign Press.* With Allied, Enemy, and Neutral Press Supplements. Issued by the General Staff, 1916-1920.

Bulletin d'informations roumaines. Weekly organ of the Romanian Delegation, March 25 to June 3, 1919.

La Roumanie, Paris. Weekly organ of the Romanian National Council, January 1918 to June 1919.

Le Temps, Paris. Daily.

Times, London. Daily.

The New York Times. Daily.

INDEX OF NAMES